美 國務省 韓國關係 文書

INTERNAL
AFFAIRS OF KOREA

1940~1944

（Ｉ）

韓國學資料院

해 제

I

1980년대에 들어서면서 우리가 놓여있는 현실과 관련하여 소위 해방전후 시기에 대한 관심이 크게 고조되었고, 따라서 이 시기의 역사를 학문적으로 정리해 보려는 노력이 꾸준이 이루어져 왔다. 특히 한반도의 분단과 전쟁 그리고 냉전의 구조적 정착이라는 민족적 비극이 일차적으로는 외세의 개입에서 비롯되었다는 인식 아래 현실적으로 한국문제에 가장 큰 영향력을 행사했던 미국의 역할을 새롭게 조명하는데 초점이 모아졌다. 그러나 이 과정에서 국내 연구자들은 한가지 큰 어려움에 부딪쳤다. 그것은 다름아닌 실질적으로 이용가능한 자료의 빈곤이었다.

비교적 최근에 이르러서야 한림대학교 아시아문화연구소를 비롯한 몇몇 출판사에서 미군정 관련자료들이 발간되면서 일단 기본적 연구조건이 갖추어지기 시작했다. 그러나 이것은 어디까지나 시작에 불과하다. 특히 해방 이전 미국의 대한정책 수립과정과 관련해서는 편자들이 임의로 취사선택한 단편적인 자료들이 소개되고 있을 뿐이다.[1] 또한 우리는 해방직전 국외에서 활동하고 있던 한인 독립운동단체들의 움직임과 국내 사정에 대해서도 제한된 지식만을 갖고 있다. 이러한 사정으로 말미암아 지금까지의 국내 연구동향을 살펴보면 '해방'을 전후한 역사가 분절적으로 이해되고 있는 감이 없지 않다. 이같은 연구경향은 아직 뚜렷한 학문적 논쟁없이 한국 근대사와 현대사의 분기점을 해방으로 잡는 시각과도 무관하지 않을 것이다. 그러나 적어도 미국의 대한정책을 분석할 때 일본의 패전이라는 결과 보다는 일본과의 전쟁 개시 자체가 갖는 의미가 중요하다. 왜냐하면 1941년 12월 초 일본의 하와이 진주만 기습공격을 계기로 미국의 동아시아정책은 전면적인 수정이 불가피했기 때문이다. 바로 이 시점에서 미국은 전후 한반도문제를 본격적으로 검토하기 시작했다.

이후 한반도문제와 관련된 미국의 정치적, 전략적 고려가 그렇게 단순하지 않았다는 점은 그들의 국립문서관에 보존되어 있는 국무부, 합동참모본부(Joint Chiefs of Staff), 육군부(War Department) 산하 기획작전국과 민간업무국, 전략정보처(Office of Strategic Services), 그리고 각 부처간에 서로 정보를 교환하고 의견을 조정하기 위한

---

1) 해방 이전의 자료들은 原主文化社에 출간된 『미국외교문서：한국편(1942-1948)』과 『韓國分斷史資料集』(申福龍 編), 『解放前後史資料集：美軍政 準備資料』(李吉相 編) 등에 부분적으로 들어가 있다.

i

여러 위원회의 기록에 한국문제가 거의 빠짐없이 등장하고 있다는 사실에서 쉽게 확인할 수 있다.2) 이들 자료에 대한 분석·검토는 그동안 주로 미국 내에서 이루어졌던 바 적지 않은 연구성과가 축적되어 있다. 그러나 아직 모든 문제가 만족스럽게 해결된 것은 아니다. 특히 기존의 연구들이 거의 대부분 미국측 자료--그것도 일정한 기준에 따라 비밀 분류에서 해제된 자료--에 의존하여 문제를 풀어가고 있기 때문에 핵심적인 사안에 대한 미국 정부의 본래 의도가 가리워지거나 또는 잘못 해석되었을 가능성을 전혀 배제할 수 없다. 실제로 우리는 미국이 한반도문제에 개입하면서 추구하고자 했던 이익--그것이 한반도에 국한될 수도 있고, 또는 동아시아 나아가 세계전략적 차원의 일환일 수도 있다-- 이 어떠한 것이었으며, 또 그 이익을 얻기 위하여 어떠한 수단들이 동원되었는가에 대한 확정적인 해답을 얻지 못하고 있다.

아울러 우리가 한가지 더 염두에 두어야 할 점은 전후 한반도의 문제가 미국만의 유일한 관심사는 아니었다는 사실이다. 당시 미국측 정책입안자들이 인정했듯이 한반도에 관한 한 중국과 소련이 보다 더 직접적인 이해관계를 갖고 있었고, 따라서 미국의 대한정책 결정과정에 있어서 주요한 변수는 중국 및 소련의 태도였다. 그러나 이 두나라 특히 소련의 한반도에 대한 관심과 전략의 구체적 내용에 대해서는 당시는 물론이고 오늘날에도 제대로 밝혀지지 않고 있다. 미국이 일본과의 전쟁 개시 직후부터 한반도문제를 내부적으로 검토하기 시작했음에도 불구하고 전쟁 종결에 이르기까지 신탁통치를 실시한다는 원칙만을 세웠을 뿐 그 세부적인 내용을 확정짓지 못한 것도 전후 한반도의 주변정세가 유동적인 상황에서 소련의 의도를 정확히 예측하기 어려웠기 때문이다. 중국 국민당의 경우에는 미국이 그 내부사정을 어느정도 알고 있었고, 또 그들에 대한 현실적인 압력수단을 갖고 있었기 때문에 소련만큼 심각하게 의식했던 것 같지는 않다.

어떻든 제2차 세계대전기 미국의 대한정책 수립과정을 논의할 때 우리는 미국 정부의 기본입장 못지않게 중국과 소련의 한반도문제에 대한 개입의지와 그 구체적 전략을 폭넓게 고려해야 한다. 이와 더불어 생각할 것은 중국 국민당과 공산당 그리고 소련은 각각 그들의 세력범위 내에서 활동하고 있는 한인단체들을 보호 내지 후원하고 있었다는 사실이다. 즉 중국 관내지역의 대한민국임시정부와 조선독립동맹 및 소련 영내에 새로 근거지를 마련한 동북항일연군 가운데 김일성을 중심으로 한 일단의 한인부대가 그것이다. 한편 미주지역의 여러 한인단체들도 미국의 공식적인 승인과 지원을 얻기 위하여 노력하

---

2) 해방전후 시기 미국 국립문서관에 소장된 한국관계 자료의 소개에 대해서는, Jack Saunders, "Records in the National Archives Relating to Korea, 1945-1950," Bruce Cumings ed., *Child of Coflict : The Korean-American Relationship, 1943-1953* (Seatttle and London: University of Washington Press, 1983), pp. 309-326 참조. 번역서로는 1987년에 청사에서 출판된 『한국전쟁과 한미관계, 1943-1953』, pp. 365-387 참조.

고 있었다. 해방 후 한반도에 대한 미·소의 개입이 각각 그들의 영내에서 활동하고 있던 한인단체 또는 인물을 매개로 이루어졌던 점을 고려할 때 해방직전 단계에서의 이들의 동향 또한 보다 세밀히 추적할 필요가 있다. 중국 역시 대일전쟁 종결 후 곧 바로 내전에 돌입하지 않았다면 어떠한 형태로든 한반도문제에 개입했을 것이고, 이때 그들은 대한민국임시정부나 조선독립동맹과의 관계를 최대한 활용하리라는 것은 쉽게 짐작할 수 있는 일이다.

II

앞서 제시한 몇가지 문제와 관련하여 이번에 출간되는 자료집의 출처와 특징을 살펴보기로 하자.

본 자료집의 출처는 미국 정부의 중요한 기록유산을 보존·정리하고 있는 국립문서관(National Archives)이다. 이 기관에 소장된 자료들은 대체로 민간문서국(Civil Archives Division), 군사문서국(Military Archives Division), 일반문서국(General Archives Division)으로 나뉘어 정리되고 있는데, 그 중 민간문서국의 외교분과에는 국무성의 모든 문서를 포함한 미국의 외교문서가 망라되어 있다. 통상적인 국무성의 일반문서(Record Group 59)에는 각국에 파견된 외교 및 영사관원들에게 보낸 지시와 또 그들로부터 접수된 보고서, 국무성과 재미 외교사절과의 교환각서, 국무성 관리들이 작성한 비망록, 그리고 미국 행정부의 다른 부서와 민간단체 및 개인들과의 통신문 등이 포괄되어 있다. 방대한 이들 문서는 국무성 자체의 십진분류 문서철체계에 따라 정리되고 있는데3), 그 가운데 "십진문서철 895"(Decimal File 895)에는 한국과 관련된 일반 외교문서들이 들어있다. 이 외교문서들 중 일정시기가 경과한 후 소정절차를 밟아 공개된 문서들이 자료보존과 이용의 효율성을 높이기 위하여 마이크로필름으로 제작되고 있는 바 그 가운데 일부가 이번에 원주문화사를 통하여 출간되기에 이른 것이다.

이 자료집에 수록된 문서들은 시기적으로 1940년부터 1944년까지 한정되어 있는데, 그 대체적인 내용은 우선 문서목록(List of Papers)을 통하여 확인할 수 있다. 즉, 이 목록를 보면 국무성의 문서분류 기준에 따른 고유번호(File No.와 SUB No.)가 각 문서마다 매겨져 있고, 그 다음에는 문서의 작성자(또는 기관)와 작성일자 및 수신인(또는 기관), 그리고 문서의 요지가 간략히 기록되어 있다. 많지는 않지만 목차에 들어가 있는 문서가 본문에서 빠지는 경우도 더러 있다. 그 반대로 목차에는 나오지 않지만 본문에 수록된

---

3) 국무성의 문서분류 방법에 대해서는 이 자료집 제1권의 앞 부분에 수록된 "Introduction to the SR Microfilm Edition"을 참조하라.

문건의 경우 편집하는 과정에서 문서번호와 발신인 및 발신일자를 목차에 기입했다. 그리고 중국과 필리핀 관계문서가 잘못 들어간 부분이 있었는데 본문에서 삭제했다. 이외에도 똑같은 문서가 잇달아 나올 경우 그 가운데 하나만을 남겨 놓았다. 물론 이러한 문제들은 모두 사소한 것들로서, 자료집의 원상을 손상하지 않는 범위 내에서 조심스럽게 이루어졌음을 밝혀둔다.

이 자료집에 수록된 문서들은 그 성격으로 보아 크게 보아 두가지 범주로 나눌 수 있다.

첫째는 중국 중경에 근거를 두고 있던 대한민국임시정부와 미주 내 한인단체들이 미국 정부에 보낸 각종 청원문이다. 이 가운데 가장 많은 비중을 차지하고 있는 것이 '한국위원회'(Korean Commission)의 위원장 이승만과 중한민중동맹단(Sino-Korean People's League)의 대표 한길수가 보낸 문건이다. 이승만은 이때 중경의 임시정부로부터 대미외교의 전권을 위임받고 있었는데, 그가 보낸 청원문은 주로 임시정부 승인과 광복군에 대한 군사적 지원획득에 초점이 모아지고 있다. 한편 중일전쟁 발발 후 재미한인사회에서 이승만의 유력한 경쟁자로 부상하고 있던 한길수는 조선의용대 미주후원회 및 그 후속단체인 조선민족혁명당 미주지부와 연계하여 이승만의 외교선전활동에 제동을 걸고 있었다. 이외에도 대한인국민회가 주도한 재미한족연합위원회(United Korean Committee in America)와 이승만의 외교활동을 측면에서 지원하고 있던 한미협회(Korean-American Council), 기타 몇몇 단체와 개인들, 그리고 중경의 임시정부가 직접 미국 정부에 제출한 문건들이 자료집에 수록되어 있다.

둘째는 미국 정부의 공문서로서, 국무부에서 작성했거나 또는 국무부에 접수된 다른 행정부처와 재외공관의 문서들이다. 이들 문서에서 거론하고 있는 문제는 무척 다양하다. 그러나 가장 많이 언급되는 문제는 중경의 임시정부를 비롯한 한인망명단체의 승인여부이다. 이와 관련하여 국무부는 재미한인단체 및 주요인물들의 동향을 개인면담, 편지검열, 정보기관의 사찰 등의 방법으로 예의 주시하는 한편 중경 임시정부의 실상을 그곳에 주재하고 있는 자국 외교관원을 통하여 수시로 보고받고 있었다. 또한 국무부는 전후 한국의 독립과 임시정부의 승인문제를 놓고 중국 국민당 및 영국 정부의 입장을 타진하고 있다. 이외에도 한반도 내에서의 무장봉기의 가능성과 더불어 전술적 차원이기는 하지만 국외한인의 인적자원을 미국의 대일전쟁에 활용하는 문제가 신중히 검토되고 있었음을 알 수 있다.

전체적으로 볼 때 이 자료집에 수록된 문서들은 일정한 체계가 없어 무척 산만하다는 느낌을 줄 뿐만 아니라 전후 한반도문제에 대한 미국 정부의 기본입장이나 또는 정책결정 과정에 있어서 국무부와 다른 정부 부처간의 견해차이를 보여주는 주요 문건들이 쉽게 눈에 띄지 않는다. 이 때문에 공개된 국무부 일반문서는 "정부의 온갖 종류의 쓸모없는 하찮은 서류들을 내버리는 쓰레기장"이라는 극단적인 비판이 제기된 바 있다. 또 외교문서를 관장하는 당사자들도 국무성 문서분류 체계의 결함과 더불어 결정적인 문서의 사본들이 그 가운데 종종 빠져있음을 인정하고 있다.[4) 이러한 결함들은 국립문서관에 소장된 다른 정부 부처의 문서들에 의하여 보완될 수 있겠지만 이들 문서 또한 일정한 검토를 거쳐 공개되고 있는 만큼 완전한 자료의 복원이란 사실상 기대하기 어려운 일이다. 따라서 우리는 어차피 공개된 자료를 가지고 꼼꼼히 검토하는 가운데 의도적이었든 아니면 본래 그러한 것이었든 지워진 공백부분을 메꾸어 나갈 수밖에 없다.

이러한 시각에서 바라볼 때 우리가 이 자료집 수록된 문서들을 통하여 얻을 수 있는 것은 무엇일까.

첫째는 대한민국임시정부가 추진했던 대미승인교섭의 구체적 내용이다. 주지하듯이 임시정부는 출범 직후부터 외교노선에 치중했고, 특히 미일전쟁이 발발한 이후에는 미국의 승인을 얻기 위하여 최대의 노력을 기울였다. 그 노력이 얼마만큼 집요했는가는 임시정부와 재미한인단체들이 미국 정부에 제출한 각종 청원문의 분량만을 보더라도 쉽게 짐작할 수 있을 것이다. 이들 문서들을 종합적으로 분석·검토하게 되면 가장 중요한 고비에 임시정부의 승인외교가 갖고 있던 한계와 문제점을 파악할 수 있을 것이다.

둘째, 미국무부는 현안으로 제기된 국외 한인단체의 승인여부를 놓고 중국 국민당 및 영국정부와 긴밀히 협의했던 바 그 논의과정에서 서로 의견이 엇갈리는 부분을 면밀히 검토해 보면 이들 세 정부가 궁극적으로 전후 한반도문제를 어떻게 처리하려고 했는가 하는 점에 대하여 일정한 시사를 받을 수 있을 것이다. 왜냐하면 특정 한인단체의 승인문제는 전후 한국의 독립 및 새로 등장할 집권세력의 성격과 직결된 매우 민감한 사안이었기 때문이다. 이 자료집의 상당부분이 한국의 임시정부 승인문제와 관련되어 있는 것도 이 문제가 갖고 있는 상징적 중요성을 반영하는 것으로 받아들여야 할 것이다.

세째는 미국무부가 입수하고 있던 한국관련 정보의 총량과 그 질에 대한 파악이 가능하다. 사실 우리는 그동안 미국이 국외한인의 독립운동과 한반도 내의 사정에 대하여 얼마만한 정보를 갖고 있었으며, 또 어떻게 인식하고 있었는가 하는 문제를 거의 간과해 왔다. 그러나 이 문제에 대한 충분한 검토없이는 전전 미국의 대한정책 수립과정을 제대로 설명하기 어려울 뿐 아니라 전후 한반도에 진주한 미군정과 한국민의 관계에 대해서도 겉으로 드러난 현상으로 밖에 달리 이해할 길이 없다. 한편 해방직전 단계에서의 재미한인단체와 주요인물들의 동향 및 성격을 파악하고자 할 때에도 미국무부가 입수하고 있던 정보분석은 필수적이다. 아울러 중국 중경주재 미국 외교관원들의 임시정부에 대한 각종

---

4) 앞의 Jack Saunders의 글 가운데 p. 317 참조.

보고서도 이 시기 임시정부의 실상을 파악하는데 적지않은 도움을 줄 것이다.

 마지막으로 이 자료집만을 놓고 볼 때 미국은 대한정책 수립에 있어서 몇가지 한계를 갖고 있었던 것으로 보인다. 즉, 미국은 재미한인단체 및 중경 임시정부의 요구사항과 그 내부사정에 대하여 나름대로 파악하는 바가 있었지만 소련 및 만주 접경지대 그리고 중국관내 공산당의 관할지역에서 활동하고 있던 한인단체와 무장부대에 대해서는 무척 소략한--또는 시기가 지났거나 과장된--정보만을 갖고 있었다. 그것은 미국이 이 지역에 독자적인 정보망을 갖고 있지 못한 필연적인 결과라고 할 수 있다. 한편 일제 식민통치와 한반도 내의 사정에 대해서는 그 이전에 축적된 지식과 또 귀환하는 선교사들의 증언을 통하여 어느정도 알고 있었지만 과연 한국민 특히 일반민중의 불만과 요구를 얼마만큼 이해하고 있었는지는 의심스럽다.

 물론 해방 이전 미국이 대한정책을 수립함에 있어 가장 신경을 썼던 부분은 한국민의 다수의사가 아니라 연합국 열강의 한반도에 대한 관심과 이해관계였다. 그러나 이 문제에 국한해서 말한다 하더라도 미국은 정치적, 군사적으로 한반도문제에 실질적인 영향력을 행사할 수 있는 소련의 의도를 정확히 파악하지 못하고 있었다. 이렇게 된 직접적인 이유는 소련의 대일참전이 마지막 순간까지 유동적이었고, 따라서 미국은 그 이후의 사태진전을 예견하기가 무척 어려웠다. 이 점은 소련의 참전 후 불과 일주일만에 일본이 무조건 항복했다는 사실에서 뚜렷이 읽을 수 있다. 요컨대 일본의 패전 후 한반도문제가 미국의 의도대로 순조롭게 풀려나가지 않은 것은 그들의 정책결정에 있어서 한국민의 다수의사를 이해하고 그것을 반영시키려는 문제의식이 결여되어 있었다는 점과 더불어 소련의 한반도문제에 대한 개입을 예상했음에도 불구하고 그에 대한 견제수단과 대안을 충분히 갖추고 있지 못했기 때문이 아닌가 하는 것이 필자 나름의 생각이다.

1993년 11월 12일

포항공과대학 교양학부
한국근대사 고 정 휴

INTERNAL AFFAIRS OF KOREA 1940–1944

Records of the U.S. Department of State
relating to the
Internal Affairs of Korea, 1940-1944

- - - - - - - - - - - - -

Department of State Decimal File 895

Library of Congress Cataloging-in-Publication Data

Records of the U.S. Department of State relating to
   the internal affairs of Korea, 1940-1944 [microform].

   Includes index.
   1. Korea—History—Japanese occupation, 1910-1945—
Sources.   2. United States. Dept. of State—Archives.
I. United States. Dept. of State.   II. Title:
Records of the U.S. Department of State relating to
the internal affairs of Korea, 1940-1944.
[DS916.54]   016.9519'03   86-15424
ISBN 0-8420-3017-4

This microfilm edition © 1986
by Scholarly Resources Inc.

PUBLISHER'S NOTE

The materials in the Department of State file have been microfilmed in the exact order and condition in which they appear in the holdings of the National Archives and Records Administration. Those documents that have not yet been declassified were removed prior to filming and replaced with notices identifying the item and the reason for its removal.

ACKNOWLEDGEMENT

This publication is produced with the cooperation of the National Archives and Records Administration.

DECLASSIFICATION NOTICE FOR USERS OF THIS PUBLICATION

Documents in this microfilm publication were declassified by
appropriate authorities of the Federal Government in accordance
with the provisions of current Executive orders. Copies of
documents bearing national security classification markings
which are reproduced from this publication should be labeled as
follows:

DECLASSIFIED
E.O. 11652 or E.O. 12356
NATIONAL ARCHIVES AND RECORDS ADMINISTRATION

Documents determined to contain still sensitive national
security classified information were withdrawn prior to the time
of filming. Any withdrawn document is briefly described on a
"Withdrawal Notice" filed and filmed in its place. Some
withdrawn documents may have been reviewed again, declassified
and released to the public subsequent to the preparation of this
publication. Inquiries about such releases should be addressed
to:

Diplomatic Branch
Civil Archives Division
National Archives and Records Administration
Washington, DC 20408

TRUDY HUSKAMP PETERSON
Acting Assistant Archivist
for the National Archives

Introduction to the
SR Microfilm Edition of
**RECORDS OF THE U.S. DEPARTMENT OF STATE RELATING TO THE
INTERNAL AFFAIRS OF KOREA, 1940-1944**

This publication reproduces the U.S. Department of State Decimal File 895, titled **Records Relating to the Internal Affairs of Korea** for the years 1940 through 1944. The documents found in this file are predominantly instructions to and despatches from U.S. diplomatic and consular staff regarding political, economic, military, social, and other internal conditions and events in Korea. Other types of documents represented are reports and memoranda prepared by State Department staff, communications between the State Department and foreign governments, and correspondence with other departments of the U.S. government, private firms, and individuals.

Decimal File 895 is part of the General Records of the Department of State, Record Group 59.

ABOUT THE DECIMAL FILING SYSTEM

From 1910 to 1963, the State Department used a decimal filing system to organize its central files, which subsequently became known as the "Decimal Files." This filing system is basically a numerical subject index; documents are assigned file numbers according to the subject they cover. The numerical-subject listing for Class 8 records follows this introduction, and is also reproduced in the printed Guide for this microfilm.

Each document's file number includes four elements of classification. An example is given below:

8   95   ·   24 / 446
(1)   (2)   (3)   (4)

(1) Class Number. The decimal filing system begins with nine major classes, each corresponding to a broad subject area. All the documents in this publication are in Class 8, which designates materials on the internal affairs of states.

(2) Country Number. Every country was assigned by the Department of State an identifying number. All documents in this publication have the country number of 95, designating Korea.

(3) Subject Number (follows the decimal point). Within each Decimal File class, a numerical outline of subjects is developed to allow filing of documents by topic. Subjects can be as general as "Political Affairs" and as precise as "Disposal of the Dead." In this example, the numerical-subject outline for Class 8 reveals that this document deals with subject 24, which is "Military equipment and supplies."

- 3 -

(4) Document Number (follows the slash). Within each subject group, documents are filed in chronological order and then numbered. In this example, the document is the 446th to be filed on the subject of military equipment. From July 1944 on, the document number reflects the date of the document's creation. For example, a document dated November 20, 1944, would be numbered 11-2044. This numbering system is also used for documents that were created before July 1944 but not filed until after this date.

THE LIST OF PAPERS AND THE PURPORT CARDS

The State Department prepared a List of Papers, or purport list, for each Decimal File. This list records the documents in numerical order, as they appear in the file, and provides for each the date sent, the sender and recipient, an abstract of its contents, and other information. Beginning in 1944, the State Department switched to recording the same general information for each document on individual Purport Cards. The selection of the List of Papers or Purport Cards corresponding to the documents on each roll of microfilm appears at the beginning of the roll. This can be used conveniently as a table of contents for the roll.

A page from the List of Papers, a Purport Card, and an example of a first page of a document are shown in the printed Guide, with annotations pointing out the location of specific information the researcher will find useful.

LOCATING DOCUMENTS ON THE MICROFILM

Because of the organization of the Decimal File, this is a particularly easy collection for researchers to access. When looking for information on a particular topic, follow these steps:

(1) Check the numerical-subject listing for Class 8 records, located both in the Guide and on this roll of film, to determine the subject number of the topic of interest to you.

(2) Check the Roll Contents, located both in the Guide and on this roll of film, to determine the roll or rolls of film on which documents with your subject number appear.

(3) With an appropriate roll of film in the reader, start at the List of Papers or Purport Cards at the beginning of the roll, and read the abstracts for documents with your subject number, noting the document number of any that seem promising.

(4) Turn in the roll of film to the documents you wish to inspect.

NUMERICAL-SUBJECT LISTING FOR

CLASS 8 RECORDS

Note: Asterisks (as in 8**.00) indicate Country Numbers.

8**.00   Political Affairs.
     Elections, political parties, political refugees, amnesty, revolutions, riots, and political conspiracies.
     8**.00B Bolshevism. Communism. Communist activities.
        .00F Fascism. Fascist activities.
        .00N Nazi. Nazi activities.
        .00S Socialism. Socialist activities. Industrial Workers of the World.
        .001 Chief executive. Sovereign.
        .002 Cabinet. Ministry.
     8**.01 Government.
        Mandates, recognition, constitution, citizenship, political rights, and flag.
     8**.02 Executive departments of government.
     8**.03 Legislative branch of government.
     8**.04 Judicial branch of government.
     8**.05 Mixed (international) courts.

8**.10   Public Order, Safety, Health, and Works. Charities and Philanthropic Organizations.
     8**.11 Regulations governing residence, trade, travel, firearms, explosives, liquor, drugs, and sex relations.
     8**.12 Public health.
     8**.13 Correction and punishment.
     8**.14 Charities.
     8**.15 Public works.

8**.20   Military Affairs. Army. Army Posts. Fortifications. Defenses.
     8**.21 Army maneuvers.
     8**.22 Personnel.
     8**.23 Movement of troops.
     8**.24 Equipment and supplies.

8**.30   Naval Affairs. Navy. Naval Vessels.
     8**.31 Naval maneuvers.
     8**.32 Personnel.
     8**.33 Movement of naval vessels.
     8**.34 Equipment and supplies.

8**.40   Social Matters.
     8**.41 History.
     8**.42 Education.
     8**.43 Societies.
     8**.44 Special mention of citizens or subjects of country ** not otherwise classifiable.
     8**.45 Etiquette.
     8**.46 Entertainment.
     8**.48 Calamities. Disasters.

8**.50   Economic Matters.
         8**.51   Financial conditions.
         8**.52   Lands.
         8**.54   Intellectual and industrial property.
         8**.55   Immigration.
         8**.56   Emigration.
8**.60   Industrial Matters.
         Monopolies, concessions, franchises, contracts, bounties, subsidies,
         cartels, trades. expositions, and exhibitions.
         8**.61   Agriculture.
         8**.62   Animal husbandry.
         8**.63   Mines. Mining.
         8**.64   Engineering.
         8**.65   Manufactures. Manufacturing.
8**.70   Communication and Transportation.
         8**.71   Post.
         8**.72   Telegraph.
         8**.73   Cable.
         8**.74   Wireless telegraph.
         8**.75   Telephone.
         8**.76   Wireless telephone.
         8**.77   Railway.
         8**.78   Street railway.
         8**.79   Other means of communication and transportation.
8**.80   Navigation.
         8**.81   Waterways.
         8**.82   Aids to navigation.
         8**.83   Menaces to navigation.
         8**.84   Taxes on navigation.
         8**.85   Merchant vessels.
         8**.86   Seamen.
         8**.88   Foreign carrying trade.
8**.90   Other Internal Affairs.
         8**.91   Public press.
         8**.92   Science. Philosophy.

Note: ** and ++ indicate Country Numbers.

Subject: **Political Affairs – Chosen.**

727

-1940-

SUB No.	FROM—	DATE	TO—	SUB No.	PURPORT	
727	Korean Student Federation of North America (Chicago, Ill.) Seunghak Cho	Nov.15	FE Sur...		Closing of churches and schools in Korea by the Japanese. Transmits translations of certain articles with regard to pressure being brought in --	
727	Sino-Korean Peoples' League (Haan, Kilsoo K) fe	-1941- May 13			America's sympathy toward Korea. Requests President Roosevelt to express -- for freedom and independence in nationwide radio broadcast.	50
728	Sino-Korean Peopl's League (Haan, Kilsoo K) fe	May 16			DITTO: DITTO: ncloses clipping from New York Times, May 16.	53
729	State Dept. PA/H (Hornbeck)	Aug.20	PA/H Confidential File	MEMO	Approach made by leading representative of Korean nationalists. Memo attached regarding --. NOTE 895.01	54
730	Philippines High Commissioner of US(R. C. Ross) FE PA/H	Nov 21			Independence of Korea. Transmits letter from Edward Lim, regarding question of,-	64
731	Censorship, Office of	Jan.30			Letter from Philip K. S. Pyun, Wahiawa, Oahu, T. H. to Private Kenneth H. Pyun, Mississippi: Transmits report of -- informing of the Koreans' hatred of Japan.	72
732	Sino-Korean Peoples League (Haan, Kilsoo K.)	May 5			Fight of the Korean National Federation against Japan. ... eleven points in the belief that it will be of some value in the decision of arriving at more effective policy giving aid in regard to --	73
833	Korean-American Council Washington, D. C. (Summerfield, Aletta)	1942 Apr.30	fe a-b/h		News items relating to Korea. Transmits mimeographed copy of--.	78
834	DESCRIPTIVE ENTRY	Apr. 28	fe a-b/h		DO: Mimeographed copy of -- sent by Korean-American Council.	
835	Korean National Front Federation (Haan)	Aug 12	fe		How Japan Plans to Win: Encloses recently translated book entitled --.	83
		Aug 17	Sino-Korean People's League (Haan) fe	835	DO: Acknowledges receipt of book entitled --.	
836	Korean National Front Federation Washington, D.C. (Haan)	Aug.15	FE PA/H A-B		Various Korean activities. Expresses views in respect to --.	88
		Aug 24	Sino-Korean Peoples League (Haan) FE FE PA/H au	836	DO: Acknowledges receipt of letter expressing views in respect of --.	
837	State Dept. European Affairs (Cannon)		au	MEMO	Free Korea movement: Submits memorandum regarding --	93
838	Sino-Korean Peoples League	Aug 31	FE		Script entitled "VICTORY STARTS AT HOME": Encloses copy of radio talk -- in regard to Korea.	105

See sheet #28.

895.00

LIST OF PAPERS

Subject Political Affairs – Chosen.

839   1942

ICS No.	FROM—	DATE	TO—	SUB No.	PURPORT	
839	Junkin, Edward L.	Dec. 20		NOTE	Korean independence and United States strategy. Letter regarding the –. See 811.001 Roosevelt, F.D /737	104
840	State Department Far Eastern Affairs (Hamilton)	1942 Oct. 10	FE	MEMO	aspirations of the Koreans for freedom. Submits a suggestion for a constructive way in which to approach the Korean question.	105
841	Rhee, Syngman	Dec. 7	FE		Present and ultimate aims of the Korean Provisional Government. Copy of memorandum prepared at request of Dr. Victor Hoo, the Chinese Under Secretary of Foreign Affairs on the –. Note to 794.95	109
842	Hyrarrd, Norman E.	Jan. 8			Korean government. Transmits letter to Henry Wallace in regard to –.	114
843	China (Chungking) #2214 (Gauss)	Feb. 23	CA TS		Conditions in Korea: Encloses despatch No. 17, February 3, 1944, from the Secretary on detail at Sian reporting on –.	116

FORM DS-46
10/12/45

DEPARTMENT OF STATE

LIST OF PAPERS

005.01

SUBJECT

Government. Korea (Chosen)

SUB NO.	FROM	DATE	TO	SUB NO.	PURPORT	
48	Provisional Government of Republic of Korea (Kin Ku)	1941 Feb. 25	FE		Recognition of Provisional Government of Korea, Requests –.	122
49	Faddis, Charles I. USS.	Dec. 8	FE		Independence of Korea: Suggests recognition of Korea's provisional government would be an encouragement to movements already mentioned and would be of distinct assistance in defeating Japan.	132
49½	Korean Commission (So-ang, Joe)	June 6	Korea's status: Informs of –, and advises that Dr. Syngman Rhee has been appointed official diplomatic representative of Gov't. in U. S.		Korean provisional government at Chungking: Heads the recognise–, also informs Koreans in April offer services.	134
50	United Korean Committee in America, Tel.	Dec 10	FE			147
51	Korean National Association (Kim, Yongjeun)	Nov 15			Korean rights as affected by present Japanese situation, refers to visit of Sayuru kurusu to Washington and to –, and expresses hope for a favorable settlement that will not deprive Korea of rights. Held in Third and Eighth joint declarations of both the president and r. See 711.94/.36	148
51½	Navy Dept.	Nov. 24	Possible Korean National activity: Attaches document, copy of information intercepted by British censors at Hongkong.			149

Subject: Government– Korea (Japan)

5d   1—207   1941

SUB No.	FROM—	DATE	TO—	SUB No.	PURPORT
52	State Dept. Far Eastern Affairs (Langdon)	Dec. 13	A–B/H FE	Memo	Korean organizations in the U.S. Memorandum stating that there are three organizations of Koreans ... 153
52½	State Dept. Far Eastern Affairs (Salisbury)	Dec. 23 A–B/H	Korean Independence and Allied Questions:Memo of conversation between Mr. J.Jerome Williams, John W.Staggers and Mr.Salis- F. E. bury re.—	MEMO 52	in the U.S. ... the Korean Commission, headed by Dr. Syngman Rhee, and the Sino-Korean Peoples League, represented in this country by Kilsoo Han. Disbanding of each. ... 156
Memo	State Dept. Foreign Activity Correlation (Hoskins)	Dec.17			Re: Memorandum submitting copy of Free Korea which is a dissertation on — for attention of Mr. Hornbeck
		Dec. 17	Faddis, Charles I. FE CI PA/H FE	49	Independence of Korea. No answer is given to all questions such as — and expresses thanks for bringing the matter to attention of Dept.
FW	United Korean Committee Honolulu (Won Soon Lee) Tel/FE PA/H	Dec 17		53	Government of Korea. Desires that status should be clarified so that they will not be subjected to the enemy alien treatment.
53	President (Watson) FE PA/H	Dec18			Do:– Transmits telegram from United Korean Committee. ... 161
54	State Dept. PA/H (Hornbeck)	Dec 16		MEMO	Do:– Transmits three documents which should be regarded as not yet received by the State Department. ... 163
FW	State Dept Division of Far Eastern Affairs (Langdon) PA/H	Dec 20		54 MEMO	Do:– States no definite decision should be made on matter at the present time.
		Dec 23	China(Chungking) Tel # 320 6 PM FE PA/H	54	Do:– Information desired regarding the Republic of Korea claiming to have its seat in Chungking.
55	Korean National Association Ho Kim Tel A	Dec.31 1942	FE FC		Convention of the Korean National Association: Message of gratification to Cordell Hull from —. ... 170
56	China (Chungking) Tel.#12, 3pm Gauss	Jan. 3 1941	FE PA/H		Provisional Government of the Republic of Korea. Information concerning an investigation of —. ... 172
57	State Dept. PA/H (Hornbeck)	Aug.20 –1942–		OTE	Approach made by leading representatives of Korean nationalists. Copy of papers left at Department by Dr. Syngman Rhee on July 4 regarding Korean Government. Information given to Dr. Syngman on Department's attitude in matter. — 895.00/729 ... 184
57½	Haan, Kilsoo K. Tel.#—; 5:30 am	Jan.5	Request as Washington representative of the Korean Volunteer Army in China and Sino-Korean Peoples League that the U.S.Gov't permit Korea to join the 26 Anti-Axis powers: Submits —.		... 185
58	Haan, Kilsoo K. Tel.—	Dec.26 1942			Cordial Christmas greetings to Secretary Hull. ... 188
59	Gillette, Guy M. USS	Jan.6 1942	FE PA/H		Adherence of Provisional Korean Gov't to the Twenty-Six Nation Pact upon recognition of the Gov't by the U.S. Comments concerning —, and probable effects. ... 190
60	Williams, Jay Jerome Staggers, John W. Harris, Frederick Brown	Jan.10	FE		Korean independence movement. Transmits copy of memorandum prepared for support of —. ... 196

See Page 106

Subject: Government - Korea(Chosen)

60-1/26   1-307   -1941-

SUB No.	FROM—	DATE	TO—	SUB No.	PURPORT	
60-1/26	State Department Foreign Activity Correlation(Hoskins)	Dec. 9		MEMO	"Free Korea":Memorandum of conversation between Dr.Syngman Rhee, head of the Korean Commission in Washington and Mr. Hoskins re.-.	202
60-2/26	Rhee, Syngman(Dr) Korean Commission Washington, D. C.	Dec. 9			Request that Koreans in this country be allowed to carry on their business unmolested:Submits -.	206
60-3/26	Sino-Korean Peoples' League Washington, D.C. (Haan, Kilsoo K.)	Dec. 12			"Free Korea":Requests that Koreans in this country be permitted to assist in the defense of America and its security in the Pacific.	204
60-4/26	Rhee, Syngman(Dr)	Dec. 17			Aid for the Koreans fighting in China:Reports on conversation with Major Wallace H. Moore of the Army Intelligence Service who promised he would endeavor to secure -.	211
60-5/26	State Department PA/H(Hiss)	Dec.18		MEMO	Korean activities in the United States:Memo of conversation between Dr. Syngman Rhee, of the Korean Commission and Mr. Hiss re.-.	215
		-1942-				
60-6/26	State Department A-B/H(Hoskins)	Jan. 2		MEMO	Free Korean Movement:Informs he will handle discussions or correspondence regarding -.	218
60-7/26	Kim, Yongjeung	Jan. 9			Status of Koreans in the U.S. and Hawaii with regard to the recent freezing order of the U.S.Treasury: Requests that Treasury Dept. announce publicly that the freezing of Korean funds is solely for protective purposes and that the Koreans are friendly aliens.	219
60-8/26	State Dept. Foreign Activity Correlations	Jan.19		MEMO	Free Korea:Informs the procedure to be adopted re.registration of Koreans as enemy aliens.	222
60-9/26	Justice Dept.	Jan.26			Registration of Koreans :Encloses copy of letter from Haan, Kilsoo K. inquiring as to status of -.	223
60-10/26	Staggers,John W.	Jan.30			DO:Encloses copy of letter addressed to Mr.Kilsoo K. Haan regarding his activities in connection with -, on behalf of Dr.Syngman Rhee, Chairman of the Korean Commission.	228
60-11/26	State Dept. PA/H(Hornbeck)	Feb. 4		MEMO	Free Korea:Memo of conversation between Dr. Syngman Rhee and Mr.Hornbeck re.problems in connection with -.	230
60-12/26	United Korean Committee in America,Honolulu T.H. (Dunn, J.Kyuang)	Feb.19			Exclusion of Koreans from the enemy alien registration:Expresses appreciation for the -,recently effected by the Department of Justice.	
60- /26	State Dept. PA/H(Hiss)	Mar. 27		MEMO	Korean Provisional Government:Informs Colonel Zia ,an assistant military attache at the Chinese Embassy in Washington is well informed as to the -.	233
60-14/26	Hahn, Soon K.	Mar. 19			DO:Informs of his forthcoming visit to Washington to discuss Korean problems.	234
60-15/26	Rhee, Syngman(Dr)	Apr.9			Reorganization of Korean Volunteer Corps in China:Copy of telegram from T.Josowang,Chungking re.-.	

See Pg3

Subject: __Government - Korea(Chosen)__

-1942-

SUB No.	FROM—	DATE	TO—	SUB No.		PURPORT	
16/26	Haan, Kil Soo Sino Korean Peoples League Tel.-	Apr.18				Congratulations on Bombing Tokyo: Transmits -.	235
17/26	State Department Foreign Activity Correlation (Hoskins)	Apr.28				Korean Independence: Discusses original draft of telegram re.- and gives reasons for sending it.	236
18/26	Haan, Kil Soo K. Sino Korean Peoples League	May 5				Newly formed Korean National Front Federation,composed of four Korean political parties in the Far East: Submits eleven point program on behalf of the -, to aid the Dept. in arriving at some effective policy giving aid to the Korean National Front Federation.	239
19/26	Haan, Kilsoo K. Sino Korean Peoples League	May 4				Korean Census in U.S. and Hawaii: Inquires whether all the Koreans must comply with the request of the Korean Commission to submit to the -.	243
20/26	Jhung, C.	May 8				Korean Provisional Government: Submits suggestions regarding Korea and the Korean people.	248
		May 12	Jhung, C. A-B/H	60-20/26	DO:	Acknowledges receipt of letter submitting suggestions re.-.	
21/26	Coordinator of Information(Langer)	May 14				Korean Independence Movement: prepared in the Research and Analysis Branch of the Coordinator's office Transmits copy of Report No.41 re-	252
22/26	DISCRIPTIVE ENTRY	May 23				Korean Strength in Free China Consolidated under one Command:Excerpt from the CHINESE NEWS SERVICE, NYC, dated May 23, 1942.	259
23/26	State Department A-B/H(Hoskins)	June 1			MEMO	Kilsoo Haan:Memo of conversation between Mr. Hoskins and Mr.-,who outlined his ideas regarding Korea.	265
24/26	Haan, Kilsoo K.	June 17				Future of Korean Independence: Informs of willingness to withdraw from the Korean political field to prove his sincerity.	274
25/26	State Department A-B/H(Hoskins)	June 17			MEMO	Korean Revolt said to have taken place in Northern Korea on Feb.2-6, 1942:Memo of conversation with Mr.Kilsoo K. Haan who left the attached memorandum re-.	275
		May 8	Haan, Kilsoo K. FE	60-19/26		Korean Census in U.S. and Hawaii: Informs State Dept.has no knowledge of the rumored -.	

See Page #6

Subject: Government - Korea (Chosen)

1942

SUB No.	FROM—	DATE	TO—	SUB No.	PURPORT	
61	Senate, U.S. President of	Jan.14	fe		DO: Letter from Norman E. Nygaard of Los Angeles, California, urging recognition and encouragement of a provisional Korean Government which represents the people of the hermit kingdom. States that the Koreans have never accepted Japanese rule.	280
62	China (Chungking) (Gauss) #248	Dec.20	FE PA/H		Letter from "Tjosowang, Foreign Minister of The Provisional Gov't of the Republic of Corea" to the President. Encloses —.	282
63	King, Samuel W., MC	Jan.19	fe		Government - Korea (Chosen) Discussion of difficult position of people of Korean nationality or descent who reside in Hawaii due to their technical status as nationals of Japan. Suggests that Korean nationals in America be put in a separate category from that of Japanese nationals, so that they may not be classified as enemy aliens. Note 740.00115 Pacific War.	
64	Gillette, Guy M., USS	Jan.20	fe :a/h		Possible recognition of the Korea Provisional Government by U. S. Appreciates and commends views of Department concerning—.	288
		Jan.19	Gillette, Guy M. USS FE:PA/H:A-B:	59	Investigation of certain pro-Axis activities, particularly relating to the Far Eastern situation, and to the possible recognition by this Govt. of the Korean Provisional Govt. Acks. receipt of letter in regard to —.	
65	United Korean Committee in America (Lee)	Jan.23	FE		Appeal for recognition of the Provisional Government of the Republic of Korea. Makes urgent appeal, encloses open appeal for —.	289
		Jan.26	Williams, Jay Jerome A-B FE	60	DO: Informs that points set forth in memorandum regarding — will be given careful consideration.	
		Jan.26	Nygaard, Norman E. A-B FE	61	DO: Assures him that careful consideration will be given views re.—.	
66	Gillette, Guy M. USS	Jan.22	EU PA/H		Article by Geraldine T. Fitch in the publication, "Amerasia". Encloses photostatic copy of an excerpt from —; requests the copy be returned after reading it.	314
		Jan.30	Gillette, Guy M. USS FE PA/H A-B/H DE	56	Article entitled "Korea's Hope of Freedom" published in Jan. issue AMERASIA. Expresses appreciation in sending the excerpt — and advises that copy if being returned after having made a copy for Dept's file.	
		Jan.29	King, Samuel Wilder MC A-B/H FE A-B PA/H	63	Situation of Korean nationals and possible recognition by this Govt. of Korean Provisional Govt. Encloses copy of statement released from Attorney General regarding —.	

See Page #7

LIST OF PAPERS

Subject: Government - Korea (Chosen)

67

SUB No.	FROM—	DATE	TO—	SUB No.	PURPORT	
67	Korean Commission (Rhee)	Feb. 7	FE PA/H SR		Present situation of American-Korean affairs. Transmits letters to President and State Department relative to —.	319
		1942				
68	China (Chungking) (Gauss) Tel # 80 10 am	Jan 31		ECIE	Tjosowang, Mr. Application has been made by a German, — to visit the US to attend a foreign confer ence as the representative of the Provisional Government of Korea at the invitation of Korean Commission at 1766 Hobart St. Wash, D. C. of which Dr Syngman Rhee is understood to be the head. SEE 811.111-Tjosowang, Mr.	322
		Feb 12	Great Britain (G) Tel # 551 MIDNIGHT FE EU PA/H A-B/H A-B	68a	Participation by Koreans in the war effort. Views of Government of US on approach made by various Korean groups in US working for Korean independence regarding	
69	Great Britain Winant Tel. #730 12pm	Feb.16	FE EU PA/H A-B/H	A-B	DO: Informs of discussion with foreign office relative to —.	325
70	Imperial Mutual Life Insurance Co Los Angeles.Cal (Frank P. Tibbetts) FE	Feb.14			Recognition of Provisional Government of Korea. Suggests,—	327
		Feb.13	Rhee, Syngman PA/H FE A-B	67	Present situation of American-Korean affairs: Acknowledges receipt of letter of Feb. 7th concerning — and encloses copy of Dept's press release of Dec. 10, 1941 concer ing policy regarding "Free Movements" in the US.	
71	Welch, Richard J., MC	Feb.19	fe		Recognition of provisional Go vernment of Korea. Letter from Frank P. Tibbetts requesting that some action be taken for—.	330
72	State Department A-B (Hoskins)	Feb.12		MEMO.	DO: Telephone conversation with Mr. Singman Rhee concerning his rea son for return of various offi cial documents covering request for— to Dr. Hornbeck.	333
73	Great Britain Tel. #962,3pm (Matthews)	Feb.28	RE EU PA/H A-B/H A-B		DO: Quotes memorandum received which sets forth the views of the Foreign Office toward—, and informs of activities and approa ches made by Mr. Tjoso Wang, Mr. Ching Jo-Shan, and Mr. Yong Jeung Kim.	336
74	United Korean Committee in America (KIM, F. Y.) Executive Vice Chairman	Feb.28	FE FC Los Angeles,Calif.		23rd Anniversary of declaration of independence of Korea and founding of Korean republic. Informs of meeting of — and reaffirm loyalty to America,democracy and freedom.	356
		Feb.26	Welch, Richard J. MC A-B/H FE PA/H	71	Recognition of provisional Govt. of Korea. Transmits copy of reply sent to Dept. from Frank P. Tibbett s, Feb. 23, regarding —.	

LIST OF PAPERS

Subject: Government - Korea(Chosen)

75

SUB No.	FROM	DATE	TO	SUB No.	PURPORT	
75	United Korean Committee in America, Los Angeles, California Kim, F.	Mar 2	FE		Independence of Korea. Reports that at a mass meeting to commemorate the twenty-third anniversary of the proclamation of the — they adopted a resolution to petition Secretary and to formally recognize the provisional government of Korea.	357
76	Great Britain (Matthews) Tel. No 0. 6pm	Feb 27		NOTE	Government - Korea. Inquires regarding statement made by the Attorney General that Koreans who had not owned allegiance to Japan before a certain date would not be treated as enemies.	359
77	Dongjihoi Society, Los Angeles, Calif. Officers and Members Tel. 4	Mar 4	FE PA/H		Independence of Korea. States that they are most grateful for consideration for recognition of Korea.	360
78	United Korean Committee in America, Los Angeles, Calif.	Mar.2	fe		Recognition of Provisional Government of Korea. Copy of resolution adopted at mass meeting of the Committee on March 1,1942 urging the Secretary of State to recognize this government now in exile in Chungking.	363
79	State Department Far Eastern Affairs (Langdon)	Feb.20	U AB FE	MEMO	Some aspects of the question of Korean independence. Reports on	366
		Mar.3	KIM, P. Y A-B/H PA/H fe	75	Recognition of Provisional Government of Korea. Assures that petition will be brought to attention of interested officials of State Dept. and will be given due consideration.	
80	Korea Provisional Government of (Kim Ku)T.I FE.	Mar 10			Do:- Requests.-	385
81	China(Chungking) (Gauss) # 297 FE - PA/H SR	Feb 12			Provisional Government of Korea. Transmits copy of letter from Tjosowang, Minister of Foreign Affairs of,- with enclosures which contains information on,-	390
82	Bird, Remsen D.	Feb.14			Korean for Victory Movement, in the United States. Encloses letter to Doctor Syngham Rhee, regarding.-	307
83	Korean Liberty Conference Washington, D.C.	Mar.1			Korean Liberty Conference held at LaFayette Hotel, Washington, D.C. Feb. 27, 28 and March 1, 1942, sponsored by the United Korean Committee in America and the Korean American Council. Transmits resolutions, press releases and program relative to.-	412
84	United Korean Committee in America, L. A. Calif. Korean-American Council, Washington D.C.	Feb.27			DO: Invitation to .-	435

See Page #9

LIST OF PAPERS

Subject: Government - Korean (Chosen)

1942

SUB No.	FROM—	DATE	—TO—	SUB No.	PURPORT	
MEMO.	State Department Far Eastern Affairs (Langdon)	Mar.3		FW84	Korean Liberty Conference held at the Lafayette Hotel, Washington D.C. on February 27-28 and Mar.1. Comments on –.	
85	Sino-Korean Peoples League Tel.#	Mar.3			Korean Independence. Expresses hearty appreciation for Mr.Welles sympathy towards –.	447
86	State Dept. Far Eastern Affairs (Salisbury)	Mar.6	pa/h a-b/h fe.	FW6	Objectives of Koreans in the United States: Informs of call of Mr.Soon K.Hahn to discuss – in respect to becoming unified and serving the United States.	448
MEMO	State Dept. Far Eastern Affairs (Salisbury)	Mar.7	pa/h a-b/h fe FW	86	DO: Informs of call of Mr.Hahn re –; discusses various Koreans and Korean activities in the U.S. and war plan submitted to President Roosevelt by Mr.Hahn.	
MEMO	State Dept. Far Eastern Affairs (Salisbury)	Mar.14	pa/h a-b/h u fe FW	86	DO: Informs of call of Mr.Hahn re possibility of the Amer.Govt. recognizing the "Korean Provisional Govt.at Chungking"in connection with –.Dr.Syngman Rhee is the Wash.representative of this regime;recognition granted to this regime prior to unification of various Korean groups in the war effort would rival the Korean Provisional Govt.	
		Mar.20	China Tel.#199 9pm FE PA/H EU A-B/H	56	Provisional Government of the Republic of Korea. Comments regarding recognition of – and requests information regarding the Korean question.	
12710	State Department A-B/H (Hoskins)	Mar.13		FW 56	DO: Suggests revision of final paragraph emphasizing idea of issuing statement determining future attitude of Chinese Govt.	
		Mar.20	Great Britain. Tel.#1172 10pm FE PA/H EU A-B/H	73	Recognition of Provisional Government of Korea. Informs that Department coincides with views of Foreign Office and refers to statement made at press conference in regard to –, see radio bulletin of March 2.	
87	Korean Commission (Rhee)	Mar.24	PA/H FE A-B		DO: Desire of Korean govt. to be advised how U. S. Govt. regards the enclosed treaty between the two countries.	468
88	China(Chungking) Tel.#285. 9 am (Gauss)	Mar.28	FE PA/H EU A-B/H		Provisional Govt. of the Republic of Korea. Information concerning –.	462
89	State Dept. PA/H	Mar 17	u a-b/h pa/h a-a fe		"Recognition" of Korea: Discusses possible ways of handling pressure on the Dept. for the, –	467
90	Soon K. Hahn	Mar 17	fe pa/h		Interview with Acting Sect. Welles: Requests, – to discuss Korean problems.	469
		Mar 25	Soon K. Hahn FE pa/h a-b/h	90	DO: Regrets, – cannot be granted because of pressure of official business.	

see page #10

895.01

File No.

LIST OF PAPERS

Subject: Government -- Korean (Chosen)

91

-1942-

SUB No.	FROM—	DATE	TO—	SUB No.	PURPORT	
91	Haan, Kilsoo K.	Feb. 12	PA/H		Activities of Dr. Syngman Rhee: Informs concerning the --.	471
		Feb. 18	Haan, Kilsoo K. PA/H FE A-B/H	91	Do: Informs that letter of Feb. 12th concerning the -- will be brought to attention of officers of Dept. who are concerned with matters relating to --.	
		Apr. 7	China (Chungking) Tel. #283.9pm fe pa/h a-b/h a-b	8*	Recognition of Korea: requests continued expression of views in connection with --.	
92	Staggers, John W.	Jan. 30			Activities of Mr. Kilsoo K. Haan in behalf of the Korean cause: Encloses copy of letter to Mr. Haan concerning --.	475
93	Justice Department	Jan. 23			Certificates of Identification for aliens of enemy nationalities: Encloses photostatic letter to Mr. Kilsoo K. Haan, informing that Koreans who registered under the Alien registration act of 1940, are not required to apply for --.	486
94	Frederick Harris John W. Staggers Jay Jerome Williams	Feb. 4	FE PA/H		Korean revolution against the Japanese and the question of Korean independence: Copy of letter sent to the Navy Department concerning the question of a --.	488
		Feb. 11	War Department pa/h fe a-b	92	Recognition of the Korean Commission by the State Department as an official representative of the Provisional Government of Korea: Encloses memorandum commenting on certain statements made in a letter addressed to Mr. Kilsoo K. Haan, by Mr. John W. Staggers.	
		Feb. 14	Justice Department pa/h fe a-b/h a-b	92	DO: DO:	
		Feb. 11	Navy Department pa/h fe a-b/h a-b	92	DO: DO:	
95	War Department	Feb. 22	fe		DO: Acknowledges receipt of letter relative to --.	492
96	China (Chungking) Tel. #381. 10am (Gauss)	Apr. 10	fe pa/h		Recognition of the Korean Provisional Government: Information concerning the proposal for immediate --, submitted by Sun Fo and supported by certain party members.	495
		Apr. 11	China (Chungking) Tel. #283.6pm FE PA/H	96	DO: Requests that before the Chinese Government takes any definitive action with regard to the -- it will make available its views and conclusions.	
97	China (Chungking) (Gauss) Tel. #411. 10am	Apr. 15	FE PA/H		DO: Reports that they will notify in advance any informed developments and Chinese Government's views in regard to --.	524
98	China (Chungking) Tel. 287- 11am (Gauss)	Mar. 28	a-p		DO: United press report is based upon an address by Sun Fo before a local cultural association which subsequently appeared in the Chinese language press in abbreviated form. Extracts reported by the United Press correspondent	525
98		Mar. 28 (Continued)				527

"To Help China, Let's Help Korea Too!"

SINO-KOREAN PEOPLES' LEAGUE

101 D Street, N. E.   WASHINGTON, D. C.   May 15, 1941

President Franklin D. Roosevelt
White House
Washington, D. C.

Your Excellency:

May I humbly repeat my sincere request: that if humanly
possible - your Excellency express America's sympathy toward the
aspiration of 25-million Koreans for freedom and independence in
the coming nationwide radio broadcast.
"To help China, let's help Korea too!" seems to be timely
and strategically necessary in stirring up the slowly rising fire
of Korean nationalism which the Jap militarists fear and dread.

Oriental Point of View - America's radio and the press are
filled with controversial issues, largely out of confusion through
"Over-emphasis" of "Aid Britain" policy.

From my observations and evaluation of public opinion
throughout the country (I have traveled 35,000 miles in America
in 2½ years - gave 179 talks before American public - interviewed
hundreds of Americans of all classes in 90 cities and 35 states)
I believe there is a definite necessity for temporarily diverting
the public mind from "Aid Britain" to pointing out "Japanese
Menace" in the Pacific aiding Hitler's aggression in Europe.

Frankly I have found the American public underestimates
Japan's naval and military strength - hence a great majority of
the ones I have interviewed were willing to tackle Japan in the
Pacific while reluctant to aid Britain in fear of Germany's power
in Europe and the Atlantic.

Psychologically when a family is thrown into some controversial issue which tends to divide the spirit of unity, a wise father
or mother would soon inject an issue, seemingly foreign in aspect
yet threatening the common interest of the family's security, hoping
to have all the members unite in defense of their common interest
forgetting the controversial issue.

I believe that American public opinion should be temporarily diverted.   There were times in the past when leaders
of many countries have when on the verge of national

disintegration or civil strife have created a sudden new foreign menace even to the extent of a foreign war, thus uniting its national spirit defending its national rights while forgetting the much confused and dangerous controversial issues threatening national defense.

<u>Our Humble and Sincere Suggestions:</u> -

The following suggestions were sent to me by our men in Japan. These men as Your Excellency may have noted have been in Japan all their lives, they know the Japanese officials, the Japanese people and the Japanese militarists. On March 25,1941, I wrote to the Secretary of State informing him that these men predicted the "Reshuffling" of Japanese Cabinet April 3, 1941 (this was confirmed A.P.Report 4-4-41); Signing of the Russo-Japan Non-Aggression Pact before April 29th (this was confirmed last Easter Sunday); and recruiting a million Chinese laborers (confirmed) (5-5-41, Christian Science Monitor - it said the Japanese are recruiting 1,300,000 Chinese laborers).

I have great respect for their observed and experienced suggestions - therefore I am with prayerful heart submitting their suggestions, which are as follows:

A. Immediately close Panama Canal to Japanese shipping - make a dramatic and sudden move.

B. Freeze Japan's funds in U. S. A.

C. Tighten export of oil and other lubricants. Request British and American oil firms in Dutch East Indies to cease sale of oil and lubricants to Japan.

D. Convoy American and British ships - only in the Pacific - from Australia, New Zealand, India, etc., to the Red Sea. Convoying question in the Atlantic would become less controversial in 60 days after this move.

E. Express Your Excellency's sympathy and desire to see Korea's freedom in East Asia through Your Excellency's letter to our League. Mention the gallant fight of the Korean Volunteer Army beside the Chinese Nationalist Army in China during the past 2½ years. This letter to be made public at the proper moment.

Our men believe that if Your Excellency made such a diplomatic move soon it would be like throwing a bomb into the midst of the Japanese Supreme War Council of the Japanese Army and Navy. The reason it would be so great in the Orient is that they believe a Pacific conflict may be averted.

Hitler and Stalin have the "Oriental mind" like the Japanese militarists - hence their minds click - they think and act alike. The Japanese militarist mind is like the mind of an "Egomaniac". An insane person can be very cunning and yet so brutal - however their only fear is force and the baptism of fire.

In any type of war - diplomatic or military - the strategists first seek the weakest link of the chain of the enemy's defense. Japan is the weakest link of the Axis chain of defense as well as their offense. Therefore this weak link must be cut off, must be pounded into confusion and disintegration first before America makes positive move in the Atlantic. Once this is done I am certain the American public opinion will be able to fathom the need of an all out aid to Britain.

Time: Talk and act upon the menace of Japan's position in the Pacific aiding Hitler against Britain and the danger to U. S. National Defense for 30 days - will bring about the desired result.

The above request and humble Oriental suggestions are sincerely submitted.

Very prayerfully yours,

Kilsoo K. Haan

P. S. The above suggestions were received by me May 12, 1941, sent to me by our men in Japan.

THE NEW YORK TIMES, FRIDAY, MAY 16, 19

May 16, 1941

President Franklin D. Roosevelt
White House, Washington D.C.

Your Excellency:

Congratulation for your statement urging the people of France to rise up and fight for Democracy.

Could your Excellency do the same for Korea? The response would be so much more different — I assure you.

We need your sympathetic understanding and help now — very soon. The Korean Volunteer Army in China, for 2½ years fought the Jap-militarists. Our men in Korea and Japan are praying for your sympathy and material help.

The longer America help Japan to use Panama Canal — sell oil and get U.S. financial aid as U.S.A. did for years — the harder Japan will hit U.S.A. aloha

Kilsoo K. H

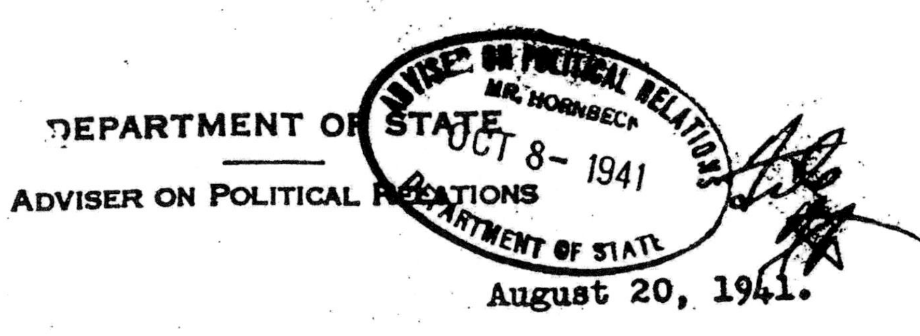

DEPARTMENT OF STATE
——————
ADVISER ON POLITICAL RELATIONS

August 20, 1941.

The papers here attached are copies of papers which
Dr. Syngman Rhee brought to me on July 14. At that time,
Dr. Rhee took the original papers from his pocket, said
that he and his Korean associates wanted to send the said
papers to the addressees or to have me take them and forward them, but that before doing so he wished to ask my
opinion as to the advisability of their so proceeding.
I looked over the papers, which were finished off with
seals, et cetera, and I said that I had doubt regarding
the advisability of Dr. Rhee's organization taking the
step indicated, that I would not myself wish to receive
the papers without first having consulted certain of my
associates, and that if Dr. Rhee would be willing to leave
the papers with me tentatively, I would give him a reply
within a few days. I added that I greatly feared that
my ultimate advice would have to be advice discouraging
the taking of the step which he had in mind.

I conferred with Mr. Hamilton and Mr. Ballantine and
Mr. Welles. Mr. Ballantine conferred with Mr. Hackworth.

The upshot of the matter was that on July 22 I asked
Dr. Rhee to call. I then said to him that the question
involved

involved had been given careful consideration and I found
it necessary to suggest that he hold these papers and
neither present them to me nor send them to the addressees.
I expressed the opinion and gave reasons in support that
it would not advance the cause to which Dr. Rhee has
given his adult life were this approach to be made here
at this time. Dr. Rhee received this statement with all
the appearance of having expected it and expressed real
appreciation of our having given the matter the careful
and sympathetic consideration of which there was clear
indication in the statement of reasons which I had given
him. He said that he would continue to watch developments
in the international situation in the hope that an appropriate and opportune time would arrive.

PA/H:SKH:ZMK

<u>COPY</u>

The Korean Commission
Washington, D.C.

To His Excellency
Secretary of State
The Department of State.

The Korean Commission

Washington, D.C.

Translation from
Korean-Chinese script.

June 6, 1941.
23rd year of the
Republic of Korea.
Chungking, China.

Honorable Cordell Hull
Department of State,
Washington, D.C.

Sir:

I have the honor to inform Your Excellency that in February this year, the Executive Chief of the Provisional Government of the Republic of Korea, now situated temporarily in Chungking, China, submitted a memorandum relating to Korea's status to Mr. Laughlin Currie, who was visiting here, with the request that he present it to the President of the United States; and later when Mr. James Roosevelt, son and representative of the President, was here another document was handed to him for the same purpose. I hope they have been brought to the attention of Your Excellency also.

This Government has been co-operating with China in its resistance to Japan. We are determined to continue our fight until the cause of democracy is securely upheld in the Far East, and Korea's lost freedom has been completely restored. In this task we need the material support of the United States. So long as the Chinese and the Koreans have sufficient supplies of munitions and war materials, our victory is assured.

May I remind Your Excellency of the fact that the American-Korean treaty of 1882 is still in effect and now is the time, we feel, when we should respectfully ask the United States to fulfill its treaty obligations by exerting its "good offices" in behalf of Korea.

Out of our sincere desire to cooperate with all the democratic forces now
engaged in our common cause, Dr. Syngman Rhee,
Chairman of the Korean Commission in Washington,
has been appointed as the official diplomatic
representative of this Government and has received full power and authority which he may
exercise at his own discretion in all official dealings with the United States.

I trust Your Excellency will extend
to Dr. Rhee a cordial, friendly reception,
advice and assistance.

Let me assure Your Excellency of my
high personal regards to you and best wishes
for the United States.

Yours respectfully,

(Signed) Joe So-ang,
Minister of Foreign Affairs,
Provisional Government of
The Republic of Korea.

(SEAL)

<u>COPY</u>

The Korean Commission

Washington, D.C.

C R E D E N T I A L

The Korean Commission

Washington, D.C.

Translation from Chinese.

CREDENTIAL

BE IT KNOWN, that I, Kim Ku, Chief Executive
of the Provisional Government of the Republic of
Korea, by and with the approval of the Cabinet
Ministers of the Provisional Government, have
appointed Dr. Syngman Rhee, Chairman of the Korean
Commission in Washington, D.C., U.S.A., as the
official representative of this Government, invested with full power and authority which he may
exercise at his own discretion in all diplomatic
dealings with the Government of the United States.

DONE in Chungking, China, on the sixth day
of June, in the year of our LORD one thousand nine
hundred and forty one, in the twenty-third year of
the Republic of Korea, and in the National Year of
Korea, the four thousand two hundred and seventy-
fourth.

<pre>
              (Signed) Kim Ku,
                        Executive Chief of the Provisional
                        Government of the Republic of Kore

              (Signed) Joe So-ang,
                        Minister of Foreign Affairs of the
                        Provisional Government of the
                        Republic of Korea.

     (SEAL)
</pre>

The Korean Commission
Washington, D. C.

To His Excellency

President of the United States of America.

COPY

The Korean Commission
  Washington, D. C.

Translation from
Korean-Chinese script.

June 6, 1941.
23rd year of the
Republic of Korea.
Chungking, China.

To His Excellency
Franklin D. Roosevelt,
President of the United States of America,
Washington, D. C.

Sir:

        I have the honor to remind Your Excellency
of the fact that, although the diplomatic intercourse
opened between the United States and Korea in 1882
was forcibly suspended in 1905, the cordial, friendly
spirit and good will existing between our two peoples
has never been interrupted. Now the changed situation
in the Far East warrants the restoration of that friendly relationship for mutual benefit.

        The Provisional Government of the Republic
of Korea, temporarily situated in Chungking, China,
earnestly desires to re-open that friendly intercourse
and it is hoped that their desire may be reciprocated
by the Government and the people of the United States.

        At a recent meeting of the Cabinet Ministers
of the Korean Provisional Government, Dr. Syngman Rhee,
Chairman of the Korean Commission in Washington, was
appointed as the official representative of this Government, invested with full power and authority which
he may excercise [sic] at his own discretion in all diplomatic dealings with the Government of the United States.

By virtue of the authority vested in me as
Executive Chief of the Korean Provisional Government,
I beseech Your Excellency to receive him and the
message he is instructed to present in behalf of the
23,000,000 Korean people suffering under an alien
domination.

I take this occasion to assure Your
Excellency of my highest consideration and best
wishes for your great Republic.

Yours very respectfully,

(Signed)   Kim Ku,
            Executive Chief of the
            Provisional Government
            of the Republic of Korea.

            [Seal]

NOVEMBER 21, 1941

The Honorable
The Secretary of State,
Washington, D. C.

Sir:

There is enclosed for such disposition as the Department may deem appropriate a letter dated November 7, 1941, addressed to me by Dr. Edward Lim, with regard to the question of the independence of Korea.

This office has acknowledged receipt of the letter and has informed Dr. Lim that it is being forwarded to the Department of State in view of the fact that the Department is charged with the conduct of the foreign affairs of the United States.

Very truly yours,

For the High Commissioner:

E. C. Ross
Acting Executive Assistant
to the
United States High Commissioner

Enclosure:

Original letter of
November 7, 1941.

The Honorable
     The Secretary of State,
          Washington, D. C.

Sir:

     There is enclosed for such disposition as the De-
partment may deem appropriate a letter dated November 7,
1941, addressed to me by Dr. Edward Lim, with regard to
the question of the independence of Korea.

     This office has acknowledged receipt of the letter
and has informed Dr. Lim that it is being forwarded to
the Department of State in view of the fact that the
Department is charged with the conduct of the foreign affairs of the United States.

                         Very truly yours,

                    For the High Commissioner:

                              E. C. Ross
                         Acting Executive Assistant
                                to the
                         United States High Commissioner

Enclosure:

   Original letter of
   November 7, 1941.

朝鮮義勇隊駐非律濱通訊處

嗎尼刺通訊處

DR. EDWARD LIM
712 ONGPIN ST.,
MANILA, PHILIPPINES

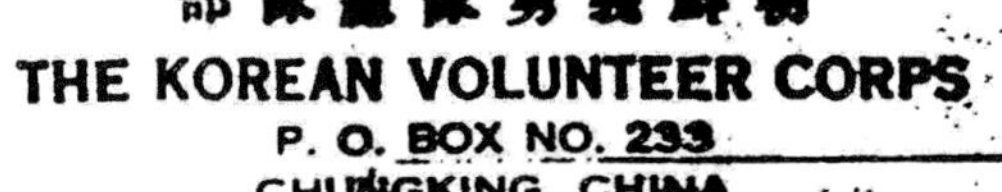

朝鮮義勇隊進隊部

THE KOREAN VOLUNTEER CORPS
P. O. BOX NO. 233
CHUNGKING, CHINA

Nov. 7, 1941.

NOV 10 1941

16471

Hon. Francis B. Sayre,
U.S. High Commissioner,
Manila, Philippines.

Your Excellency:

With your kind permission, may I remind you a few facts, concerning the Far Eastern situation as well as the United States? I believe you might be interested.

At the latter part of ninteenth century, Admiral Shufelt of the United States Navy knocked at the door of the Kingdom of Korea, and asked her to open treaty relations with the United States, promising assistance in case of trouble. So, the Treaty of Defensive and Offensive Alliance between the United States of America and the Kingdom of Korea was conclude in the year of 1882. The first article of this treaty contained what is known as the amity clause, which reads as follows:
" If other powers deal unjustly or oppressively with either government, the other will exert its good offices, on being informed of the case, to bring about an amicable arrangement, thus showing friendly feelings."

The United States Senate and the President of the United States, as well as the State Department, all gave approval and affixed their signatures to the treaty, thus making it a law of the United States. President Chester A. Arthur proclaimed of the treaty, that " every clause and article must be observed and fulfilled with good faith by the United States and the citizens thereof."

The Korean government granted special privileges and concessions to the citizens of the United States, such as franchise for the first railway lines and trolley-car lines in Korea, and the richest goldmines in the country. Above all, the Koreans loved and respected the Americans, and believed in American religion. Hundreds of Christian churches were erected all over the country, and more than two-hundred-thousand people were converted into Christians within a few years. The people considered the Americans as God-sent angels.

But in the year of 1906, at the end of Russo-Japanese War, Ex-president Theodore Roosevelt recognized Japanese protectorship over Korea, very much against the will of the Koreans, breaking the promise which the United States

處訊通濱律非駐隊勇義鮮朝

處訊通剌尼眠
DR. EDWARD LIM
712 ONGPIN ST.,
MANILA. PHILIPPINES

部 隊 總 隊 勇 義 鮮 朝
THE KOREAN VOLUNTEER CORPS
P. O. BOX NO. 233
CHUNGKING. CHINA

the United States Government so solemnly made before God and men. Then, in 1910, the United States was the first one who recognized the Japanese annexation of Korea, the remorseless subjugation which was but the beginning of Japan's program of invasion and conquest of Asiatic mainland, which she euphemistically designated with the plan of Toyotomi Hideyoshi, Napoleon of Japan, three hundred years ago.

The United States was under the treaty obligation to help Korea in such a critical moment of life and death, but President Theodore Roosevelt denied it and forsook his ally, Korea. Why? President Roosevelt had a secret pact with Japan through Baron Kaneko, Japan's liaison man in America, that the United States was to recognize the Japanese occupation of Korea, and Japan was to recognize the American possession of the Philippines (see page 605 of History of the United States, by Ralph Voleney Harlow. H. Holt, New York City). Can this be enough reason for such a heroic and freedom-loving nation as the United States to break the solemn oath and throw the helpless little sister away to the merciless murderer? Another excuse for America to break the promise was: " The Korean Emperor was weak, officials corruted, and the people ignorant and supine," reported by E. V. Morgan, the United States Minister to Korea. But this cannot serve ass an excuse for the Koreans were same when the treaty was signed by the governments of U.S.A. and Korea.

Japan, after annexing Korea, the stepstone to the Asiatic continent seized Manchuria, setting up a puppet regime, the so-called Manchukuo (fo which she is threatening the United States to recognize or accept her sword), then penetrated into North China regardless of international law or treaties, challenging all good people in the world.

The poor Koreans, after losing their beloved country which has a histiry of more than four thousand years, have been waiting for last thir years for the Americans to reilize what grave mistake they have made in recognizing Japan to annex Korea, who so imploringly looked up America fo help. While suffering the tortures, deaths and starvations under the iro heels merciless invaders, the Koreans, with undying spirit, struggled incessently for freedom and independence. So, there was national uprising in 1919, students' uprising in 1929, all proclaiming independence. The Koreans are still looking up the United States who will certainly come one day to rescue Korea, the once forsaken ally.

Now, the time has come. " The question of peace and war in the Pacific will be decided by whether the United States and Japan understand

處訊通賓律非駐隊勇義鮮朝

處訊通剌尼岷
DR. EDWARD LIM
712 ONGPIN ST.,
MANILA. PHILIPPINES

部隊總隊勇義鮮朝
THE KOREAN VOLUNTEER CORPS
P. O. BOX NO. 233
CHUNGKING, CHINA

and respect each other's positions. If the United States recognizes Japan's leadership in East Asia, Japan would recognize the United States' leadership of the Americas. If the United States refuses to understand the real intention of Japan, Germany and Italy in concluding an alliance for possitive co-operation in creating a new wold order, and persist in challenging those powers in the belief that the accord is a hostile action, there will be no other course than to go to war," said Prince Konoye on October, 1940.
" The United States is not prepared to fight on both Pacific and Atlantic Oceans at same time," said Chugai Shinbun, the well-known news paper in Japan, meaning that this the time for Japan to fight the Americans. The United States helped Japan in the Treaty of Portsmouth and in annexing Korea, thus making her big and strong. Now, she is challenging the United States!

I, as the represemtative of Korean Volunteer Corps in China, humbly request the citizens of the United States to do justice to Korea, your ally, whom you refused to exert good offices when she was unjustly and oppressively dealt by a third power. Please help the Koreans now. It is not too late. In fact, the Koreans are better fit for an independent nation now than ever, after thirty years of bitter experiences. May it please Your Excellency to deliver this message through some means to your nation.

We are twenty-three millions in number, twenty millions in Korea, three millions without. There are approximately two millions in Manchuria and Siberia, with bitter enmity against the Japanese for we were driven out by them and their economical policy. We have nearly half million, mostly men, in China Proper, who are more than willing to fight for both China and Korea. There are more or less than ten thousand in the United States and Hawaii, mostly in the latter, who proclaimed that they " owed no allegiance to any country but the United States," in 1940.

The Korean Volunteer Corps in China is organized by young Koreans, 75% of whom are graduates from both Huangpu Military Academy, established by late Dr. Sun Yat Sen, and Central Military College, established by Generalisimo Chiang Kai Shek. We have knowledge and experiences in war, but we are not able to render much service for lacking in necessary materials. Commander Kim Yak San, the commandant of the Korean Volunteer Corps, informed me that he is able to organize two-hundred-thousand Korean youngmen as an independence army if he had funds, arms, ammunitions, etc. I also believe it myself.

朝 鮮 義 勇 隊 駐 非 律 濱 通 訊 處

處 訊 通 刺 尼 眼
DR. EDWARD LIM
712 ONGPIN ST.,
MANILA. PHILIPPINES

朝 鮮 義 勇 隊 總 隊 部
THE KOREAN VOLUNTEER CORPS
P. O. BOX NO. 233
CHUNGKING. CHINA

Now, the war is inevitable, as Japanese say. If they say so, it i
time for the United States to take necessary action to defend its freedom and democracy and to protect its interest in Far East. So, I appeal
to Your Excellency to find us a chance to fight side by side with you ag
ainst our common enemy. Please do not discourage us again. We have wai
thirty years for this one opportunity when you raise your hand to smash
that rattle snake which is so poisonous to humanity and civilization.

Even though ignorant and supine we were thirty years ago, I dare
say that we are one of the most courageous people in the world. I cannot
go into the details of the various happenings between Koreans and Japanes
for last thirty years, but suffice it to say that the Koreans can make
much better soldiers than the Japanese. One Korean battalian is suffici
to defeat one Japanese division, I dare say, according to our experiences
on Manchurian and Siberian borders. Please help us.

Awaiting your kind consideration, I remain, Your Excellency,

Very Respectfully Yours,

Edward Lim,
Representative, Korean Volunteer Corps in China. Ex-Major-General, Medic
Director, Chinese National Army.

Extract of letter from:
Dr. Edward Lim
712 Ongpin Street
Manila, Philippines

The Korean Volunteer Corps
P. O. Box No. 233
Chungking, China

I, as the representative of Korean Volunteer Corps in
China, humbly request the citizens of the United States to
do justice to Korea, your ally, whom you refused to exert
good offices when she was unjustly and oppressively dealt
by a third power. Please help the Koreans now. It is not
too late. In fact, the Koreans are better fit for an independent nation now than ever, after thirty years of bitter
experiences. May it please Your Excellency to deliver this
message through some means to your nation.

We are twenty-three millions in number, twenty millions
in Korea, three millions without. There are approximately
two millions in Manchuria and Siberia, with bitter enmity
against the Japanese for we were driven out by them and
their economical policy. We have nearly half million, mostly
men, in China Proper, who are more than willing to fight
for both China and Korea. There are more or less than ten
thousand in the United States and Hawaii, mostly in the
latter, who proclaimed that they "owed no allegiance to any
country but the United States," in 1940.

The Korean Volunteer Corps in China is organized by
young Koreans, 75% of whom are graduates from both Huangpu
Military Academy, established by late Dr. Sun Yat Sen, and
Central Military College, established by Generalisimo
Chiang Kai Shek. We have knowledge and experiences in war,
but we are not able to render much service for lacking in
necessary materials. Commander Kim Yak San, the commandant
of the Korean Volunteer Corps, informed me that he is able
to organize two-hundred thousand Korean youngmen as an independence army if he had funds, arms, ammunitions, etc.
I also believe it myself.

Now, the war is inevitable, as Japanese say. If they
may so, it is time for the United States to take necessary
action to defend its freedom and democracy and to protect
its interest in Far East. So, I appeal to Your Excellency
to find us a chance to fight side by side with you against
our common enemy. Please do not discourage us again. We

have

have waited thirty years for this one opportunity when you raise your hand to smash that rattle snake which is so poisonous to humanity and civilization.

Even though ignorant and supine we were thirty years ago, I dare say that we are one of the most courageous people in the world. I cannot go into the details of the various happenings between Koreans and Japanese during last thirty years, but suffice it to say that the Koreans can make much better soldiers than the Japanese. One Korean battalion is sufficient to defeat one Japanese division, I dare say, according to our experiences on Manchurian and Siberian borders. Please help us.

Awaiting your kind consideration, I remain, Your Excellency,

Very Respectfully Yours,

Edward Lim,
Representative, Korean Volunteer Corps in China. Ex-Major-General, Medical Director, Chinese National Army.

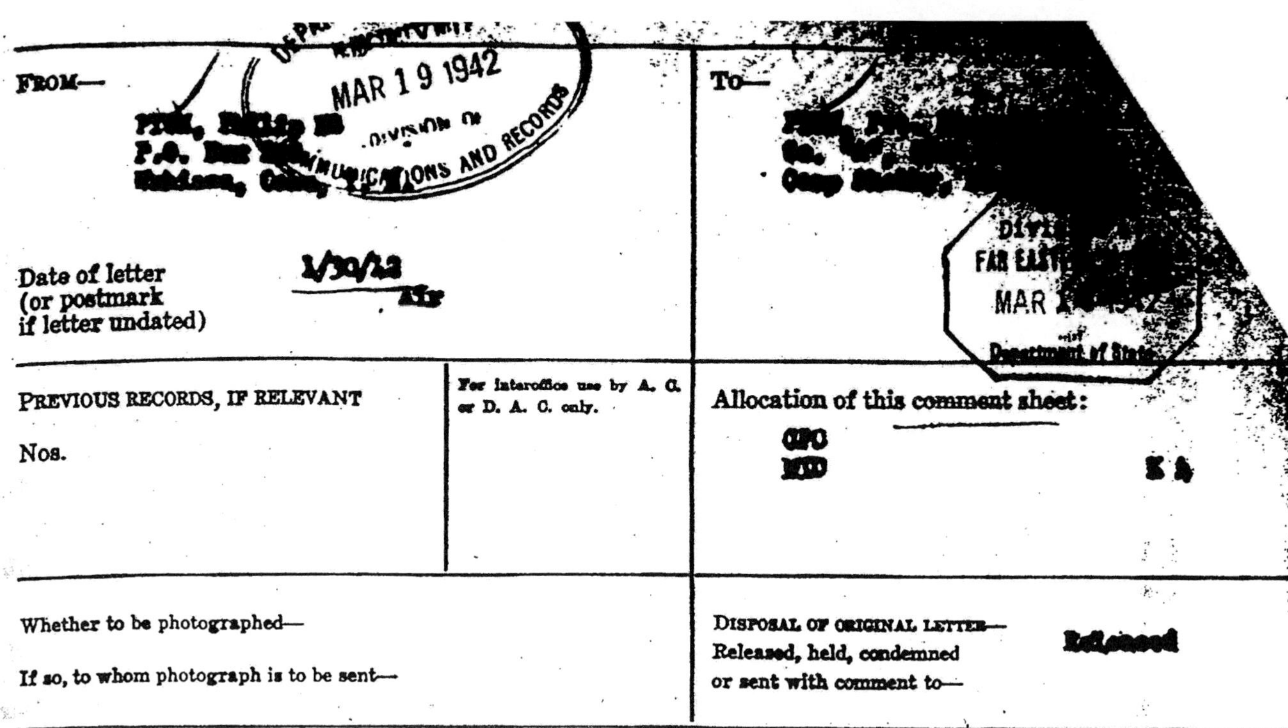

FROM—	TO—

MAR 19 1942

Date of letter (or postmark if letter undated): 1/30/42   Air

PREVIOUS RECORDS, IF RELEVANT	For interoffice use by A. C. or D. A. C. only.	Allocation of this comment sheet:
Nos.		CPC MID X A

Whether to be photographed—

If so, to whom photograph is to be sent—

DISPOSAL OF ORIGINAL LETTER— Released, held, condemned or sent with comment to—   Released

COMMENT

English

POLITICAL

A Korean writer, in a letter to his brother, states that although his people are technically Japanese Nationals, the Koreans have more hatred for Japan than any of the countries now at war with Japan. He infers that he disapproves of Japanese military, political and social tactics. The writer believes that the United States puts more trust in the Koreans than it does in the true Japanese, and he expresses the hope that Washington will take action to give the Koreans a standing apart from the Japanese.

ADB	IMM
AG	INT
BEW	LO
BP	MC
CAA	MID
COO	ONI
CIAA	PO
COI	RFO
COM	~~SD~~
CPC	T
DL	BF
ED	BR
FBI	CAN
FCC	JSM
FR	MEW
FSA	SO
FTC	

MAR 17 1942

Division (or section)	TABLE	EXAMINER	D. A. C.	DATE
	4	74	42	2/44

SINO-KOREAN PEOPLES LEAGUE
101 D Street N.E.
Washington, D.C.

May 5, 1942

His Excellency Cordell Hull
Secretary of State
Department of State
Washington, D. C.

Your Excellency:

The Sino-Korean Peoples' League, representing the newly formed Korean National Front Federation, composed of four Korean political parties in the Far East, do humbly and sincerely submit to your Excellency the aims and activities outlined by the Sixth Plenary Session of the Korean National Revolutionary Congress recently held in Chungking, China.

We submit the following eleven points in the belief and hope that it will be of some value to your Excellency in the decision of arriving at some effective policy giving aid or aids to the Korean National Front Federation in their fight against our common enemy, Japan.

The Eleven Points:

1. To overthrow Japanese Imperialist rule and to establish in Korea a free, independent and a democratic republic.

2. To summon a peoples' assembly which is to frame a constitution and make arrangement for holding a general election.

3. To eliminate the vestiges of old feudal system, detrimental to the future welfare of Korea.

4. To confiscate the property of all Japanese imperialists.

5. To afford special protection for the welfare and business enterprises of those citizens who have opposed the Axis Powers interests.

6. To institute an agrarian policy and redistribute the land among the tenants and farmers.

7. To reduce working hours and put into force various measures of social security for the benefit of the workers.

8. To establish political, economic and social equality of the sexes.

9. To institute freedom of speech, publication, assembly and of worship.

10. To institute compulsory education, vocational training and social insurance at the expense of the State.

11. To seek cooperation with all countries on a basis of equality, mutual assistance in the security of national defense, in the pursuit of peace and happiness of mankind.

The eleven points were unanimously approved and accepted by all four Korean party representatives. These representatives represented large numbers of Koreans in Siberia, North China, Manchuria, Korea and Japan.

We Urge America to Face Reality in the Far East

More than five months have elapsed since the Jap Envoy Kurusu sang the Pearl Harbor lullaby song to the officials of the United States. And as reported by our men in Japan last March, 1941, Japan did carry out its "U.S.-Japan War Plan".

"There must be diplomatic conversation as usual in some form or other, at least until the initiation of military action...During the first period of four months the Japanese fleet will be free to carry on its activities throughout the Pacific and there will exist no strong opposing forces in the Pacific to interfere." Quotations from the book "How Japan Plans to Win" pages 202 and 208.

Unless America soon checks the Japs they will soon be in all strategic position to attack the Aleutians, Alaska, Hawaii and the Pacific Coast States. Based on the Jap War Plan the first period of U.S.-Japan war is over, the second period will soon begin.

If the Department of State will check the reports of our agents during the past years your Excellency will realize that the time and events did prove that their reports were of much value to the United States security. It will further show that these Koreans will be of much value to America now more than in the past. Their strategic positions in Japan and Korea should not be overlooked.

Though the United States officials ignored their warning reports in past years, I have been asked to convey this message to your Excellency. These patriotic Koreans' message declared: "Every sense of our loyalty and honor oblige us to offer our services to the cause of America and Korea to win this war. We pledge full cooperation with your honorable government to clear out from the Far East and in the Pacific waters our mutual enemy, Japan."

America's diplomatic records will show that in the early period of the American Korean diplomatic relationship America took a realistic policy in the Far East. Immediately after the signing of the American Korean Treaty, May 22, 1882, the Hon. John Russell Young, minister to China, wrote to the Department of State these wise and realistic words: "I think it very important that the U.S. should have a footing in Korea and that having opened the door we should not close it or give any other power precedence."

The treaty had in it these innocent but fateful words which so often in diplomatic documents may mean much or nothing according to interpretation: "If other powers deal unjustly or oppressively with either government the other will exert its good offices, on being informed of the case, to bring about an amicable arrangement, thus showing its friendly feelings."

Perhaps it was fate, that the U.S.A. chose to ignore its moral if not its legal obligation toward Korea. Perhaps again it was fate, - why the State Department in recent years ignored the Koreans' continued warning reports, even up to the eve of the Japanese attack on Pearl Harbor last December 7, 1941.

Time and events have taught all peace loving citizens of the United States to awaken to the fact that only effective unity of purpose and unity of quick action alone will defeat the Axis Powers. In so doing even small countries like Korea in the Far East should not be overlooked. In 1904 Japan declared, Korea was "pistol pointed at the heart of Japan". Today, because England and America ignored Korea and the geo-strategic position of Korea, this same pistol is pointed at the heart of China and Siberia. Restore Korea to its former status, again Korea will be the "pistol pointed at the heart of Japan".

Internationally speaking, Korea has become both the exponent and the finished example of Japanese totalitarian ambition.

Willard Price a few years ago wrote these prophetic words for all of us to stop and think:

"Those who wish to get a glimpse of the trend of future events in Asia should not neglect to study that vivid object lesson, Korea."

The international events of the past decade proved beyond doubt that - because England and America blindly aided and built up Japan at the expense of their own security and the security of Korea and of China, today we are facing the brute force of the "Frankenstein" Japan.   Therefore morally, spiritually and legally, unless England and America realize their mistakes and win this war against Japan, there will be no lasting peace in the Pacific. "Reason and free inquiry are the only effective agents against error", advised Thomas Jefferson.

<u>Everywhere Koreans Beg America for a Chance to Fight the Japs</u>

In the blood of all good Koreans flows a hatred of all things Japanese - a hatred that dates back three hundred fifty years to a day in 1592 when three hundred thousand Jap soldiers on orders from the regent Hideyoshi, swarmed the coasts of the ancient Kingdom of Korea, laying waste her cities, her farmlands and treasure. Today all Korea is under the bondage of Japan - and today, as all Koreans have for ten generations back, the man of Korea still lives for the day when he can settle the score for three and a half centuries of humiliation against the Jap.   Koreans are a distinct people, being neither like their ancient friends, the Chinese, nor like their ancient enemies, the Japs.

In the backyard of the Jap strategic military naval and air bases, millions of Koreans are eager to do what they can to defeat the Japs.

America Can Help Koreans to Reorganize the Refugee Provisional Government in China

In March 1, 1919 within 10 years after annexation of Korea by Japan, the Koreans in Korea revolted against the Japanese overlords. Soon it established a Korean Provisional Government in Shanghai, China.   As adverse circumstances and events were forced upon them, the Korean Provisional Government moved whenever and wherever the Chinese Nationalist Government moved.   During the past 23 years the Koreans were forced to undergo much hardship. Numerous appeals to England and America were repeatedly made.   Time after time England and America closed their diplomatic doors against the Korean patriots.

Due to continuous and constant rebuff met by these struggling patriots, they were forced to seek help wherever and from whomever they can get such help to fight the Japs. In the meantime, dissension forced many Koreans to break with the Provisional Government. Some turned to Soviet Russia and some to China. As a result of these unavoidable political, economic and diplomatic difficulties two schools of thought have carried on the war on Japan, each believing that their method would eventually win the hearts of the Democratic Powers to assist them to whip Japan out of Korea.   Since 1938 the Chinese Nationalist Government has given financial aid to the Korean Volunteer Army in China, under the command of Commander Yak San Kim.

Koreans like all nationals and races struggling for freedom and independence under similar political and economic conditions have met regrettable experiences and the existence of some disunity among themselves. History shows the French revolution leaders, the Chinese revolution leaders and the Soviet revolutionary governments too faced similar internal political and governmental problems as the Koreans now face. The struggles of these patriots were many, they have reaped dissension among fellow patriots, doubt - even civil wars and the bitter price of costly mistakes.   Soviet Russia and China both bear the scars of political, social, economic and religious struggles for freedom and independence.

Remember Early Period of U. S. Revolutionary Leaders

Even this great country, the U.S.A., was torn with dissension. One wonders if the American Revolutionary leaders did not get the moral and material aid from some Europeans and European Powers if they could have won the Revolutionary war in 8 years; Perhaps George Washington may have had to undergo a few more "Valley Forges". Even today one can with a little imagination hear the challenging voice of Benjamin Franklin: "Either we all hang together or hang separately."

Some U. S. officials repeatedly say that the Koreans are not united, they are trying to use this as an issue in refusing to give early consideration to aiding Koreans to fight the Japs. Koreans are not angels, we as the American forefathers did, are forced to undergo the unavoidable transition of political growth. Americans are apt to forget, while the U.S. has fought the Japs only 5 months, the Koreans have been fighting the Japs since 1910.

After the Jap "stab in the back" attack on Pearl Harbor, Dec. 7, 1941, several conferences were held, written appeals were made; with prayers, faith, hope and great anxiety we have waited for an official reply, one way or another. We pray our prayers and appeals have not been made in vain. Korea needs America's moral and material aid now as did the American forefathers. We sincerely and most humbly once more submit this plea for an early reply and for a favorable consideration by the Department of State soon.

Whatever the reason or excuse the U. S. officials have in delaying the use of millions of Koreans who are so anxiously awaiting U.S. official O,K. - Koreans everywhere pray and urge the United States to attack Japan at her heart. I say this, knowing full well that when the American bombers range over the industrial cities of Jap-dominated Korea my people will be killed. But I say, and my people say, let it come - we would rather die by American bombs than live as servants to the Japanese.

In the interest of effective cooperation and for an early and complete victory of the United Nations against the Axis Powers,

Gratefully yours,

KILSOO K. HAAN

Korean National Front Federation
Korean Volunteer Army in China
Sino-Korean Peoples League

Hon. Fletcher Warren
Department of State
Washington D.C.

THE KOREAN-AMERICAN COUN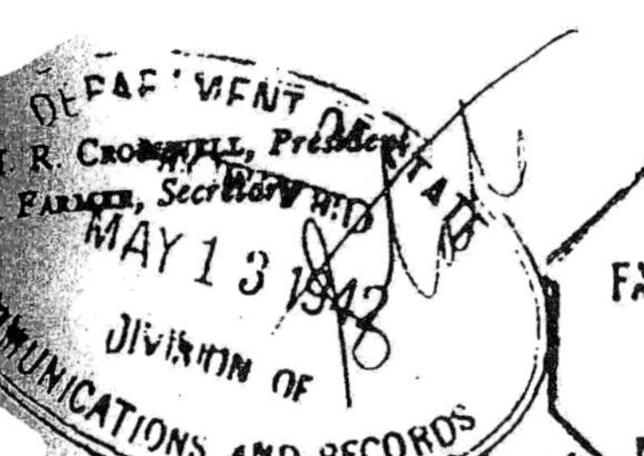

COLORADO BUILDING

WASHINGTON, D. C.

April 30, 1942

RESPECTFULLY REFERRED
TO THE
DEPARTMENT OF STATE

M. H. McIntyre

Secretary to the President

Dear Mr. President:

Knowing your interest in oppressed and enslaved
nations is very real, we are sending you herewith a mimeographed copy of news items relating to Korea.

This information is being sent to Koreans and
Americans who are interested in the Korean cause, or who
would be interested if they knew the facts.

It is superfluous to remind you of the unceasing
struggle of Korean patriots during the past forty years.
At this time, Korea's hopes for independence are brighter
than at any time since Japan enslaved that small but
highly cultured country in 1905.

In 1919 the people of Korea formed a Provisional
Government, with Dr. Syngman Rhee as its first President.
That government is functioning in exile in Chungking, China,
at the invitation of the Chinese Government. Kim Ku is its
President and the Korean Commission is its representative
in Washington. Dr. Syngman Rhee is now Chairman of the
Korean Commission.

Mr. President, we realize how busy and full your
days are, but it is our sincere hope that you will find
time to read the enclosed items and give them your earnest
consideration. We shall be glad to send you similar
information from time to time as we receive it and compile it.

May God guide and protect you in these troublous
times.

Sincerely yours,

THE KOREAN-AMERICAN COUNCIL

By *Aletta Summerfield*
Assistant Secretary

The President
The White House
Washington, D. C.

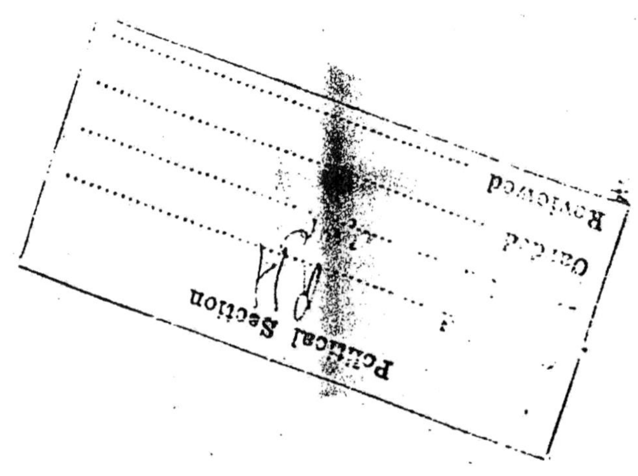

Political Section
Reviewed

327 Colorado Building
Washington, D. C.

April 28, 19

NEWS ITEMS RELATING TO KOREA

N. Y. Herald-Tribune CHUNGKING (AP) Feb. 24, 1942....Generalissimo
Chiang Kai-shek has returned from his visit to India, a government
spokesman announced today.

..... The spokesman welcomes President Roosevelt's rejection of
defensive strategy in favor of an Allied offensive, and said that
the President's promise of independence for Japanese-held Korea
"shows clearly that this war is conceived by Allied statesmen as
a war for Asiatic freedom."

- - -

Radiogram, CHUNGKING, March 22, 1942

Dr. Syngman Rhee, Washington, D. C.

"Under joint auspices of Chinese Peoples Oriental Cultural
Association China Branch of International Peace Campaign Dr. Sun Fo
President of Legislative Yuan insisted before large audience today
upon absolute independence of Korea and immediate recognition of
Korean Provisional Government. Tjosowang Foreign Minister of
Korean Provisional Government."

- - -

Radiogram, CHUNGKING, March 22, 1942

Dr. Syngman Rhee, Washington, D. C.

Korean Provisional Government spoke on outline of national
reconstruction and said recognition of Korean Provisional Government must come now from Chungking, Washington, London and Moscow
if Allies wish Korea to contribute her part to defeat Japan. KIM KU

- - -

SUN FO SAYS CHINA NOW HAS POWER
AND WILL TO HELP KOREAN FREEDOM

CHUNGKING, March 23 (CNS*)....... Korea is the country from
which Japan started her invasion of the Asiatic continent and in
Korea she will find her own grave, declared Dr. Sun Fo, President
of the Legislative Yuan, in a lecture on Korea before a large
audience in Chungking yesterday.

The lecture was sponsored by the People's Foreign Relations
Association, the Eastern Cultural Association and the China Branch
of the International Peace Campaign.

Outlining the relationship between China and Korea, Dr. Sun
said that the two countries have been on friendly terms for more
than four thousand years. They have mutual friendship and welfare.
Dr. Sun continued to say that the international political goal
should be the assisting of weak nations and the liberation of
enslaved races. The Second World War broke out because they
have overlooked these principles but the conclusion of it
will see a just and lasting peace with freedom for every nation.
Dr. Sun.

(*) - Chinese News Service

The Koreans were enslaved for the past thirty years and the tragedy of their slavery should still be fresh in the minds of Koreans of this generation. The organization of these 30,000,000 Koreans will not only mean the downfall of Japanese imperialism, it will also shorten the present World War, Dr. Sun declared. He asserted that after more than four years of resistance China finds herself stronger than ever. Before, China was unable to help the Korean Provisional Government, but after these years China not only has determined to help Korea but has the power to assist her, Dr. Sun emphatically declared. He concluded with the assurance that history has shown that China will not become an imperialist. She is only too anxious to extend her helpful arm to her friendly neighbor.

- - -

Radiogram, CHUNGKING, April 10, 1942

Dr. Syngman Rhee, Washington, D. C.

"Chinese Foreign Ministry requested its government for our recognition Dr Wang Chunghui, Secretary General of Chinese Defense Council, insisted on the necessity of speedy recognition. Korean Volunteer Corps will be reorganized under Korean National Army. Your radiograms on Dr. Sun Fo's address and other two, have been published in all Chinese papers here. Tjosowang, Foreign Minister of the Korean Provisional Government."

- - -

Radiogram, CHUNGKING, April 10, 1942

"China soon is expected to recognize the provisional (anti-Japanese) Government of Korea and similar recognition by the United States and Great Britain will follow, Korean Foreign Minister Tjosowang said.

"On the eve of the 23rd anniversary of the Korean Independence Movement the Provisional Government under President Kim Ku held a reception for the diplomatic corps here.

"Among the guests were the Czech Minister, Stanislaus Minovsky, and representatives of the United Nations.

"The Korean Provisional Government is the world's earliest anti-aggression regime," the President of the Executive Council of the Provisional Government said. "Not a single one of the Chinese people is opposed to extending immediate and full recognition to us."

- - -

MOBILIZATION OF 30,000,000 KOREANS TO
FIGHT AGGRESSION PLEDGED ON KOREA DAY

CHUNGKING, April 11 (CNS)..... In Chungking the Provisional Government has announced that it is determined to mobilize 30 million Koreans to fight against aggression until the world can enjoy a just and lasting peace. The declaration was made by KIM KU, President of the Korean Provisional Government at a meeting held in Chungking yesterday in observance of the 23rd anniversary of the founding of the Korean Provisional Government. General Wu Te-chen, Secretary General of the Kuomintang, said in a speech that China was not only fighting a war for the recovery of her lost territories but was also fighting against aggression. The day of final victory would mean the liberation of the Koreans and all oppressed nations of the world, declared General Wu.

- - -

The Koreans were enslaved for [illegible]
tragedy of their slavery, should [illegible]
Koreans of this generation. The [illegible]
Koreans will not only mean the downfall of Japan [illegible]
will also shorten the present World War, Dr. Sun [illegible]
asserted that after more than four years of resistance [illegible]
herself stronger than ever. Before, China was unable [illegible]
Korean Provisional Government, but after these years China
has determined to help Korea but has the power to assist [illegible]
Dr. Sun emphatically declared. He concluded with the [illegible]
history has shown that China will not become an imperialistic [illegible]
is only too anxious to extend her helpful arm to her friendly
neighbor.

- - -

Radiogram, CHUNGKING, April 10, 1942

Dr. Syngman Rhee, Washington, D. C.

"Chinese Foreign Ministry requested its government for our
recognition Dr Wang Chunghui, Secretary General of Chinese Defense
Council, insisted on the necessity of speedy recognition. Korean
Volunteer Corps will be reorganized under Korean National Army. Your
radiograms on Dr. Sun Fo's address and other two, have been published
in all Chinese papers here. Tjosowang, Foreign Minister of the
Korean Provisional Government."

- - -

Radiogram, CHUNGKING, April 10, 1942

"China soon is expected to recognize the provisional (anti-
Japanese) Government of Korea and similar recognition by the United
States and Great Britain will follow, Korean Foreign Minister
Tjosowang said.

"On the eve of the 23rd anniversary of the Korean Independence
Movement the Provisional Government under President Kim Ku held a
reception for the diplomatic corps here.

"Among the guests were the Czech Minister, Stanislaus Minovsky,
and representatives of the United Nations.

"The Korean Provisional Government is the world's earliest anti-
aggression regime," the President of the Executive Council of the
Provisional Government said. "Not a single one of the Chinese people
is opposed to extending immediate and full recognition to us."

- - -

MOBILIZATION OF 30,000,000 KOREANS TO
FIGHT AGGRESSION PLEDGED ON KOREA DAY

CHUNGKING, April 11 (CNS)..... In Chungking the Provisional
Government has announced that it is determined to mobilize 30 million
Koreans to fight against aggression until the world can enjoy a just
and lasting peace. The declaration was made by KIM KU, President of
the Korean Provisional Government at a meeting held in Chungking
yesterday in observance of the 23rd anniversary of the founding of the
Korean Provisional Government. General Wu Te-chen, Secretary General
of the Kuomintang, said in a speech that China was not only fighting
a war for the recovery of her lost territories but was also fighting
a war against aggression. The day of final victory would mean the
liberation of the Koreans and all oppressed nations of the world,
declared General Wu.

- - -

Radiogram, CHUNGKING, March 30, 1942   10 a.m.

A Korean Volunteer Corps has been organized and will operate
under the orders of the Chungking regime.

KOREAN NATIONAL FRONT FEDERATION

SINO-KOREAN PEOPLES' LEAGUE

KILSOO K. HAAN
Washington Representative

TRinidad 8500

101 D Street, N. E.
WASHINGTON, D. C.

Lincoln 8167

August 12, 1942

Honorable Cordell Hull
Wardman Park Hotel
Washington. D.C.

My dear Sir:

$45.00   With warm admiration for your generous desire to create a new kind of peaceful world and your sympathetic understanding of Korea and our struggle for freedom, I extend my deep appreciation and thanks for what you have done what you have done for us.

I am sending in a separate packet my recently translated book How Japan Plans To Win.

God bless you.

Very truly yours,

Kilsoo K. Haan

SINO-KOREAN PEOPLES LEAGUE
101 D Street N. E.
Washington, D. C.

June

His Excellency Cordell Hull
Secretary of State
Department of State
Washington,   D. C.

Your Excellency:

The Sino-Korean Peoples' League, representing the newly formed Korean National Front Federation, composed of four Korean political parties in the Far East, do humbly and sincerely submit to your Excellency its aims and war activities outlined by the Sixth Plenary Session of the Korean National Revolutionary Congress recently held in Chungking, China, November 1941.

We submit the following eleven points in the belief and hope that it will be of some value to your Excellency in your decision in arriving at some effective policy giving aid or aids to the Koreans. Today we need more than honorable intentions and friendly gestures of friendship. We need positive help from America, both moral and material aid.

The Eleven Points Are:

1. To overthrow Japanese Imperialist rule and to establish in Korea a free, independent and a democratic republic.

2. To summon a peoples' assembly which is to frame a constitution and make arrangement for holding a general election.

3. To eliminate the vestiges of old feudal system, detrimental to the future welfare of Korea.

4. To confiscate the property of all Japanese imperialists.

5. To afford special protection for the welfare and business enterprises of those citizens who have opposed the Axis Powers interests.

6. To institute an agrarian policy and redistribute the land among the tenants and farmers.

7. To reduce working hours and put into force various measures of social security for the benefit of the workers.

8. To establish political, economic and social equality of the sexes.

9. To institute freedom of speech, publication, assembly and of worship.

10. To institute compulsory education, vocational training and social insurance at the expense of the State.

11. To seek cooperation with all countries on a basis of equality, mutual assistance in the security of national defense, in the pursuit of peace and happiness of mankind.

The eleven points were unanimously approved and accepted by all four Korean party representatives from Siberia, North China, Manchuria, Korea and Japan.

Sincerely submitted,

Kilsoo K. Haan
Washington Representative
Sino-Korean Peoples League

August 17, 1942

In reply refer to
FE

My dear Mr. Haan:

The receipt is acknowledged of your letter of
August 12, 1942, stating that you are sending under
separate cover a copy of the book entitled "How
Japan Plans to Win".

Your courtesy in supplying us with this
volume is appreciated.

Sincerely yours,

For the Secretary of State:

George Atcheson, Jr.,
Assistant Chief
Division of Far Eastern Affairs

Mr. Kilsoo K. Haan,
Sino-Korean People's League,
101 D Street, N.E.,
Washington, D. C.

FE:AKS:MS
8/15/42

DIVISION OF FAR EASTERN AFFAIRS

August 20, 1942

PA/H
Mr. Hornbeck:

A-B
Mr. Berle:

Reference underlying letter of August 15,
1942 from Mr. Kilsoo K. Haan in which he
quotes in part a statement recently released
to the press by the Korean-American Council,
of which Mr. James H. R. Cromwell is believed
still to be the President, adversely critical
of the Department's policy regarding the
Korean question.

FE is studying the question whether there
is any action which the Department might
take in regard to the press release of the
Korean-American Council.

FE:Salisbury:MBW

My dear Mr. Haan:

The receipt is acknowledged of your confidential
letter of August 1b, 1942, in which you express your
views in respect of various Korean activities.

Your courtesy in bringing your views to the attention
of the Department is appreciated.

Sincerely yours,

For the Secretary of State:

George Atcheson, Jr.
Assistant Chief
Division of Far Eastern Affairs

Mr. Kilsoo K. Haan,
Washington Representative,
Sino-Korean Peoples' League,
101 D Street, Ne.,
Washington, D. C.

Division of
FAR EASTERN AFFAIRS
AUG 1 7 1942
Department of State

Aug., 15, 1942

Confidential

August 24, 1942

KNAN
Representative

Hon. Cordell Hull
U.S. Secretary of State
Department of State
Washington D.C.

Honorable Sir:

Today I have received a press release distributed by the Korean-American Council. August 14, 1942. I am enclosing a copy of same.

I do hope that the State Department will issue a public statement clarifying its stand, specifically similar to your letter of May 20 to Hon. James H. R. Cromwell & his letter of May 5, 1942.

I am afraid if Dr. Rhee and Mr. Cromwell will issue and continue issue such state- ments derogatory toward America it may be used by the Axis Powers creating anti American sentiments.

KOREAN NATIONAL FRONT FEDERATION

SINO-KOREAN PEOPLES' LEAGUE

TRinidad 8500   101 D Street, N. E.   Lincoln 5187
WASHINGTON, D. C.

O K. HAAN
Representative

The press release said   quote

"Not only the Koreans but subjugated people everywhere are growing suspicious because for days, weeks and months since Dec. 7, we have avoided taking any action which would make good our promise.

Why is it that the State Department refuse to implement the Atlantic Charter and make it a thing a deeds rather than of words?

Is it because the State Department, or a group of individuals in it, is unwilling to and steps which might arouse resentment on the part of the Japanese Government?" Unquote

May I call your attention to the above state ment as very dangerous one and I fear far reaching repercussion against the cause of Korea and the United Nations if the Japs get hold of the above statement — so misleading and ambiguous. Such a statements will only aid the Japanese an will confuse the Koreans more and more

KOREAN NATIONAL FRONT FED[ERATION]

SINO-KOREAN PEOPLES' LEAGUE

TRinidad 8500   101 D Street, N. E.   Lincoln 5187
                       WASHINGTON, D. C.

KILSOO K. HAAN
Washington Representative

Already Dr. Syngman Rhee's official publication the Pacific Weekly — editorialized Jan. 16, 1941 — cautioning Koreans in their attempt to report anti-American Jap activities in Hawaii. Again on May 27, 1942 his control representative Secretary Jacob Dunn of the United Korean Committee of Honolulu published a letter to the editor of Honolulu Star Bulletin two column appeasement letter —

You already are aware of the continued statement of Dr. Rhee and Cromwell that they will not encourage the Koreans to fight the Japs not until Department of State recognize his group — diplomatic recognition as a government.

It would be a real service if you could make these fears public and warn the Koreans it will help many oof us to consolidate our morale and spirit into aiding America 100 per cent. By and large Koreans are for America and for the freedom of Korea — even Dr. Rhee is for it — but his selfish greed for power has eclipsed all reason and common

KOREAN NATIONAL FRONT FEDERATION

SINO-KOREAN PEOPLES' LEAGUE

TRinidad 8500   101 D Street, N. E.   Lincoln 5187
                       WASHINGTON, D. C.

KILSOO K. HAAN
Washington Representative

Common sense. He not only refused to cooperate with Koreans who questions his conduct of policies but just because one does that publicly charges them as Communists and etc.

I trust and hope soon the Department of State can and will help us, that is those who are in your judgement are trying to carry on to the best of their ability.

All I can say — if you check the activities of our League and the Korean National Front Federation in China, Manchuria etc — you will find that we are trying our best. Ofcourse we are **not** perfect nor unblemish. We have our faults and short-comings we do made and have made mistake. However if you believe that we can do our part, please help us in a quiet way, both moral and material aid.

In the interest of United Nations Victory

Ever Gratefully Yours

Kilsoo K. Haan

Confidential

The Korean-American Council
Colorado Building
Washington, D. C.   (For release to AM Papers
   Telephone: Republic 6119   of August 14, 1942, and
                            thereafter)

The celebration of the Atlantic Charter's first anniversary bring no joy to the people of Korea.

That portion of the charter which states "...they wish to see sovereign rights and self-government restored to those who have been forcibly deprived of them" is completely meaningless and, in the opinion of Koreans, even misleading. For the Korean people, at the close of the last war, rose in revolt in response to the slogan "To make the world safe for Democracy" only to learn through "blood, sweat and tears" that their home-land had been made safe for Japanese imperialism.

The Korean-American Council wishes to call to the attention of the American people the callous disregard of the Sta te Department to the Government of a country dedicated to the democratic princples, and the military potential of 23 million Koreans who hate their enslavers, the Japanese, as only bondsman can hate cruel and tyrannical masters.

Here is the State Department's record of inertia:

Korea's plea to sign the Decalration of United Nations has not even received the courtesy of an acknowledgement.

Korea's plea for recognition of its 23-year old Government has not been acknowledged as such.

Korea's request that the State Department note the existence of the American-Korean treaty of 1882 has not even been acknowledged.

Korea's plea for military aid to help fight the Japanese has not been acted upon.

Twenty-three million Koreans are ripe for revolt, they are ready to build a huge Bonfire in the backyard of Japan. All that is needed to start the conflagration is for the State Department to fulfill the pledge made by President Roosevelt on behalf of the American people.

Nothing, however, has been done to implement that pledge and not only the Koreans but subjugated peoples everywhere are growing suspicious because for days, weeks and months since December 7, we have avoided taking any action which would make good our promise.

Why is it that the State Department refuses to implement the Atlantic Charter and make it a thing of deeds rather than of words ?

Is it because the State Department, or a group of individuals in it, is unwilling to take any steps which might arouse resentment on the part of the Japanese Government ?

****

<u>MEMORANDUM</u>

August 26, 1942

FE - Mr. Salisbury:

A-B/H:

A-B - Mr. Berle:

S - Mr. Secretary:

Mr. Paul Jones, (telephone National 2366), the Washington representative of the J. M. Hickerson Advertising Agency of New York, telephoned to say that at Mr. Berle's suggestion he wished to speak to me informally about a proposition submitted to his firm by the people interested in the Free Korea movement (James H. R. Cromwell group).

He said that his company, which is a commercial advertising concern, had been approached with a proposition which boiled down to building up pressure to influence this Government toward definite recognition of the Free Korea Government. This company would be inclined to go into the matter, he said, only if it felt that a public agitation of this question would be directly in the national interest and consequently have the approval of the the Government, and specifically of this Department. He added that he personally felt dubious about the proposition, since he had examined correspondence between Mr. Cromwell and the Department from which it was apparent to him that the Department had given, and presumably would continue to give, careful consideration to the general question, but that Mr. Cromwell had "rather deliberately failed to understand" what the Department had written in reply to his letters.

I said that I was not familiar with the particular correspondence to which he referred, but knew of course of the movement in its general outline; that other officials of the Department, had studied the question in detail and would continue to do so; and that I could see no useful purpose in building up through commercial agencies an agitation to bring about action on the part of this Government on a question which would be decided on its merits in any case.

He

He said that was all he wanted to know. His company
desires to serve the public interest, and unless we felt
that a publicity campaign would be helpful in what we had
already determined would be a sound policy he would recommend to his company that it inform Mr. Cromwell's representative that it was not prepared to take over this work at this
time.

Eu:McCannon:BJS

KOREAN NATIONAL FRONT F...
SINO-KOREAN PEOPLES' LEAGUE

August. September 5, 31, 1942

Honorable Cordell Hull
Department Of State
Washington D.C.

Honorable Sir:

I am enclosing a copy of my radio talk script, Aug. 28, 1942 – 10:30 am. W. I. N. X.

Aug. 29th was the 32nd year of the annexation of Korea.

Our yearning prayer is, May God move the hearts of America soon — so that our Commander Yak San Kim and his soldiers both the Chinese Nationalist Army and the Chinese Guerrilla Army get some help from America.

As their representative, I am daily hoping and praying that God may touch your heart and make your Excellency see our need very soon.

Gratefully Yours

Kilsoo K. Haan

Y Script 140 VICTORY STARTS AT HOME 10:30-10:45 AM Aug. 28, 194
Sylvia Milrod

ANNOUNCER-VICTORY STARTS AT HOME

MUSIC   THEME - PLAY OPENING BARS AND FADE AS B.G.

ANNOUNCER-Yes, Victory Starts at Home in your home and yours and yours.
Victory is the responsibility of those who are left on the
Home Front. Victory starts with US.

MUSIC   THEME - UP - PLAY FIVE SECONDS AND FADE OUT.

ANNOUNCER Every morning at this same time Sylvia Milrod, the director
of WINX's Victory programs, brings you the information that
you as a civilian in wartime should know.
This morning she presents a rather unusual guest with an
unusually important message - on a very timely question -
but here's Miss Milrod to tell you more about that.

MILROD   Thank you, and good morning everybody. Our guest this
morning is Mr. Kilsoo Haan - a Korean. The purpose of
today's broadcast is to acquaint you with Korea and with
the tactics of our enemy - the Japanese.
If Victory is really to Start at Home - then civilians
must be well informed not only about themselves - but also
about their friends and enemies. Therefore, the story of
Korea should be heard.
Would you tell us first, Mr. Haan - exactly where Korea
is located and just why Korea is so important to the
Allied Cause.

HAAN   Gladly, Miss Milrod. Korea is a peninsula attached to the
mainland of Asia. It lies directly between China and
Japan, and used to be an independent nation.
Korea's importance to the United Nations lies, to a great

extent, in her strategic geographical position. Being
so close to Japan, Korea could be most useful to the Allies.

MILROD   But Korea happens to be occupied by the Japanese -

Haan   That's true. Korea has been in the hands of the Japanese
for 32 years. Thirty-two years ago tomorrow, Aug. 29th,
Japan annexed Korea and in doing so took over 85,000 square
miles of new territory, and millions in population.

MILROD   And yet today - 32 years later - you feel that Koreans are
still fighting in any way possible against Japan and trying
to help the Allied Cause.

HAAN   I know it - and I can prove it to be true. Korea is still
fighting.

But Miss Milrod, perhaps you can understand just why Korea
is fighting when you hear how Japan has treated us, and see
just why Koreans will always hate the Japanese.

MILROD   Please tell us the whole story Mr. Haan.

HAAN   Well, 32 years ago Korea became the first unwilling victim
of Japanese aggression. But when Japan took Korea - that
became Japan's first stepping stone into East Asia. Japan
had to have Korea in order to plan her militarism ahead,
when Korea fell, the fate of East Asia was immediately
endangered.

The next step was Manchuria, and I need not go on to tell
you just how Japan has progressed at the expense of China
and the world. But the annexation of Korea was not an easy
matter for the Japanese. The annexation was accomplished
in 1910 - but for years before that the battle was on.
First Japan had to go to war with China and then with Russia.
Meanwhile the King and Queen of Korea made Japanese invasion

very difficult and troublesome. Especially was this true of Queen Min. She became so decidedly unmanageable and impossible to handle - she presented such strong opposition to Japan - that the Japanese were determined to kill her. You may have heard of that hideous and greatly feared Japanese Black Dragon Society. They sent their "Ronins", those famous, or rather infamous, political assassins, to Korea in 1895. That year Queen Min was murdered in her own courtyard. She was hacked to bits and burned in kerosine oil.

Fifteen years later, in 1910, Japan annexed Korea. And since 1910 the Japanese have ruled Korea with blood and iron. For 32 years the Koreans have known life under the Japanese, but for more than 32 years the Koreans have hated the Japanese, and with good reason.

MILROD

HAAN

What has it been like in Korea these past 32 years? Terrible and degrading for all Koreans. To this day, nearly every jail in Korea is overcrowded with political prisoners. One of your American missionaries, recently returned from Korea, said that at the jail in which he himself was imprisoned the cells were 11x20 feet in size. Yet 40 prisoners were crowded into that small room.

MILROD

But in addition to the treatment given to political prisoners - how has Japan treated Korea economically and otherwise?

HAAN

Like a slave state, and even worse. Out of the total national tax revenue, only one and one-half percent is ever spent on things like education. And even though Japan has been crying all these years for land, land and

more land for her increasing population, yet the Japanese
have not sent their farmers to settle in Korea. Instead
Japan sent more and more gendarmes, cruel, inhuman "carpet
bag ers", soldiers and economic exploiters. Japan cried
for more land, and yet today, after 32 years, Japan has
imported 980,000 Koreans to Japan proper, but has sent less
than 650,000 Japanese to the Korean peninsula. Of these,
more than 200,000 are gendarmes, 200,000 are soldiers, more
than 100,000 are office holders, and less than 75,000 came
to settle in Korea to till the soil and work.

MILROD   With Japan's claims of overcrowding on her small island,
this seems very strange indeed. What has been done with
those hundreds of thousands of Koreans who have been forced
to go to live in Japan?

HAAN   They have been drawn to Japan to supply cheap labor, even
cheaper than the regular Japanese labor. Right now, about
a million Koreans are so treated in Japan. And you can
well imagine how bitter is the feeling against Japan because
of this inhuman treatment. Of course, when Japan moved into
Manchuria and China many more Koreans were caught up in the
net. They had tried to escape from the Japanese, but once
again they were caught. This time some 600,000 Koreans came
under Japanese rule in occupied China, and they have been
made to pay for it.

MILROD   And yet you say, Mr. Haan, that Korea is fighting back.

HAAN   She is, indeed. In the backyard of the Japanese strategic
military, naval, and air bases, millions of Koreans are
eager to do what they can to help the United Nations and

defeat Japan.   Only a few months ago, last February and
March, there was a nation-wide revolt against the Japanese.
Koreans killed more than 3000 of their enemies.   They
destroyed the wharves and oil tanks, railroad bridges,
warehouses, hundreds of homes, and they burned many ships.
Almost a hundred war planes were burned and destroyed.
Airplane hangars also fell under the Korean fires.
You asked me before to what extent the Korean patriots
can help the United Nations war against the Japs, and I
tell you that there are 23,000,000 Koreans in Korea,
990,000 still in Japan, out of which 189,000 are employed
in Japanese defense plants.   There are half a million in
Siberia and almost two million in Japanese occupied Manchuria and China.   They can make Japan feel the full
strength of sabotage and destruction.
Only last June 17, a young Korean patriot, Park Soowon,
wounded the Japanese Premier General Tojo, and seriously
wounded the former Foreign Minister and the present official
second in command of the Black Dragon Society, Koki Hirota.
A fortnight ago, hundreds of millions of people of the Near
and Far East were thrilled to learn of America's offensive
at Solomons, at Kiska and Attu Islands.   As the Naval,
air and land battle rages down the Southern Pacific, the
people living under Jap military rule are all keenly
watching and praying for the progress of the historical
war between the Asiatic power, Japan, and the power of the
greatest democracy, America.   And, meanwhile, the American
people can well realize Korea's interest and also her role
in this people's war against the Axis powers.

MILROD   How do you feel that Americans can best show their understanding of Korea's position, Mr. Haan.

HAAN   To answer that question, I would like to quote to you from
one of your own American magazines, Miss Milrod. In the
August Supplement of Fortuno Magazine, the Editors of Fortune
printed one of their series of reports on potential courses
for democratic action. This one included Korea and here is
what they said: "As an earnest sign of friendly intentions
and as a practical means of embarrassing the Japanese
military effort wherever possible, we should give whatever
aid we can to those fighting for Korean freedom. Our Army
Air Force could form squadrons of Korean-Americans. In our
Lend-Lease arrangement with China, some provisions might be
made in favor of the Korean armed forces serving with the
Chinese Army, just as we have provided aid for the Free
French through the British Lend-Lease account."

MILROD   And you agree with those statements.

HAAN   Most decidedly, the suggestions are just and they are
constructive, and they would give us our opportunity to
fight back, be of service to the Allied Cause, and, eventually, regain our country, so as to take our rightful
place, in the family of nations, in the Far East.
If I may continue, the editors of Fortune recognized that
as well, here is what they wrote: "As for the postwar
future of Korea, a Soviet-Chinese understanding would
appear indispensable. Economically, an independent Korea
would probably be able to make ends meet. Politically,
there is a lack of administrative experience, a result of
over thirty years of Japanese rule, that might make it

advisable to provide, during a transition period, for
international assistance to Korea through the medium of
an internationally selected Korean civil service headed
by a high commissioner appointed by the Pacific Council."
That always sounds just and fair. Korea wants her independence, but she also wants to earn it. Korea bases her
hopes for the future on the Atlantic Charter, and the four
freedoms expressed therein for all people, subjugated as
well as others. Some pessimistic people of the Far East
say that the Atlantic Charter's "Four Freedoms" may suffer
the fate of President Wilson's "14 Points". They point out
that although President Roosevelt and Prime Minister Churchill
signed the Atlantic Charter a year ago, to date it has not
received the approval officially of the U. S. Congress or
the British Parliament. However, almost all of the patriotic
leaders have great faith in the spirit and integrity of the
leaders now representing the United Nations, fighting for
the freedom of all people against the Axis Powers. They
trust President Roosevelt implicitly, and they trust Prime
Minister Churchill. They know that the "Four Freedoms"
must succeed, and they look to it as the hope for the people
of the world for the future.

And we Americans feel sure they won't be disappointed.
Thank you Mr. Kilsoo Haan for joining us today on Victory
Starts At Home and giving us an insight into Korea and
through Korea into the full meaning of Japanese aggression.
Korea's story was well worth hearing - and meeting you
was indeed a pleasure.

In reply refer to
FE

My dear Mr. Haan:

The receipt is acknowledged of your letter of
August 31, 1942, enclosing a copy of the script of
a talk which you made over the radio on August 28
in regard to Korea.

Your thoughtfulness in letting us have a copy
of the script is appreciated.

Sincerely yours,

For the Secretary of State:

George Atcheson, Jr.,
Assistant Chief
Division of Far Eastern Affairs

JR

1942FT

Mr. Kilsoo K. Haan,

Sino-Korean People's League,

101 D Street, N.E.,

Washington, D. C.

FE:LES:MS   FE
9/4/42

CROSS-REFERENCE FILE

NOTE

SUBJECT Korean independence and United States strategy.
Letter regarding the -.

For the original paper from which reference is taken

See ________ Letter ________________________
        (Despatch, telegram, instruction, letter, etc.)

Dated ___ Dec. 20, 1941 ___ From| Edward L. Junkin
                             To|

File No. ___ 811.001 Roosevelt, F. D./737 ________

DEPARTMENT OF STATE

DIVISION OF FAR EASTERN AFFAIRS

<u>STRICTLY CONFIDENTIAL</u>

October 10, 1942

KOREA

A number of American citizens, a number of Koreans in this country and in China, and a number of foreign governments are especially interested in the question of Korea. Suggestions are offered in various quarters that Korean independence should be proclaimed specifically as one of the aims of the United Nations and that the Government of the United States and other governments accord diplomatic recognition to Korean regimes which have set themselves up in certain foreign countries.

There is thus some agitation for action by this and other governments; and there is a desire on the part of this Government and presumably of other governments to do what they appropriately can to further the aspirations of the Korean people for freedom.

It is suggested that a constructive way in which to approach the Korean question would be to set up a committee representing several countries to investigate the Korean question, to formulate recommendations, and to present those recommendations to the United Nations. As a logical body to initiate such action, it is suggested that the President might propose to the Pacific War Council that the Council ask a committee of the governments represented thereon to undertake this mission. The Chinese Government might be asked to act as chairman of the committee, and the other two governments represented thereon might be this Government and the New Zealand Government.

Should such a committee be set up, it would seem desirable that it be regarded as an informal, working committee; that no announcement be made of its creation; that in general the fact of its constitution be regarded as confidential; and that, if any public statement of policy is to be made, it be issued in the name of the Pacific War Council as a whole after the committee has made a report of its recommendations.

It is considered that such a committee might conceivably and to advantage arrive at conclusions which they might present to the Pacific War Council and to the United Nations for consideration and that these conclusions might include items as follows:

(a)

-2-

(a) That it be declared that the people of Korea are entitled to freedom and independence and that the Governments of the United Nations at war with Japan look forward to attainment through their efforts and those of the Korean people of that objective.

(b) That it be declared that the people of Korea should, when their native land is freed from Japan's oppression, be given opportunity to select freely their own government.

(c) That it be declared that, because the people of Korea have not since 1910 had experience in governmental processes due to their subjection to Japanese oppression, the United Nations would be prepared to cooperate with the Korean people in setting up and establishing a national government of Korea and for this purpose to assist in forming a temporary international trusteeship under which there would be given advice and technical assistance to the people and government of Korea.

(d) That upon the conclusion of hostilities and in the light of conditions then existing there be set an express period at the end of which time all such foreign technical advice and assistance mentioned in the preceding paragraph would be terminated.

(e) That Korea should undertake to cooperate with other nations in adopting and following liberal trade policies.

It is realized that it is undoubtedly premature to take up certain types of post-war problems. However, the case of Korea has certain special features which would seem to make advisable and practicable the approach suggested above.

If

If such an approach is to be given favorable consideration, it would probably be desirable before any
public announcement is made that the Soviet Government
be informed in confidence of what is contemplated. The
Soviet Government need not and probably should not be
asked to express any views. It would, however, seem
advisable to inform that Government and to give it an
opportunity, should it so desire, to make observations
or comments.

NOTE: The proposed committee might also study the
question of how the Koreans might be utilized most
usefully in the war effort.

FE:MMH:HES

THE WHITE HOUSE

WASHINGTON

December 8, 1942

MEMORANDUM FOR

        THE STATE DEPARTMENT

To do the necessary.

           F. D. R.

Enclosure

The Korean Commission

Washington, D. C.

                                    December 7, 1942

Dear Mr. Secretary:

    I have the honor to send you herewith a copy of a
memorandum prepared by me at the request of Dr. Victor
Hoo, Chinese under-secretary of state, who has asked
for a statement of the present and ultimate aims of
the Korean Provisional Government.

                            Sincerely yours,

                            SYNGMAN RHEE

Honorable Cordell Hull
Secretary of State
U.S. Department of State
Washington, D. C.

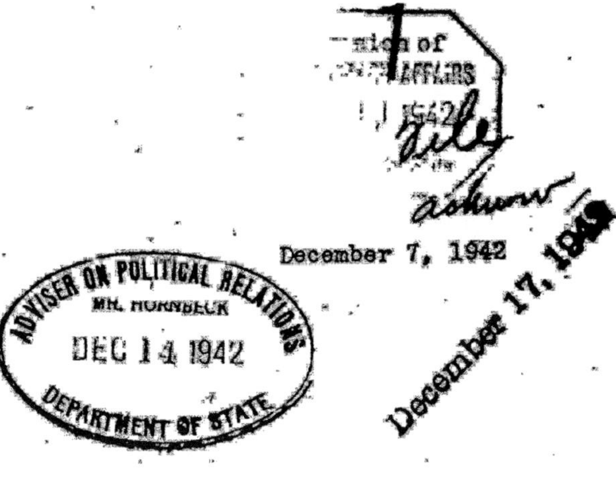

ADVISER ON POLITICAL RELATIONS
MR. HORNBECK
DEC 14 1942
DEPARTMENT OF STATE

December 7, 1942

My dear Mr. President:

I address you on this "date of infamy" with great gratitude because December 7th, as of this year marks the beginning of the training of Korean nationals for warfare against the Japanese by the American War Department. The number is small, but the purpose, my dear Mr. President, is to make use eventually of the vast reservoir of Korean manpower in Asia to defeat the island savages.

I take pleasure in enclosing herewith also a copy of a memorandum prepared at the request of Dr. Victor Hoo, Chinese under-secretary of foreign affairs, on the present and ultimate aims of the Korean Provisional Government and hope you may have the opportunity to read it.

Please be assured, Mr. President, that your understanding mention of the harsh fate of the Korean people and your authorship of the Atlantic Charter will be forever appreciated by the 23,000,000 Koreans I have the honor to represent.

Sincerely yours,

Syngman Rhee

Honorable Franklin Delano Roosevelt
President of The United States
The White House

The Korean Commission
Washington, D.C.

5

December 7, 1942

DEPARTMENT OF STATE
RECEIVED
DEC 7 - 1942
OFFICE OF THE SECRETARY

Dear Mr. Secretary:

I have the honor to send you herewith copy of a
memorandum prepared by me at the request of Dr. Victor Hoo,
Chinese under-secretary of state, who has asked for a
statement of the present and ultimate aims of the Korean
Provisional Government.

Sincerely yours,

Syngman Rhee

Honorable Cordell Hull
Secretary of State
U. S. Department of State
Washington, D. C.

December 5, 1942

My dear Dr. Hoo:

I am glad to respond to your request transmitted to me by Mr. John W. Staggers.

The immediate aim of the Provisional Government of the Republic of Korea is more actively to assist the United Nations in the war against Japan by:

(1) Adequately equipping the Korean National Army with weapons of warfare;

(2) Augmenting that army through accessions from the substantial reservoir of Korean manpower in the Far East;

(3) Establishing an espionage service both without and within Korea so that effective sabotage and revolutionary activities may be undertaken against the enemy.

I need not emphasize to you, my dear Dr. Hoo, the centuries' old and justifiable hatred of the Japanese by the Koreans, our ceaseless warfare against them during the past 37 years, the admitted skill of the Korean both as a regular and a guerrilla soldier, and our earnest desire to play a major role in crushing Japanese militarism, routing the tyrant from our homeland and instituting a democracy for the 23,000,000 enslaved Koreans.

You have been advised by American military authorities of the first initial steps to implement our aim but much remains to be done and every moment now is precious. With vigorous Chinese-American collaboration, the military potential of the Korean nation can soon be realized to the immense benefit of our common cause whereas, as you know, nearly one year since Pearl Harbor has been permitted to elapse and this potential consequently has been virtually paralyzed.

The ultimate aim of the Korean Provisional Government is the complete demilitarization of Japan. Thereafter, the following:

(1) Banishment to Japan of all of her nationals now resident in Korea.

(2) Return to Korea of all Korean nationals now held in serfdom in Japan proper.

(3) Search and recovery of all Korean books, records and works of art looted by the Japanese.

(4) Rigid restriction of Japanese fisheries, navigation (sea and aerial) and commerce.

(5) Return of Satsuma Island.

Honorable Victor Hoo
The Chinese Embassy
Washington, D. C.

(6) An

(6) An indemnity from Japan sufficient to cover her pillaging of Korean resources during the 37 years of occupation, as well as the damages which will result from the forthcoming military action in our country.

It is the purpose of the Korean Government, once the homeland is regained, to purge our nation of all Japanese influence, establish law and order, institute democratic processes, and to call for a general election wherein all adults -- male and female -- may exercise the rights of suffrage.

In the new world that will emerge from this war, a free, strong and democratic Korea can be one of the most powerful assurances of peace in the Far East.

Korea, even today, with more than one million Christians, is Christianity's greatest bastion in the Orient. And, as the future aerial gateway to Asia, it would fulfill a great role as the crucible for the tenets of Confucius and the teachings of Christ.

Korea, resuming her rightful place in the family of nations, will need the assistance of her age-old friend, China; material support and capital from America, and the understanding and friendship of her great neighbor, Russia.

Down through the 42 centuries of our existence as a nation, the Korean people have made priceless contributions to civilization -- the magnetic compass, the first moveable type, the Orient's first alphabet, solar observatory, etc., etc.-- yet the industrial revolution caught us unaware but gave the imitative Japanese their chance. We are passing through Gethsemane but our will to fight for freedom and our belief that that great document, the Atlantic Charter, should apply to us now, can be our resurrection.

Sincerely yours,

THE KOREAN COMMISSION

Syngman Rhee, Chairman

First PRESBYTERIAN CHURCH . . . of *Los Angeles*

HERMAN E. NYGAARD, *Minister*
STANLEY H. ROBERTS, *Minister of Religious Education*

2000 SOUTH FIGUEROA ST.
LOS ANGELES . . CALIFORNIA

January 8, 1942.

The Honorable Henry Wallace,
Vice-president of the United States of America,
Washington, D. C.

My dear Mr. Wallace:

You will probably not recall me although I had the privilege of meeting you on several occasions during my pastorate at Westminster United Presbyterian Church in Des Moines. I became pastor after the merger of all of the United Presbyterian churches of the city and the West--minster Presbyterian Church. During my ministry there I came, of course, to know your Uncle John and the Brownes at Indianola very well.

I am writing on behalf of my many Korean friends here on the west coast. They are greatly desirous of form--ing a provisional government similar to the governments of Czecho-Slovakia and Poland. Such a government would only have standing if it were recognized by either Great Britain or the United States.

You and Mr. Hull are undoubtedly aware of Korea's situation. Independent for centuries Korea (Chosen) came in 1910 under the rule of Japan. For seven years previously it had been nominally a Japanese protectorate.

Koreans have never accepted Japanese rule. They have an intelligently intense nationalistic fervor which will never be satisfied with anything less than complete independence. Korea also is probably more Christian today than any nation in the Far East. While the missionaries have not interfered with the political structure of the country it is true, of course, that the Christian gospel inculcates a longing for freedom.

Now that we are at war with Japan and pledged by our president to end for all time the threat of Japanese ag--gression it would seem the part of wisdom to recognize and encourage a provisional Korean government which represented the people of the hermit Kingdom. It will, to be sure, be a hermit kingdom no longer.

May I bespeak for the Koreans your interest and good will. They are a fine people and have a great longing for

Hon. Henry Wallace.   -2-

self-government and freedom.

       With warm personal regards, I am

            Sincerely yours,

NEN/ef

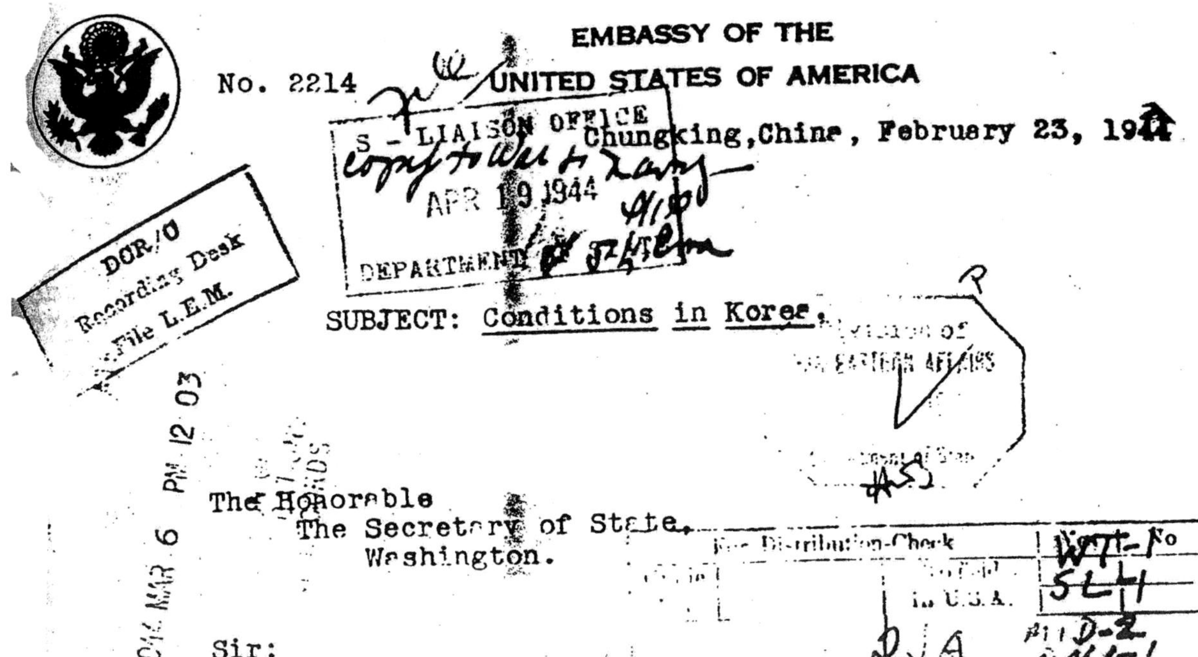

EMBASSY OF THE
UNITED STATES OF AMERICA

No. 2214

Chungking, China, February 23, 1944

SUBJECT: Conditions in Korea.

The Honorable
   The Secretary of State,
      Washington.

Sir:

   I have the honor to enclose a copy of despatch
no. 17, February 3, 1944, from the Secretary on
detail at Sian, on the subject of conditions in Korea.

   Mr. Drumright's despatch, based on an article
appearing in a Sian newspaper, contains an adequate
summary of its contents.

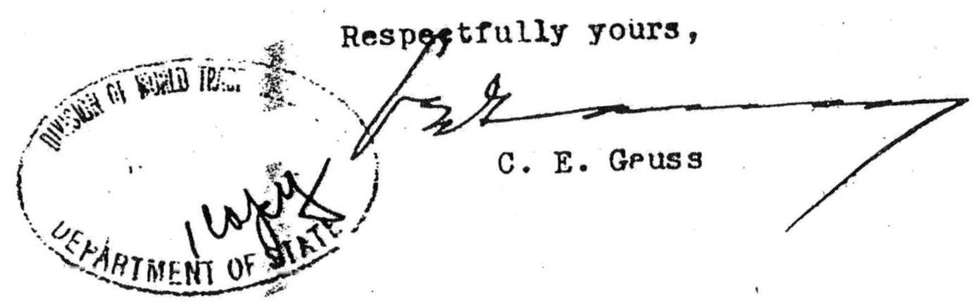

                    Respectfully yours,

                              C. E. Gauss

Enclosure:
   1. Copy of despatch no. 17, as stated above.

In single copy to the Department.

800

CHB/ccw

No. 19

Subject: CONDITIONS IN KOREA

The Honorable C. E. Gauss,
     American Ambassador,
          Chungking.

Sir:

       I have the honor to enclose herewith as of possible
interest a memorandum on the subject "Conditions in Korea".
This memorandum was prepared from an article appearing in
a Sian newspaper within the past few days, its source
reportedly being one General Li Ching-tien, Commander in
Chief of the Korean "Kwang Fu" Army.

       <u>Summary of memorandum.</u> The Korean people have been
enslaved by the Japanese, have no freedom. The Japanese are
endeavoring to "Japanize" the Korean people by intermarriage
and other means. Since the outbreak of war the Japanese
have utilized Korea as a base for the prosecution of the war.
Five organizations in Korea carry out the "New People's movement". These organizations are the vehicles by which Japan
is utilizing Korea: conscripting its manpower, increasing
the production of war materials in Korea, "Japanizing" the
population, using Koreans to help in the maintenance of
peace and order, and organizing Korean womenpower for service.
The Japanese have exploited Korean agriculture and industry
for their own ends, especially sincethe start of war. Rationing
is enforced throughout Korea, but the amount of foodstuffs
supplied is insufficient. Since 1939 some 200,000 Koreans
have been conscripted for military service. General conscription is being enforced in Korea from the spring of 1944.
Korean culture has all but been extinguished under Japanese
pressure for "Japanization" of the Korean people. <u>End of
summary.</u>

                              Respectfully yours,

                              Everett F. Drumright
                              Second Secretary of Embassy
                              on detail at Sian

Enclosure:
     1/ Memorandum

MEMORANDUM

Subject: CONDITIONS IN KOREA

Source. The following information in regard to present-day conditions in Korea is derived from an article appearing in the Hsiking Jih Pao, a daily newspaper published by the Kuomintang in Sian. The article in question is in the nature of an interview assertedly had by a Chinese news reporter with General Li Ching-tien(李青天), who is styled the "Commander in Chief of the Kuang Fu(光復軍) Army", that is a military organization composed of Koreans which is aided and supported by the Chinese Government in Chungking. (According to the local press, General Li Ching-tien, accompanied by his Chief of Staff, Chao Teh-shu(趙德樹), flew from Chungking to Paoki on January 25, 1944, arriving in Sian on January 26, 1944. The purpose of their visit to Sian was said to be to inspect the Second Unit of the "Kuang Fu" Army which is stationed at Sian. General Li is reported to have called on General Hu Tsung-nan, Vice Commander of the Eighth War Area, and General Hsiung Pin, Chairman of the Shensi Provincial Government, on January 28, 1944.)

There follows a summary of General Li's interview with a Chinese reporter as published.

General. The Japanese have occupied 98 per cent of the soil of Korea and they control 95 per cent of the wealth of Korea. Some 90 per cent of the high officials in Korea are Japanese and 70 per cent of the lower officials are Japanese. The massacre, beating, imprisonment and seizure of property of Koreans is going on constantly and without restriction. The Koreans have lost all attributes of freedom. Although the revolution of March 1, 1919 was abortive and a great many Korean patriots lost their lives, the determination of the people of Korea was kindled and revolutionary activities broke out in every corner of the country. Since the outbreak of the Sino-Japanese war Korea has become a Japanese military base, and for this reason all administrative organizations and people's organizations have assumed a military character. To facilitate their colonization tactics the Japanese have utilized propaganda to foster the Japanization of the Korean people. To bring this about the Japanese have encouraged Japanese-Korean intermarriage. Today the Japanese Government provides the marriage expenses involving the marriage of Japanese and Koreans/ Persons contracting such marriages are given preferred status in obtaining public positions, in business, in attending schools, et cetera. Everywhere in the country political pressure is applied by the Japanese to compel Koreans to adopt Japanese names and to cease using the Korean written and spoken language, the object being to convert 30,000,000 Koreans into Japanese slaves. But the revolution is on the march at the same time that the policy of enslavement is being pursued.

Political Conditions in Korea under the Japanese. There are five big organs in Korea, all under the lead of the Japanese militarists, whose object it is to carry out the "New People's Movement". These advocate the following "War first", "sacrifice first", "militarization of everything", the Japanese object being to utilize Koreans in the implementation of their own plans. The five chief organs are (1厚生省 (which might be translated "Ministry of Physical Education") whose function it is to strengthen the bodies and physical conditions of Koreans to meet war needs. Physical education is stressed among the people and in the schools, and many publications are issued on the subject. Athletic organizations have been created and playing fields built, and competition is fostered. On the surface the object is to foster physical education but there is the hidden object of asserting the physical condition of Koreans [illegible] and the [illegible]

who may be conscripted for service with the Japanese army. (2
The Production Control Board. The function of this board is to
control production and consumption and to increase the quantity
and quality of military goods and supplies.   To carry this out
this board has mobilized the manpower of Korea and made careful
investigation of the production capacity, industrial resources,
raw materials, capital and manpower of Korea. All industry other
than that producing war materials has been forced to suspend
operations, and experts are sent to factories to train workers,
augment or adjust machinery, supply added capital and raw
materials, and, in short, to perform any service that will
result in increased production of war materials.   Women have
taken the places of men factory workers who are of conscription
age and who are engaged in general factory work. Most able-bodied
men workers have been concentrated in industries turning out
important war materials.   Most clerks, conductors, ticket sellers,
letter carriers, postal employees and minor officials are now
women. (3 Cultural Control Board. The function of this organ
is to bring about the Japanization of the Korean race. The "New
People's Movement" is the vehicle by which the Japanese are
working to accomplish this object.   This board has taken over
all cultural organizations in Korea and has in addition organized new ones to carry on this work. Theatrical companys have
been created to tour the country, as well as moving picture
corps and educational corps. These organs are active throughout
the breadth of Korea endeavoring to bring the Korean people to
understand the "glorious historical past of Imperial Japan".
At the same time this board exercises great pressure on the
publishing industry to prevent the publication of any material
inimical to Japan and that country's activities. (4 National
Defense Youth Corps. Under this organization the youth of the
country are divided into two groups: those between the ages of
18 and 25 and those between the ages of 25 and 45. All able-bodied
males within these age limits are forced to join one or the other
of these organizations. Under these organizations three sub-
sidiary organizations are to be found: (1 fire-fighting units;
(2 Detective units; and (3 "Dare to die" units. The function
of these last named units is to assist the gendarmerie and police
in their work. The Detective units are officered by Japanese
or renegade Koreans. Normally these units may be put in uniforms
and used to help in theenforcement of martial law or the preservation of peace. The other two units are made up exclusively of
Koreans . But lest there be trouble these units are not supplied
with firearms. (5 Patriotic Women's Society. All Korean women
who arephysically fit must join this society. They are constantly
trained to serve as nurses and the like. They also have the
responsibility of serving as comforters of the troops and of
selling national bonds, et cetera. The main function of the
above-described organizations is to cope with the future large-
scale air raids that will be carried out by planes of the United
Nations. Recently the Japanese have established a great many
new prisons in Korea and the number of police and police expenses
have greatly increased. The recent promulgation of the
laws and the enforcement of a ban against two or more persons
assembling and talking, et cetera, have made revolutionary work
in Korea very difficult. In general revolutionists have come to
China to carry on their work of restoring Korea. Revolutionists
apprehended by the Japanese in Korea are immediately executed and
no report is ever made in the press.

Recent economic conditions in Korea. Following the absorption
of Korea by the Japanese the Korean farming system, i.e., of the
independent tiller of the soil, was abandoned, and the Korean

farmers came to be exploited by two large Japanese enterprises.
Cooperative irrigation agencies and cooperative financial
agencies were organized in more than two hundred places to
exploit the Korean farmer. Along communication lines and near
the cities and towns 90 per cent ofthe land was occupied by Japanese.
The remainder was not sufficient to support the farmers dispossessed, so they had to change their occupations or flee to
China. At present the entire production of Korean farmers is
turned over to the Japanese who in turn ration out food to the
populace. The farming population of Korea is today face to face
with starvation and death.

The industrial plants of Koreans have all been taken over
by the Japanese. With a view to meeting the needs of the Sino-
Japanese war, the Japanese trained large numbers of workers and
established war production plants. In the mountains and among
the forests and under the ground everywhere there are arsenals,
chemical plants and aircraft factories. And because the Japanese
are short of many raw materials they are busy day and night
exploiting the mineral resources of Korea. Even the very copper
and iron tools of the people andthe bells ofthe temples and
statues, iron fences, et cetera, have all been removed. At
night the use of electricity is restricted because it must be
conserved for use in the factories; the cities and villages are
plunged into darkness.

Prior to the start of the Pacific War the majority of Korean
merchants were engaged in small-scale merchandising. However,
following the application of control measures by the Japanese
and the institution of rationing and fixed prices most Korean
merchants were unable to continue in business, such business
as remained falling into the hands of petty Japanese merchants.

<u>Rationing.</u> The Japanese enforce rationing on the unit
basis in Korea. In the rationing of food the people in Korea
are divided into two classes: (1 those from 10 to to 50 years
of age are put in "A" classification; and (2 those below 10 or
over 50 years of age are placed in "B" category. These in "A"
category are given 7 "sheng"( ) of grain monthly, those in "B"
category 3½ "sheng". Of this grain 40 per cent is rice, 30
per cent beans, kaoliang, et cetera, and the remainder miscellan-
eous grains. Because this ration is insufficient for the use of
the people all the bark of the trees and the stems of the grains
are eaten in Korea. Workers in war plants and middle school
students may beissued a special ration of two "sheng" of grain
monthly (in addition to the regular ration), but the trouble
encountered in obtaining this extra ration is very great. Oil,
salt, soya sauce, vinegar and sugar are rationed to the Japanese
residents of Korea, but there are Koreans who never saw any of
these commodities in a whole year. In as much as all Korean
cotton is shipped to Japan for use in making munitions, the
Japanese supply Korea with cloth and clothing made of silk and
hemp. Koreans may only obtain the same kind of clothing whether
they are wealthy or poor. Shoes are made with wooden soles and
coats and vests without sleeves are common.

Japanese military activities in Korea. Koreans are permitted
to enter the Japanese army. In 1939 10,000 Koreans were conscripted, in 1940 20,000, in 1941 40,000, in 1942 [illegible]. In
1943 [illegible]. Thus in thespace of several years 20[illegible]
have been forced into the Japanese army. After recruiting them
a portion of these troops will soon be [illegible] to Manchuria to [illegible]
area against the Russians. But the majority has [illegible]
and are now fighting Chinese, American and British [illegible]

Korean soldiers fighting in the Japanese army in China had numbered 20,000 men. The Japanese have now decided to institute general conscription in Korea from the spring of 1944. In the latter part of 1943 they started publication in the Korean press of information pertaining to conscription and of questions and answers on this subject. Moreover, propaganda was disseminated from Korean radio stations on this subject. Following a year's training another lot of Korean youth will be sent to the front lines to face death. In the spring of 1943, the Japanese navy conscripted 4,000 Koreans for service in the navy. In north China 400 Koreans were forced by Japanese consular officials to join the navy. From the beginning of the present year Korean primary and middle school students and youths who are members of youth organizations have been undergoing examination and without soliciting their desires many students are compelled to enter the armed services. In 1942 students were selected from Korean primary and middle schools for admission into the Japanese air forces. Those with superior health and bodies and educational qualifications were selected, the number being 1500. From the same reservoir 2500 were taken for service in the armored units. In 1943 the number selected from the schools for these purposes was even greater.

Korean culture under Japanese pressure. There are no universities established in Korea. Middle and primary schools are present in small numbers, and for this reason they are divided into morning and afternoon sessions or classes. Such students as there are, therefore, have the opportunity to study only a half-day at the most. At school the students devote half their time to study and half their time to work. The proceeds of the work go/the Japanese war fund. Wealthy Koreans fear to provide funds for the opening of schools, for such funds are expropriated by the Japanese for military uses. Most Korean intellectuals who are not in jails are subject to close surveillance of the Japanese. There is a combination Japanese-Korean newspaper published in Seoul, as well as one wholly Korean language paper, but these are nothing more than translations from Japanese.

April 15, 1941

The attached letter dated February 25,
1941 addressed to the President and referred
by the White House under date of April 11,
to the Secretary of State for the necessary
action is signed by Kim Ku who styles himself
President of the Central Committee of the
Provisional Government of the Republic of
Korea. The letter indicates no return
address.

In the past (see attached file) communications of the so-called Provisional
Government have been filed without action.
It is suggested that the present communication
likewise be filed without action.

FW 895.01/48

FE:Coville:MBW

THE WHITE HOUSE
WASHINGTON

April 9, 1941.

MEMORANDUM FOR THE PRESIDENT:

Re: <u>The attached letter from the
Provisional Government of the
Republic of Korea.</u>

The attached is a plea for recognition.
I understand that such pleas have been
addressed to you before and that in the past
you have referred them to the State
Department.

Lauchlin Currie

FW
895.01/48

THE WHITE HOUSE

WASHINGTON

April 11, 1941.

MEMORANDUM FOR

THE SECRETARY OF STATE

FOR THE NECESSARY ACTION

F. D. R.

THE PROVISIONAL GOVERNMENT OF THE RE[illegible]

CABLE ADDRESS
COPOGO

25th. Feb[illegible]

To President F. D. Roosevelt,

    The White House,

        Washington, D. C.

Your Excellency:

      Our diplomatic relations with the United State[s] were begun May 23rd, 1882, when our government signed the Korean-American Commercial Treaty with your Minister in Seoul. Unfortunately when Japan forced Korea to accept the protectorial treaty [in] 1905, our sixty years of continued diplomatic relations ceased. But we are ever grateful to your Government and people for all the sympathy and consideration given to our efforts for independence. Permit us to city the special consideration given to Mr. Chang Rin-hwan in 1907; the sympathy given to our 105 imprisoned patriots in 1911; your generosity in letting Koreans residing in America use Independence Hall, Philadelphia, to conduct our Independence [First] Congress in 1919; the discussion of the Korean independence [problem] in your Senate in 1920; and also the special considerations [given] in 1940 to our students studying in America. All these generous considerations symbolize your deep interest, sympathy and friendship towards our country.

      Your Excellency has been re-elected for the third [term] as President of the United States of America because your [love for] justice and liberty, your regard for human rights, and your [opposition to] the tyranny of [illegible] dictatorship, make you [illegible]

———··———

CABLE ADDRESS
COPOGO

Pres. Roosevelt---2.

25th. February, 194

confidence in you and in your Excellency's national policy,
sure that your mission to safeguard democracy against dicta
aggression will be accomplished. Your Excellency's courageous
against imperialiststic aggression, both in Europe and Asia, wi
long in the history of mankind.

In the name of thirty million Korean people, this gover
ment is now presenting this paper to your Excellency in order to
draw your Excellency's attention to the question of Korean indepen
dence. It is our sincere wish to continue our long ceased diploma
tic relations with your Excellency's Government and with your suppor
and help to regain our independence and to establish a modern
democratiy nation. This not only will bring perpetual peace in the
Far East but also will safeguard the interests of the United Stat
in the Orient.

Allow us to present to your Excellency the following
about our Provisional Government:

(I) The Korean Provisional Government was established in 191
with the support of all those Koreans who desire to be free from
Japanese yoke and to set a new democratic nation on the basis of
political, economical, and educational equalty.

(2) Holding the principles of national consciousness, civil
zation and self- control, our people are capable of setting up an
independent democratic gevernment.

(3) Having been most inhumanly oppressed by Japanese
tien during the last thirty years, and with the lessons

CABLE ADDRESS   Pres. Roosevelt---3.
COPOGO

25th, February, 194[illegible]

...own the revolutions of China and Russia, our determination to b...
free from the Japanese yoke is unshakable. It was for this r...
that this Provisional Government was established by the represent...
tives of the thirteen Korean provinces and our independence move...
continued up to the present time.

(4) Our Independence Party is the party in which is centrali...
all our national revolutionary elements and supports this Provision...
Government.

(5) A Korean Independence Army was organized by this Government and is now fighting Japanese imperialistic aggression side by
side with the gallant Chinese Army.

On the basis of the above facts this government hops your
Excellency's Government will grant the following requests:

(1) Considering our historical relations with your country an...
your Excellency's deep interest in our country, we hope most sincer...
that your Excellency's Government will recognize this Provisional
Government.

(2) That it will aid our government in diplomatic, military,
and economic matters to strengthen our power to fight Japanese a...
aggression.

(3) To aid our war for independence more effectively, we hop...
your Excellency's Government will ask your representatives in Chun...
king to facilitate technical cooperation, economic aid and arms supp...

(4) That at the conclusion of the present world war, the
...ican government will bring up the question of Korean independen...

CABLE ADDRESS
COPOGO

Pres. Roosevelt---4.

20th. February

the peace conference and see that our representatives are permitted to participate in all the dicussions.

(5) That if a new international orgnizationis set up after the conclusion of the present world way we may be permitted to participate in this as well.

The propositions which we are present to your Excellency willnot only help us to stop Japanese imperialistic aggression, but it doubtless also agree with your Far Eastern policy. As your Excellency's country gained independence with the help of France, Spain and Holland and was first recognized by them, so we sincerely hope your Excellency's Government will approve the above five proposals in order to hasten our independence.

By this help not only will ruthless Japanese aggression in the Far East be stopped, but also democracy will be made to triump over dictatorial tyranny, and a new and glorious record in the history of mankind will be set up. Thus will it be possible to establisheinternational justice and secure the blessings of liberty for all humanity.

Yours sincerely,
President of the Central Committe of
The Provisional Government,

DEPARTMENT OF STATE

Memorandum of Conversation
DIVISION OF FAR EASTERN AFFAIRS

DATE: March 31,

SUBJECT: Recognition of Korea

PARTICIPANTS: Mr. Soon Hahn
Mr. Salisbury

COPIES TO:

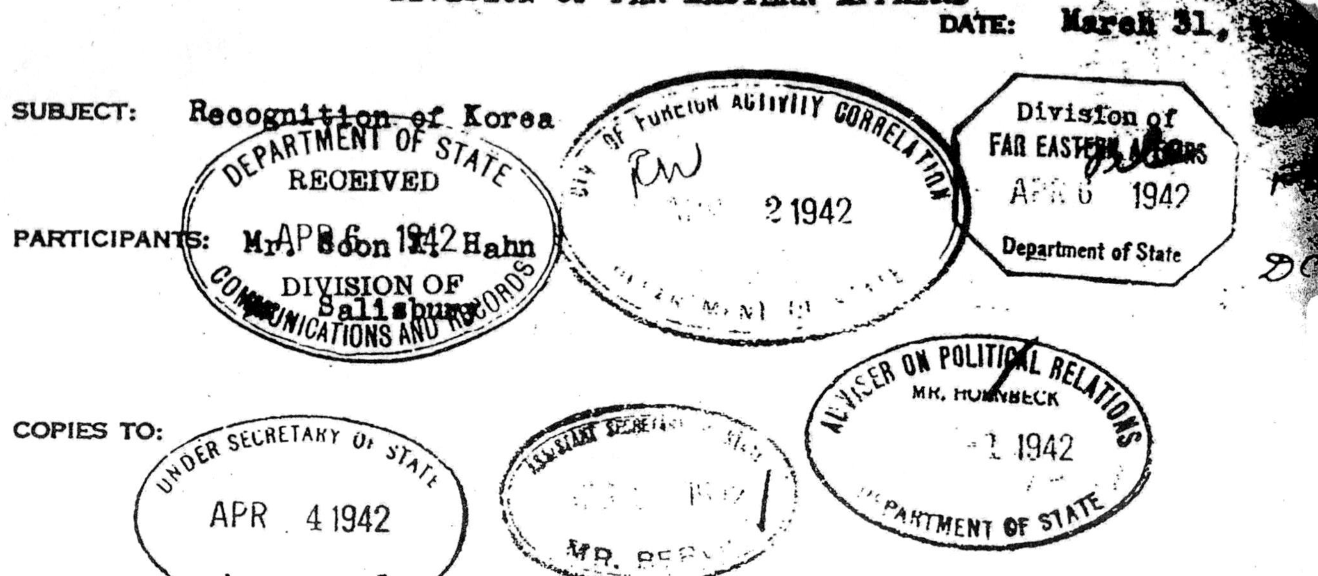

At lunch today Mr. Soon K. Hahn informed Mr. Salisbury of his views with regard to the question of unification of Korean leaders in the United States, Free China, occupied China, and the Siberian-"Manchukuo" border areas. Mr. Hahn showed Mr. Salisbury a rough chart which Mr. Hahn has made depicting the free Korean movement since 1919. This chart indicates that shortly after 1919 the movement divided into two branches, one of which is made up of those Koreans in the United States and Chungking, of which Dr. Syngman Rhee is a representative, whose primary objective is recognition of their group as the government Korea, the other branch being the "Revolutionary Koreans" in the occupied areas of China and in the border areas of Siberia and Manchuria. Mr. Hahn described the "Revolutionary Koreans"

Koreans" as having been active all these years against
Japan while the other branch, represented by Dr. Rhee, has
been passive.

Mr. Hahn stated that it was extremely important that
these two branches unite for participation in the war effort of the United Nations. He expressed the view that
the so-called revolutionary leaders will, after the successful conclusion of the war, become the leaders of a
free Korea and that Dr. Syngman Rhee and his associates
will be of little importance. He said that the revolutionary
party is regarded by Dr. Rhee and his associates as communist but that they are no more communist than the sub-
ordinates of Vice President Wallace who were attacked
recently by Congressman Dies. Mr. Hahn stated that he was
to see Mr. Staggers and Mr. Williams, associates of Dr. Rhee,
this afternoon in an effort to impress upon them that,
before recognition be granted by the United States to a
Korean Government, there should be unity among Koreans and
the Koreans should have done something for the war effort
which would deserve repayment such as recognition. Mr. Hahn
said that he felt that very likely Mr. Staggers and Mr. Williams are working for recognition of the Korean regime at
Chungking for selfish reasons and that when he recently
asked Mr. Staggers why he was so anxious to obtain recognition Mr. Staggers replied that then the United States

Government

Government would let them have lease-lend funds. Mr. Hahn then pointed out to Mr. Staggers that lease-lend funds were only a loan and would have to be repaid some day, to which Mr. Staggers replied that the United States Government was giving the money away. Mr. Hahn stated that he thought that the United States Government might be eventually embarrassed if it recognized Dr. Rhee's group and then found at the end of the war that the revolutionary leaders were the real leaders of Korea. Mr. Hahn also stated that recognition of the Provisional Government at Chungking would very likely precipitate the establishment of a rival provisional government by the so-called revolutionary leaders.

When asked what would be the activities of the Koreans in the event that Mr. Hahn were able to reconcile existing differences among Koreans, Mr. Hahn replied that, in his opinion, sabotage of Japanese activities should be their primary objective.

FE:Salisbury:MHP

Congress of the United States
House of Representatives
Washington, D. C.

December 8, 1941

The Honorable Cordell Hull,
Secretary of State,
Washington, D. C.

My dear Mr. Secretary:

Because of a conversation with some men who are quite well acquainted with affairs in the East, among them, Doctor Zia Yee-Chen and Doctor Syngman Rhee, I wish to bring to your attention the matter of recognizing the independence of Korea in connection with the present war against Japan.

No doubt this matter is among those under advisement by your department. I believe it would be a good diplomatic move as it would have the psychological effect of heartening the Korean people and give them hope that some day they will again be an independent nation. It would assist in bringing about wholly war of all the down trod Oriental peoples against the Japanese and increase the resistance of all of them because of this.

I am told there are at the present time, some 35,000 Koreans in the Chinese Army and am told that there is a well organized revolutionary movement in Korea itself. I feel sure the recognition of Korea's provisional government would be an encouragement to these movements and would be of distinct assistance in defeating Japan.

Very truly yours,

Chas. I. Faddis.

CIF:K

December 17, 1941

In reply refer to
FE 895.01/49

My dear Mr. Faddis:

The receipt is acknowledged of your letter of December 8, 1941 in regard to the question of the independence of Korea.

As you of course realize, questions such as this constantly arise. I assure you that in connection with all such questions this Department gives careful study to the problem of best safeguarding the interests of the United States and of making effective the principles and policies to which this country is committed.

Your thoughtfulness in bringing this matter to my attention is much appreciated.

Sincerely yours,

Cordell Hull

The Honorable

Charles I. Faddis,

House of Representatives.

FE:WRL:MJF/MJK   FE   PA/H   AB/H
12-13-41

To His Excellency

Secretary of State

The Department of State.

Translation from
Korean-Chinese script.

June 6, 1941.
23rd year of the
Republic of Korea.
Chungking, China.

Honorable Cordell Hull
Department of State,
Washington, D.C.

Sir:

I have the honor to inform Your Excellency that in February this year, the Executive Chief of the Provisional Government of the Republic of Korea, now situated temporarily in Chungking, China, submitted a memorandum relating to Korea's status to Mr. Laughlin Currie, who was visiting here, with the request that he present it to the President of the United States; and later when Mr. James Roosevelt, son and representative of the President, was here another document was handed to him for the same purpose. I hope they have been brought to the attention of Your Excellency also.

This Government has been co-operating with China in its resistance to Japan. We are determined to continue our fight until the cause of democracy is securely upheld in the Far East, and Korea's lost freedom has been completely restored. In this task we need the material support of the United States. So long as the Chinese and the Koreans have sufficient supplies of munitions and war materials, our victory is assured.

May I remind Your Excellency of the fact that the American-Korean treaty of 1882 is still in effect and now is the time, we feel, when we should respectfully ask the United States to fulfill its treaty obligations by exerting its "good offices" in behalf of Korea.

Out of our sincere desire to co-operate with all the democratic forces now engaged in our common cause, Dr. Syngman Rhee, Chairman of the Korean Commission in Washington, has been appointed as the official diplomatic representative of this Government and has received full power and authority which he may exercise at his own discretion in all official dealings with the United States.

I trust Your Excellency will extend to Dr. Rhee a cordial, friendly reception, advice and assistance.

Let me assure Your Excellency of my high personal regards to you and best wishes for the United States.

Yours respectfully,

(Signed) Joe Sŏ-ang,
Minister of Foreign Affairs,
Provisional Government of
The Republic of Korea.

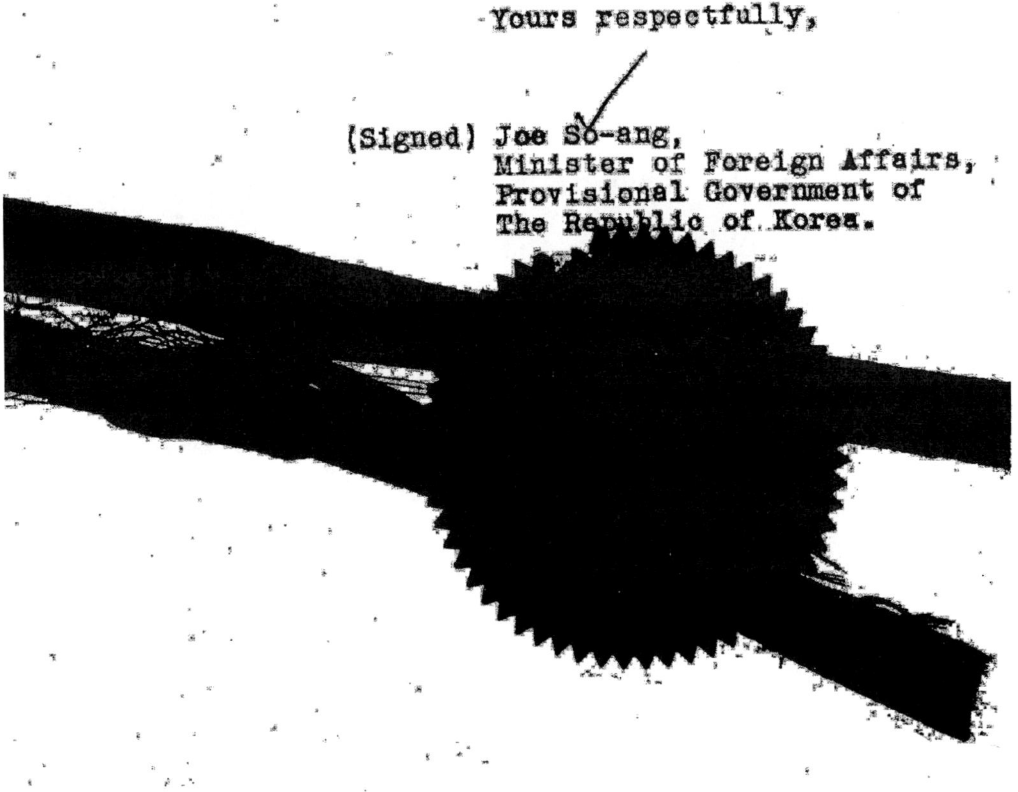

Translation from Chinese.

CREDENTIAL.

BE IT KNOWN, that I, Kim Ku, Chief Executive
of the Provisional Government of the Republic of
Korea, by and with the approval of the Cabinet
Ministers of the Provisional Government, have
appointed Dr. Syngman Rhee, Chairman of the Korean
Commission in Washington, D.C.,U.S.A., as the
official representative of this Government, invested with full power and authority which he may
exercise at his own discretion in all diplomatic
dealings with the Government of the United States.

DONE in Chungking, China, on the sixth day
of June, in the year of our LORD one thousand nine
hundred and forty one, in the twenty-third year of
the Republic of Korea, and in the National Year of
Korea, the four thousand two hundred and seventy-
fourth.

(Signed)   Kim Ku,
            Executive Chief of the Provisional
            Government of the Republic of Korea.

(Signed)   Joe So-ang,
            Minister of Foreign Affairs of the
            Provisional Government of the
            Republic of Korea.

The Korean Commission
Washington, D.C.

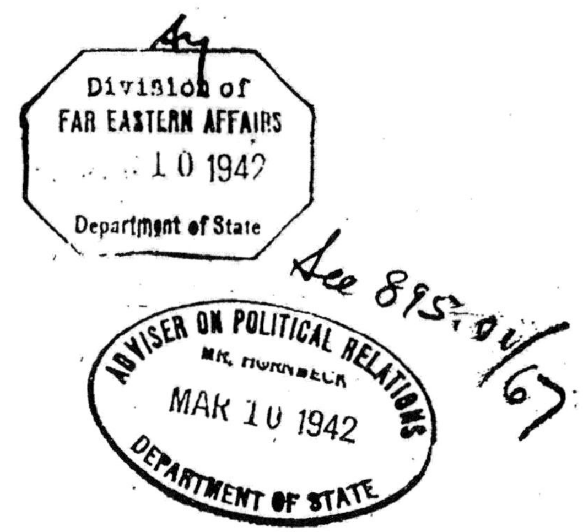

To His Excellency

President of the United States of America.

FW   895.01/49 1/2   PS/ET

FILED
MAR 12 1942

Translation from
Korean-Chinese script.

June 6, 1941.
23rd year of the
Republic of Korea.
Chungking, China.

To His Excellency
Franklin D. Roosevelt,
President of the United States of America,
Washington, D.C.

Sir:

I have the honor to remind Your Excellency
of the fact that, although the diplomatic intercourse
opened between the United States and Korea in 1882
was forcibly suspended in 1905, the cordial, friendly
spirit and good will existing between our two peoples
has never been interrupted. Now the changed situation
in the Far East warrants the restoration of that friendly relationship for mutual benefit.

The Provisional Government of the Republic
of Korea, temporarily situated in Chungking, China,
earnestly desires to re-open that friendly intercourse
and it is hoped that their desire may be reciprocated
by the Government and the people of the United States.

At a recent meeting of the Cabinet Ministers
of the Korean Provisional Government, Dr. Syngman Rhee,
Chairman of the Korean Commission in Washington, was
appointed as the official representative of this Government, invested with full power and authority which
he may excercise at his own discretion in all diplomatic dealings with the Government of the United States.

By virtue of the authority vested in me as
Executive Chief of the Korean Provisional Government,
I beseech Your Excellency to receive him and the
message he is instructed to present in behalf of the
23,000,000 Korean people suffering under an alien
domination.

I take this occasion to assure Your
Excellency of my highest consideration and best
wishes for your great Republic.

Yours very respectfully,

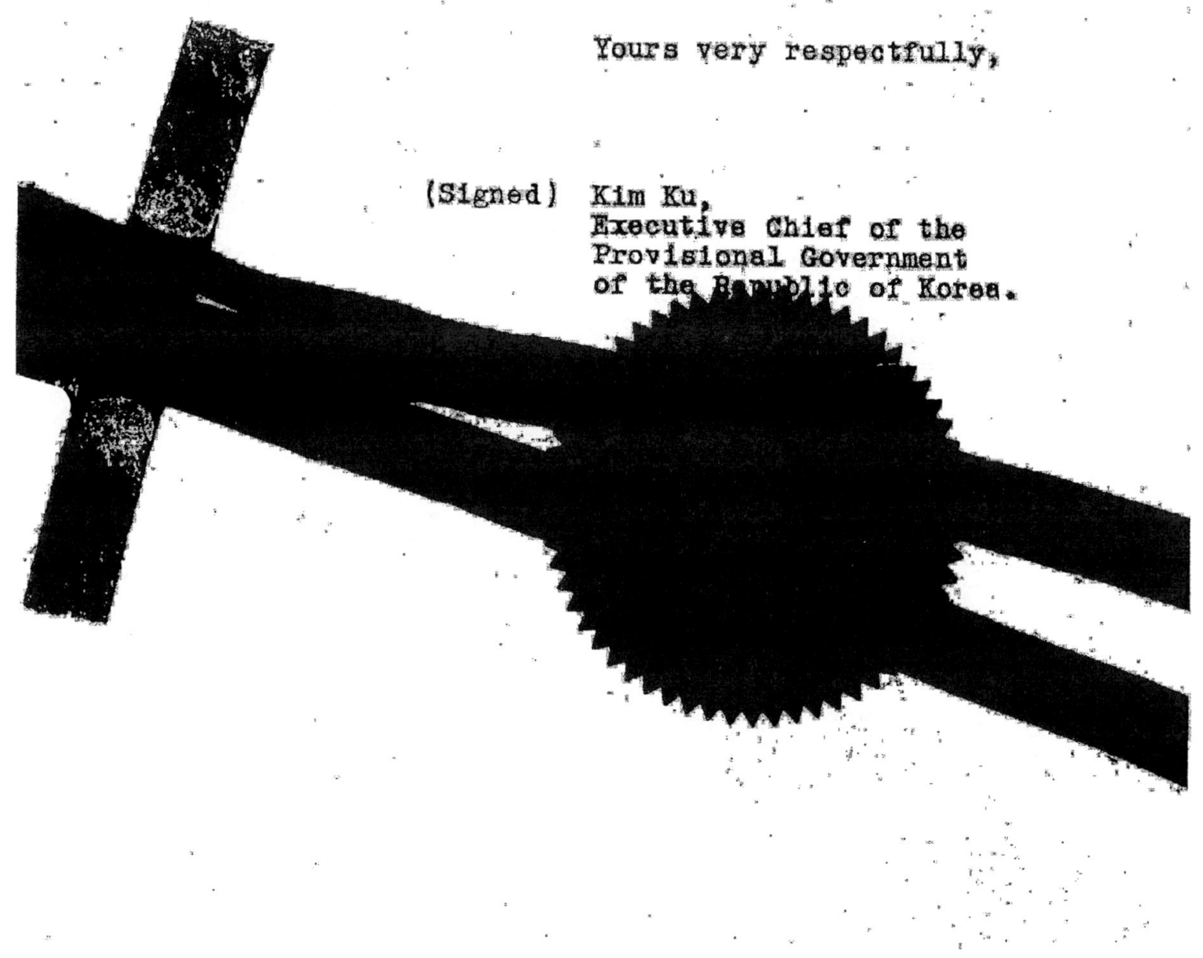

(Signed) Kim Ku,
Executive Chief of the
Provisional Government
of the Republic of Korea.

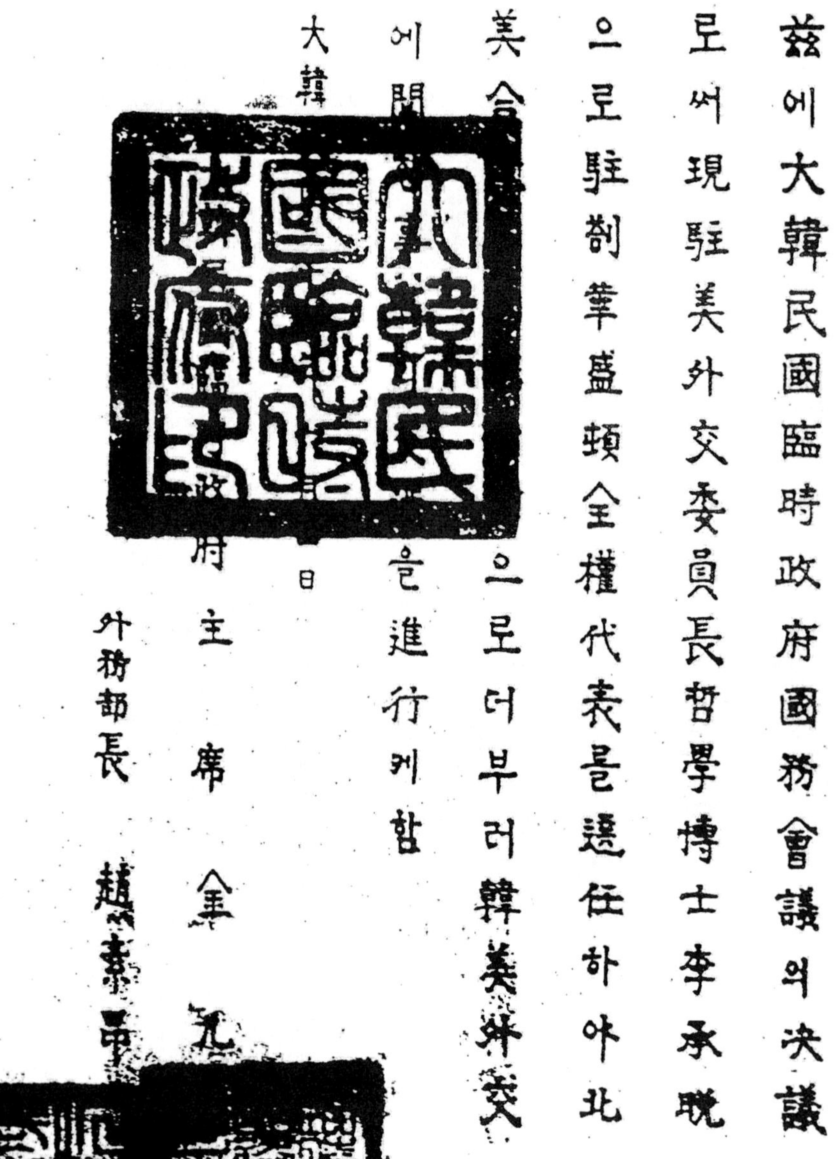

信任狀

茲에 大韓民國臨時政府國務會議의 決議로써 現駐美外交委員長哲學博士李承晩으로 駐剳華盛頓全權代表를 選任하야此美合...으로더부러韓美外交에關...을進行케함

大韓民國臨時政府 主席 金九

外務部長 趙素昻

日

大韓民國臨時政府

야 反日國際勢力과 協同하야 祖國을 光復하기 爲하야

貴我兩國民族의 友誼外交際에 對하야 繼續努力하기 爲하야

貴政府로더부러 遠東 被壓迫民族에 關한 一切問題를 商推進

行하야써 將來의 永遠平和를 奠定함에 裨補가 有케하기 爲하야

玆에 駐紮北美合衆國外交委員長 哲學博士 李承晚으로 常駐代

表를 特任하고 全權을 賦與하야

貴當局으로더부러 外交에 關한 事宜를 交涉케하오니

閣下께서 諸代表로더부러 時로

商推하심을 無任企禱하오며 아울너

閣下의 健康과

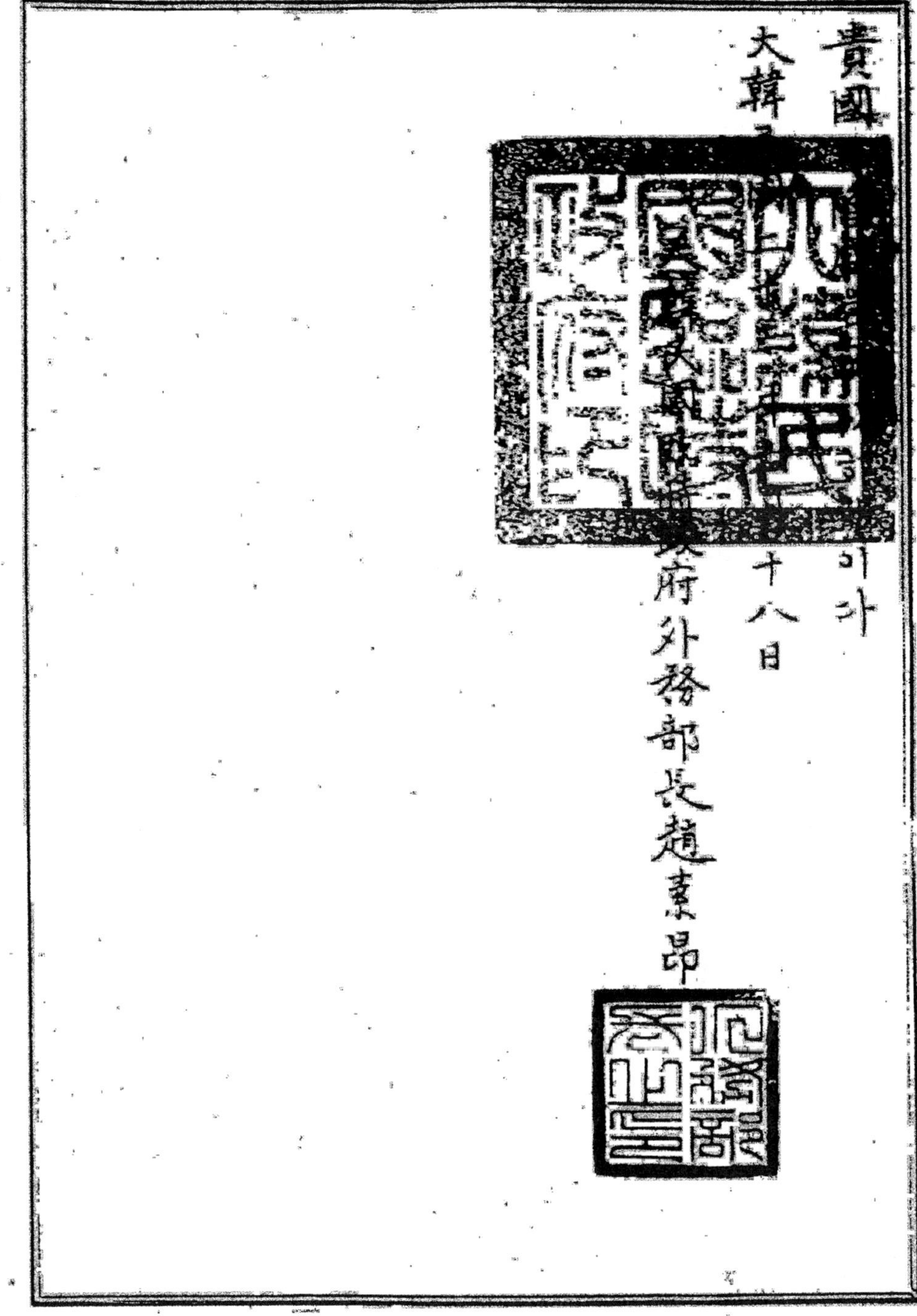

貴國

大韓

十八日

……府外務部長趙素昂

大韓民國臨時政府

大北美合衆國大統領羅斯福閣下鈞鑒敬啓者

貴我兩國이締約한以來六十年에兩國의外交가비록

形式上으로斷續은있었으나精神上으로互相信任하는

友誼는實로無間하얏나이다玆에本政府에서信任하는

駐剳北美合衆國外交委員長哲學博士李承晩을全權代

表로任命하야衷情을代陳께하오니

閣下께서該代表를接見하시고應享의禮遇를與하시며그의

陳述하는바를

聽納하야주시기를仰望하나이다敬主席이本政府를代表

하나이다

大韓民國臨時政府

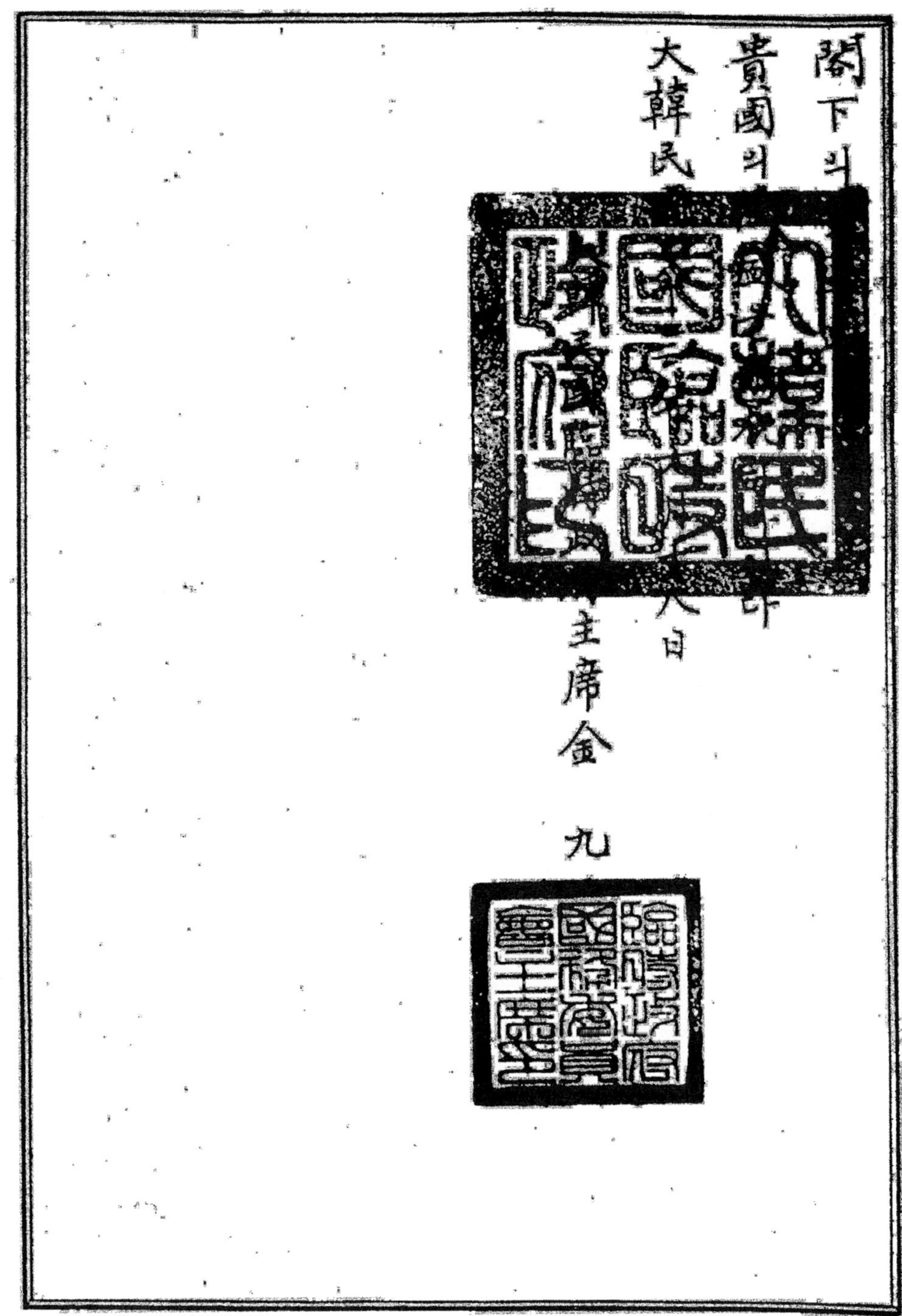

大韓民國臨時政府
閣下斗
貴國斗
大韓民
主席金九

TELEGRAM RECEIVED

FROM

3wu p 43 VIA RCA

.F HONOLULU 406P Dec 10 1941

Cordell Hull

Secretary of State Washington(passf)

Koreans in Hawaii want to render service to defend America we beg
your consideration old treaty between United States and Imperial
Korean Government we plead you recognise Korean provisional
Government at Chungking.

UNITED KOREAN COMMITTEE IN AMERICA.

715am dec 11

CROSS-REFERENCE FILE

NOTE

SUBJECT   Korean rights as affected by present
Japanese situation. Refers to visit
of Saburu Kurusu to Washington and
to -; and expresses hope for a favor-
able settlement that will not deprive
Korea of rights upheld in Third and
Eight Point Declarations of both the
President and Mr.Churchill.

LDP

For the original paper from which reference is taken

See _______________ Letter _______________
(Despatch, telegram, instruction, letter, etc.)

Dated _____ November 15, 1941 _____   From | Korean National Association
/Tb///N (Kim, Yongjeung)

File No. _______ 711.94/2535 _______

WAR DEPARTMENT
M. I. D.

November 24, 1941 /dm

SUBJECT: Possible Korean Nationalist Activity

<u>SUMMARY OF INFORMATION:</u>

RECD-G-2 APR 2 1942

Attention invited to the attached mimeographed document, copy of information intercepted by British censors at Hongkong. It alludes to a package, ostensibly containing Korean Nationalist propaganda, posted by the Young Korean Academy, P.O. Box 1, Station "D", Los Angeles, California, addressed to Li Suk Char, P.O. Box 95, Chungking, China.

Pending translation of the 13 pages of mimeographed Korean, which accompanied the list of addresses in the inclosures, it is believed Korean nationalists are on the verge of reviving their organization to harass the Japanese with political and independence agitation, while the latter are preoccupied with current political and military matters outside the Empire. It is recalled that the Korean nationalist movement gained widespread prominence during the period immediately after the Versailles Peace Conference in 1919 up to about the year 1926. A so-called provisional Korean government was organized wherever overseas Koreans resided, main centers of the movement being in Washington, Baltimore, Philadelphia and Honolulu. During the period mentioned, Dr. Snydhman(?) Rhee, President of the Provisional Korean Government, maintained his headquarters in Honolulu, and directed the movement from that place.

Suggest the activities of overseas Koreans be noted.

For the Assistant Chief of Staff, G-2:

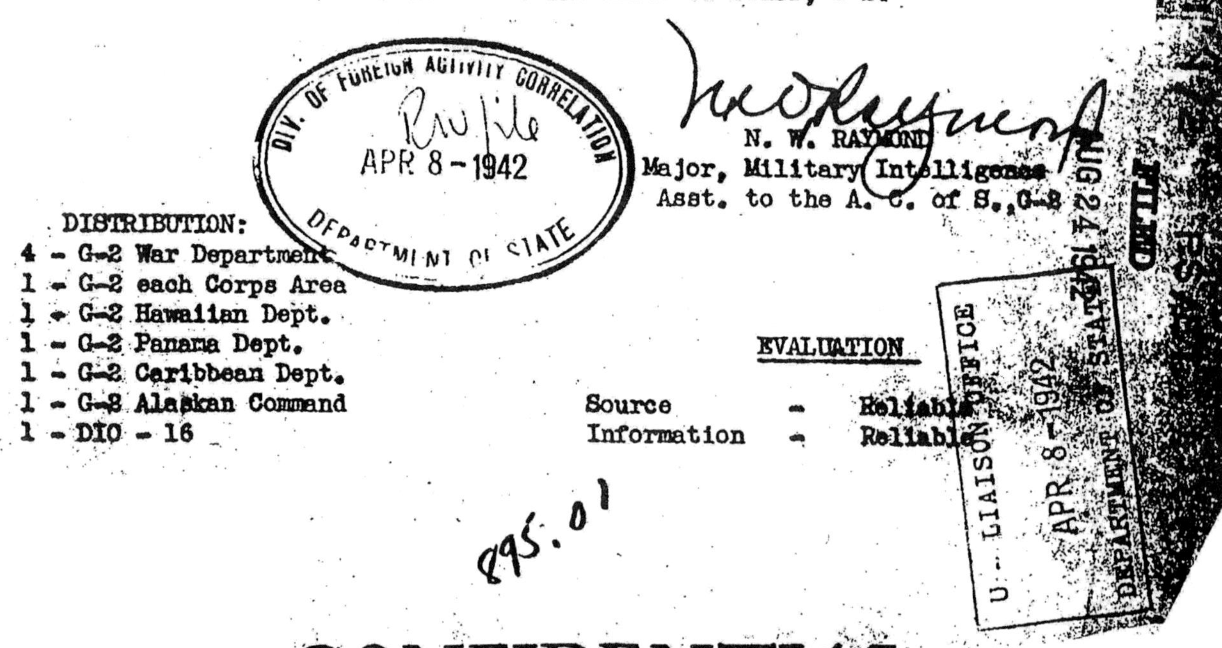

N. W. RAYMOND
Major, Military Intelligence
Asst. to the A. C. of S., G-2

DISTRIBUTION:
4 - G-2 War Department
1 - G-2 each Corps Area
1 - G-2 Hawaiian Dept.
1 - G-2 Panama Dept.
1 - G-2 Caribbean Dept.
1 - G-2 Alaskan Command
1 - DIO - 16

EVALUATION

Source   -   Reliable
Information   -   Reliable

JAPAN

POLITICAL

YOUNG KOREAN ACADEMY, CALIFORNIA

1.   The attached list of addresses in the United States, Mexico, Cuba, Hawaii and France was contained in postal package from and to the following, intercepted in the middle of September:-

    From: Young Korean Academy,
               P.O. Box 1 Station D,
               Los Angeles, California

    To: Mr. Li Suk Char,
               P.O. Box 95,
               Changking, China.

2.   With the exception of the addresses, the whole package consisted of thirteen pages of multigraphed Korean which has not yet been translated.

3.   The complete brochure bore the following Chinese title:

興 工 團 報

which might be translated as:
    "Organ of the Group for the Revival of the Knights."
    This would indicate that the letter press is probably nationalistic and does not, in any case, suggest a communistic trend.

Young R. Kim	633 W. 115th St., New York City, N.Y.
Miss Say Koon Chey	c/o Mrs. Margolies, 1841 E. 19th St., Brooklyn, N.Y.
Earl D. Park	23 Ivy St., Boston, Mass.
D. H. Kim	633 W. 115th St., New York City, N.Y.
P. William Lee	347 Madison Ave., New York City, N.Y.

Phillip Park	826 Oakdale Ave., Chicago, Ill.
Jason Hahn	6904 Glenwood Ave., Chicago, Ill.
Mrs. Frances Hahn	- do -
Young N. Kang	7627 No. Paulino Ave., Chicago, Ill.
F. T. Lee	826 Oakdale Ave., Chicago, Ill.
Henry Yim	6153 No. Broadway, Chicago, Ill.
F. H. Choy	12539 Woodrow Wilson Ave., Detroit, Mich.

Thomas T. Kim	6153 No. Broadway, Chicago, Ill.
Heuy Oak Harr	3966 Vincennes Ave., Chicago, Ill.
Sam S. Lee	5145 Liberty Ave., Pittsburgh, Pa.
James M. D. Yim	3966 Vincennes Ave., Chicago, Ill.
Hyun Chul	826 Oakdale Ave., Chicago, Ill.
Parl Lee	1303 Prospect Ave., Cleveland, Ohio.
Chin Whan Cho	530 No. Vandeventer Ave., St. Louis, Mo.,

CONFIDENTIAL

Louise Hahn	6904 Wayne Ave., Chicago, Ill.
J. William Lar	5422 No. Artesian, Chicago, Ill.
Mrs. Susana Lar	- do -
Cho Lim	3635 Lakepark Ave., Chicago, Ill.
Eugene Kang	2834 No. Kedzie Ave., Chicago, Ill.
Harry Whang	12657 Hettetal Ave., Detroit, Mich.
S. H. Chun	4636 No. Kedzie Ave., Chicago, Ill.

William Cho	P.O. Box 857, Delano, Calif.
K. H. Shinn	C.W. Kern General Hospital, Bakersfield, Calif.
E.H. Yoon	P. O. Box 61, Delano, Calif.
E.H. Oak	P. O. Box 875, Parlier, Calif.
O.D. Lar	P. C. Box 554, Delano, Calif.
Yong B. Ahn	P. O. Box 554, Delano, Calif.
Ik Doo Kang	P. O. Box 554, Delano, Calif.
T. Kim	P. O. Box 857, Delano, Calif.
Mrs. Kyung Jar Kim	" " " " " "

Mrs. Young S. Hahn	Route 2 Box 156, Delano, Calif.
C. S. Lee	Route 1 Box 162, Delano, Calif.
Chong H. Kim	P.O. Box 554, Delano, Calif.
S.D. Hahn	Route 2 Box 156, Delano, Calif.
C. W. Kim	Route 1 Box 162, Delano, Calif.
C.O. Yoon	P.O. Box 554, Delano, Calif.
C.K. Kim	P.O. Box 745, Delano, Calif.
D.B. Chun	P.O. Box 554, Delano, Calif.

Frank O. Lee	1024 W. 36th St., Los Angeles, Calif.
V.K. Park	1232 W. 11th St., Los Angeles, Calif.
S.N. Kim	1572 W. Jefferson Blvd., Los Angeles, Calif.
C.I. Song	620 E. 9th St., Los Angeles, Calif.
Diamond Kim	909 W. 36th Pl., Los Angeles, Calif.
W.K. Lee	3421 S. Catalina St., Los Angeles, Calif.
S.K. Kim	3427 So. Catalina St., Los Angeles, Calif.
P.Y. Choy	3421 So. Catalina St., Los Angeles, Calif.

Mrs. Hay Yun Kim	3427 S. Catalina St., Los Angeles, Calif.
Mrs. In Jai Lim	3724 McClintock Ave., Los Angeles, Calif.
C.H. Lim	3724 " " " " "
C.S. Lee	P.O. Box 529, Maxwell, Calif.
George Kim	3421 S. Catalina St., Los Angeles, Calif.
Henry Lang	1709 Acacia St., Alhambra, Calif.
K.T. Lee	118 East Market St., Stockton, Calif.
Lee D. Sohn	1917 W. Jefferson Blvd., Los Angeles, Calif.

D.Y. Chung	14123 Gilmore St., Van Nuys, Calif.
Mrs. Hay Kyung Chung	" " " " " "
Daniel Song	735 Pico St., San Fernando, Calif.
S.C. Myung	Route 1 Box 242, Missoula, Mont.
C.H. Choy	P.O. Box 413, Sacramento, Calif.
Paul Lim	1338 W. Jefferson Blvd., Los Angeles, Calif.
K. Y. Kim	3415 S. Catalina St., Los Angeles, Calif.
W.D. Cho	P.O. Box 431, Green River, Wyoming

Henry C. Hahn	707 W. Washington St., Los Angeles, Calif.
S.S. Whang	1321 Mason St., San Francisco, Calif.
Albert Lee	1340 W. 30th Pl., Los Angeles, Calif.
Frank Penn	2064 Powell St., San Francisco, Calif.
C.H. Kim	3421 S. Catalina St., Los Angeles, Calif.
S.T. Lim	1338 W. Jefferson Blvd. Los Angeles, Calif.
C.S. Char	663 Summit St., Pasadena. Calif.
C.I. Kim	1321 Mason St., San Francisco, Calif.
Yong S. Lee	1112 W. Pico St., Los Angeles, Calif.
Mrs. Jai Nee Lee	" " " " " "
C.K. Lim	1701 W. Jefferson St., Los Angeles, Cal.
D.S. Shynn	3724 Rosellen St., Los Angeles, Cal.
Young J. Park	1131 W. 35th St., Los Angeles, Calif.
K.S. Lee	909 W. 36th Pl., Los Angeles. Calif.
K.S. Cho	1547 W. 8th St., Los Angeles. Calif.
Thomas Lee	10063 Toluca Lake, No. Hollywood, Calif.

Donald Keng	P.O. Box 1892, Honolulu, T.H.
Powin S. Wang	P.O. Box 373, Schofield Barracks, T.H.
Phillip Chung	P.O. Box 40, Hanapepe, Kauai, T.H.
S.Y. Whang	Hawaii

Manuel Kim	Calle 54 No. 424, Merida, Yucatan, Mexico
Chong O. Lee	Apartado 229, Merida, Yucatan, Mexico.
C.S. Kim	" " " " "
D.H. Loo	" " " " "
Wan Hurh	" " " " "
H.K. Char	Apartado 273, Matanzas, Cuba
Jose Loo	" " " "
Manuel Leo	Ma Linsa Silie Y Fornando, Reparto
	Parraga Arroyo A Apolo, Havana, Cuba
Carlos Loo	Apartado 2868, Cardenas, Cuba
P.Y. Kim	P.O. Box 1 Station D, Los Angeles, Cal.
E. Emson Char	P.O. Box 229, Yorrington, Nev.
M.S. Yum	901 Kearney St., San Francisco, Calif.
O.L. Kay	P.O. Box 268, Riverbank, Calif.
Phillip Yoon	3421 S. Catalina St., Los Angeles, Calif.
D.S. Dunn	? ? ? ?
W.P. Choy	Calle 8 #185, Tiajiuana, Mexico
Juan Juanpo	Apartado 903, Mexico D.F. Mexico
Manuel M. Kim	" " " "
Myung Wun Keo	" " " "
Siokhai Tson	11 Rue Jules Chaplain, Paris, France
Yong C. Kim	7 Rue Jules Chaplain, Paris, France
Sook R. Kim	? ? ? ?
Chong Sung Kim	? ? ? ?
Soo Choong Park	? ? ? ?

December 13, 1941.

Korean Organizations in the United States.

In connection with A-B/H memorandum of December 9, memorandum of conversation with Dr. Syngman Rhee, entitled "Free Korea", the following information in regard to Koreans and Korean organizations in this country may be of interest.

The Bureau of the Census supplies the following figures of persons of Korean race in the United States as of April 1940:

	Native	Foreign Born	Total
In Continental U. S.	939	725	1,664
In Territory of Hawaii	4,461	2,390	6,851
Total	5,400	3,110	8,515

There are believed to be three organizations of Koreans in the United States: the Korean Council, Honolulu, the Korean Commission, Washington, headed by Dr. Syngman Rhee, and the Sino-Korean Peoples League, represented in this country by Mr. Kilsoo Haan.

The Korean Council is understood to be a non-political organization to advance the social status and welfare of Koreans in this country. The Korean Commission is a political organization, which has been working for many years for Korean independence. The Sino-Korean People's League claims to be the organization of Korean elements in China fighting against Japan in concert with the Chinese armies.

FE:Langdon

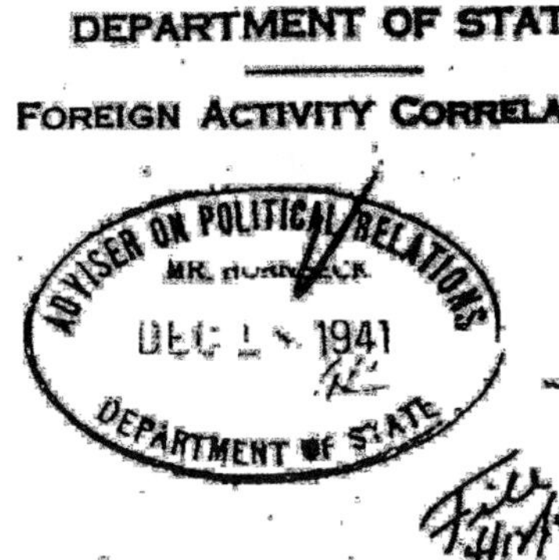

December 17, 1941

PA/H — Mr. Hornbeck:

I am returning herewith a slip attached to
Mr. Langdon's memorandum of December 13, and a
copy of my memorandum of December 9 on "Free Korea"
which apparently had not yet been seen by you.

Harold B. Hoskins

A-B/H: HBH:gw

Memorandum of Conversation.

FC - Mr. Gordon
FE - Mr. Hamilton
A-B - Mr. Berle

"Free Korea"

Dr. Syngman Rhee, head of the Korean Commission in Washington, was referred to me by Mr. Langdon in FE. Dr. Rhee reports his office as being in Room 323 Colorado Building, telephone REpublic 6119. This Commission is already registered with the State Department.

Dr. Rhee came in primarily to advise that the Aliens Registration Division of the Department of Justice had allowed Koreans to register as Koreans rather than as Japanese citizens.

In view of the war situation, Dr. Rhee was anxious that the Koreans be recognized as anti-Japanese and so treated, including among other things the question of freezing their funds. I suggested that Dr. Rhee submit a statement in writing and send a copy of it direct to Mr. L.M.C.Smith of the Defense unit of the Department of Justice.

Dr. Rhee mentioned the fact that there is a 'Free Korean Committee located in Chungking, China, and made inquiries of the possibility of some form of support being given to this same movement by the United States.

Harold B. Hoskins

A-B/HBHoskins:gw

DEPARTMENT OF STATE

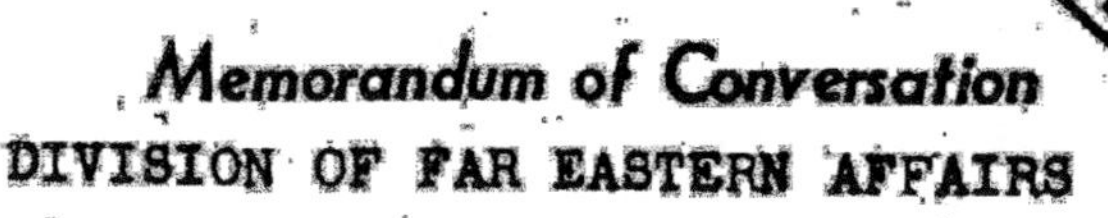

Memorandum of Conversation

DIVISION OF FAR EASTERN AFFAIRS

DATE: December 23, 1941

SUBJECT: Korean Independence and Allied Questions

PARTICIPANTS: Mr. J. Jerome Williams
Mr. John W. Staggers

Mr. Salisbury

COPIES TO:

895.01/52-1/2

Mr. J. Jerome Williams and Mr. John W. Staggers informed
Mr. Salisbury that they are lawyers in Washington, D. C., who
have long been interested in Korean affairs; that they were
calling in a private capacity as a result of conversations with
Dr. Syngman Rhee, head of the Korean Commission in Washington,
who desires their active participation in a Korean movement
for independence; and that, before entering into such activity,
they wished to know the attitude of the Department in regard
to the question of Korean independence. Mr. Salisbury replied
that he was unable to reply on behalf of the Department but
that his personal view was that activities in the United States
at the present time looking toward the independence of Korea
might have unfavorable reaction in Japan to the detriment of the
welfare of American nationals who are still in Japan and

Japanese-occupied

PS/KN

Japanese-occupied areas. Mr. Williams and Mr. Staggers immediately expressed their appreciation of this possibility, stating that it was important that nothing be done which would jeopardize those Americans. Mr. Staggers stated that he had been present recently during a conversation between Dr. Rhee and Senator Guy M. Gillette when the latter had expressed the same view.

In response to an inquiry as to the attitude of the Department toward Korean independence Mr. Salisbury replied that presumably a number of similar questions might arise during the course of the war to which the Department would give consideration but that at present the prosecution of the war was paramount and that it would seem too early to reach decisions of the sort referred to.

Mr. Williams expressed the opinion that it would be important to encourage Koreans to undertake activities detrimental to Japan and that encouragement on the part of the United States would accelerate such activities. Mr. Salisbury replied that he felt that this was a question which deserved serious consideration. In connection with this subject, Mr. Williams and Mr. Staggers stated that, according to Dr. Rhee, the Koreans fighting under General Chiang Kai-shek now number more than 40,000.

Mr. Williams inquired whether Mr. Salisbury perceived

any objection

any objection to Mr. Williams' continuing his association
with Dr. Rhee's organization, which is primarily concerned
with distributing in the United States information with
regard to Korea and Koreans. Mr. Salisbury replied that
he personally saw no objection to Mr. Williams' continuing
that association with activities such as Mr. Williams
described.

During the conversation Mr. Staggers stated at one
point that Dr. Rhee had informed him that Dr. Rhee's organization had recently desired to make a public denunciation
of Mr. Kilsoo Haan, leader of another Korean faction, because
of Mr. Haan's undesirable character as indicated by his past
association with the Communist Party but that Dr. Rhee had
succeeded in preventing this on the grounds that it would be
inadvisable to give publicity to dissidence among Korean
groups.

Following further conversation along lines similar to
those indicated above, Mr. Williams and Mr. Staggers left,
stating that for the present they would not take any part
in activities looking toward Korean independence and that they
would get in touch with Mr. Salisbury at a later time.

FE:Salisbury:MHP

FOREIGN ACTIVITY CORRELATION

1-2-42

A-B/Mr. Berle:

I am planning to send this
memorandum to Mr. Hamilton if
you approve.

Harold B. Hoskins

A-B/H:HBH-gw

January 2, 1942.

TO: FE - Mr. Hamilton:

SUBJECT: Free Korean Movement.

I am advising Mr. Berle of our conversation in which
you agreed that discussions or correspondence regarding a
"Free Korean" movement had best be centered in one individual, and that you are agreeable to its being handled
by me under Mr. Berle's direction, as contemplated in
Departmental Order No. 995.

I am therefore retaining recent correspondence on this
subject, including Mr. Salisbury's memorandum of conversation of December 23, 1941. I shall keep FE fully informed on all developments as they occur. I have also
noted your general point of view that we must be extremely
cautious in taking any positive action that might endanger
the treatment of American citizens still in Japan or in
that part of China occupied by Japan.

                                    Harold B. Hoskins

A-B/H:HBH:gw

THE WHITE HOUSE

WASHINGTON

December 18, 1941.

Respectfully referred to the

Secretary of State for attention.

EDWIN M. WATSON
Secretary to the President

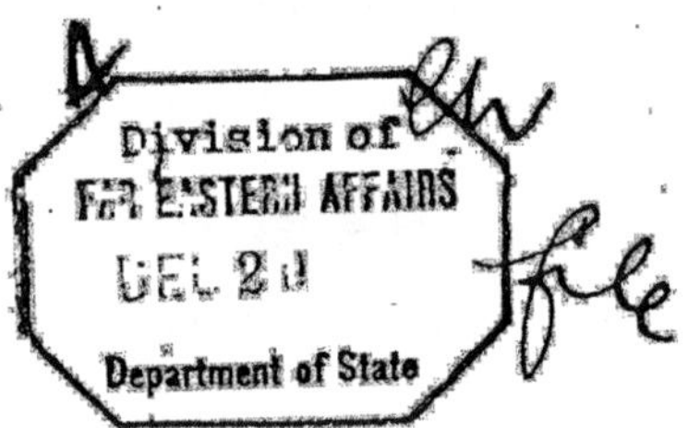

PO12 259 WIRELESS (MRT DIV) PASHU

HONOLULU DEC 17 1941 437P

PRESIDENT ROOSEVELT

WASHINGTONDC

WITH FIRM BELIEF IN ULTIMATE AND SPEEDY VICTORY OF THE FREE
WORLD NAND UNQUALIFIED CONFIDENCE IN LEADERSHIP OF UNITED
STATES AMONG DEMOCRATIC NATIONS WE BEG YOUR SPECIAL
CONSIDERATION OF KOREA AS ONE OF THEM AND AN ALLY WOULD YOU
PLEASE EXERCISE YOUR INFLUENCE TO HAVE THEM RECOGNIZE
KOREAN PROVISIONAL GOVERNMENT AND LEAD THE MOVEMENT BY GIVING
IT DE JURE STATUS THIS WILL MEAN GREATEST MORAL BOOST NOT ONLY
TO KOREAN PEOPLE WHO HAVE BEEN SUFFERING UNDER THE FIGHT AGAINST
THE OPPRESSOR NOW PRONOUNCED ENEMY OF AMERICA BUT TO ALL
THOSE PEOPLES THROUGHOUT THE WORLD WHO HAVE LOST
THEIR FREEDOMAND ARE NOW ENGAGED IN STRUGGLE TO REGAIN IT MAY
AMERICAN PRINCIPLES THAT RESULT OF AGGRESSION SHALL NOT BE
RECOGNIZED BE APPLIED TO KOREA AS TO OTHER NATIONS MAY WRONG BE
RIGHTED ONCE FOR ALL WE APPEAL TO YOUR LEADERSHIP FURTHER WE
BEG YOU TO GRANT US KOREANS IN UNITED STATES CLEAR STATUS.
FIRST FREELY SEPARATED FROM JAPANESE WHICH WE HAVE NEVER BEEN AND
WILL NEVER BE FOR ALIEN REGISTRATION LAST YEAR DEPT OF JUSTICE
PERMITTED US TO REGISTER AS KOREANS NOT JAPANESE CENSUS
REPORTS LIST KOREANS SEPARATE FROM JAPANESE STATE AND LABOR
GRANTED SEPARATELY TO KOREAN STUDENTS AND REFUGEE

December 16, 1941.

The papers here attached are self-
explanatory. The three documents and the
three addressed envelopes should be regarded
as not yet having been <u>received</u> by the
Department.

Will FE please be so good at this
stage as to give the question dealt with in
the last paragraph of Dr. Rhee's letter to
me of December 9 appropriate consideration.

895.01/54

PS/MCD

PA/H:SKH:FLB

DR. SYNGMAN RHEE

1766 Hobart Street, N. W.

Washington, D. C.

December 9, 1941

Dr. Stanley K. Hornbeck,
State Department,
Washington, D. C.

Dear Dr. Hornbeck:

    The inevitable clash has at last come, but now that it is here we have to do everything under the sun to crush Japan. The Koreans are seeking every opportunity to serve the cause of the United States.

    .   .   .   .

    I leave these papers with you to see if there is any change to make. If not, I know you will find the first opportunity to present them to the President and the Secretary of State. Kindly advise me the proper procedure.

        Yours most cordially,

            SYNGMAN RHEE

TELEGRAM SENT

Department of State

23   "SC"

Washington,

December 18, 1941

AMEMBASSY,

CHUNGKING (CHINA).

The Department desires that you make very discreet
inquiries of the National Government in regard to the
so-called provisional government of the Republic of
Korea, claiming to have its seat in Chungking. Information as to the extent of the physical following and
organization of the so-called government, as to the
number and sphere of operations of its armed volunteers,
as to its contacts with any revolutionary forces that
might exist in Korea and Manchuria, and as to the
attitude of the National Government toward it and relations
with it would be of interest.

Carbon copies
destroyed.

FE:WRL:MJF   FE   PA/H   CR

DEC 22 1941 PM

December 22, 1941.

24

A-B.
Mr. Berle:

I am initialing the telegram.

am reserving opinion regarding the views expressed in FE's memorandum.

PA/H:SEH:ZME

December 20, 1941.

Reference FE's memorandum of December 16,
question of presentation to the President of
Dr. Syngman Rhee's credentials as official representative in the United States of the provisional government of the Republic of Korea.

FE is of the opinion that it would be
preferable not to undertake to make a definitive
decision on this question at this time, but to
defer such definitive decision until the subject
of the restoration of the independence of Korea
can be thoroughly studied and, in the light of
that study, this Government adopts a definite
policy toward Korea. In that study it would
seem desirable to take into account, for example, factors such as the attitude toward Korean
independence of China, Russia, Great Britain, and
perhaps our other associates in the war. Isolated action on our part might involve responsibilities which in the light of later events it
might have been better for this Government not
to have assumed.

In the meantime FE believes that it would
be preferable that Dr. Rhee's credentials be
returned

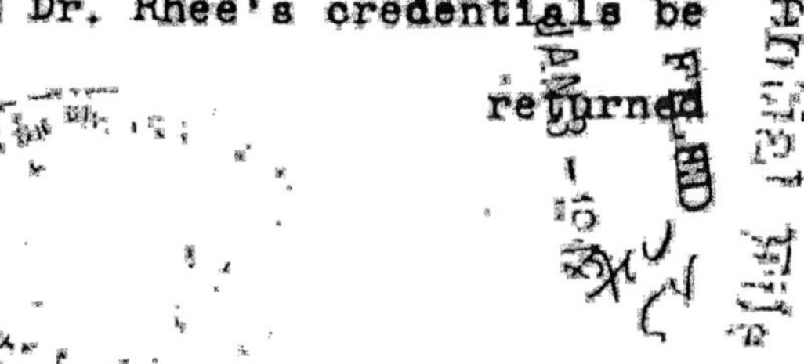

returned to him with the statement that the
question of their presentation to the President
cannot, in the nature of things, be decided in
a hurry. While FE considers that the action
suggested in the preceding sentence is the most
advisable course, it perceives no strong objection to the acceptance by the Department of
Dr. Rhee's credentials. Should this be done,
it is suggested that it be made clear to Dr.
Rhee that the credentials are simply being
placed on file in this Department as record
of documents received by the Department.

There is attached a draft telegram to
Chungking (in very confidential code) directing
the Ambassador to learn what he can of the
provisional government of the Republic of Korea
and of its organization and physical following.

GA

FE:Langdon:HES

March 13, 1942

TO: A-B/ Mr. Berle:

You will be interested in seeing the attached cable
which you will note represents the views of FE and PA/H.
The general tenor is, I think, in agreement with your
ideas, but I am suggesting a revision of the final paragraph emphasizing again our idea of issuing the statement
referred to in the first paragraph of this cable.

Harold B. Hoskins

Attached:

Suggested Revision of ~~Final Paragraph~~ Page 4

A-B/H:HBH-gw

TELEGRAM RECEIVED

74WU Y 122

wr LosAngeles Calif 12?0p Dec 31 1941

Hon Cordell Hull,

Secretary of State Washn.

Our Dear Secretary Hull:-

In behalf of the thirty fifth annual
convention of the Korean National Association representing
all members in America Cuba and Mexico we earnestly pray to
our Almighty God that he may give you your health His wisdom
and His guidance at this critical hour.when the world democracy
is on a balance and its salvation depends upon your leadership
and that you may bring the everlasting peace and happiness to
this heartbroken world. We, the Koreans as one body pledge
to your our loyal and humble support and sympathy until the
final victory is won we also want to express our deep appreciation
for safety peace happiness and freedom that we have enjoyed
under your protection respectfully yours.

Charles Ho Kim, Chairman,

Of Convention.

605p

January 2, 1942

Dear Mr. Kim:

By reference from the Secretary of State your telegram of December 31 on behalf of the 35th Annual Convention of the Korean National Association has been given to me for acknowledgment and thanks.

The Secretary much appreciates your message and the spirit which prompted you to telegraph him.

Sincerely yours,

Harold B. Hoskins
Executive Assistant

Mr. Charles Ho Kim, Chairman,
35th Annual Convention of the Korean National Association
Los Angeles, California.

A-B/H:HBH:RW:JKF:SS   1/2/42

MEV

TELEGRAM RECEIVED

Chungking

This telegram must be
closely paraphrased be-
fore being communicated
to anyone. (SC)

Dated January 3, 1942

Rec'd 1:12 p.m.

FROM

Secretary of State

Washington.

January 3, 6 p.m.

Department's 320 December 22, 6 p.m.

The result of investigation and study which the
Foreign Office is now making with regard to the Provisional Government of the Republic of Korea will
determine the future attitude of the Chinese Government. I gather that the present attitude is not
enthusiastic. Information with regard to the physical following and organization of the Provisional
Government is not yet available here. There are reported to be no more than 200 Koreans in this area.
There is a small corps of armed Korean volunteers with
the Chinese army. The local representative is named
Tjosowang who describes himself as Foreign Minister.
The extent of his contacts with revolutionary Korean
forces is difficult to ascertain. The Provisional
Government is understood to be dominated by the moderate Korean Independence party, the strength of which
is not known. I am told that the left wing national
revolutionary party has a large following among Koreans
in Manchuria, but that it is not accorded a place in
the so-called Provisional Government.

GAUSS

26

PARAPHRASE

A strictly confidential telegram of January 3, 1942 from the American Ambassador at Chungking reads substantially as follows:

The future attitude of the Chinese Government toward the Provisional Government of the Republic of Korea will be determined by the results of investigation and study which is now being made by the Foreign Office. The present attitude, I infer, could not be characterized as enthusiastic. The local representative of the Provisional Government describes himself as Foreign Minister and his name is Tjosowang. It is not known, and it is furthermore difficult to ascertain, how extensive are his contacts with revolutionary Korean forces. Information is not yet available here in regard to the organization and physical following of the Provisional Government. The Chinese Army contains a small volunteer corps of armed Koreans. It is understood that the Provisional Government is under the domination of the Moderate Korean Independence Party, whose strength is unknown. The Left Wing National Revolutionary Party has, I am told, a large Korean following in Manchuria, but that the so-called Provisional Government accords it no place. According to reports the maximum number of Koreans in the Chungking area is 200.

FE:HPF/LES:ALM
1-6-41

TELEGRAM SENT

Department of State

27

*This cable must be sent in confidential Code,
or should be carefully paraphrased before
being communicated to anyone.*

Washington,
March 18, 1942.
9 pm

CHUNGKING (CHINA).

199

895.01/56c

Reference your telegram no. 12, January 3, 3 pm.

On February 10 the Department requested the Embassy at
London to inform the British Government that this Government
has been approached by various Korean groups in this country
interested in independence and participation in war effort;
that, although this Government desires to obtain all active
support possible of opponents of the Axis, we are not at this
time contemplating QUOTE recognizing UNQUOTE any organization
of Koreans as the primary movement for Korean opposition to
Japanese oppression or making any commitment as to future
recognition of Korea; that we were giving thought to the
possibility of issuing some general statement to the press
expressing the interest of this Government in the efforts of
the Korean people to end Japanese oppression; and that we
should be pleased to receive the views of the British Government in regard to this whole question.

On February 28 the British Foreign Office handed to the
Embassy a memorandum which was, in part, to the effect that
there were not enough Koreans in the United Kingdom to form

an organization; that after the outbreak of war Mr. Tjo So
Wang and representatives of other Korean organizations at
Chungking made approaches to the British Embassy there similar to those made to the American Embassy; that the British
Ambassador gained the impression that there was considerable
disunity in the Korean ranks and was told by the Chinese Ministry
for Foreign Affairs that, although the Koreans in free China
were aiming at independence, they differed widely in their
politics; that Chinese authorities found them useful for
anti-Japanese activities but declared that there could be
no question of any sort of recognition of a free Korean
movement until factional differences were composed, to which
end they were lending their good offices; that the British
Foreign Office believed that the possibilities of effective
Korean opposition to Japan in Japan itself and in Korea
were very small, although in Manchuria and occupied China
the possibilities were perhaps greater; that as long as the
present successes of Japan continue any formal declaration
or act of recognition on the part of the United States or
United Kingdom would be unlikely to arouse a response on
any effective scale among Koreans generally in areas

Enciphered by _______________________

Sent by operator _______________ *M.,* _______________, *19*____, _______________

1—1461   U. S. GOVERNMENT PRINTING OFFICE

under Japanese control; that when the tide turned against the Japanese, however, a well-timed declaration might produce results; that for the present the Foreign Office considers that the reply to further approaches from Koreans outside Japanese areas should be confined to assurances of sympathy with efforts toward the realization of Korean aspirations for national freedom; that this was the attitude adopted by the Chinese Minister of Foreign Affairs in a letter addressed on October 25 last to Yong Jeung Kim; that, in view of the interest of the Chinese Government in Korean matters, it might be well to concert with that Government any action tending toward recognition; and that the British Foreign Office would be glad to support any action the Department might eventually decide to take in the Korean question.

The Department is informing the British Foreign Office that the British Government's views as indicated in the memorandum coincide in general with those of this Government. The attention of the British Foreign Office is being brought to a statement which I made at my press conference on March 2 (see Radio Bulletin no. 51).

The Department

TELEGRAM SENT

Department of State

30

—4—   *Washington.*

The Department would appreciate any comment on your
part which you think might be helpful to the Department
in regard to the Korean question. Specifically will you
give us your opinion as to the advisability of this Department's issuing in the near future a general statement
expressing the interest of the American people in the
efforts of the Koreans to end Japanese oppression? As
you may have been informed, there recently was held here
in Washington a QUOTE Korean Liberty Conference UNQUOTE
sponsored by the United Korean Committee in America and
the Korea American Council, organizations affiliated with
the Chungking group, to publicize the Korean question and
urge QUOTE recognition UNQUOTE of Korea. Although the
attendance of Koreans was small and reportedly only partially representative of the Korean community in this
country and although the agenda apparently did not repeat
not include consideration of positive measures which
Koreans might take looking toward the achieving of their
independence or their participation in the war effort,
the conference served in some degree to focus public
attention on the question of Korean QUOTE recognition
UNQUOTE. In addition this group is making an effort to

TELEGRAM SENT

Department of State

31

-5-

Washington,

develop American public opinion toward urging American
recognition, and a considerable amount of publicity for
their views is being obtained in various parts of the
United States.

In such conversations as you may have with the
Chinese Government on this matter you may in your discretion use such parts of the information contained in
the foregoing paragraphs as you may think appropriate.

Acting

<u>CONFIDENTIAL</u> 32

<u>P A R A P H R A S E</u>

A telegram of March 20, 1942 to the American Embassy
at Chungking reads substantially as follows:

The Department instructed the American Embassy at
London under date February 10 to inform the British Government that various groups of Koreans in this country interested
in participation in the war effort and independence of Korea
have approached the American Government; that, although the
American Government is desirous of obtaining as much active
support as possible from opponents of the Axis powers, it
(the American Government) is not contemplating at the present
time recognizing any Korean organization as the principal
movement for Korean opposition to the oppression of Japan
nor is it giving any commitment in regard to recognition
of Korea in the future; that thought is being given by the
American Government to the possibility of issuing to the press
some general statement expressing the American Government's
interest in the attempts of the Korean people to terminate
Japanese oppression; and that the American Government would
be pleased to receive an expression of the British Government's
views concerning this entire matter.

The British Foreign Office gave the American Embassy a
memorandum under date February 28 in part to the effect that
there were not in the United Kingdom a sufficient number of

Koreans

Koreans to form an organization; that approaches similar
to those made to the American Embassy im Chungking were made
to the British Embassy there after the outbreak of war by
representatives of various Korean organizations at Chungking,
including Mr. Tjo So-wang; that the impression gained by
the British Ambassador was that a great deal of disunity existed
among the Koreans and he was informed by the Chinese Minister
for Foreign Affairs that there was a wide difference in the
politics of the Koreans in free China although they were
aspiring to independence; that although the Koreans were
useful to the Chinese for activities against the Japanese,
the Chinese authorities said that the question of recognition
of any sort of a free Korean movement could not be considered
until factional differences were settled, an end which the
Chinese were endeavoring to assist the Koreans in achieving;
that it is the opinion of the British Foreign Office that
although there might be some possibility of effective Korean
opposition to Japan in occupied China and Manchuria, the
possibility of such opposition in Korea and in Japan itself
was quite small; that as long as Japan continued to meet with
success as at present, it would be unlikely that any active
recognition or formal declaration by the United Kingdom or
the United States would arouse a response to any effective

extent

extent among Koreans in general in Japanese-controlled areas;
that, however, results might be produced by a well-timed
declaration when the tide turned against Japan, but the
British Foreign Office is of the opinion that for the
time being the reply to further approaches made by Koreans
outside the Japanese-controlled areas should be composed
only of assurances of sympathy with attempts toward bringing
about a realization of Korean desires for national freedom;
that this attitude was taken by the Chinese Minister for
Foreign Affairs in a letter addressed to Yong Jeung Kim on
October 25; that, considering the Chinese Government's interest in the Korean question, it might be advisable to act in
concert with the Chinese Government in any action looking
toward recognition; and that the British Government would be
pleased to support any action which the American Government
might decide eventually to take in this matter.

The British Government is being informed that its views
as set forth in the above-mentioned memorandum are in accord
in general with the views of the American Government. The
British Government's attention is being invited to a statement
made on March 2 by the Acting Secretary of State at his press
conference. In this connection see Radio Bulletin No. 51.

Any

-4-

Any comment from the American Ambassador at Chungking
which might be helpful in consideration of the Korean question
would be appreciated by the Department. The Ambassador's
opinion is especially desired concerning the advisability
of the issuance by the Department in the near future of a
general statement expressing the American peoples' interest
in Korean efforts to bring about an end to oppression by the
Japanese. Recently there was held in Washington, as the
Ambassador may know, a "Korean Liberty Conference" under the
sponsorship of the Korea-American Council and the United
Korean Committee in America, organizations affiliated with
the group in Chungking. The purpose of the "Conference" was
to publicize the Korean question and urge that Korea be
recognized. To some extent the conference served to focus the
attention of the public on the question of Korean "recognition"
although there was a small attendance of Koreans which
according to reports represented only partially the Korean
community in the United States and although apparently
consideration of positive measures which might be taken by
Koreans looking toward their participation in the war effort
or the achieving of their independence was not included in
the agenda of the conference. This group is trying also to

develop

United States toward urging
develop public opinion and in various parts of
recognition by their large amount of publicity is
the United States own views. The American Ambassador
being obtained in his discretion, in any conversations
is authorize on this subject with the Chinese Government,
which he as of the foregoing information as he may consider
such p.
advi

ONI } 3-21-42
MIA }

FE:EGC:MBW
3/21/42

FE

CROSS-REFERENCE FILE

NOTE

SUBJECT Approach made by leading representative of Korean
nationalists.

Copies of papers left at the Department by Dr.
Syngman Rhee on July 14 regarding Korean Government.
Information given to Dr. Syngman on Department's
attitude towards.-

FLH

For the original paper from which reference is taken

See ________________ **memorandum** _______________________
(Despatch, telegram, instruction, letter, etc.)

Dated ___August 20, 1941___ From |
                            To | ___State Department___
                                            PA/H (Hornbeck)

File No. ____895.00/729_______________________

develop public opinion in the United States toward urging
recognition by this Government and in various parts of
the United States a rather large amount of publicity is
being obtained for Korean views. The American Ambassador
is authorized to use in his discretion, in any conversations
which he may have on this subject with the Chinese Government,
such portions of the foregoing information as he may consider
advisable.

FE:EGC:MBW
3/21/42

FE

CROSS-REFERENCE FILE

NOTE

SUBJECT: Approach made by leading representative of Korean
nationalists.

Copies of papers left at the Department by Dr.
Syngman Rhee on July 14 regarding Korean Government.
Information given to Dr. Syngman on Department's
attitude towards,-

FLH

For the original paper from which reference is taken

See ______________ **memorandum** ________________________________

(Despatch, telegram, instruction, letter, etc.)

Dated ___**August 20, 1941**___ From / To } ___**State Department**

PA/H (Hornbeck)

File No. ______**895.00/729**________________________________

DEPARTMENT OF STATE

DIVISION OF FAR EASTERN AFFAIRS

November 23, 1942

Reference underlying telegram of January 4, 1942 addressed to the President by Kilsoo Haan in which Kilsoo Haan states that if the United States Government refuses his request that it "permit us to join the 26 anti-Axis powers in its pledge to fight the Axis powers until victory" then "all the proclamations, talk of humanity, the sanctity of international justice, the spirit of democracy will become nothing but an empty gesture".

This telegram, although dated January 4, 1942, was received in the Department only on November 18, 1942. In view of this fact and of the tenor of the telegram, it would seem advisable that no acknowledgment be made.

FE:Salisbury:MJF

PRESIDENT ROOSEVELT

WHITE HOUSE

HON SIR: IN BEHALF OF 26 MILLION KOREANS WHO SINCE THE ANNEXATION OF KOREA FOUGHT THE ENEMY OF DEMOCRACIES, I AS WASHINGTON REPRESENTATIVE OF THE KOREAN VOLUNTEER ARMY IN CHINA, AND SINO-KOREAN PEOPLES LEAGUE SINCERELY PLEAD AND HUMBLY REQUEST THAT THE UNITED STATES GOVERNMENT PERMIT US TO JOIN THE 26 ANTI-AXIS POWERS IN ITS PLEDGE TO FIGHT THE AXIS POWERS UNTO VICTORY.

UNITED STATES OF AMERICA DEFINITELY OWES ITS MORAL AND SPIRITUAL OBLIGATION TO THE 26 MILLION KOREANS UNDER THE SPIRIT OF THE AMERICAN KOREAN TREATY OF MAY 22, 1882 TO GRANT OUR PRESENT REQUEST.

PLEASE DO NOT DENY US THIS GOD GIVEN RIGHT TO FIGHT FOR OUR FREEDOM AGAINST OUR COMMON ENEMY, JAPAN.

(END SHEET 1)

WKB14 SHEET 2 WASHDC PRESIDENT ROOSEVELT WHITE HOUSE

FRANKLY SPEAKING IF U.S.A. REFUSES OUR REQUEST NOW IT WOULD MEAN
THAT ALL THE PROCLAMATIONS, TALK OF HUMANITY, THE SANCTITY OF
INTERNATIONAL JUSTICE, THE SPIRIT OF DEMOCRACY WILL BECOME
NOTHING BUT AN EMPTY GESTURE — WHICH OBVIOUSLY WILL PROVE A
BOOMERANG AGAINST U. S. A. AND WHICH OBVIOUSLY WILL EVENTUALLY
DEFEAT THE PRESENT PLEDGE TO DEFEAT THE AXIS POWERS.

AS WASHINGTON REPRESENTATIVE OF THE KOREAN VOLUNTEER ARMY IN
CHINA WHO HAVE ALREADY FOUGHT THE JAPS FOR 3 YEARS AND OF THE
SINO-KOREAN PEOPLES LEAGUE WHO HAVE FOR THE PAST 8 YEARS GIVEN
UNSTINTED VOLUNTARY SERVICES TO U.S.A. IN ITS PREPARATION FOR
NATIONAL DEFENSE, I HUMBLY BEG YOUR EXCELLENCY TO GRANT MY
URGENT REQUEST PERMITTING US TO JOIN THE 26 DEMOCRATIC NATIONS.

TRUSTING FOR YOUR SYMPATHETIC CONSIDERATION AND AN EARLY
GRANT OF PERMISSION TO JOIN THE 26 NATIONS.

HUMBLY SUBMITTED

KILSOO K HAAN

101 D ST NORTHEAST WASHINGTON DC

TEL. LIN. 5187.

536AM JAN 5.

WAC72 FT=WASHINGTON DC

SECRETARY OF STATE CORDELL HULL=

DEPT OF STATE=

WISHING YOU THE UTMOST IN HEALTH, HAPPINESS AND PROSPERITY
DURING THE YULETIDE SEASON. MAY ALL THE DAYS THROUGHOUT THE
COMING YEAR BRING FULL JOY AND HAPPINESS=

KILSOO K HAAN.

DEPARTMENT OF STATE

DIVISION OF FAR EASTERN AFFAIRS

January 16,
1942.

Mr. Secretary:

    This letter has been
redrafted in accordance with
the suggestion made by you.

    I have also added a para-
graph incorporating an idea
suggested by Mr. Hornbeck.

FE:MMH:HES

January 14, 1942.

Mr. Secretary:

I am sending this forward to you as drafted.

I would suggest, however, that there be added a paragraph to read in substance as follows: "In passing, may I say to you I cannot but wonder why this should not have come to me directly from the Army and the Navy expressions of solicitude similar to those which have apparently been made to you by intelligence officers of those services regarding this matter. Further, might I suggest that in any matters of this sort which may be brought to your attention by officers of those services, you, after having heard what they may wish to say, suggest to them that they also inform me on similar lines."

PA/H:SKH:FLB

United States Senate

WASHINGTON, D. C.

January 6, 1942

My dear Secretary:

As you know, I have been tremendously interested in certain phases of our relationship with the Far East.

You will recall that you were gracious enough to accord me an opportunity of discussing a Resolution which I had offered in the Senate looking to the investigation of certain pro-Axis activities, particularly relating to the Far Eastern situation. You suggested at the time that it might be preferable to postpone the stirring up of the situation by publicity attendant on such an investigation. I acceded to your wishes, as suggested.

One of the sources of information concerning these activities and many other such activities that are adverse to the interest of our Nation has come to me through certain representatives of the Korean people. There is no doubt that there are sources of news which will be of inestimable value to our Army and Naval forces that are located in Japan and in position to acquire much secret information for our Service Departments. Many of these contacts are people of Korean ancestry or closely related to them.

Recent press reports suggested that a move was planned for the adherence of the Provisional Korean Government to the Twenty-six Nation Pact, and certain proclamations have been published, both in English and in Korean, urging that every pressure be exerted to secure recognition by the United States of the Provisional Korean Government as an independent entity and the adherence of this Provisional Government, when so recognized, to the United Nations' Pact. The publication of these articles and the American news releases have seriously disturbed the Intelligence Units of the Army and the Navy, who have called upon me to discuss this attitude of concern. It is their fear that the recognition of the Provisional Government of Korea at

this time or a publication of the adherence of the Provisional
Government to the United Nations' Pact would militate seriously
against the work they are trying to do and would bring down upon
the agents, upon whom they are strongly relying, the wrath of the
Japanese Government. They not only feel that their sources of
information would be destroyed, but they feel that there might
be wholesale murder of any suspected agents.

If their fears are properly grounded, it occurs to me
that the evil resulting from such a move at this time would
greatly offset any possible benefit of the present adherence or
recognition.

I am taking the liberty of presenting this matter to
you after consultation with them and at their request. I
sincerely hope that you will not consider this letter presumptuous.
It is written merely for the purpose of presenting this viewpoint
to you in the conviction that any decision which you reach will be
a sound one. I share to the utmost the confidence of the American
people in you, but felt the liberty to present the viewpoint
which I have just outlined.

With sincere regard, I am

Respectfully,

GUY M. GILLETTE

The Honorable Cordell Hull
Secretary of State
Washington, D.C.

19, 1942

My dear Senator Gillette:

This will acknowledge the receipt of your letter
of January 6 in which you refer to a conversation we
had relating to a Resolution which you had offered in
the Senate looking to the investigation of certain pro-
Axis activities, particularly relating to the Far Eastern situation, and to the possible recognition by this
Government of the Korean Provisional Government and its
adherence to the Washington Declaration by United
Nations.

With regard to your call some months ago at which
time you were so good as to discuss with me your Resolution under reference, I mentioned various factors in the
then existing international situation in order that you
might be in position to reach a decision with full
knowledge thereof. I think you will recall that I said

that

The Honorable
     Guy M. Gillette,
          United States Senate.

that knowledge of those factors would also enable you,
in case you should decide to go ahead with the Resolution and in case there should ensue difficulties, to
share with us any appropriate responsibility.

With regard to the possible recognition of the
Korean Provisional Government and its adherence to the
Declaration by United Nations, this matter has, as you
know, been brought to our attention, and I appreciate
your courtesy in presenting me with your views which
will, I can assure you, be given careful thought. We
have no intention of taking any action until all phases
of the situation have been examined and, in this connection, your opinion is of great value to this Department.

Might I add in passing that I believe that it
would be helpful if you could, when officers of the War
or Navy Departments bring to your attention views which
they hold in reference to matters such as that under
discussion in the preceding paragraph, say to them, if
opportune occasion arises, that you believe that I would
be interested in their views and that you suggest that,
if they have not already done so, they might care to com-
municate their views to me or to other officers of this
Department?

Department? We are very glad to have knowledge of the development of which you are so good as to give account in your letter, and your thoughtfulness in the matter is much appreciated.

Sincerely yours,

Cordell Hull

February 10, 1942.

I am trying to find a letter alleged
to have been addressed by Messrs. Frederick
Brown Harris, John W. Staggers and Jay Jerome
Williams to the Secretary of State on January 10 and an alleged State Department
acknowledgment thereof.

These papers are supposed to relate to
Korean matters.

DCR states that these papers are tallied
to FE.

Receipt of this file would be greatly
appreciated by

Stanley K. Hornbeck

PA/H:SKH:ZMK

DEPARTMENT OF STATE

DIVISION OF FAR EASTERN AFFAIRS

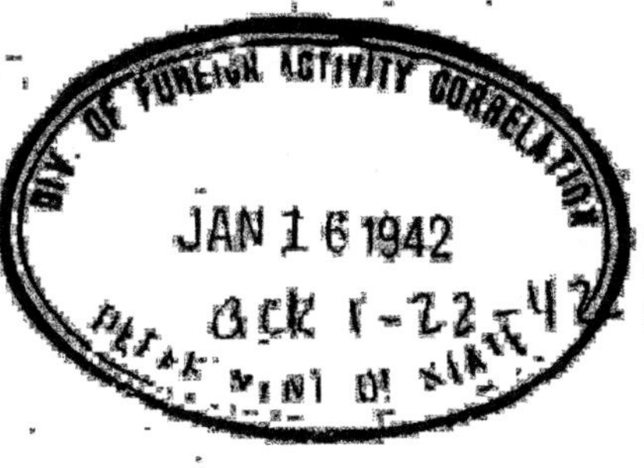

JAY JEROME WILLIAMS
WASHINGTON, D. C.

1764 Lanier Street,
January 10, 1942

Dear Mr. Hornbeck:

The undersigned American citizens have been interested for more than twenty years in the Korean independence movement without receipt of compensation and with no thought of receiving same.

We have prepared, for presentation to the President of the United States, a memorandum of the Korean situation, and in order to keep you advised we are attaching a copy of the memorandum herewith.

We have already been in contact with the State Department and Messrs. Staggers and Williams have been granted, within the next fortnight, a most courteous reception by one of your aides, Mr. Laurence E. Salisbury.

On that occasion, Mr. Salisbury informed us that the Department felt it should take no action on the request of the Korean Provisional Government for recognition until such time as the United States arranged with Japan for the safe conduct and transfer of those American citizens who, on the outbreak of the war, were in Japan, Japanese-occupied China, and now those sections of the Philippines which also are occupied by the enemy.

While our first thought naturally is of the safety and well-being of our fellow-nationals, we also feel that each day the recognition of Korea is delayed is a day wasted in the utilization of the efforts of 23 million Koreans against the enemy. Moreover, we are of the opinion that our consideration for our fellow-nationals is not shared by an enemy who, as you have so

February 10, 1942.

I am trying to find a letter alleged
to have been addressed by Messrs. Frederick
Brown Harris, John W. Staggers and Jay Jerome
Williams to the Secretary of State on January 10 and an alleged State Department
acknowledgment thereof

These papers are supposed to relate to
Korean matters.

DCR states that these papers are tallied
to FE.

Receipt of this file would be greatly
appreciated by

Stanley K. Hornbeck

PA/H:SKH:ZMK

DEPARTMENT OF STATE

DIVISION OF FAR EASTERN AFFAIRS

JAY JEROME WILLIAMS
WASHINGTON, D. C.

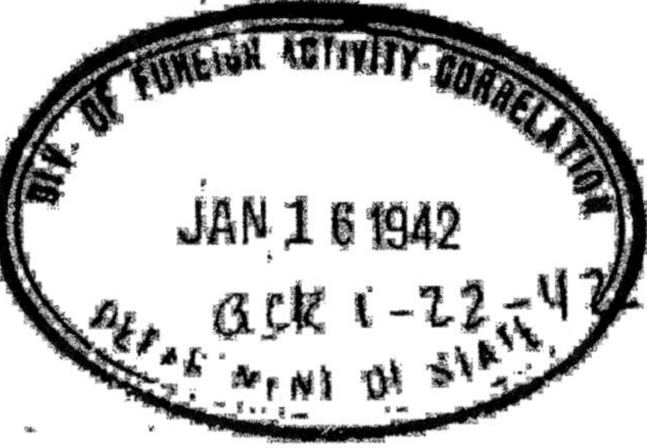

1736 L Street
January 10, 1942

Dear Mr. Secretary:

The undersigned American citizens have been interested for more than twenty years in the Korean Independence movement, without receipt of compensation and with no thought of special gain.

We have presented, for presentation to the President of the United States, a memorandum on the Korean situation, and in order to keep you advised we are attaching a copy of the memorandum herewith.

We have already been in contact with the State Department and Messrs. Staggers and Williams have been granted, within the past fortnight, a most courteous reception by one of your aides, Mr. Laurence E. Salisbury.

On that occasion, Mr. Salisbury informed us that the Department felt it should take no action on the request of the Korean Provisional Government for recognition until such time as the United States arranged with Japan for the safe conduct and transfer of those American citizens who, on the outbreak of the war, were in Japan, Japanese-occupied China, and now those sections of the Philippines which also are occupied by the enemy.

While our first thought naturally is of the safety and well-being of our fellow-nationals, we also feel that each day the recognition of Korea is delayed is a day wasted in the utilization of the efforts of 23 million Koreans against the enemy. Moreover, we are of the opinion that our consideration for our fellow-nationals is not shared by an enemy who, as you have so

Hitler said, has descended to the lowest level of animal savagery in his

conduct toward American citizens in the city of Manila.

We are very anxious to do all in our power to aid the cause of

Korean recognition and respectfully solicit your advice in the matter.

Sincerely yours,

Frederick Brown Harris
Frederick Brown Harris

John W. Staggers
John F. Staggers

Jay Jerome Williams
Jay Jerome Williams

Hon. Cordell Hull
Secretary of State
Washington, D. C.

(C O P Y)

THE KOREAN SITUATION

January 9, 1942

A tremendous opportunity for the United States and the nations united with it in the war against the Axis powers and the Japanese particularly lies at hand in the Korean situation.

The Korean people, with an existence of 42 centuries as a nation, were the first victims, to use the language of President Roosevelt, in Japan's "blood-stained course of conquest." And again, to quote the President's inspiring words that one of our war aims is the "objective of liberating the subjugated nations," the liberation of 23 million Koreans must and should be accomplished.

Beyond the practical advantages to the United States in the recognition of Korea as an independent nation, there exists an inescapable moral obligation to take this step.

There still is in existence a treaty of amity and mutual protection -- dating from 1882 -- between the United States and Korea, this treaty having been made by our State Department at the request of the American naval officer who persuaded the Korean Emperor to open his country for commerce with the western world. This treaty, ratified by the United States Senate in 1883, has never been abrogated.

Neither have the Korean people ever accepted Japanese rule. A provisional government of the Republic of Korea is functioning today. It

has been given hospice by the Chinese Government and maintains its headquarters in Chungking, China. Moreover, a Korean national army now is in
the field, with Chinese forces, fighting the common enemy, the Japanese.

The Korean cause has been ably represented by Dr. Syngman Rhee,
first president of the Korean Republic, and leader of the 1919 revolt
against the Japanese. Great friend of Woodrow Wilson, whose student he was
at Princeton University, Dr. Rhee now is in Washington and has presented to
the State Department his credentials as the accredited envoy of the Korean
Provisional Government, as well as that Government's request for American
recognition.

Many American citizens believe in the justice of the Korean
cause. These citizens now see a two-fold opportunity of the first magnitude.
They believe their country, in the new era unfolding under the leadership of
President Roosevelt, should morally uphold the sanctity of its treaty obligations. They further believe 23 million Koreans, inspired by recognition by
the American Government, will be made powerful allies in the war against
Japan.

The undersigned American citizens have been interested for more
than twenty years in the Korean independence movement.

(Sgd) Frederick Brown Harris
Frederick Brown Harris

(Sgd) John W. Staggers
John W. Staggers

(Sgd) Jay Jerome Williams
Jay Jerome Williams

Mr Zetzschmy FE

Memo now attached
— will you
read & return
it & the letter?
Hoskins

memo now
attached
RW

A- B
Mr Hoskins
No memorandum
was attached when
this letter reached
FE.
I made a memo
of the conversation
referred to and I
stated only my view,
not the Dept's views_

January 26, 1942

In reply refer to
A-B/H

My dear Mr. Williams:

The Secretary of State has referred to me for
acknowledgment your letter and memorandum of January 10,
regarding your wish, and that of Mr. Harris and Mr. Staggers,
to see this Government recognize the Korean Provisional
Government.

This matter has, as you know, already come to the
attention of the Department of State, and you may be
assured that the points set forth in your memorandum will
be given careful consideration.

Your courtesy in writing and your interest in the
question are much appreciated.

Sincerely yours,

Harold B. Hoskins
Executive Assistant

Mr. Jay Jerome Williams,

JAN 23 1942PM   1700 Eye Street, N. W.,
JAN 26 1942PM
                   Washington, D. C.
    A-B/H:HBH:RW:JKF   1/22/42

DEPARTMENT OF STATE

FOREIGN ACTIVITY CORRELATION

December 9, 1941

Memorandum of Conversation.

FC - Mr. Gordon
FE - Mr. Hamilton
A-B - Mr. Berle

"Free Korea"

Copy in FE

Dr. Syngman Rhee, head of the Korean Commission in Washington, was referred to me by Mr. Langdon in FE. Dr. Rhee reports his office as being in Room 323 Colorado Building, telephone REpublic 6119. This Commission is already registered with the State Department.

Dr. Rhee came in primarily to advise that the Alien Registration Division of the Department of Justice had allowed Koreans to register as Koreans rather than as Japanese citizens.

In view of the war situation, Dr. Rhee was anxious that the Koreans be recognized as anti-Japanese and so treated, including among other things the question of freezing their funds. I suggested that Dr. Rhee submit a statement in writing and send a copy of it direct to Mr. L.M.C.Smith of the Defense unit of the Department of Justice.

Dr. Rhee mentioned the fact that there is a "Free Korean Committee located in Chungking, China, and made inquiries of the possibility of some form of support being given to this same movement by the United States.

Harold B. Hoskins

A-B/H:HBH:gw

December 9, 1941

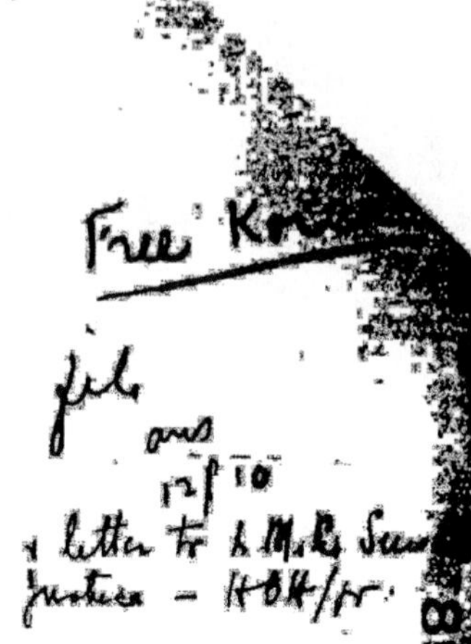

Mr. Harold B. Hoskins,
State Department,
Washington, D. C.

My dear Mr. Hoskins:

Since the Alien Registration Act was put into effect in July 1940, the United States authorities officially declared that the Koreans in this country shall be permitted to register as Koreans, not as Japanese. All the Korean aliens in America and Hawaii have registered as a distinct Korean group. As such they have been allowed to carry on their business unmolested even by the Fund Freezing Acts, enacted later.

Since yesterday, I have received several telegraphic and telephone messages from Los Angeles and Chicago, complaining that local authorities had ordered them to close their bank accounts and stop their business.

Please wire instructions to the local officers to let these few Koreans continue their business as usual. The situation has changed and there is every reason for the United States to treat the Koreans as a friendly people. It is proverbial that the Koreans are loyal to the United States and hereditarily inimical to Japan.

I am waiting to hear favorably from you.

Sincerely yours,

Syngman Rhee

SINO-KOREAN PEOPLES' LEAGUE

101 D Street, N. E.   WASHINGTON, D. C.   Lincoln 5187

KILSOO K. HAAN
Washington Representative

December 19, 1941

Secretary of State Cordell Hull
U. S. State Department

My dear Sir:

I am enclosing copy of a letter to Mr. Fletcher Warren, of the Visa Division, requesting him to grant Koreans to travel in the United States and also not to classify Korean aliens as Japanese subjects.   I trust that you will be able to read my letter to Mr. Warren setting forth my reasons why we should not be classified as Japs.   Technically we are, but in reality we are not Japanese.   In fact, we are friends of America, and have been friends of America for many, many years.

Strategically speaking, Koreans can be most useful in carrying out certain type of activities within Korea, Japan, Manchuria, as well as in Hawaii and America.   I believe the results of my work proves itself.

May I humbly plead that the State Department grant our request as soon as possible so that we will be able to assist in the defense of America and its security in the Pacific.

In the interest of National Defense, I am.

Very sincerely yours,

Kilsoo K. Haan

Kilsoo K. Haan

December 12, 1941

Honorable Fletcher Warren
U. S. Department of State
Visa Division
Washington, D. C.

My dear Mr. Warren:

Since Japan's dastardly attack on peaceful Hawaii, the Koreans have unfortunately been classified as enemy aliens in all matters such as travel and freezing of funds in the banks.

August of 1940 the Justice Department, Director of Alien Registration, Hon. Earl G. Harrison, after consideration of my request that Koreans in Hawaii and America be permitted to register as Koreans and not as Japanese subjects according to the usual practice based on international law, granted our request.

This was hailed by all Koreans as a special honor and an exception - contrary to the practice of international law - in fact the Justice Department faced the reality and acted accordingly.

After all, my opinion is that what the State Department does is none of the Japs' business and that after all if the Justice Department or the State Department gives favorable and sympathetic consideration to the Koreans it is purely a domestic policy which has no bearing on foreign policy.

In view of the Japanese action against America and in view of the precedance set by the Justice Department regarding the registration of Korean aliens as Koreans and not as Japs, may I humbly and urgently request that the State Department give early consideration in ruling that Koreans in Hawaii and America will not be classified as Japs, and I further request that the Koreans be permitted to travel as the Chinese citizens do.

There is one other factor which I sincerely desire to call to your attention. For many years my men and myself, voluntarily and at our own risk and expense, investigated anti-American Japanese activities and turned in to the State Department, Justice Department, and Army and Navy Intelligence Departments information which cost us thousands of dollars, time, and much risked danger. In the Far East 46 of our men lost their lives.

If a careful check is made you will find that much of our information has been verified and the events of the international situation during the past year show that our men's reports were correct.

- 209 -

As references may I urge you to call up the U. S. Army G-2 or Senator Guy M. Gillette, or check the files of the State Department of my reports.   You will agree with me that we have done our best to serve America and for the best interest of the security of America in the Pacific.

Significant Factor to Koreans and particularly
to Sino-Korean Peoples League

Because the State Department classified Koreans as Japs, our work will suffer, in fact we will be forced to cease operation.

No matter how much our League desires to help America, our hands will be tied, we will be forced to undergo much humiliation and economic suffering.

Strategically, in purely a military sense, I cannot see any sane reason why the State Department should have the Koreans stop helping American Defense activities, especially the intelligence service work.

If the State Department persists and insists on classifying Koreans as Japs and restricts us from giving voluntary help to America by freezing our funds so that we cannot carry on our work or travel, the Japanese militarists in Japan, Hawaii and America will be very happy.

In reality the Jap militarists will construe that the State Department is helping Japan's war on America.

Please do consider throwing overboard the technical international legal points and grant our sincere request in the interest of America's defense.

Very sincerely yours,

Kilsoo K. Haan

In reply refer to
FE 895.01/49

My dear Mr. Faddis:

The receipt is acknowledged of your letter of
December 8, 1941 in regard to the question of the independence of Korea.

As you of course realize, questions such as this
constantly arise. I assure you that in connection with
all such questions this Department gives careful study
to the problem of best safeguarding the interests of
the United States and of making effective the principles
and policies to which this country is committed.

Your thoughtfulness in bringing this matter to my
attention is much appreciated.

Sincerely yours,

The Honorable

    Charles I. Faddis,

        House of Representatives.

FE:WRL:MJF/MJK   FE   PA/H
12-13-41

December 10, 1941.

My dear Mr. Smith:

You have received from Dr. Syngman Rhee of the Korean Commission in Washington a letter that I suggested he address to you in regard to the status of Koreans both in the United States and in Hawaii.   Dr. Rhee has been for years known to this Department as opposing strongly the Japanese domination of his country. He succeeded in connection with the Aliens Registration Act in getting permission for Koreans to register in this country as Koreans and not as Japanese.

I hope in connection with the work of your Department you can be of assistance to see that Koreans are given a status distinct from the Japanese in various matters, including the unfreezing of any funds which may have been frozen through a misconception of their relations to the Japanese,

Yours sincerely,

Harold B. Hoskins
Executive Assistant

Mr. L. M. C. Smith,
     Special Defense Unit,
          Department of Justice,
               Washington, D.C.

A-B/H:HTH:gw

December 10, 1941

In reply refer to
A-B/H

Dear Dr. Rhee:

    This will acknowledge the receipt of your letter of December 9. I have written to Mr. Smith of the Department of Justice urging consideration for the status of Koreans in this country and in Hawaii, and suggest that you follow this matter up with Mr. Smith.

Yours sincerely,

Harold B. Hoskins
Executive Assistant

Dr. Syngman Rhee,

  The Korean Commission,

    1766 Hobart Street, N.W.,

      Washington, D.C.

A-B/H: HBH:gw

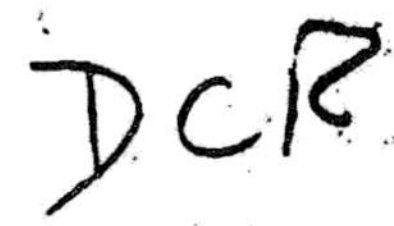

In reply refer to

My dear Mr. Haan:

In reply to your letter of December 9, 1941 in regard to the freeing of funds and property of Koreans in the United States from the restrictions on the funds and property of enemy aliens, you are informed that this Government is giving consideration to this matter. It has also been brought to the attention of the Department of Justice.

Note has also been taken of your correspondence on this subject with officials of the Treasury Department.

Sincerely yours,

Maxwell M. Hamilton
Chief
Division of Far Eastern Affairs

Mr. Kilsoo K. Haan,
   101 D Street, Ne.,
      Washington, D.C.

FE:WFL:HDW (EDH)
12/12/41

DR. SYNGMAN RHEE
1766 HOBART STREET. N. W.
WASHINGTON, D. C.

Dec. 17, 1941

Dear Dr. Hornbeck:

Yesterday afternoon, I had a very interesting conversation with Major Wallace H. Moore of the
Army Intelligence Service.   He said it was at your
suggestion that the Army wants to find out what they
can do to help Korea.   He said he would do all he
could to secure aid for the Koreans fighting in China.

The following cable message was received
from Chungking the other day:

  KOPOGO(Korean Provisional Government) declared
  war against Japan, announced to Ambassadors here
  Please urging American Government recognize
  KOPOGO Details mail.   Josoang.

Josoang is Mr. Cho Soang, Foreign Minister of the Korean
Provisional Government.   He and Kim Ku were given by me
a letter of introduction to Dr. Quo Tai Chi soon after
his return to Chungking as Chinese Foreign Minister.
Dr. Quo assured them that the Chinese Government would
formally recognize the Korean Provisional Government.
On Nov. 25, the following cablegram was received:

  CHINESE GOVERNMENT SENT US OFFICIAL DOCUMENT
  RECOGNIZING KWANGPOKUN(Korean National Army)
    (Signed) KOPOGO (Korean Provisional Gov)

    Yours sincerely,

    Syngman Rhee

Overseas Convention And United Korean Committee

Coming as a climax to many months of careful study and concerted effort by responsible leaders of the Korean community here and on the mainland, the first convention of overseas Korean delegates was held in Honolulu April 19-29 this year with 15 representatives from 7 major organizations present.

The convention resulted in a success. All of the important issues bearing on the present and future welfare of the Korean people have been settled and a comprehensive program looking toward materialization of these issues was formulated.

One noteworthy feature of the convention was the birth of the United Korean Committee in America with two co-ordinating headquarters, the first the seat of Directors' committee in Honolulu and the other the seat of administrative committee in Los Angeles.

Mr. Won Soon Lee heads the local committee as general chairman with Mr. Won Kiu Ahn as vice chairman: Mr. Warren Kim, English secretary; Mr. C. H. Tough, Korean secretary; Mr. Henry K. Kim, chairman of the National Defense Aid subcommittee; Messrs .S. W. Sohn and P. Y. Cho co-treasurers: Mr. Shinho Char, auditor. Other members of the Board of Directors include Mr. S. W. Lim, Mrs. Youngsin Shim, Mr. S. H. Kang and Mrs. Yinsik Min.

The staff of the administrative body in Los Angeles include Mr. Ho Kim, chairman: Lee Kyung Sun, secretary; C. I. Song. treasurer and Mr. Sidai Hahn, P. Y. Kim.

The local National Defense Aid Committee. organized soon after the convention with a staff of 9 live-wires. has done and continue to do admirable piece of work in furtherance of the UKC function. This body includes subcommittee on information—David Youth, C. H. Tough, Father Noah K. Cho: subcommittee on training—Walter Jhung. Young Kee Kim, Donald Kang ; and subcommittee on relief—Rev. C. H. Min. Thomas Yoon. H. K. Ahn.

FINANCES

To carry on the vast work formulated by the United Korean Committee, a considerable sum of money is needed. The Convention decided to raise at least $20,000 per year—$15,000 from Hawaii and $5,000 from the mainland—to support three institutions dedicated to the independence movement: the Korean Provisional government, the Restoration Army and the Korean Commission at Washington, D. C.

There has been an unexampled manifestation of spontaneous interest and loyalty in responding to the call for Toknipkeum by Hawaii Koreans. To date, over $17,000 has been pledged by local people, an astounding feat! It went over the top by a substantial margin.

CONCLUSION

To the young Koreans of Hawaii, we wish to urge a 100% loyalty, cooperation and willing service in behalf of America's National Defense program which appears more imperative today in view of rapidly changing world situation. Let the entire Korean community in Hawaii and the mainland put up a united solid front behind the United Korean Committee in America in assisting this important piece of national policy. It is our duty, our privilege as well as our obligation.

With Japan-America relations now strained to the breaking point, a show-down in Pacific looms almost a certainty. This is the chance we have been praying for since the fateful year of 1910 While the older people are doing their part to support the independence movement, we urge every young Korean in the United States to pitch in and do their share too. This is decidedly a world of youthful activities. Without your active interest and cooperation, our work would fall short of success.

———O———

Resolutions Adopted By The Oversea Convention

I. UNIFICATION OF INDEPENDENCE FRONT

1. Koreans should transcend the "isms" and principles and concentrate all their strength and resources to resist Japan.

(Reason: Regardless of the difference in beliefs among our people; let it be known that Japan is the common enemy of Korean people. Koreans should therefore unite to overthrow her.)

2. All Korean publications should maintain a unified stand on the world situation as it exists today.

(Reason: For cooperative work we need to have the same spirit and plans. Therefore, all publications must agree in spirit, purpose and methods.)

3, Mottos or slogans should be formulated to stimulate team-work.

(Reason: To visualize our program and to accelerate the activity by coining simple suggestive words.)

II. SUPPORTING PROVISIONAL GOVERNMENT

1. All Koreans and their organizations should place absolute trust and faith in the integrity of the Korean Provisional government and support it with spirit and matter.

(Reason: Because of the failure in the past of the people to trust and support the Provisional Government, it had great difficulties. From now on, we should, therefore, trust and support that central organization with all our heart and strength.)

2. Every Korean and every Korean organization should observe the decrees issued by the Provisional Government.

(Reason: By observing the decrees, we may sanctify and strengthen it.)

3. For the sanctity of the government and the discipline of the people we should ask the Provisional Government not to change the form of the present government until the people demand it.

(Reason: We ask this for fear of coup-de-tat and of the diminution of the efficiency of the government.

III. MILITARY ACTION

1. Every Korean political organization abroad should emphasize the idea that every Korean is a unit of the military force and should train himself for it.

(Reason: We know it is our duty to be a soldier for the independence movement. But we need to place strong emphasis on it in this emergency and to train the people to be the vanguards of the movement.)

2. Kwangbokkoon and Euiyondai should come under the control of the Provisional Government without any condition to put up a united front against Japan.

(Reason: We, believing the great significance of unity in our movement, should ask the Government to incorporate these two military units under the control of the Government.)

IV. DIPLOMATIC ACTION

1. We should establish a diplomatic commission in Washington, D. C.

(Reason: Because Washington is the center of word diplomacy, a diplomatic organ at that spot would well serve our purpose.)

2. For the time being we should send one representative to be a full-time worker. According to the development of the work and the situation, the number of officers may be increased.

(Reason: Owing to financial conditions and for simplicity of the procedure, one person takes charge of the work. Later, as conditions warrant, the number of representatives may be augmented.)

3. The diplomatic commission should initiate its action after finishing the legal procedure of the Provisional Government.

(Reason: It is necessary to have the approval of the government for appointment of its staff personnel).

4. The expenses of the diplomatic commission shall be paid by the Koreans abroad.

(Reason: Because the financial power is practically in the hands of the Koreans in America (U.S.A., Hawaii, Cuba, et al), they are to have this responsibility.

5. Dr. Syngman Rhee is elected as the representative of the diplomatic commission

6. The above four items should be presented to the Provisional Government for approval. The commission will start to function when it is approved by the government.

V. AID TO U. S. NATIONAL DEFENSE PROGRAM

1. The United Korean Commission should proclaim to the Koreans to render their services to the United States national defense program, directly or indirectly, both morally and materially.

2. A representative should be elected to be of service to the national defense project. The expense of the representative shall be paid by the Koreans in America.

3. Mr. Kilsoo K. Haan is elected as service man to aid the U. S. National Defense.

VI. FINANCE FOR INDEPENDENCE MOVEMENT

1. All contributions for the Independence movement should be named "Toknipkeum." This should be collected and in a unified method in different organizations of the locality, according to the economical, industrial and labor conditions of the individual. The organization should all co-operate to bring best results in this respect.

2. All other terms used for the contributions in the connection by various organizations should be abolished from now on.

3. The Budget of Toknipkeum: Of the total collection of Topnipkeum two-thirds shall be sent to Provisional Government and the remaining one-third used for the diplomatic and National Defense aid service.

4. The details of the finances will be stated

VII. ESTABLISHMENT OF UNITED COMMITTEE

1. The United Korean Committee in America is hereby established.

2. The committee shall consist of two parts: Directors' Committee and Executive Committee. Directors' Committee is organized by the representatives from Hawaii while the Executive Committee is organized by the representatives from the Mainland.

3. The regulations of the Committee will be stated hereafter.

REGULATIONS GOVERNING THE UNITED KOREAN COMMITTEE

1. This organization shall be called the United Korean Committee in America.

2. The purpose of this committee is to attain the independence of Korea. As the first step toward this goal, the organizaiton will unite the war front to win victory over Japan. Meantime, the organization will do various cooperative work for the betterment of the Korean society abroad.

3. The committee shall cooperate with all Korean political organizations abroad.

4. The committee shall put into practice a representative system. The members of the Committees are all of the delegates to the Convention of Overseas Koreans and the presidents of the Korean National Association of Hawaii, of Dongji Hoi and of the Korean National Ass'n of North America.

5. The Director's Committee shall consist of the representatives in Hawaii, The Executive Committee shall consist of representatives in America. Supplementation is done by the appointment of each particular organization.

6. The unit organization shall make every effort to collect toknipkeum and send same to the United Committee.

7. Every unit organization shall observe the duty to collect and send toknipkeum cordially.

8. The unit-organizations should be obedient to the regulations and agreements and should not do anything contradictory to the spirit and rules of the Committee.

9. The appointees of the Committee shall follow the supervision of the Committee faithfully.

10. The Committee shall supervise the work of the National Defense Aid service.

11. The financial regulations will be stated hereafter.

12. Details of the expenditures of the Committee shall be paid after the approval of Directors' Committee.

13. The Committee has no regular meeting. Temporary meetings may be held through an agreement made by the Directors' and Executive Committees in time of urgent need.

BY-LAWS OF THE TREASURY

1. The Executive Committee supervises the disposal of Toknipkeum.

2. The Toknipkeum is sent to the Directors' Committee in Hawaii and to the Execuitve Committee in America. Each committee has two treasurers.

3. The minimum amount of Toknipkeum for each individual shall be at least $15 per annum. The method of collection is determined by the respective committee according to local situation.

4. The collection of Toknipkuem shall be operated following the approval of the Committee.

5. The Executive Committee shall report income and expenses of Toknipkeum monthly.

The delegates to the Convention pledge to support all the resolutions of the convention fully and make every effort to fulfill them.

The above 7 resolutions, supplements and by-laws of the treasury shall become operative from May 15, 1941. Donations collected by the unit organizations up to May 14 shall be sent to the treasury of Provisional Government or elsewhere directly by the respective organizations.

April 29, the 23rd year of Korean Republic (1941). By the following delegates in attendance at the Convention:

(Sgd) S. D. Hahn, KNA of North America.
" Ho Kim, KNA of North America.
" C. Y. Song, KNA of North America.
" H. K. Ahn, Dongji Hoi.
" W. S. Lee, Dongji Hoi.
" C. H. Tough, Donji Hoi.
" W. K. Ahn, KNA of Hawaii.
" H. C. Kim, KNA of Hawaii.
" W. Y. Kim, KNA of Hawaii.
" S. H. Char, Sino-Korean Peoples' League.
" S. H. Kang, Korean National Independence League.
" S. W. Lim, Hawaii Chapter, Korean Independence Party.
" Doin Kwon, Korean Volunteer League in America.
" Y. S. Shim, Korean Women's Relief Society in Hawaii.
" Hamna Min, Korean Women's Relief Society in Hawaii.

———O———

Memorandum of Conversation

DATE: December 1[?]

SUBJECT:

PARTICIPANTS: Dr. Syngman Rhee, of the Korean Commission, Washington, D.C.

Mr. Alger Hiss.

COPIES TO:

At Dr. Hornbeck's direction I received Dr. Rhee in Dr. Hornbeck's stead.

Dr. Rhee left with me for Dr. Hornbeck the attached letter dated December 17 addressed to Dr. Hornbeck. In this connection he said that this morning Major Moore, who is referred to in the letter under reference, had told him to get in touch with Major Goodfellow, of the Military Intelligence Division.

Dr. Rhee also left with me the attached printed leaflet relating to Korean activities in the United States. He pointed out that on page 2 the statement is made that Mr. Kilsoo K. Haan has been appointed by the Korean Commission to assist United States National Defense.

Dr. Rhee

Dr. Rhee said that he had known Mr. Haan since
the latter was a small boy whom he had taught in school.
He said further that Mr. Haan, in his opinion, was
courageous and anti-Japanese, but that he was unable to
have confidence in him. His comments about Mr. Haan were
rather vague and expressed with some emotion. At some
point in his comments he stated that Mr. Haan had once
been "a Japanese spy" but he reiterated his opinion that
Mr. Haan is anti-Japanese. The impression which I gathered
was that Dr. Rhee considers Mr. Haan somewhat lacking in
judgment but not in spirit.

The main emphasis made by Dr. Rhee was upon the
urgency of getting supplies to Chungking before the Burma
Road is out. He stated that it was inevitable that the
Road would soon be out. In this connection his main
interest was that supplies be sent to Chungking for the
use of what he referred to as the National Korean Army
which he said is now operating in China and which, as
stated in his letter under reference, he asserts has been
recognized by the Chinese Government.

He asked that I tell Dr. Hornbeck that Dr. Hornbeck
should suggest to Dr. Hu or to Mr. T. V. Soong that the
Chinese Government should also recognize the so-called
Korean Provisional Government. This he said would enable
his organization to receive Lend-Lease assistance.

JAN 1 0 1942

A-B/H
Mr. Hoskins:

 Reference your memorandum of January 2, 1942, in which you state that you are agreeable to handling discussions or correspondence regarding a "Free Korean" movement and that you will keep FE fully informed on all developments as they occur:

 FE would be glad to cooperate with you in this manner and believes that the procedure agreed upon represents sound administrative practice. It is understood of course that there will be a full interchange of information between your office and FE and full discussion between the two offices in reference to any question relating to decisions on policy.

FE:Salisbury:HES

FILED
MAR 20 1944

January 2, 1942.

TO: FE - Mr. Hamilton:

SUBJECT: Free Korean Movement.

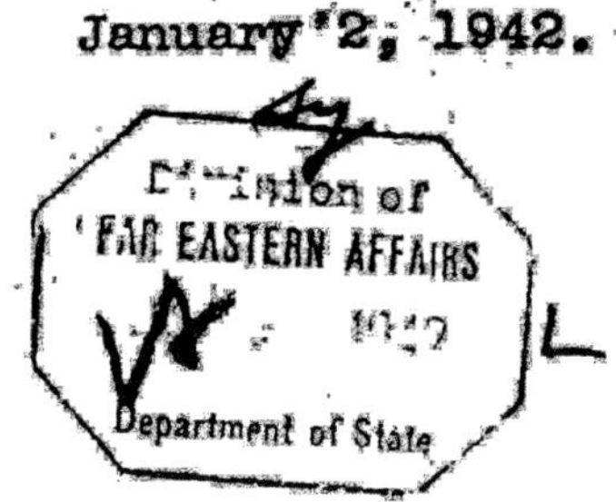

895.01/60-6/26

I am advising Mr. Berle of our conversation in which you agreed that discussions or correspondence regarding a "Free Korean" movement had best be centered in one individual, and that you are agreeable to its being handled by me under Mr. Berle's direction, as contemplated in Departmental Order No. 995.

I am therefore retaining recent correspondence on this subject, including Mr. Salisbury's memorandum of conversation of December 23, 1941. I shall keep FE fully informed on all developments as they occur. I have also noted your general point of view that we must be extremely cautious in taking any positive action that might endanger the treatment of American citizens still in Japan or in that part of China occupied by Japan.

Harold B. Hoskins

A-B/H:HBH:gw

THE HAY-ADAMS HOUSE

WASHINGTON, D.C.

9th January, 1942.

Mr. H. B. Hoskins,
Room 178, State Department
Washington, D. C.

My dear Mr. Hoskins,-

May I take this opportunity to express my sincere
appreciation for your sympathetic understanding of our
problem.

Complying with your request, I am enclosing a copy
of my letter to Mr. H. F. Slade, of the Federal Reserve Bank
of San Francisco.

Our people will appreciate very much if you would be
so good as to relieve them from the predicament they are now
confronted with, as soon as possible.

With my best regards, I am————

Very respectfully yours,

Yongjeung Kim

재미한족련합위원회

United Korean Committee in America

**1368 WEST JEFFERSON BOULEVARD
LOS ANGELES, CALIFORNIA**

Copy

December 26, 1941

Mr. H. F. Slade
Assistant Cashier
Federal Reserve Bank of San Francisco
San Francisco, California

My dear Mr. Slade,

I am taking this opportunity to express my sincere appreciation for your sympathetic understanding of our problem. I returned home with much hope and courage.

The United Korean Committee in America, representing all Korean Organizations in the United States and the Territory of Hawaii, wishes me to request your good offices to bring about a satisfactory arrangement of our status in the recent freezing order of the United States Treasury.

May I, in this connection, recall to your attention the following facts: After the Japanese seizure of our native land, we Koreans in the United States and its possessions have been enjoying our pursuit of happiness only under the government of this country, to which we give and owe our loyalty and support. We shall not neglect our duty to this land of our adoption.

The Koreans, both in and out of their mother country, have never recognized the right of Japan to rule over Korea. For more than thirty years we have been fighting the aggressor with all our means, wherever and whenever possible. This has been un unequal struggle but now we have on our side the greatest democratic power, the United States. We know our victory is assured, and that with it the peaceful and liberty -loving people in Korea will be freed from the Japanese oppression.

While we are fighting the common enemy, unfortunately our funds were frozen together with those of the Japanese under the technicality that Korea is an occupied territory. Our misfortune makes Japan happy but brings discouragement to our people. Our brethren in Korea are suffering under the Japanese yoke. How can we in this country suffer and be punished for the treacherous conduct of our enemy?

We would greatly appreciate it if the Treasury Department would announce publicly--and give the widest publicity to such an announcement--that the freezing of Korean funds is solely for protective purposes; that the Koreans are "friendly aliens" who will operate their business as usual under the general licensing system; and that they have a status the same as that of the Chinese. This will build up our morale and preserve our self-respect in the eyes of the American public. On behalf of the United Korean Committee in America, may I sincerely ask you to respond to our earnest appeal and to exert your best efforts to give us the "equal treatment" to which, by our profession and our performance we feel that we are entitled.

Very respectfully yours,

Yongjeung Kim
Director of Public Relations
United Korean Committee in America

January 19, 1942

Regarding "Free Korea".

Mr. Salisbury of FE telephoned to say that Mr. Hamilton and Mr. Hornbeck had been consulting with him and had no objection to the plans of the Department of Justice for distinguishing between Koreans and Japanese in the United States, and that if Koreans were required to register, they should be allowed to register as Koreans rather than as Japanese. I advised Mr. Marvin Coles about this fact in the Department of Justice, and understand from him that the procedure they will probably adopt will be to exempt Koreans from having to register as enemy aliens when new registration requirements of February 2nd are put into effect.

H. B. H.

A-B/H:HBH:gw

Earl G. Harrison

615 Pennsylvania Avenue, N.W.

January 26, 1942.

33

<u>MEMORANDUM FOR MR. HOSKINS</u>

In accordance with Miss Wellington's request, I am
sending you herewith a copy of the letter sent to me by
Mr. Kilsoo Haan, together with a copy of my reply.

Best regards.

EARL G. HARRISON
Special Assistant to the Attorney General

EGH:P

Encls.

PS. It occurs to me that you might like to have a copy of
the telegram received from Mr. Haan on Saturday last.

EGH

FILED
MAR 27 1944

34   January 14, 1942

Hon. Earl G. Harrison
Director of Alien Registration
Department of Justice
Washington, D. C.

My dear Hon. Harrison:

        Your department on August, 1940, granted us the honor and
privilege to register as Koreans and not as Jap citizens.

        We now read in the press report that all "enemy-aliens" will
be re-registered.

        Since your department has permitted the Koreans to register
as Korean - I assume the Koreans are not considered as "Enemy-Aliens", hence
are exempted from this re-registration.

        Kindly let me know. I would like to inform my people as to
their true status.

        Assuming that if we are forced to re-register as "Enemy Aliens"
I am sure every Korean in Hawaii and the United States would consider such
an act contrary to all the good intention proclamations proclaimed by the
State Department.

        God has made us Koreans - even He cannot change our nationality
and race. Contrary to this natural law, Japan forcefully attempted to
change our nationality - but the Japs have failed.

        If, however, the United States of America attempts forcefully
to change our God-given rights to live and breathe as Koreans into Japs -
what difference is there between Japan's inhuman treatment of subject
people and of the United States?

        Please do not force the Koreans to re-register as Japs, and as
"Enemy Aliens". If your department does such an unjust and inhuman act,
you will be trying to attempt an act obviously even the Almighty God cannot
do. I would rather be shot than to re-register as a Jap - and an "Enemy
Alien".

        I am enclosing a photostat copy of recent newspaper clippings
which beyond doubt will prove that I am loyal to America and to Korea and
that I desire to serve America with all my heart, with all my mind and with

loyal spirit to win this war for democracy.

If and when the Justice Department forcefully makes Koreans the hateful Japs - hence "Enemy Aliens" - it would mean one thing and that is, that American stupid policy would aid the Jap-militarists to murder more and more young Americans in this war between Japan and the U.S.A.

Undoubtedly because of our helpless situation there would be no means of doing anything. But I have faith in the democratic spirit and the sportsmanlike and fair play spirit of the millions of thinking American people in these United States.

In the interest of U. S. security,

Very gratefully yours,

s/ Kilsoo K. Haan
Kilsoo K. Haan

<u>C O P Y</u>

Harrison

sylvania Avenue, N.W.

January 23, 1942.

Mr. Kilsoo K. Haan,
Sino-Korean Peoples' League,
101 D Street, N.E.,
Washington, D.C.

Dear Mr. Haan:

I am now in position to answer your letter of January 14.

The regulations, just adopted, governing Certificates of Identification for aliens of enemy nationalities provide that Koreans who, under the Alien Registration Act of 1940, registered as Koreans, are not required to apply for Certificates of Identification, providing that such persons have not at any time voluntarily become German, Italian or Japanese citizens or subjects.

I am sure you will be glad to learn of this official action.

I was a little disappointed that after your informal visit to me several days ago, at which time I told you that we were still working on the matter, and that I would not be able to give you final word for several days, you should have issued a statement to the newspapers. This was certainly a little premature and might have been quite embarrassing all around, if the newspaper men had not been good enough to call me on the telephone for a confirmation. While I of course confirmed the fact that I had made the statement which you attributed to me, I told those who called that no final action had been taken and that publication of the matter at this time would be premature.

I suggest that in situations of this kind it would be better to clear with the person you intend to quote before giving statements to the press. I am sure that you forgot this in the pleasure of learning what would probably be the case regarding Koreans in connection with the new registration program.

With best regards, I am

Sincerely yours,

EARL G. HARRISON
Special Assistant to the Attorney General

EGH:P

<u>C O P Y</u>

Telegram

11:45 a.m. 1/24/42

Hon. Earl G. Harrison
Special Assistant to Attorney General
615 Pennsylvania Avenue
Justice Department
Washington, D. C.

Million thanks for your letter of 23 official ruling Koreans are not
enemy aliens and need not reregister. Regret premature press release.
My happiness in your assurance made me like to shout out to the whole
world. Again I thank you.

                              Kilsoo Haan

C O P Y

January 30, 1942

Mr. Harold B. Haskins
State Department
Washington, D. C.

Dear Mr. Haskins:

I have been instructed by Dr. Syngman Rhee,
Chairman of the Korean Commission to mail you, for
your information, a copy of the enclosed letter.
This letter was addressed by me to Mr. Kilsoo K.
Haan and is self-explanatory.

Sincerely yours,

J. W. STAGGERS

JWS:e
Encl.

January 30, 1942

Mr. Kilsoo K. Haan
101 D Street, N. E.
Washington, D. C.

Dear Mr. Haan:

As Counsel for the Korean Commission, I have been
asked to write you in reference to your activities in
behalf of the Korean cause.

In your earnest and enthusiastic efforts to help
you have in some instances caused confusion and misunder-
standing.

One recent incident is the publication by you of
information on the registration of Koreans. This was
made public by you without consulting with the Korean
Commission which had an understanding with the officials
in the Department of Justice that it would not be released until the Department saw fit to do so.

The Korean Commission is recognized by the State
Department as the official representative of the Provisional Government of Korea. It, therefore, follows
that the proper procedure would be for you to submit to
the Korean Commission, to be forwarded through official
channels, any communication which you wish to address to
any of the Departments in Washington.

This letter is to further advise you unless you
are willing to conform to the Commission's wishes in
this matter you will be requested by it and the Provisional Government of Korea to cease all activities in connection with the Korean cause.

I am sure you recognize the necessity for a concerted and harmonized effort on the part of the Koreans
at this time and that you would not knowingly do anything
which would cause or bring about confusion.

A copy of this letter will be filed with the State
Department, War Department, Navy Department and Department
of Justice.

Very truly yours,

J. W. STAGGERS

JWS:s

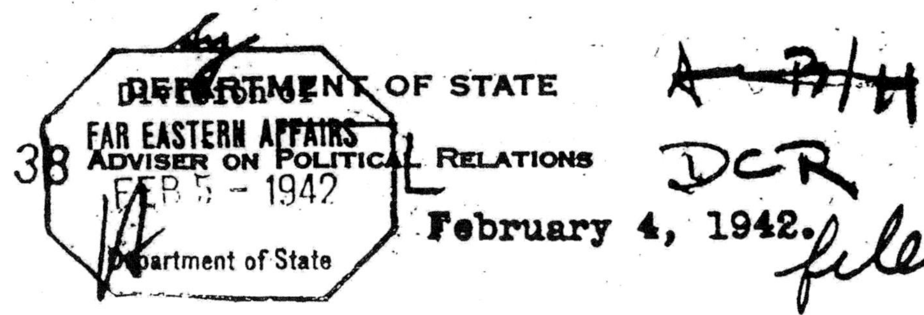

DEPARTMENT OF STATE
ADVISER ON POLITICAL RELATIONS

February 4, 1942.

<u>Reference</u>, Dr. Syngman Rhee's letter to
me of December 9, my memorandum of
December 16 and FE's memorandum to me of
December 20 regarding papers offered by
Dr. Rhee.

Dr. Rhee called on me, at his request
today. Our conversation related to various
matters of concern to Koreans active in the
Korean independence movement which raised
questions of interest and concern to the
American Government.

Having in the interval since December 20
discussed with officers of FE and most recently
with Mr. Hoskins the question of the documents
which Dr. Rhee had offered, I, at an opportune
moment in this conversation, took up with
Dr. Rhee the question of possession of those
documents. I stated that it appeared that the
time had not yet arrived when it would be opportune and would serve a useful purpose for
those documents to be presented to the
President, the Secretary of State and the
Department; and I summarized, in other parts
of the conversation, reasons for that opinion.
Dr. Rhee indicated that he in no way dissented
from that opinion and that he was perfectly
willing to have the documents continue to be
withheld. I then said that it seemed to me
that the documents might either continue to
be held by me or might be given back by me

to

to Dr. Rhee; that I was willing to follow
either procedure but I thought that it would
be better for Dr. Rhee to take them. I said
that the fact that these documents had been
offered was a matter of record and was known
to Mr. Hamilton, Mr. Hoskins and myself,
and that the matter had been mentioned to the
Secretary of State. Dr. Rhee said that it
would be perfectly agreeable to him for me
to hand the documents back to him. I thanked
Dr. Rhee and gave the documents over to him.

SKH

PA/H:SKH:FLB

December 20, 1941.

Reference PA/H's memorandum of December 16,
question of presentation to the President of Dr. Syngman
Rhee's credentials as official representative in the
United States of the provisional government of the
Republic of Korea.

FE is of the opinion that it would be preferable not
to undertake to make a definitive decision on this question
at this time, but to defer such definitive decision until
the subject of the restoration of the independence of
Korea can be thoroughly studied and, in the light of that
study, this Government adopts a definite policy toward
Korea. In that study it would seem desirable to take into
account, for example, factors such as the attitude toward
Korean independence of China, Russia, Great Britain, and
perhaps our other associates in the war. Isolated action
on our part might involve responsibilities which in the
light of later events it might have been better for this
Government not to have assumed.

In the meantime FE believes that it would be preferable
that Dr. Rhee's credentials be returned to him with the
statement that the question of their presentation to the
President cannot, in the nature of things, be decided in
a hurry. While FE considers that the action suggested in
the preceding sentence is the most advisable course, it
perceives no strong objection to the acceptance by the
Department of Dr. Rhee's credentials. Should this be done,
it is suggested that it be made clear to Dr. Rhee that the
credentials are simply being placed on file in this Department
as record of documents received by the Department.

There is attached a draft telegram to Chungking (in
very confidential code) directing the Ambassador to learn
what he can of the provisional government of the Republic
of Korea and of its organization and physical following.

FE:Langdon:HES

Reference, attached copy of a
telegram to Chungking and Mr. Hoskins'
penciled inquiry.

On January 2, 1942 Dr. Rhee
told me that a Colonel Zia had
recently become an assistant
military attaché at the Chinese
Embassy in Washington. He said
that Colonel Zia is particularly
well informed as to the "Korean
Provisional Government" and had
had dealings with that organization
in Chungking.

The Division of Protocol informs
me that Colonel Zia Yee Chen has been
listed by the Chinese Embassy since
May 22, 1941 as an assistant officer
in the office of the Military Attaché.
Colonel Zia's name does not appear in
the blue book and he is not regarded
as having diplomatic status.

PA/H:AHiss:BGT

IMPORTERS

CHINESE — PERSIAN

ORIENTAL RUGS AND CARPETS

LINENS AND ART GOODS

900 S. WABASH AVENUE
CHICAGO, ILL., U.S.A.

PHONE WABASH
CABLE ADDRESS
"DONGHAHN CHICAGO"
COMMERCIAL
BENTLEY'S

Suite 210 - 245 Fifth Ave.,
New York City, N. Y.
March 19th, 1942

Mr. Harold B. Hoskins,
Foreign Activity Co-Relation,
Department of State,
Washington, D. C.

Dear Mr. Hoskins:

I am glad to take this opportunity to thank you for your many kindnesses extended to me during my several interviews with you.

Ever since I became acquainted with you, I have given you my honest opinion as to the personalities and the relationships of the different Korean political organixations in this country and in the Far East.

I also have been trying my best to unite the different factions in order to give our maximum service to the United States in her efforts to win the war. I am glad to inform you there is a good prospect in the near future of accomplishing that end.

I plan to return to Washington the first of next week, and I shall be glad to pay my respects to you again.

With my sincere appreciation and gratitude for your personal interest in the Korean cause, in which I hope you will further avail yourself of my knowledge and services, I am,

Sincerely yours,

SOON K. HAHN

I have seen Maj. Moore

SKH/MH

WA 17

WT WASHINGTON DC 815A APR 28 1942

PRESIDENT FRANKLIN D ROOSEVELT

WHITE HOUSE WASHINGTON DC

CONGRATUALTIONS FOR BOMBING TOKYO WE KOREAN KNOW DEMOCRACY WILL

WIN. WE PLEDGE OUR ALL TO USA VICTORY

KILSOO HAAN SINO KOREAN PEOPLES LEAGUE.

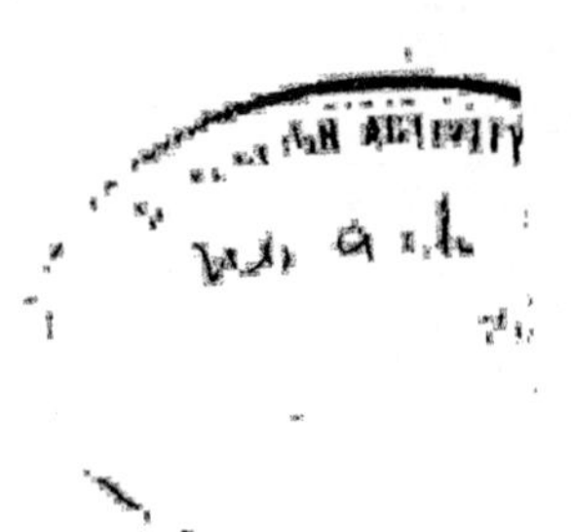

DEPARTMENT OF STATE

FOREIGN ACTIVITY CORRELATION

April 28, 1942.

MEMORANDUM

A-B - Mr. Berle

If you agree with the reasoning in the attached memorandum, I
hope you will continue to urge the
sending of the original telegram
or at least the compromise suggestion rather than the new draft
proposed by FE and Eu.

Harold B. Hoskins

April 28, 1942.

<u>MEMORANDUM</u>

A-B: Mr. Berle

"DIPLOMATIC DEFENSIVE WILL NOT WIN THE WAR"

(To paraphrase the title of a recent book)

The telegram regarding Korean Independence that you initialled has been thoroughly emasculated in the new draft attached. This has been done

    (a) by elimination of the last sentence in paragraph five, page four that stated this Government's willingness to join with China and other United Nations immediately concerned in announcing support for Korea's aspirations to freedom.

    (b) by elimination of the next to last sentence of paragraph six on page five stating that if China should recognize a Provisional Government of Korea this Government would re-examine its position in the light of that new step.

I still hope that the telegram as originally drafted can be sent, however, with an additional sentence to be added to paragraph five. This sentence makes point three of the Atlantic Charter the basis for the suggested action; and since both Great Britain and Russia have accepted the principles of this document, there would appear to be no reason for their objecting to our proposal or for their not being advised in advance of our proposed plan.

The reasoning that might be suggested in support of such action follows a line of aggressive political warfare

fare to aid our still limited military efforts rather than of more defensive diplomatic action. It may be summarized as follows:

(1) To win this war we must aim at obtaining full support and active, not passive, assistance from all peoples everywhere who oppose or can be induced to oppose the Axis.

(2) Our experience in the Far East particularly has indicated that where these peoples have definite assurances of freedom they will effectively aid our united cause - e.g. China and the Philippines. On the other hand, where no such assurances of freedom have been given - Burma, Malaya, Dutch East Indies to mention three examples - the native populations have not given the active assistance that might have turned defeat into victory.

(3) Chiang Kai-Chek returning from India and Burma has concluded that recognition of a Provisional Government of Korea would be advisable and helpful to our cause. It would seem that his judgment in this matter might, in the absence of serious objections, warrant our active support of this political effort rather than a "safe" and more negative statement.

(4) There are 21,000,000 Koreans, many of whom admittedly can never be expected to give us effective active assistance, but this again would not appear to be a valid reason for our not trying to gain from them the greatest measure of support possible for our war effort.

(5) The Atlantic Charter and the Declaration of United Nations, Mr. Roosevelt has stated, apply to all parts of the world and therefore include Korea. Even if the recognition of Korea's aspiration to freedom did prove of only limited practical value it is likely to prove of even greater value in helping us to gain the active support of other Asiatic populations whose help we need to win this war. To them this step can be effective evidence of the sincerity of our pledges and an honest specific application of the general principles of the Atlantic Charter.

(6) Since

(6)   Since British diplomacy in this Asiatic area can hardly claim to have given very effective results, their opposition to the more aggressive policy proposed by the Generalissimo is probably subject to change; and their stand might be more readily reversed if this Government indicated its willingness at least to make a statement regarding Korea's aspiration to freedom even if no Provisional Government were recognized.

If, in spite of the above reasoning, it is decided that we are not at the moment ready to go as far as suggested in the original telegram can we not go at least part way and leave the matter of a final decision on our part for re-consideration if China acts as she plans? A revision of the telegram along these lines has been prepared and is attached herewith.

I should like to make one final point on the policy proposed in regard to Korea. We have for months been trying to find a formula for dealing more effectively with various free movements in this country. We wish on the one hand to rally to our aid all the latent opposition to the Axis of aliens in the United States, in this hemisphere, and even within the Axis-occupied or controlled territories. On the other hand, we are also anxious, so far as we can, to obtain such support without the accompanying responsibility of _our_ having to choose from among perhaps several aspirants one individual or group to whom some form of "recognition" might be given. If the suggestion made in this Korean case were adopted, it would appear that a similar policy might with advantage be applied to other free movements - of recognizing the aspiration of a people to freedom without at the same time recognizing specifically any individual or group that might at some later date prove unacceptable to the people of their country of origin.

Harold B. Hoskins

A-B/HHBH:VRC

SINO-KOREAN PEOPLES LEAGUE
101 D Street N.E.
Washington, D.C.

His Excellency Cordell Hull,
Secretary of State
Department of State
Washington D. C.

May 5, 1942

Your Excellency:

The Sino-Korean Peoples' League, representing the newly formed Korean National Front Federation, composed of four Korean political parties in the Far East, do humbly and sincerely submit to your Excellency the aims and activities outlined by the Sixth Plenary Session of the Korean National Revolutionary Congress recently held in Chungking, China.

We submit the following eleven points in the belief and hope that it will be of some value to your Excellency in the decision of arriving at some effective policy giving aid or aids to the Korean National Front Federation in their fight against our common enemy, Japan.

The Eleven Points:

1. To overthrow Japanese Imperialist rule and to establish in Korea a free, independent and a democratic republic.

2. To summon a peoples' assembly which is to frame a constitution and make arrangement for holding a general election.

3. To eliminate the vestiges of old feudal system, detrimental to the future welfare of Korea.

4. To confiscate the property of all Japanese imperialists.

5. To afford special protection for the welfare and business enterprises of those citizens who have opposed the Axis Powers interests.

6. To institute an agrarian policy and redistribute the land among the tenants and farmers.

7. To reduce working hours and put into force various measures of social security for the benefit of the workers.

8. To establish political, economic and social equality of the sexes.

9. To institute freedom of speech, publication, assembly and of worship.

10. To institute compulsory education, vocational training and social insurance at the expense of the State.

11. To seek cooperation with all countries on a basis of equality, mutual assistance in the security of national defense, in the pursuit of peace and happiness of mankind.

The eleven points were unanimously approved and accepted by all four Korean party representatives. These representatives represented large numbers of Koreans in Siberia, North China, Manchuria, Korea and Japan.

We Urge America to Face Reality in the Far East

More than five months have elapsed since the Jap Envoy Kurusu sang the Pearl Harbor lullaby song to the officials of the United States. And as reported by our men in Japan last March, 1941, Japan did carry out its "U.S.-Japan War Plan":

"There must be diplomatic conversation as usual in some form or other, at least until the initiation of military action...During the first period of four months the Japanese fleet will be free to carry on its activities throughout the Pacific and there will exist no strong opposing forces in the Pacific to interfere." Quotations from the book "How Japan Plans to Win" pages 202 and 208.

Unless America soon checks the Japs they will soon be in all strategic position to attack the Aleutians, Alaska, Hawaii and the Pacific Coast States. Based on the Jap War Plan the first period of U.S.-Japan war is over, the second period will soon begin.

If the Department of State will check the reports of our agents during the past years your Excellency will realize that the time and events did prove that their reports were of much value to the United States security. It will further show that these Koreans will be of much value to America now more than in the past. Their strategic positions in Japan and Korea should not be overlooked.

Though the United States officials ignored their warning reports in past years, I have been asked to convey this message to your Excellency. These patriotic Koreans' message declared: "Every sense of our loyalty and honor oblige us to offer our services to the cause of America and Korea to win this war. We pledge full cooperation with your honorable government to clear out from the Far East and in the Pacific waters our mutual enemy, Japan."

America's diplomatic records will show that in the early period of the American Korean diplomatic relationship America took a realistic policy in the Far East. Immediately after the signing of the American Korean Treaty, May 22, 1882, the Hon. John Russell Young, minister to China, wrote to the Department of State these wise and realistic words: "I think it very important that the U.S. should have a footing in Korea and that having opened the door we should not close it or give any other power precedence."

The treaty had in it these innocent but fateful words which so often in diplomatic documents may mean much or nothing according to interpretation: "If other powers deal unjustly or oppressively with either government the other will exert its good offices, on being informed of the case, to bring about an amicable arrangement, thus showing its friendly feelings."

Perhaps it was fate, that the U.S.A. chose to ignore its moral if not its legal obligation toward Korea. Perhaps again it was fate, - why the State Department in recent years ignored the Koreans' continued warning reports, even up to the eve of the Japanese attack on Pearl Harbor last December 7, 1941.

Time and events have taught all peace loving citizens of the United States to awaken to the fact that only effective unity of purpose and unity of quick action alone will defeat the Axis Powers. In so doing even small countries like Korea in the Far East should not be overlooked. In 1904 Japan declared, Korea was "pistol pointed at the heart of Japan". Today, because England and America ignored Korea and the geo-strategic position of Korea, this same pistol is pointed at the heart of China and Siberia. Restore Korea to its former status, again Korea will be the "pistol pointed at the heart of Japan".

Internationally speaking, Korea has become both the exponent and the finu
example of Japanese totalitarian ambition.

Willard Price a few years ago wrote these prophetic words for all of us t(
and think:
"Those who wish to get a glimpse of the trend of future events in Asia sho
not neglect to study that vivid object lesson, Korea."

The international events of the past decade proved beyond doubt that - because
England and America blindly aided and built up Japan at the expense of their ow
security and the security of Korea and of China, today we are facing the brute i
of the "Frankenstein" Japan.   Therefore morally, spiritually and legally, unles
England and America realize their mistakes and win this war against Japan, there
be no lasting peace in the Pacific.   "Reason and free inquiry are the only effec
agents against error", advised Thomas Jefferson.

<u>Everywhere Koreans Beg America for a Chance to Fight the Japs</u>
In the blood of all good Koreans flows a hatred of all things Japanese - a
hatred that dates back three hundred fifty years to a day in 1592 when three hun
thousand Jap soldiers on orders from the regent Hideyoshi, swarmed the coasts of
ancient Kingdom of Korea, laying waste her cities, her farmlands and treasure. T
all Korea is under the bondage of Japan - and today, as all Koreans have for ten
generations back, the man of Korea still lives for the day when he can settle the
score for three and a half centuries of humiliation against the Jap.   Koreans ar
a distinct people, being neither like their ancient friends, the Chinese, nor lik
their ancient enemies, the Japs.

In the backyard of the Jap strategic military naval and air bases, millions
Koreans are eager to do what they can to defeat the Japs.

America Can Help Koreans to Reorganize the Refugee Provisional Government in Chin

In March 1, 1919 within 10 years after annexation of Korea by Japan, the Kore
in Korea revolted against the Japanese overlords.   Soon it established a Korean Pr
sional Government in Shanghai, China.   As adverse circumstances and events were
forced upon them, the Korean Provisional Government moved whenever and wherever th
Chinese Nationalist Government moved.   During the past 23 years the Koreans were
forced to undergo much hardship.   Numerous appeals to England and America were
repeatedly made.   Time after time England and America closed their diplomatic doo
against the Korean patriots.

Due to continuous and constant rebuff met by these struggling patriots, they
were forced to seek help wherever and from whomever they can get such help to figh
the Japs.   In the meantime, dissension forced many Koreans to break with the Provi
sional Government.   Some turned to Soviet Russia and some to China.   As a result of
these unavoidable political, economic and diplomatic difficulties two schools of
thought have carried on the war on Japan, each believing that their method would
eventually win the hearts of the Democratic Powers to assist them to whip Japan out
of Korea.   Since 1938 the Chinese Nationalist Government has given financial aid t
the Korean Volunteer Army in China, under the command of Commander Yak San Kim.

Koreans like all nationals and races struggling for freedom and independence
under similar political and economic conditions have met regrettable experiences an
the existence of some disunity among themselves.   History shows the French revoluti
leaders, the Chinese revolution leaders and the Soviet revolutionary governments t
faced similar internal political and governmental problems as the Koreans now face.
The struggles of these patriots were many, they have reaped dissension among fellow
patriots, doubt - even civil wars and the bitter price of costly mistakes.   Soviet
Russia and China both bear the scars of political, social, economic and religious
struggles for freedom and independence.

Remember Early Period of U. S. Revolutionary Leaders

Even this great country, the U.S.A., was torn with dissension. One wonders if the American Revolutionary leaders did not get the moral and material aid from some Europeans and European Powers if they could have won the Revolutionary war in 8 years? Perhaps George Washington may have had to undergo a few more "Valley Forges". Even today one can with a little imagination hear the challenging voice of Benjamin Franklin: "Either we all hang together or hang separately."

Some U. S. officials repeatedly say that the Koreans are not united, they are trying to use this as an issue in refusing to give early consideration to aiding Koreans to fight the Japs. Koreans are not angels, we as the American forefathers did, are forced to undergo the unavoidable transition of political growth. Americans are apt to forget, while the U.S. has fought the Japs only 5 months, the Koreans have been fighting the Japs since 1910.

After the Jap "stab in the back" attack on Pearl Harbor, Dec. 7, 1941, several conferences were held, written appeals were made; with prayers, faith, hope and great anxiety we have waited for an official reply, one way or another. We pray our prayers and appeals have not been made in vain. Korea needs America's moral and material aid now as did the American forefathers. We sincerely and most humbly once more submit this plea for an early reply and for a favorable consideration by the Department of State soon.

Whatever the reason or excuse the U. S. officials have in delaying the use of millions of Koreans who are so anxiously awaiting U.S. official O.K. - Koreans everywhere pray and urge the United States to attack Japan at her heart. I say this, knowing full well that when the American bombers range over the industrial cities of Jap-dominated Korea my people will be killed. But I say, and my people say, let it come - we would rather die by American bombs than live as servants to the Japanese.

In the interest of effective cooperation and for an early and complete victory of the United Nations against the Axis Powers,

Gratefully yours,

KILSOO K. HAAN

Korean National Front Federation
Korean Volunteer Army in China
Sino-Korean Peoples League

SINO-KOREAN PEOPLES' LEAGUE

TRinidad 8500   101 D Street, N. E.   Lincoln 5187
WASHINGTON, D. C

May 4, 1942

SOO K. HAAN
— Representative

Honorable Maxwell Hamilton
Chief, Far Eastern Division
Department of State
Washington D.C

My dear Honorable Hamilton;

The New Korea a bilingual Korean weekly published in Los Angeles, Calif in its April 30 1942 - issue under the caption of (In Korean

"Special Notice
Census Of Koreans

The gist of the article (You can have it translated say that; According to the Korean Commission in Washington D.C (headed by Dr. Syngman Rhee) the Commission has asked the Koreans to sent out the Census Questionaires as soon as possible

The reason of this Korean Census and the haste are that the U. S. State Department

SINO-KOREAN PEOPLES' LEAGUE

2

likewise requires this Census taking
as the Korean Commission do, because
of the following two reasons.

First: To get an accurate number
of Koreans in Hawaii and America

Second: Aside from the possibility of getting
some help after the census when a person
get into difficulty — it would mean
personal help to the Korean who comply,
with this Census Requirement.

One of the significant matter
would be if after the completion of
this Korean Census of all Koreans in
overseas area — when a person have
neglected to do so or have done so,
there will arise much personal
difficulties befall on the person who
have refused or neglected to comply
to this Korean Census.

Obviously any thinking layman can see what
would this mean — it is purely and simply

3

an attempt to indirectly force the control of all the Koreans in Hawaii, America under the "Political Power" of the Korean Commission (Dr. Syngman Rhee) and his political groups namely the United Korea Committee – of which Rhee and his group are now in control.

Please Let Us Know The Truth.

This same group and this same weekly (New Korea) in the past published articles saying that Senator Gunse have introduced resolutions in the Senate to recognize the Korean Provisional Government. Another Weekly "The Pacific Weekly" – Dr. Rhee's official organ published on Jan. 2?, 1942 – that Congressman Faddis of Penn – introduced a Resolution in the House of Representative that Korean Provisional Government be recognized.

Both these publications, published false & both news items were refuted as not a fact. Congressman Faddis – emphatically denied & personally to me in writing

May I also call your attention that the

SINO-KOREAN PEOPLES' LEAGUE

4.

same United Korean Committee — a yes man Committee of Dr. Syngman Rhee published articles on several occasion gave out special notice that "Any Korean who have the means but refuse to donate money to the United Korean Committee will be considered enemy to Korea

Based upon the past acts of falsity in their attempt to create the impression to the Koreans that the Korean Commission and the United Korean Committees acts are approved by the State Department and other U.S. Governmental officials —

We desire to know the truth — whether or not the State Department have requested or have conveyed the State Departments desire to have all the Koreans to submit to this Korean Census under the United Korean Committee and the Korean Commission in Washington D.C.

If so, Does it mean all the Koreans must comply to their request? Will the Koreans who refuse be made miserable? What about the U.S. 1940 Census?

Kindly let me know soon — Gratefully Yours

Kilsoo K. Haan

May 8, 1942

reply refer to
/H

My dear Mr. Haan:

I refer to your letter of May 4 to Mr. Hamilton in regard to a notice of a census of Koreans which appeared in the April 20 issue of "New Korea".

Matters relating to the census of persons in the United States are outside of the jurisdiction of the State Department, and the Department has no knowledge of the census referred to in your letter.

Sincerely yours,

Harold B. Hoskins
Executive Assistant

Mr. Kilsoo K. Haan,
Washington Representative,
Sino-Korean People's League,
101 D Street, N.E.,
Washington, D. C.

Phoenix, Arizona
May 8th 1942.

DEPARTMENT OF STATE
Washington, D. C.

"HAROLD B. HOSKINS Esq.
Executive Assistant,

Dear Sir:

It may be presumptuous on my part
in addressing you further in regard Korea,
and help to the Korean people. However, it
is of such personal concern to me that I
would offer as a suggestion certain matters
as herein stated.

(I) Under the Land Lease plan now in full
operation by this government, toward other
nations, what method or plan could be instituted
wherein small bands of guerrilla soldiers
recruited from the Provisional Army, provided
with proper equipment and divided into platoons
or companies, with full instructions to infil-
trate the occupied country, harass and destroy
all and every thing used and useful to the
Japanese in their occupation. To arouse the people

a of the Korean people.

o increase this help as time goes on and
tions warrant such action by the United
tes.

he country is especially adapted to such
dure, mountainous in most part, and difficult
ness. In its remote regions they could
r on and work most effectively, doing much
to the Japanese occupational forces.

Young men from the Provisional Army selected
ir service training, thereby learn to them
plements of war essential in this terrible
list.

Some recognition of the Korean Provisional
rnment, publicly proclaiming interest and
dship in their just cause, something in manner
s Free French.

All this can be done in one way only, that is
rsonal contact with the people exiled in China,
y people familiar with all conditions pertaining
ch a venture, knowing first hand the points
laces most vulnerable, seasons and time formation,
probability of success in any given direction.

Caution should be used in that no advance notice
ven to any one who by word or act would inform

action strike fast and effectively, and all this

will tend to hold up the morals of the people,

soldiers and crews.

This may all appear confusing to you

Mr. Secretary; but I am firmly of the opinion that

a great help would be accomplished by some of the

matters set out herein.

Believe me , I am

Respectfully Yours

C. Jhung

612 South Seventh Street
Phoenix, Arizona.

May 12, 1942

Dear Mr. Jhung:

Thank you for your letter of May 8, 1942 and for your further suggestions regarding Korea. This matter is at present under consideration, and I shall see that in this connection your letter is brought to the attention of the proper officials.

Sincerely yours,

Harold B. Hoskins
Executive Assistant

Mr. C. Jhung,
125 South Seventh Street,
Phoenix, Arizona.

A-B/H:HBH:RW:JKF   5/12/42

May 14, 1942

Mr. George A. Gordon
Acting Chief, Division of
  Foreign Activity Correlation
Room 178
Department of State
Washington, D. C.

Dear Mr. Gordon:

  I am transmitting herewith a
copy of Report No. 41, "Korean Independence Movement," prepared in the Research
and Analysis Branch of the Coordinator's
office, and classified as confidential.

      Sincerely yours,

      William L. Langer
      Acting Director, Branch
      of Research and Analysis

Enclosure

KOREAN INDEPENDENCE MOVEMENT

The following brief survey of the Korean independence movement includes a short history of the growth of the independence parties, recent developments in the movement in China and the current situation in America.

I. HISTORICAL SURVEY OF KOREAN INDEPENDENCE PARTIES

Organized movements for the freeing of Korea from Japanese domination began in 1919, although their origins reach back before that date. On March 1, 1919, a group of leading Koreans signed and made public a declaration of Korean independence, while their countrymen throughout the peninsula celebrated the event by shouting and waving flags. The Japanese were completely surprised. They ruthlessly crushed what they feared would be an armed revolt and killed and imprisoned thousands of the people. Other thousands fled.

From the beginning there were two viewpoints as to how Koreans should oppose the Japanese conquest. One group operated underground, secretly planning to kill, sabotage, strike and destroy the Japanese on every available occasion. They were the direct-actionists, the Korean guerrillas. The other group hoped for a more peaceful fulfillment of their aims, and in about 1919 organized a refugee Provisional Government in Changhai. Its main purpose was to enlist the support of other powers in resurrecting Korea. There was no conflict in the beginning between these two groups; each was doing its part for Korea.

One of the famous early Korean rebels in Manchuria was YI Tonghwi, who even before 1919, had organized many guerrilla bands and had incessantly fought the Japanese. One of his associates after 1919 was KIM Yuksan, the present leader of the Korean partisans in China, and another was YI Chiengch'on, now General-in-chief of the Korean Provisional Government Army. Thousands of Koreans followed these men into Manchuria and many of them crossed the border into Soviet Siberia as well. Korean colonies, composed of refugees who had fled from Korea during the earlier years of Japanese occupation, were thus rapidly enlarged.

The Korean Provisional Government in Shanghai elected Dr. Syngman Rhee (YI Sungman) president and selected YI Tonghwi to head the military activity of the new government, with the title of Prime Minister. Differences in opinion among the members soon resulted in a split. Dr. Rhee soon left Shanghai and later organized the Tongji-hoe (Korean Comrades Association) in Honolulu. Those who opposed Rhee belonged to the Kungmin-hoe (Korean National Association) with headquarters in San Francisco and later in Los Angeles. Before long these rival groups, both of which were related to the Provisional Government, were at odds. The Korean National Association was fathered by AN Ch'angho, one of the ministers of the original Provisional Government and the man who replaced Rhee in leadership there. Another important leader was KIM Kyusik, a well-educated patriot who opposed Rhee and was also a member of the original cabinet. He was sent by the Provisional Government to Versailles in 1919 and has since continued to be active in various independence movements.

The chief differences between the Korean Comrades Association and the Korean National Association seem to have been these: (1) Personal rivalry between Syngman Rhee (YI Sungman) and KIM Kyusik, with AN Ch'angho favoring KIM, but mediating between them to maintain solidarity; (2) Syngman Rhee and the Korean Comrades Association were dominantly south Korean, while KIM Kyusik, AN Ch'angho and the Korean National Association were dominantly north Korean; (3) Syngman Rhee's group stressed the importance of diplomacy and foreign recognition in the struggle for independence, while the other group thought that self-improvement and the education of Korean leadership at home and abroad was more important.

In 1924 in Shanghai, representatives of various Korean groups met together to plan a joint program and to unite their combined forces. The direct-actionist groups, which had become quite leftist in ideology, were represented also. No common ground was found. The result of this conference seems to have been to estrange still more the various groups rather than to bring them together. The Provisional Government which survived was still largely dominated by the AN Ch'angho group, and KIM Kyusik went over to the side of the leftist groups.

Although AN Ch'angho failed to achieve unity among the Koreans at this time, he was able to extend his influence into Korea in a very active way. Under Governor-General Saito the Japanese policy in Korea had been liberalized. Permission was therefore granted for the organization of the Young Korea Academy, a society devoted to advancing the physical, intellectual and moral growth of the youth of Korea. AN Ch'angho had long held up this ideal, and, although he was a refugee, he worked indefatigably to promote the Academy. His lieutenant who went to Korea was YI Kwangsu. The Young Korea Academy, whose membership included the leading Koreans within Korea, was therefore unofficially related to the Korean National Association and the then declining Korean Provisional Government. Although the Academy could not officially engage in political activity in Korea, it promoted Korean nationalism in many ways, such as in the study of Korean language and history and in encouraging young Koreans to excel in sports. In 1937 this society was disbanded by government order.

During this period the direct-actionists were becoming

better organized and increasingly active. Some of the leaders attended military schools in Russia and China. The largest group of these partisans were called the Yinul-dan (Heroic Retribution Society), and they operated chiefly in Manchuria and Siberia, where they had a large following in the Chientao region and in the Maritime Province. This organization was communistic. It carried on extensive propaganda even in Korea among students and laborers. Its leader was KIM Yaksan one of the earlier associates of YI Tonghwi. (YI Tonghwi died in 1928.)

After 1931, when Japan occupied Manchuria, the activity of Korean nationalist groups accelerated. Dr. Phee went to Geneva to plead Korea's cause. The Provisional Government was reorganized under the presidency of KIM Ku, while AN Ch'angho continued to guide its activity. In 1932 (after the Shanghai bombing incident, when a bomb hurled by a Korean killed and injured several prominent Japanese officials) AN Ch'angho was captured by the Japanese authorities and sent to Korea for trial. After several years imprisonment, he was released on parole, and despite the restrictions, he had much influence upon other Koreans until his death in 1938.

During the early 1930's the direct-action groups became especially active in Manchuria. They joined the Chinese who were fighting the Japanese and grew rapidly in numbers. KIM Yaksan became the acknowledged leader of these groups when a "united front" was formed in 1936. KIM Kyusik, who had heretofore been active in the Provisional Government group, was also associated with them as a "spiritual godfather."

II. RECENT DEVELOPMENTS IN THE INDEPENDENCE MOVEMENT IN CHINA

A new chapter began in 1937. The Provisional Government and the Korean Volunteer Corps, as KIM Yaksan's followers who had joined the Chinese partisans came to be called, both were aided by the Chinese. It is reported that Generalissimo Chiang Kai-shek provided special transportation for the Koreans of the Provisional Government and their associates when they evacuated Shanghai and Hanking. The Generalissimo and his wife financially aided the organization of a Korean Provisional Government Army in 1939, officered by Koreans but commanded by Chinese. Reports vary as to the size of this army. The Generalissimo is also reported to have aided the Korean Volunteer Corps. Various Korean guerrilla units are given important assignments in north China as the occasional news from China indicates. The total number of Koreans now fighting or training to fight with both the Provisional Government Army and the Volunteer Corps is estimated by responsible Koreans to be about 35,000 men. The number is reportedly increasing rapidly. There are also a great number of Koreans in various units of the Soviet Far Eastern Army, an unverified estimate being 40,000 men.

There is apparently still a strong rivalry between the Provisional Government supporters and the Korean Volunteer Corps. The main differences are these: (1)In economic ideology, the Provisional Government is conservative and the Volunteer Corps is radical; (2) the Provisional Government is dominated by older men who hark back to the "old" Korean philosophy and way of life, and are still inclined to depend upon aid from abroad, whereas the Volunteer Corps is young and vigorous and has very little use for old Korean customs and still believes in direct action; (3)personal affiliations and loyalties which have been strong for many years likewise separate the two groups.

III. RECENT DEVELOPMENTS IN AMERICA

Unity among Koreans in America has been more effectively achieved than in China. The two major parties, the Korean National Association and the Korean Comrades Association, both of which are conservative, began to work together after 1939. Probably the real reason for the new-found friendship was the threatening growth of a minority group representing the Korean Volunteer Corps. In 1933, KIM Kyusik, the famous patriot who had turned from the Provisional Government to the direct-actionist, came to America where he stimulated the activity of the direct-actionist sympathizers. The Korean Comrades Association had been the strongest group in Hawaii, while the Korean National Association was strongest in the United States proper. These two societies soon realized that they were in danger, especially after Kilsoo Haan (HAN Kilsu, a very active propagandist, supported by several direct-actionist groups (nominally the Sino-Korean People's League of Hawaii), came to Washington and began to gain the spotlight. Dr. Rhee, who had for sometime been in Washington, was tacitly recognized as the spokesman for Korea by the Korean National Association as well as the Korean Comrades Association.

In 1940 and 1941, Mr. C. Ho Kim (KIM Ho), a wealthy farmer of California, together with several other leaders, started a movement for unification. Mr. Kim had formerly been a Comrades Association man, but had changed to the National Association. He was anxious that all Korean groups be represented in a united organization, including those supporting the Korean Volunteer Corps. A conference was held in April 1941 in Los Angeles. The outcome of this conference was the organization of the United Korean Committee in America (Yonhap-hoe), officially representing nine Korean nationalist organizations:

(1) Kungmin-hoe (Korean National Association)
(2) Tongji-hoe (Korean Comrades Association)
(3) Tongnip-tang (Korean Independence Party)
(4) Kungmin-tang (Korean Nationalist Party)
(5) Uiyongdan (League to Aid Korean Volunteers in China)
(6) Sino-Korean People's League
(7) Women's Auxiliary, Korean National Association
(8) Women's Auxiliary, Korean Comrades Association
(9) Women's Auxiliary, League to Aid Korean Volunteers in China

Several of these were women's auxiliaries, but the Committee in-

cluded members from the Korean Comrades Association, Korean
National Association and the League to Aid Korean Volunteers in
China. Mr. C. Ho Kim was elected chairman and four sub-commit-
tees were selected: (1) Defense, (2) Public Relations, (3)
Finance and (4) Executive. The organizations represented (including the Sino-Korean People's League) decided to pool their
financial resources and to support both Dr. Rhee and Mr. Kilsoo
Haan as Washington agents. Rhee was paid $200 and Haan $150 per
month. The Korean Provisional Government in Chungking approved
of this representation.

Smooth progress in unity was not to be the result,
however. Rhee and Haan differed widely in temperament and aims
and cooperated perfunctorily. The direct-action minority com-
plained on inadequate representation in the United Korean Committee. In January 1942 two members of the Committee were sent
from Los Angeles to Washington to investigate certain charges
against Kilsoo Haan. They recommended that the Committee stop
supporting him, and their recommendation was approved. Dr. Rhee's
salary and office allowance, however, was raised to $600 per month.

Despite the ouster of Mr. Haan by the Committee, the
League to Aid Korean Volunteers in China did not immediately
secede, although one of its members resigned. Mr. D. S. Shinn,
another of its representatives, kept his membership in the Committee. Mr. Haan went to California in February and returned
to Washington early in April. He claims that he urged his
followers not to take any disunifying action. Recent information (April 14, 1942), however, indicates that they have formally
withdrawn from the United Korean Committee. There are thus two
major parties in this country, the United Korean Committee and
the League to Aid Korean Volunteers in China.

Excerpt from the Chinese News Service,
New York, of May 23, 1942.

__Korea.__

KOREAN STRENGTH IN FREE CHINA
CONSOLIDATED UNDER ONE COMMAND

CHUNGKING, May 21 (CNS)....With a view to
consolidating the Korean revolutionary strength the
National Military Council has ordered the incorporation
of the Korean Volunteer Corps into the Korean Independent
Army. It will be renamed "First Flying Column" of the
Korean Independent Army and will be placed under the
direct command of General Li Ching-tien, Commander-in-
Chief of the army. General Kim Yak-shan, Commander of
the Korean Volunteer Corps will be deputy Commander-in-
Chief of the army.

DEPARTMENT OF STATE

DIVISION OF FAR EASTERN AFFAIRS

May 29, 1942.

The underlying press report from Chungking of May 21 indicates a step toward
unification of the two principal Korean
groups. According to this report, the
National Military Council has ordered the
incorporation of the Korean Volunteer Corps
into the Korean Independent Army. The
Korean Volunteer Corps, under the leadership of Kim Yak-shan, has not heretofore
been associated with the "Korean Provisional
Government" but has been regarded as belonging to the so-called radical Korean groups
in Manchuria.

FE:Salisbury:MJK

- 263 -

CHINESE NEWS SERVICE

1250 6TH AVENUE

NEW YORK, N. Y.

Phone: CIrcle 6-5225

Cable Address: SINONEWS

New York, May 23, 1942

VOICE OF CHINA
(China News by Shortwave Radio)

<u>War Communiques</u>

300 KILOMETER CHEKIANG FRONT ACTIVE;
ENEMY ESTIMATED AT 30 TO 40 THOUSAND

CHUNGKING, May 21 (CNS)....Japanese forces pushing in a southwesterly direction on the 300 kilometer front in East Chekiang are now about 80 kilometers from Kinhua which is apparently their main objective, declared the military spokesman at today's press conference in Chungking.

The spokesman revealed that the enemy, who launched his drive last Friday, had made an advance of approximately 80 kilometers by Sunday. Fighting is raging on the whole front with unabated severity. Chinese forces battling against great odds are doing their utmost to stem further enemy advances.

Referring to the total Japanese strength on this front the spokesman disclosed that so far five enemy divisional designations had been found. However, the enemy strength may not be as great as five divisions. It is believed that between 30,000 and 40,000 men are actually in the field with 40,000 or more held in reserve in Hangchow and its vicinity.

Divided into four columns the Japanese concentrated their main strength in the Chekiang-Kiangsi Railway zone. Here a Japanese column moved southward from Hsiaoshan on the south bank of the Chientang River and reached Chuki on Sunday. The enemy has now advanced to points southwest of Chuki.

Supporting this column another enemy contingent based at Fuyang and Yuhang near Hangchow battled its way along both banks of the Fuchun River. Farther to the east a fourth Japanese column from Fonghua, after advancing 40 kilometers southwest of Fonghua, is continuing its drive in the direction of Tientai.

The spokesman further disclosed that roughly 20,000 Japanese had lately concentrated in the Nanchang area in Kiangsi. The purpose of this concentration, he said, is unascertainable as they have not yet made any move. Should they make a drive eastward they may attempt to control the Chekiang-Kiangsi Railway, the spokesman said.

<u>Korea</u>

KOREAN STRENGTH IN FREE CHINA
CONSOLIDATED UNDER ONE COMMAND

CHUNGKING, May 21 (CNS)....With a view to consolidating the Korean revolutionary strength the National Military Council has ordered the incorporation of the Korean Volunteer Corps into the Korean Independent Army. It will be renamed "First Flying Colun" of the Korean Independent Army and will be placed under the direct command of General Li Ching-tien, Commander-in-Chief of the army. General Kim Yak-shan, Commander of the Korean Volunteer Corps will be deputy Commander-in-Chief of the army.

(Shortwave Broadcast, "Voice of China," over XGOY, Chinese International Broadcasting Station at Chungking, picked up by Chinese News Service; broadcast of May 21)

CHINESE NEWS SERVICE

1250 6TH AVENUE

NEW YORK, N.Y.

Phone: CIrcle 6-5225

Cable Address: SINONEWS

VOICE OF CHINA
(China News by Shortwave Radio)

W E E K L Y   I N D E X

May 18 to May 23, 1942

Excerpt from the <u>Chinese News Service</u>,
New York, of May 23, 1942.

<u>Korea</u>.

KOREAN STRENGTH IN FREE CHINA
CONSOLIDATED UNDER ONE COMMAND

      CHUNGKING, May 21 (CNS)....With a view to
consolidating the Korean revolutionary strength the
National Military Council has ordered the incorporation
of the Korean Volunteer Corps into the Korean Independent
Army. It will be renamed "First Flying Column" of the
Korean Independent Army and will be placed under the
direct command of General Li Ching-tien, Commander-in-
Chief of the army.- General Kim Yak-shan, Commander of
the Korean Volunteer Corps will be deputy Commander-in-
Chief of the army.

Propaganda – Radio

FEDERAL COMMUNICATIONS COMMISSION
WASHINGTON, D. C.

February 10, 1943

Mr. Bernard Guffler
Special Division, State Department
Washington, D. C.

Dear Mr. Guffler:

  Enclosed is an extraction from a recent broadcast which might be of interest to you.

       Very truly yours,

       Goodwin Watson,
       Chief, Analysis Division
       Foreign Broadcast Intelligence Service

Enclosure

Tokyo in Japanese at 240 AM 1/13 to West Coast of North America

In connection with the outrageous attack made on our hospital ship in Rangoon port, the enemy is again carrying out counter-propaganda. This incident concerning the attack made on the hospital ship exposes the real nature of the enemy by shedding the mask of love of humanity which the enemy professes and has aroused extreme indignation among government officials and civilians on the spot.

The outrageous acts of America and Britain do not limit themselves at this point. On Dec. 20 the enemy had carried out bombing attacks on civilians, moslems temples, and hospitals all of which are non-military installations.

The present attack on our hospital ship occurred despite the fact that our government had notified the enemy on this matter in accordance with International Law and the ship had been marked with the insignia of the Red Cross. Shortly after this outrageous act was reported the enemy now that this matter has reached this point is greatly excited and his carrying out a surprising false propaganda without any sense of humiliation saying that the ship subject to attack was not a hospital ship and was a merchantman of the 10,000-ton class.

Compared to the repeated outrageous acts of the enemy, our military has established a well equipped anti-airdraft emplacement even in the prison camp in Rangoon and consequently British prisoners interned are grateful to the magnanimous attitude of our forces.

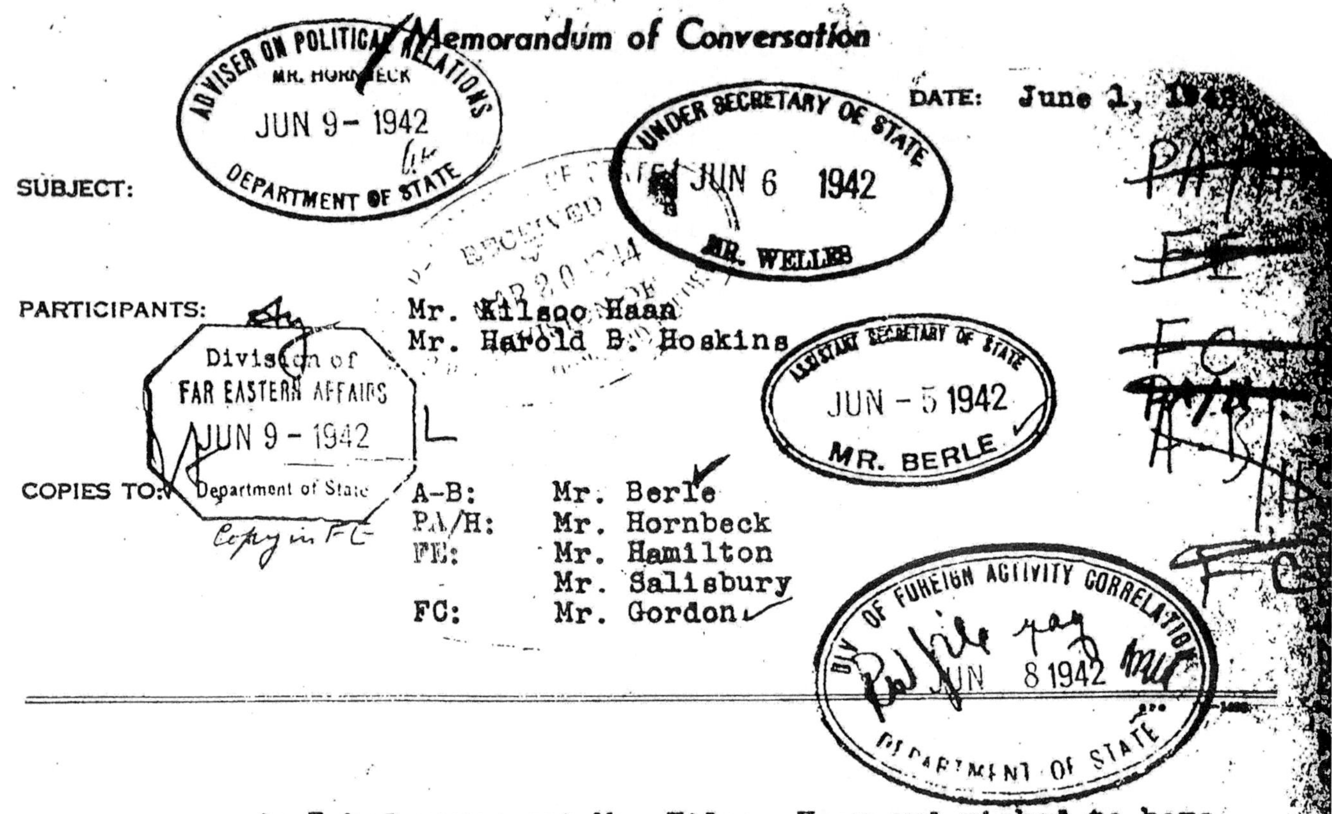

SUBJECT:

PARTICIPANTS: Mr. Kilsoo Haan
Mr. Harold B. Hoskins

COPIES TO: A-B: Mr. Berle
PA/H: Mr. Hornbeck
FE: Mr. Hamilton
Mr. Salisbury
FC: Mr. Gordon

As I had never met Mr. Kilsoo Haan and wished to have
a personal estimate of him, I telephoned him and asked him
to come in and see me at the State Department.

Mr. Haan gave me in considerable detail information
already in the State Department files regarding his past
activities and particularly the difficulties he ran into in
his attempt first to learn about Japanese penetration in
Hawaii and later in his unsuccessful efforts to impress on
American officials the dangers involved in the situation.
Mr. Haan brought with him a good sized scrap book containing letters and articles relating to his work. I gathered
that he has systematically made it a policy to get all the
publicity he could and have it available for future reference.

Later in the conversation Mr. Haan outlined his ideas
regarding Korea which again followed the lines of his
letters already in our files. The only new development
that came out of his conversation related to his recogni-
ion of the necessity for uniting the various Korean groups
together, in place of the open conflict that he realizes

has

has been damaging to the cause of Korean independence both in this country and in Chungking. As proof of his willingness to cooperate he gave me the same information referred to in Mr. Salisbury's memorandum of May 29 in regard to the incorporation of the Korean Volunteer Corps into the Korean Independent Army. He stated however that his efforts in this connection had been made very difficult by the announcement that the Korean Volunteer Corps had been dissolved whereas he had advised his supporters (many of whom had only reluctantly agreed) that it had not been dissolved but had been incorporated into the Korean Independent Army. Mr. Haan left with me a photostat of a letter from General Kim Yak-San in regard to this change. He also left with me a mimeographed copy of his radio talk of May 22 in regard to the American Korean Treaty. Both of these documents are attached to this memorandum.

I carried away from this conversation a definite impression that Mr. Haan, more clearly than before, felt the advisability of developing a united Korean front both in China and in the United States. At the same time he seemed to think there was little chance of Dr. Rhee's agreeing to such a step unless the State Department took the initiative by insisting on such a course. I expressed the opinion that any unity imposed from without would obviously hold only as long as the outside pressure was applied, and that any solution along these lines could hardly be considered a very sound one.

Harold B. Hoskins

A-B/H:HBH:JKF

朝　鮮　義　勇　隊

THE KOREAN VOLUNTEER CORPS

COMMANDER

Y. S. Kim

Chungking, Szechwan.

c/o Prof. Y. S. King
College of Agri.
National Central Univ.

Mr. Kilsoo Hann
Sino-Korean People' League
101 Street. N. E.
Washington, D. C.
U. S. A.

Dear Mr. Hann:-

I have received your letter of Nov. 6th. I agreed with you and at the same time I am accepting all of your demands. So far we have not co-operate with the Korean Provincial Government. It will take some time to co-operate with the old fellows. Time has not come for the Koreans in China to unify all of the revolutionists. Now The Korean Volunteer Corps is directly under the Chinese National Government Military Council and General Chiang Kai-Chek is directing our volunteers. Our volunteer Corps will be changed into Korean Army. As soon as our volunteer is changed into Army I will let you know at once.

Hoping you are struggle for the rights of the Koreans in the U. S. A.

With kind regards, I remain

Sincerely yours,

Yak San Kim

Commander of the Korean Volunteer Corps

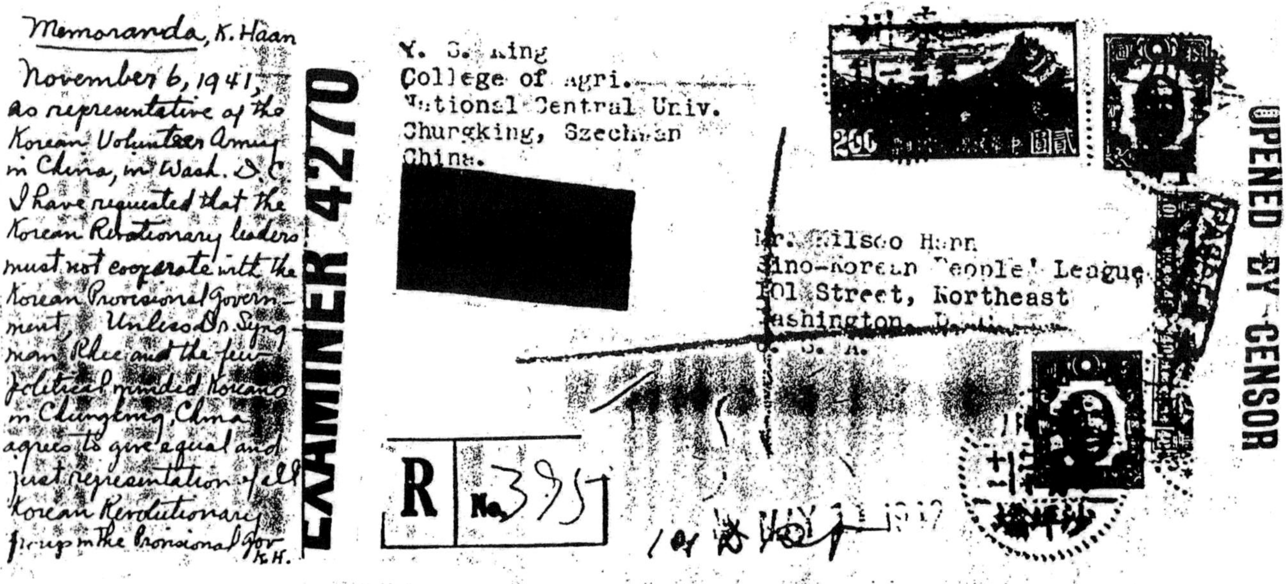

THE AMERICAN KOREAN TREATY

60 Years Old This Month 1882-1942

By KILSOO K. HAAN
Washington Representative
SINO-KOREAN PEOPLES LEAGUE
Radio Talk WINX 7:45 to 8 P.M. May 22, 1942

Since the attack on Pearl Harbor last December 7th, the forgotten people of Korea have loomed into the horizon in the Far East. Korea and the Koreans have become the topic of some serious consideration in the capital of the United Nations.

Sixty years ago the United States of America casually entered negotiating the American-Korean Treaty. Probably no treaty to which America entered has had greater influence on the course of events in the Far East. On its face, Commodore Shufeldt's convention was completely a harmless agreement providing for American seamen who might be shipwrecked on the coast of Korea, and for the opening of Korea to commercial and diplomatic intercourse with the West. From an international point of view, and in the light of subsequent events, the treaty of 1882 is seen to mark an important step in the rivalry of China and Japan over Korea, Russia over Korea.

The Treaty of 1882 was the first to be negotiated between Korea and any Western power and in this respect it marked a distinct break with traditions running back into distinct past. Korea no longer remained a Hermit Kingdom, she received the treaty with open arms and looked upon America as her benefactor.

American Korean Treaty Worth Reconsideration

Internationally speaking, Korea has become both the exponent and the finished example of Japanese totalitarian ambition. Willard Price a few years ago wrote: "Those who wish to get a glimpse of the trend of future events in Asia should not neglect to study that vivid object lesson, Korea."

Korea, or Chosen, is a Florida-like peninsula that hangs down from Manchuria, Southeast of the peninsula, across the island-dotted Korea Strait, lies Japan. About 23 million people live in Korea, which approximates Utah in size. Utah has a little over one-half of one million. That spells a good deal.

U. S. Realistic Attitude in 1882

About the time the new treaty was being sent to the Senate for ratification, Seoul, the capital of Korea, was upset by palace revolution. On July 23, 1882 (two months after the signing of the American-Korean treaty), the Japanese legation was burning and the Minister with his legation staff fled for their lives. The disturbance was quelled only after the simultaneous arrival of Chinese and Japanese troops.

American-Korean Treaty

The disorders of July 23, 1882, furnished the first occasion after the completion of the treaty for American action relative to Korea. Mr. John Russell Young, who accompanied General Grant on his around the world trip, and who was fully in the confidence of the Arthur administration, arrived in the Far East in the summer of 1882 as the new minister to China. On reaching Shanghai he learned from the Japanese consul of the disturbances in Seoul. Evidently the situation was grave. Without waiting for instructions from Washington, he initiated a course of action based upon his own conception of American obligation, moral, if not legal, under the still unratified treaty of previous May. On August 1, 1882 he telegraphed the State Department asking that a naval vessel be sent to Korean waters for protection there of American interests. The U.S.S. Monocacy, under Commander Cotton, was promptly placed at the disposal of the American minister. Young's instructions to Cotton were to offer his friendly offices for the settlement of existing differences while maintaining an attitude of strict neutrality. He was to say that the President had "heard with sorrow" of the attack on the Japanese legation; it was expedient, however, that the Japanese should look upon the coming of the U.S.S. Monocacy as an act of courtesy. Cotton was not to join the Japanese in any demonstration for an indemnity, and if such action were proposed he was to try to dissuade the Japanese from it.

Commander Cotton's mission was successful although he was unable to arrange a meeting with the Japanese representative, Mr. Hanabusa; the latter expressed his appreciation of American sympathy in a note which made up in courtesy what it lacked in cordiality. The Chinese authorities, on the other hand, were not slow in voicing their gratitude.

Mr. Young's action in 1882 was looked upon as an "armed intervention" and believed diplomatic force was used in conformity with the American-Korean Treaty. Consequently it had been hailed with great joy by the King and the populace. The U. S. minister to China, Hon. John Russell Young, fulfilled his realistic interpretation. It was he who advised the Secretary of State after the signing of the American Korean Treaty: "I think it very important that the U. S. should have a footing in Korea, and that having opened the door, we should not close it or give any other power precedence."

The treaty had in it these innocent but fateful words which, as so often in diplomatic documents, may mean much or nothing according to interpretation:
"If other powers deal unjustly or oppressively with either government, the other will exert its good offices, on being informed of the case, to bring about an amicable arrangement, thus showing its friendly feelings."

U. S. Moral Obligation?

The result of this treaty of 1882 was that the U. S. assumed a certain moral and legal obligation connected with the question of Korea's status as an independent power, and to the extent that the treaty upset the balance of power between China and Japan and later Japan and Russia. The U. S. was responsible in no small measure for the subsequent course of events, ultimately so disastrous to the cause of peace in the Far East. If the United States had adopted a strong policy toward maintaining Korea's independence it could also have eliminated the Sino-Japanese war of 1894-95, the Russo-Japan War of 1904-1905, thus possessing the key to permanent peace in the Far East and the guarantee of the Open Door in Asia.

Korea's fatal error lay in her failure to differentiate between "good" and "intervention" as interpreted by Secretary Olney. However, looking over early diplomatic relation, the Korean government could not be wholly blamed for believing that the words "good offices" were meant other than "intervention". The earlier demonstrations of friendship of the American government contrasted sadly with the subsequent unrealistic acts contrary to the best interest of U.S. security and peace in the Pacific.

Japan Annexes Korea 1910

The annexation of Korea by Japan came about not quite like the annexation of Austria by Germany: but as the result also of a complicated chain of events. The peninsula had been a kingdom - which in 1864 passed under a rigorous regency. For nine years there was "Korea for the Koreans" with a vengeance. "The Hermit Nation" became Korea's sobriquet, Japan was the first to crack the shell, with a treaty in 1876, getting in return an open port for trade. Two other ports opened later. Second concession to the outside world was a treaty with the USA, secured by Commodore Shufeldt in 1882. Not little by little, but much by much, control of all Korean affairs went over into the hands of Japan. The final annexation on August 29, 1910, Korea as an independent, treaty-making nation had ceased to exist and our treaty of 1882 became a matter merely of affectionate memory.

That memory is to be revived by the Koreans on May 22, not by way of exciting rebellious feelings nor of recrimination or accusation, but in appreciation of the old-time Korean-American friendship and the many aids the country received. Americans, they say, have done much for Korea, and it is remembered. And our state department was liberal in "good offices" though it couldn't see that "intervention" would be an anagram.

Everywhere Koreans Beg America for a Chance to Fight the Japs,

In the blood of all good Koreans flows a hatred of all things Japanese - a hatred that dates back three hundred fifty years to a day in 1592 when three hundred thousand Jap soldiers on orders from the regent Hideyoshi, swarmed the coasts of the ancient Kingdom of Korea, laying waste her cities, her farmlands and treasure. Today all Korea is under the bondage of Japan - and today, as all Koreans have ten generations back, the man of Korea still lives for the day when he can settle the score for three and a half centuries of humiliation against the Jap. Koreans are a distinct people - being neither like their ancient friends, the Chinese, nor like their ancient enemies, the Japs.

In the backyard of the Jap strategic military, naval and air bases, millions of Koreans are eager to do what they can to defeat the Japs. We are ready. The Koreans have already set up a Provisional Government in China.

What is holding up America's decision to recognize Korea as the 27th member of the United Nations? One cannot surmise it without some regret. We strongly urge the State Department to recognize the Korean Provisional Government.

Koreans everywhere pray and urge the United States to attack Japan at her heart. I say this, knowing full well that when the American bombers range over the industrial cities of Jap-dominated Korea my people will be killed. But I say, and my people say, let it come - we would rather die by American bombs than live as servants to the Japanese.

Evacuees eligible for compensation

3-7-'42

S.F. Daily

Japanese moving out of the state of California in the event of evacuation will still be eligible for the State Unemployment Compensation, it was revealed today through the Department of Employment. Unemployed persons who have been contributing towards this Insurance may apply for returns to their state from any state in the nation, it was stated.

100,000 JAPANESE STILL AWAITING EVACUATION

4-16-'42

A temporary lull was experienced this week in orders removing Japanese from strategic areas.

So far about 10,000 have been evacuated, another 5,000 moved out voluntarily, and about 100,000 still remain to be shifted.

Lieut. Gen. John L. DeWitt and Col. Karl Bendetsen have announced that removals would be speeded as soon as assembly and reception centers are available.

A group of Los Angeles Japanese were removed Tuesday on orders issued last week to Santa Anita, one of the 16 assembly centers established by the Wartime Civil Control Administration, directing the evacuation.

8,010 ENEMY ALIENS HELD SINCE BEGINNING OF WAR

1942

WASHINGTON, April 16.—The Federal Bureau of Investigation has arrested 8,010 enemy aliens as possibly dangerous to the national safety since the war began, the justice department announced yesterday.

This was an increase of 441 since March 31. The total included 4,443 Japanese, 2,140 Germans and 1,127 Italians.

YOUTH "LEARNS LOT" ENGLISH IN 2 WEEKS

1942

SPOKANE, Feb. 25—Federal authorities said that Ryoji Kasai, 19, Japanese, who was arrested February 9 in a railroad yard, "learned a lot" while in custody.

After his arrest he answered all questions with a broad grin and two words: "No Savvy", but today, he spoke perfect English when he learned he was detained no longer.

NISEI WILL RETAIN RIGHT TO VOTE IN CALIFORNIA

1942

SACRAMENTO, Calif., April 15. American-born Japanese being evacuated from prohibited areas in California will not lose their rights to vote in the state's primary and general elections, Deputy Attorney General Jess Hession declared this week.

Local officials working with the Wartime Civil Control Administration on the evacuation said approximately 54,000 Japanese-American citizens would be entitled to participate in the elections and probably would cast absentee ballots at assembly centers or the resettlement areas.

Alien Japanese Given 5 Years

Honolulu—3-31-1942

For having in his possession 53 pounds of poison and a map showing location of military installations, Kanematsu Yanagida, 42, alien Japanese living at Kailua, was fined $5,000 and sentenced to five years in Oahu prison at hard labor late Monday in provost court.

In passing sentence Lt. Col. John R. Hermann, provost judge, said: "My only regret is that I can't give you a heavier sentence."

Yanagida was found to have in his possession:

Fifty pounds of arsenic; one pound of arsenate of lead; two pounds of Fungi-bordo, a poison; eight copies of U.S. Naval Institute proceedings; a world map showing naval installations of the United States, Japan and Great Britain; examination papers of an army extension course, and a map of Nakashima-ken, Japan.

Alien Mother Listens To Tokyo Broadcast, Family Loses Radio

N. Jiji—3-23-1942

A family will be minus any radio for the duration of the war for having violated General Order 74 that prohibits enemy aliens from listening in to short wave radio broadcasts from Japan.

In provost court Saturday, Mrs. Kana Nakata, 52, born in Japan, and her three sons, Herbert Saburo, Harry Yoshio and Jiro, all American citizens, admitted having listened to broadcasts together "frequently."

Atty. Gen. Biddle upon whom properly has been placed the larger portion of the blame for obstructing the evacuation of, or restraining enemy aliens, particularly Japanese, on the West Coast has not performed a pleasing service to the nation's security. The Attorney General Biddle through actual [illegible] has released on parole to "citizen sponsors," a large number of the suspected Japanese aliens listed in California, Oregon and Washington by the F.B.I. [illegible]

3-16-1942 N.T.

日本人の布哇支配陰謀云々
と例に依つて出鱈目な放言

Nippu Jiji

5-29-40

It's Damaging to Hawaii Itself

Editorial 3-31-40

In plain words, to quote the old proverb, [illegible] is cutting his nose to spite himself.

If the allegations he makes are true, then [it] would be a different story. But actually they are all fabrications—utterly, positively, false charges.

THE WASHINGTON POST: SUNDAY, APRIL 12, 1942

BOOKS

A WEEKEND REVIEW OF CURRENT PUBLICATIONS

How The Japs Propose To Beat Us

Two Years Ago Mr. Matsuo Explained It All

By Robert E. Runser

MONTHS AGO there was some rumor and gossip here in Washington about a "secret document" which was supposed to disclose the exact line of attack the Japanese army and navy would (and subsequently did) take against the United States. We know now that what was meant was a book published openly enough at Tokyo in 1940 under the title, "The Three Power Alliance and the U. S.-Japanese War."

Mr. Kilsoo K. Haan, a Korean nationalist, managed by secret and devious means to purloin a copy of the book brought to California by two Japanese officers who were members of the notorious Black Dragon society, the religio-political organization which for some time has been the de facto government of Japan. Mr. Haan made the contents of the book known to various United States Government departments, including the Army and Navy, many weeks before the attack on Pearl Harbor.

The present volume is Mr. Haan's unabridged translation of the book. It gives one Kinoaki Matsuo's conception of what the Pacific war would be like, and what will be its result.

KILSOO HAAN

Harris & Ewing

The resourceful Korean who filched a copy of the Matsuo thesis from a Japanese officer and made its contents known to the U. S. Government

ACCORDING to Mr. Matsuo, the United States is solely to blame for the United States-Japanese crisis. Jealous and nervous about our possessions in the Pacific, we naturally hated the powerful though peace-loving Japanese. We are, it seems, extremely imperialistic, ready to grab anything which might fall in our way, such as the many islands bases in the Atlantic and Caribbean which we stole from the British under the pretext of offering aid. Moreover, the United States has a black record in China where we tried to thwart Japan's altruistic plan of coprosperity for the Oriental races. To top this off, we were building the largest fleet in the world, dickering for additional spheres of influence in the Pacific, and were conscripting our citizens for a huge army under the pretext of National Defense when it was generally known that our military forces were already more than adequate to protect our shores. Obviously, then, the United States was making ready for a big land grab and the finger pointed at innocent Japan. So much for the *casus belli*, as envisaged by Mr. Matsuo.

"Japan," says Mr. Matsuo, "is a country entirely different from the aggressive United States. For her history to date has not even a single page showing that she has encroached upon other countries." But things had already come to a pretty pass. Despite many concessions in favor of peace, Japan, unless she acted quickly, was doomed to fall before the military and capitalistic power of the United States. Her one salvation lay in joining the Three Power Alliance, that agreement among the underlings of the world which promised to put an end to the imperialistic capitalism to assure a cooperative and peaceful world.

With the moral support of Germany and Italy, the fateful shadow that hovered over Japan became less grim, but nevertheless war was still inevitable. When it

came, what would be Japan's plan of operation? Kinoaki Matsuo, doffing his disguise of outraged idealism becomes most sober and realistic in his ideas on this point. He analyzes the naval and military strength of the United States and shows how these would be used against Japan. The United States would immediately assume the offensive, send fleets and expeditionary forces to her Pacific possessions, blockade Japan, and commence raiding the Japanese mainland.

Unless Japan could frustrate such an offensive, she would be doomed. Her alternative was to take the offensive herself. A surprise-attack fleet could be dispatched to the United States Pacific Coast and to the Panama Canal to destroy or weaken the United States Fleet as soon as it departed on its Japanese mission. While Japanese trade was being protected in the China and Japan Seas, submarines would be sent to raid on the United States Atlantic Coast, to create a diversion and so hold the Atlantic Fleet in the Atlantic. Russia could be wooed into at least armed neutrality and the Philippine Islands swiftly occupied.

FOLLOWING the Philippine occupation, Hongkong, Singapore and the Dutch Indies—all vulnerable to Japanese attack—would be taken solely to keep them from being used, as American naval bases. Forced to use Hawaii, which is actually a little too far away, as a base against Japan, the United States Fleet would concentrate there. Then the Japanese would launch a surprise attack and cripple our fleet while submarines would play havoc with shipping and lines of communication on the Pacific Coast.

Further surprises would await the remnant of the United States Fleet on its way to Japan. Small Jap naval forces would whittle

away at our fleet without offering open battle. Through such tactics, the American force would be severely damaged, dispersed, or even destroyed by the courageous Japanese navy and by the Japanese air force which "would show a courage a hundred times higher than ordinary."

Only by the greatest bit of luck could the United States hope to break through the Japanese cordon. Our great losses, to Mr. Matsuo thought, would force us to drop offensive tactics and to withdraw. In so doing we would undoubtedly give up Hawaii or else leave it in such a weak state that it could be taken by the Japanese, though not without great cost. So, too, the Panama Canal, which if necessary to the Japanese victory, could be destroyed or taken. Swept from the seas and driven from her territories in the Pacific, the United States could only give up the struggle and promise thereafter to mind her own business. Japan would thus "see her great ideal realized" and have a free hand in the Far East.

THIS EXTRAORDINARY testament by an officer of the Japanese naval intelligence had as its purpose the winning of Japanese support for the Japanese militarists. It was evidently an attempt to convince conservative members of the admiralty that a war with the United States was not necessarily an act of suicide. Some of the pictures the author draws have been justified by events.

Thus it gives us some reason to ponder about the value of the work as a blueprint of what is yet to come. However, the book is written in pretty general terms, which may account for its correspondence with events. It was not a secret document, at least in Japan, nor does it appear to bear any official indorsement. Interesting as it is,

Other Informative Books About Our Pacific Enemy

this book is scarcely a reason for further alarm or any special blame for those who knew about this work prior to December 7, 1941.

"HOW JAPAN PLANS TO WIN," by Kinoaki Matsuo, translated by Kilsoo K. Haan. (Little, Brown, $2.50.)

FBI Seizes Alien, Flares

SANTA CRUZ, March 3.—(INS)—Sixty-nine packing cases of what were described as "highly powerful" sky rockets, colored flares and other fireworks were seized today by FBI agents and local police officers in the beach-front residence of an alien Japanese.

Arresting officers tested the sky rockets and flares and stated that they were powerful enough to be seen for miles out on the Pacific Ocean.

The packing cases, found in the residence of George Nakamura, were as large as office desks. Nakamura was arrested. The majority of the fireworks had been manufactured in Japan, a few in China.

'Cook' Was Jap Captain

SAO PAULO, Brazil, April 1—Police yesterday arrested a Japanese army captain who for the past five years has masqueraded as a woman cook. He was employed in the house of the director of a large concern which supplies war materials to the democracies.

Jap Spy Network Reported in Chile

SANTIAGO, Chile, March 3.—(P)—The Socialist newspaper Critica reported today that a "powerful Japanese espionage network" was at work in Chile and operating a short wave radio station at Puerto Montt in southern Chile for the transmission of military and political information.

The radio station, the newspaper said, transmits weather conditions and other information "connected with the possible Japanese aerial and naval action in the extreme south of Chile." This area includes the strategic Straits of Magellan.

It was charged that the Japanese were seeking to foment differences among the American nations, especially Chile and Argentina."

The First Reader

By HARRY HANSEN

Japanese Naval Officer Outlined in 1940 the Strategy That Tokyo Has Followed in War with U. S.

In October, 1940, a member of the Japanese Naval Intelligence, Kinoaki Matsuo, outlined the strategy that Japan must pursue in making war against the United States. Alarmed by preparations to augment the United States navy, made by that "incarnation of the devil army of democracy," President Roosevelt, Matsuo advocated the immediate use of the surprise-attack, the seizure of Guam and the Philippines, the attempts to destroy the United States Navy piecemeal and the march south that Japan has since followed. Japan is David with the slingshot and the United States is the lumbering Goliath in this startling forecast, which, translated by a Korean, Kilsoo K. Haan, is published today as How Japan Plans to Win. (Little, Brown, $2.50.)

It may amaze Americans to see themselves as this analytical foreigner sees them—following the British formula of using foreign colonies for trade, seizing raw material, sending it home to be worked and selling the products back to the outside world, instead of recognizing the "new order," to make parts of the world self-sustaining. They will also learn that the "surprise-attack fleet" was fully visualized by this author, who in 1940 outlined the way to attack Pearl Harbor and showed that without bases in the East the United States could not threaten the life-line of Japan or bomb its home ports. Matsuo expected diplomatic negotiations to continue "until the initiation of military action" and hoped it would be before the Atlantic and Pacific fleets could be combined. But if the fleets joined up and then moved westward from Pearl Harbor, "Japan cannot lose even a second; she should launch a naval action like a lightning flash." She did.

Says We Cannot Bomb Toyko Successfully.

So much of Matsuo's plan has been realized by Japan that the book seems a diabolical history. On one or two points the plan went awry. The Philippines are not yet conquered and the United States Asiatic fleet got away. Of interest is Matsuo's contention that, despite the inferiority in numbers of the Japanese navy, Japanese battleships can fire five seconds faster than American battleships—and "even this little difference of five seconds determines victory or defeat." He considers the defeat of the American fleet essential to victory: if the United States will not yield after it loses the fleet—and Matsuo does not expect it to—then Hawaii must be occupied. He tells how the fleet must be fought to be destroyed. This is the war game the Japanese children play—not the Americans.

Of considerable interest is his analysis of the possibilities of bombing Tokyo. He believes the United States will have to use airplane carriers, with about 100 airplanes making a flight of 1000 miles, at 120 miles an hour, during which the airplane fleet hovers near. While he does not underestimate the danger to Tokyo (especially if incendiaries and gas are used), he thinks only 20 out of 100 planes will reach Tokyo and that "Japan places much hope in her submarine warfare." Thus a "United States raid on Tokyo is nothing to be feared," but a Russian raid from Vladivostok would be a "genuine menace."

Gas warfare seems important to Matsuo, for he says repeatedly that the United States is manufacturing huge quantities of gas at Edgewood, the largest plant of its kind in the world. "Perhaps America, whose favorite words have always been peace and humanity, will not venture to commit such an inhumane action," says he. This is practically his only fear, and it sounds ominous.

Maybe He Overlooked Something.

This is the plan that the pro-war Japanese fed the "America-fearing" citizens. They said they could carry on. Expenditures will be far below America's "notorious extravagance." Distances are too great to send an expeditionary force to the East. It will be a naval war, and Japan will win it by superior fighting ability, says Matsuo. His calculations omit one or two points. Obviously he considers the British no help to America, and Australia enters his mind only as a place to seize. He does not combine Japan's fortune with Hitler's. Also he takes no account of the acceleration of American war pro-

duction, especially in planes. His point is that they can't reach the objective.

Thus this book bears out the oft-repeated criticism of the Japanese—they live according to blueprints but can't deal with the accidentals.

Wash. Post. 4-12-'42

Hawaii's Japanese

There can be only academic interest now in the fact that a labor commission, sent to Hawaii nearly 20 years ago, reported back to the State Department that the Japanese there were a "military menace." Such claims have been made, officially and unofficially, for more than 40 years. Moreover, similar claims have been made about the Japanese in California. The interesting thing, however, is that while California's Japanese are being moved out of strategic areas, Hawaii's Japanese remain in our Mid-Pacific bastion. Some of them have been interned. But for most of them the prevailing island spirit is reportedly one of toleration. This, of course, is in line with civilian Hawaii's traditional attitude. Moreover, there is reason to believe that it accords with the exigencies of the situation, as sized up by the intelligence services.

For to exclude from Oahu all persons of Japanese blood would involve a mass transportation which, at present, would be unthinkable, considering the many thousands of persons who would be involved. Also, it goes without saying that such a move would cripple the island economy just when it must be sustained. Yet it is a fact that because of the prevailing situation on Oahu, it remains impossible to handle this country's Japanese "problem" with uniformity. This is to be regretted, for it is perfectly obvious that disloyal Japanese in Hawaii constitute a more serious threat than do their compatriots in California.

Jap. Naval Strategy Map Out of Jap. Matsuo's First Book.

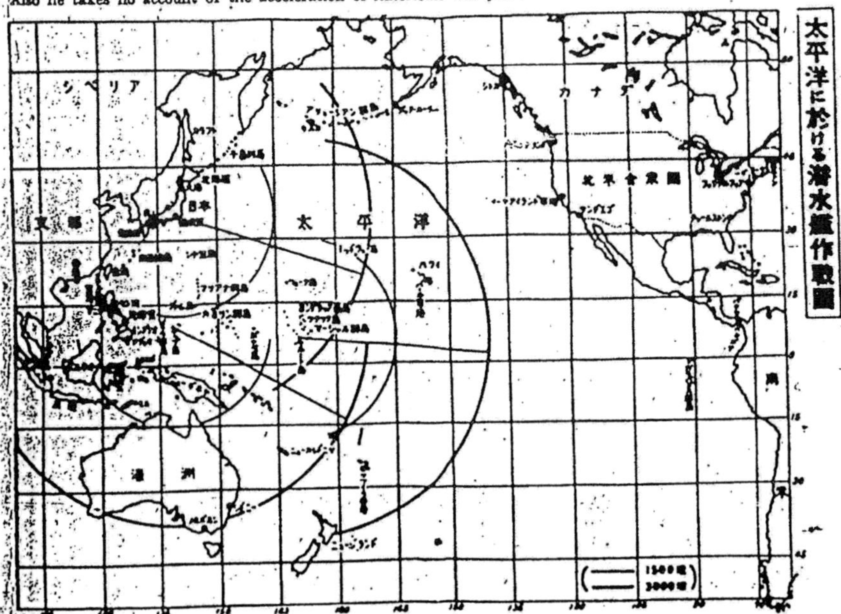

"Buy Defense stamps and Bonds, — now —."

SINO-KOREAN PEOPLES' LEAGUE

701 D Street, N. E.
Washington, D. C.

Lincoln 5187

June 17, 1942

Honorable Harold B. Hoskins
Department of State,
Washington, D. C.

My Dear Sir:

I thank you for the honor of having had a frank
discussion with you this morning in regards to the
future of Korea in relation with the unity of the
Koreans in general and of the future official
attitude of America toward the Korean Independence.

As I have already stated, I will do everything to
make this unity a reality and if necessary I will
fade out of the Korean political field to prove to
the leaders of Chungking, Hawaii and Dr. Syungman Rhee
of my sincerity, I repeat that I have not dreamed of
going to Korea in connection with any political
movement, this, I am sure, will make Dr. Rhee very
happy.

I trust and pray that America will help Korea in the
very near future and recognize the independence of
Korea.

Ever gratfully yours,

Kilsoo K. Haan

DEPARTMENT OF STATE

Memorandum of Conversation

DATE: June 17, 1942

SUBJECT:

PARTICIPANTS: Mr. Kilsoo K. Haan
Mr. Harold B. Hoskins

COPIES TO:
A-B: Mr. Berle
PA/H: Mr. Hornbeck
FE:
FC: Mr. Gordon

Mr. Haan came in to see me at his own request to give me the attached memorandum regarding a Korean Revolt said to have taken place in Northern Korea on February 2-6, 1942. Mr. Haan said that he had supplied this same information to Colonel Pettigrew of the Far Eastern Division of MID.

In addition Mr. Haan said he had been thinking over our recent conversation and had decided to submit the attached letter in which he offers to withdraw himself and his group of two or three dozen Koreans in the United States from active opposition to the Korean Provisional Government represented by Dr. Rhee if by so doing the United States Government can be induced to recognize Korean independence.

I reminded Mr. Haan that in our previous conversation I had not said that this Government would necessarily take any definite action if there were unity among Koreans in this country. What I had pointed out was that in my opinion there was no possibility of any action by this Government at least until unity had been attained among the various Korean elements. I also reminded him of the differences among the Koreans in China and mentioned again the primary interest of China in the question of Korean independence.

Mr. Haan

Mr. Haan then referred to a two and one-half hour conversation he had had with Mr. T. V. Soong about two months ago and a further talk with Mr. Victor Hoo who is associated with Mr. Soong. Mr. Haan said that it was a result of his conversation with Mr. Hoo that arrangements were finally worked out so that the two Korean military groups in China had been consolidated under the name "First Flying Column" under a Korean General representing the Korean Provisional Government, General Li Ching-tien. General Kim Yak-shan, Commander of the Korean Volunteer Corps, was made second in command. I thanked Mr. Haan for the information he had supplied and told him that I would discuss with other officers in the Department his suggestions and get in touch with him at a later date if we would have further comments or suggestions to make.

After Mr. Haan's departure I telephoned Mr. Hoo and obtained confirmation from him of Mr. Haan's visit and of the statements Mr. Haan had made regarding his conversation. I also learned from Mr. Hoo that Dr. Rhee had recently been in touch with them and had inquired whether the Chinese Government would recognize the Provisional Government of Korea if Dr. Rhee came to terms with Kilsoo Haan's group. Dr. Hoo stated that he had told Dr. Rhee that such a united front on the part of Koreans in this country would undoubtedly hasten some action but that there were other considerations also involved and that no definite promise of recognition could at this time be made if a united front were actually worked out.

Harold B. Hoskins

A-B/H:HBH:JKF

SINO-KOREAN PEOPLES' LEAGUE

101 D Street, N. E.
WASHINGTON, D. C.

Lincoln 5187

June 17, 1942

Honorable Harold B. Hoskins
Executive Assistant
Department Of State
Washington D.C.

My dear Sir:

The enclosed unconfirmed information cause me to pointedly request the following reply if humanly possible. This is impeled by the sincere interest as to the desire and hope on our part to help U.S.A. to win the war in the Far East and in the possible aid we can give the patriotic Koreans in Korea, Manchuria, Siberia, China and Japan an opportunity to set up a free and independent Korea.

The last time we met – you frankly told me that nothing can be done for Korea and Koreans until there is "Unity Among Koreans".

895.01 I am ready to instruct my comrades in the inner circle that at all cost we must unite even if necessary to give up all and every position to the opposing side for the sake of unity of Koreans. For if this is the only means of getting aid – then we do not want to be the cause of disunity.

Sir: Please tell me in writing – what would U.S.A. do – if we would unite as you suggest? Will U.S.A. recognize Korean Independence? Will U.S.G. give us the much need material aid?

I am sure if U.S.A. is sincere the reply would be yes. Otherwise – we would know where we stand.

SINO-KOREAN PEOPLES' LEAGUE

TRinidad 8500   101 D Street, N. E.   Lincoln 5187
WASHINGTON, D. C.

KILSOO K. HAAN
Korean Representative

Attached is a news clipping which proves the Free French vainly are trying to get help while they knew deep down in their heart the chances were 100 to one — getting the much needed help from the British

America is unlike the British — America can give the much needed moral, political and material aid to the Koreans. Unlike the Free French — we can depend on U.S.A. if only America take the chance and give the Koreans a just trial.

The "Free French Fought On, Hoping for British Aid That Never Came" — but Koreans know U.S.A. will come to our aid.

There is no alternative for us — but to be frankly request your reply; When I do receive this reply, I will immediately convey it to the proper parties and bring about the unity you mentioned as the only condition. I know — I have the confidence that it can be done if we receive your written reply soon In the interest of U.S.A victory over the Japs —

Gratefully yours

Kilsoo K. Haan

Memoranda. From our agent via South America
Koreans Revolt in Northern Korea Feb: 2 to 6th 1942.
<u>Unconfirmed - Have Requested To U.S. Army</u>
<u>G-2- To check This For Us.</u>

Total Korean dead   2,185 ⎫ agent insist these are
Total Korean wounded + arrested   18,500 ⎬ very conservative
Jap civilian dead   400 ⎬ figures.
Jap soldiers, police, gendarmes dead 680 ⎭

Port of Yuki, Woongkee in Korean
Nearest Korean Port to Vladivostok
6 Oil tanks dynamited and 1 warehouse destroyed by f

Heizyo or Peyng Yang in Korean
161 miles North of Seoul
Police and Gendarmes' Headquarters stoned and burned 2 A.M. 2-
2 Airplane Hangers and 22 planes burned.
68 Japanese residences completely burned.

Seoul the Capital of Korea
Police and Gendarmes' headquarters attacked and set fire. First atta
at 1 AM. Feb. 2, 1942.   180 Japanese homes at Honmachi
(the Japanese section of the Capital) completely burned.
12 Warehouse including 2 ammunition warehouses burned.
200 nearby were badly damaged.

Singisyu or Senenjyu in Korean
308 miles North of Seoul.
4 Warehouses burned.   8 Railroad Cars loaded with arms and munit
blown up.   1 Paper Mill completely burned and destroyed. Forest
fires raged for 2 whole days before putting it under control.
The bridge crossing the Yalu River to Antung (Manchuria) was
dynamited - but with little damage.

Gensan or Wonsan in Korean:
140 miles Northeast of Seoul - Jap. Naval base - Japan Sea
3 large warehouse burned including 2 naval munition warehouses. 92 Motor.
boat fishing - burned.   2 Oil tankers dynamited. Hundreds of home damaged
Note: March 1, 1919 Korean Revolt news did not come out months after.

January 28, 1942

My dear Dr. Nygaard:

By reference from the Vice President I have been given for acknowledgment your letter to him of January 6, regarding your wish t see this Government recognize the Korean Provisional Government.

This matter has, fo course, already come to the attention of the Department of State, and you may be assured that the point of view you expressed in your letter and your reasons therefor, will be given careful consideration. Your courtesy in writing and your interest in the question are much appreciated.

Sincerely yours,

Harold B. Hoskins
Executive Assistant

Rev. Norman E. Nygaard,

2000 South Figueroa Street,

Los Angeles, California.

A-B/E:HBH:RW:JKF   1/21,22/42

Office of the Vice President

Washington, D. C., _____January 14_____, 1942

Respectfully referred to

State Department for direct reply

895.01

895.01/61

FAR EASTERN AFFAIRS

Department of State

H. A. Wallace
Vice President.

PS/LC

Out of file

American Embassy,

Chungking, China.

March 9, 1942.

MEMORANDUM for the filing department,

Department of State:

Reference Chungking's despatch no. 248 of December 20, 1941.

Please change the file number of this despatch to "801 - Korea".

J.S.S.

cwf

correction made
L.E.C. aug. 15, 1950

Correction Desk
a.

EMBASSY OF THE
UNITED STATES OF AMERICA

No. 248.   Chungking, December 20, 1941

Subject: Letter from "Tjosowang, Foreign
Minister of The Provisional
Government of the Republic of
Corea" to The President.

Air mail

The Honorable

The Secretary of State,

Washington, D. C.

Sir:

I have the honor to enclose a letter addressed
to the President under date of December 11th, by
"Tjosowang" who represents himself as "Foreign
Minister" of "The Provisional Government of the
Republic of Corea".

Mr. Tjosowang called in person at the Embassy
and was received by a Secretary of Embassy to whom
he presented the attached letter requesting that it
be forwarded to the President. At the same time he
requested information as to the number of casualties
sustained by the Korean population during the Japanese
attack on Honolulu. He was told that this information
was not available to the Embassy.

Mr. Tjosowang stated that his Government is
anxious that the United States recognize the independent Government of Korea. Asked whether his

"government"

- 287 -

3

AIR MAIL

"government" had been recognized by China, he stated
that it is only a question of time until such recognition is extended.

My British colleague tells me that he has similarly
been approached by Mr. Tjosowang. There is no present
indication that Mr. Tjosowang's "Provisional Government
of the Republic of Corea" will be recognized by the
National Government of China.

Respectfully yours,

C.E. Gauss

Enclosure:

1. Letter dated December 11, 1941
   from Mr. Tjosowang

Original to the Department by airmail
Three copies to the Department

710
801-Korea
CEG:MCL

THE PROVISIONAL GOVERNMENT OF THE REPUBLIC OF COREA

MINISTRY OF FOREIGN AFFAIRS

TJOSOWANG
P. O. Box No. 95
CHUNGKING, CHINA

CABLE ADDRESS
COPOGO

Chungking, December 11, 1941.

His Excellency,
President Franklin D. Roosevelt,
White House,
Washington, D. C.,
U. S. A.

[...] people of Corea I pay [...] for dealing [...] on aggressive [...] aggressor is to be eliminated there would be no hope for the democratic countries in the Pacific to unanimously direct their entire forces against the Axis in Europe. And unless the democracies make a united effort against Nazi Germany hope of crushing her would be very slim.

Re-establishment of Far Eastern order is only possible after the elimination of militarist Japan. It is hoped that following the victories of the democracies all the countries, large or small, in this part of the world will be enabled to [...] freedom and independence.

Regarding free Corea's attitude towards the Pacific War I propose to say the following:

1. The whole body of the Corean people participates in the anti-aggression campaign and declares war on the Axis.
2. The so-called State-Amalgamated Treaty of 1910 and all other unequal treaties are invalid; whereas privileges and rights of anti-aggression nations in Corea are to be respected and maintained.
3. The people of Corea are most resolute to help fighting Japanese forces until final victory is won by the democracies.
4. Corea will intensify her co-operation with China and will never recognize the puppet organizations at Changchun and Nanking.
5. Corea is in full support of the declaration jointly issued by President Roosevelt and Premier Churchill.
6. Corea prays for ultimate triumph of the democratic bloc.

I wish Your Excellency and your nation every success in the launching of anti-aggression campaign.

Yours respectfully,

Tjosowang,
Foreign Minister.

Congress of the United States
House of Representatives
Washington, D. C.

January 19, 1942

Honorable Cordell Hull,
Secretary of State,
Washington, D.C.

Dear Mr. Secretary:

Because a substantial number of people of Korean nationality or descent reside in Hawaii I have been asked on several occasions to intercede in their behalf. According to the 1940 census there are a total of 2,206 Korean nationals in Hawaii and 4,555 people of Korean descent who are citizens of the United States, making a total of 6,761 in this group.

These aliens have frequently been inconvenienced and embarrassed by their technical status as nationals of Japan. Since the outbreak of the war with Japan their situation has become most difficult. Their funds have been frozen and their ability to earn a livelihood in the United States has been curtailed. I have discussed this problem with Dr. Syngman Rhee, representing the Korean Mission in Washington, and with outstanding leaders of the Korean group in Hawaii.

Aside from administrative action which might relieve the situation it has occurred to me that the recognition of Korea as an independent nation might be the best solution of the problem if it accords with our national policy. Apart from the service which might be rendered by the small number of Koreans in the United States, the moral effect on the 23,000,000 Koreans in Asia might help us in the prosecution of the war with Japan.

I therefore should like to suggest that the Korean nationals in America be put in a separate category from that of the Japanese nationals in order that they may not be classed as enemy aliens, and that the possibility of including Korea as one of the Governments-in-Exile be given consideration.

With highest personal regards, I am,
Sincerely,

In reply refer to
A-B/H

        My dear Mr. King:

        I have received your letter of January 19 with
regard to the situation of Korean nationals and to
the possible recognition by this Government of the
Korean Provisional Government.

        The question of recognition has, of course, al-
ready come to the attention of the Department of
State, and you may be assured that the views you
expressed in your letter, and your reasons therefor,
will be given careful consideration.

        In connection with the status of Korean nationals
in the United States, the Attorney General has just
released a statement, a copy of which I enclose for
your information.

        Your courtesy in writing and your interest in this
question are much appreciated.

                Sincerely yours,

Enclosure:
   Copy of statement.   Cordell Hull

The Honorable
   Samuel Wilder King,
        House of Representatives.

CR
JAN 28 1942

A-B/H:HBH-RW-gw   1-26-42   FE   A-B   PA/H

United States Senate

COMMITTEE ON FOREIGN RELATIONS

January 20, 1942

My dear Mr. Secretary:

This acknowledges the receipt of your very courteous
and helpful letter of January nineteenth in response to an
inquiry which I had addressed to you under date of January 6,
1942, particularly relating to possible recognition of the
Korean Provisional Government by the United States.

I appreciate and commend your views, as expressed
in your letter to me.

Respectfully,

GUY M. GILLETTE

The Honorable Cordell Hull
Secretary of State
Washington, D.C.

895.01/64

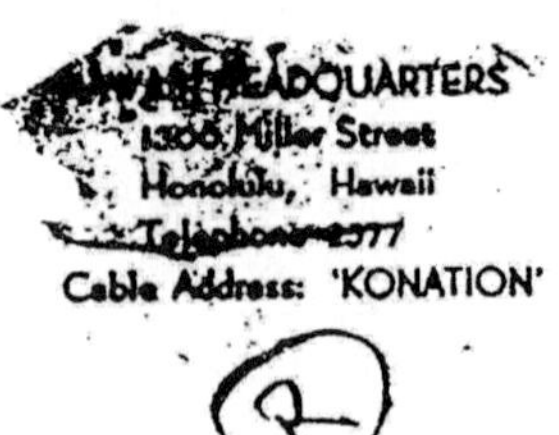

UNITED KOREAN COMMITTEE
in America

HONOLULU,   January 23,

His Excellency Franklin D. Roosevelt,
President of the United States of America,
Washington, D. C.

Sir:

We are enclosing, herewith, an open appeal by the
United Korean Committee in America to the United States of
America and the Allied Powers to recognize the Provisional
Government of the Republic of Korea.

The Provisional Government of the Korean Republic has
been in existence since 1919 with present headquarters at
Chungking, China. This Provisional Government declared war
on Japan December 11, 1941, and allied itself with the cause
of the democratic governments in exile.

This appeal gives, in brief, the history and background
of Korea together with a summary of some of the atrocities
and cruel treatment received by the Korean people at the
hands of the Japanese Empire that is now at war with the
United States.

We most earnestly request that you use your good offices
to obtain the immediate recognition of the Provisional Government of Korea and the restitution of its souvereignty and
territorial integrity at the conclusion of the present conflict.

                    Most Respectfully,

          UNITED KOREAN COMMITTEE IN AMERICA

          By Wonn Soon Lyel
                Chairman.

THE WHITE HOUSE
WASHINGTON

January 31, 1942

Respectfully referred to the

Secretary of State.

M. H. McINTYRE
Secretary to the President

TO THE PRESIDENT

THE UNITED STATES OF AMERICA

"KOREA'S APPEAL TO THE ALLIED POWERS
THROUGH THE UNITED STATES OF AMERICA"

SUBMITTED BY

the

UNITED KOREAN COMMITTEE IN AMERICA

HONOLULU

TERRITORY OF HAWAII

<u>KOREA'S APPEAL TO THE ALLIED POWERS
THROUGH THE UNITED STATES OF AMERICA.</u>

The United Korean Committee in America, which is the official organ representing the people of Korean ancestry resident in the United States and its Territory of Hawaii, desires to express its loyalty to the United States especially at this time and to bring to the attention of its government the suffering that the Koreans have had to bear by reason of Japanese oppression. It is also the desire of the committee to extend any and all aid to the United States in this present conflict with Japan; and that upon the successful determination of this war, the sovereignty of Korea be re-established as it existed in 1882 when a treaty of amity and commerce was entered into between the United States of America and the Kingdom of Korea, in which the United States agreed in Article I of said treaty,

> "If other Powers deal unjustly or oppressively with either Government, the other will exert their good offices, on being informed of the case, to bring about an amicable arrangement, thus showing their friendly feelings."

Koreans throughout the United States who were born in Korea, which was unjustly annexed as a part of the Empire of Japan in 1910, have been considered as Japanese by race, allegiance and nationality. The Koreans, however, are not Japanese by race or sentiment, nor do they in fact have any real allegiance to Japan. A little of the history of Korea will show that she has never been a voluntary subject of Japan and is and has been anti-Japanese ever since her subjugation.

There are three main phases of Korean history that should be considered: (1) the period of 4215 years prior to 1882 during which she maintained her own independence; (2) from 1882 to 1905 when she depended and relied on treaties with the world powers to maintain her sovereignty, and (3) the period of 1905 to the present, which is the era of her subjugation by Japan.

(1) The Korean people were a nation, with a language and a culture of their own, before Japan ceased to be a land of warring tribes and unlettered people.

Japan, as early as 1500 A. D., seeking territorial expansion of her island empire, repeatedly invaded Korea, which invasions ended in failure. The most destructive was the war of Hideyoshi, the Napoleon of Japan, in 1592, which, even though it ended in Japan's defeat by the Sino-Korean allied armies, left Korea, which was the battleground, so helplessly devastated that it never completely recovered. The Japanese returned to their islands laden with trophies, "among which were the ears of ten thousand Koreans who had been butchered in the frays." (Collier, History of Nations, Vol. 6, p. 37).

As a result of this war, Korea concluded that the only way to maintain peace was to isolate herself. This was done so meticulously that it became known as the "Hermit Kingdom" and for a period of 300 years enjoyed profound peace.

(2) In 1882, at the request of the United States, she established the open door policy and relied upon the treaties of nations of the world. In addition to the United States, she made treaties of friendship, commerce and navigation with Austria-Hungary (June 23, 1892); Belgium (March

23, 1901); China (Sept. 11, 1899); Denmark (July 15, 1902);
France (June 4, 1886); Germany (Nov. 26, 1883); Great Britain (Nov. 26, 1883); Italy (June 26, 1884); and Japan (Feb.
26, 1876). All these treaties recognized the sovereignty
and territorial integrity of Korea.

It is interesting to note some of the provisions
of these treaties.

Germany, Italy, Great Britain and France agreed
that "in case of differences arising between one of the High
Contracting Parties and a third Power, the other High Contracting Party, if requested to do so, shall exert its good
offices to bring about an amicable arrangement."

Article I of the treaty of Feb. 26, 1876, with Japan
stated,

> "Chosen being an independent state enjoys
> the same sovereign rights as does Japan.
>
> "In order to prove the sincerity of the
> friendship existing between the two nations,
> their intercourse shall henceforward be car-
> ried on in terms of equality and courtesy,
> each avoiding the giving of offense by arro-
> gance or manifestation of suspicion.
>
> "In the first instance, all rules and
> precedents that are apt to obstruct friendly
> intercourse shall be totally abrogated, and in
> their stead, rules, liberal and in general
> usage fit to secure a firm and perpetual peace
> shall be established."

During the Sino-Japanese War of 1894-5 the Japanese
occupied portions of Korea, and, although by the Treaty of
Shimonoseki (April 17, 1895), she compelled China to recognize the "full and complete independence and autonomy of
Korea", she did not wish to leave Korea herself and, because
of Korea's Queen Min, who was using all her power to expel
them, Japan, through her minister to Korea, Viscount Miura,
plotted her murder which was carried out by Japanese troops

and hired thugs. The Queen was "cut down, her body hacked
to pieces, wrapped in woolen blankets, saturated with kero-
sene (oil) and burned in the courtyard" of the Palace. The
Japanese desire to keep Korea at this time was frustrated
by the pressure brought by Germany, France and Russia through
the active presence of their eastern fleets, and Japan, under
this display of armed might, withdrew from Korea and henceforth began to arm herself.

Miura was later tried in Japan for the murder of
Queen Min and the justification put up by his counsel which
was adopted by the court was,

> "He did only his duty, as he was in charge of
> peace and order in Korea. The root of political
> trouble, the effects of which would have lasted
> for a long time to come, was torn up. Consider-
> ing the class of diplomacy prevailing in Korea,
> Viscount Miura has accomplished a triumph."

The culprit, although admittedly guilty, was discharged.

The European powers and the United States endeavored to, and did for a period of time, maintain and establish
the open door policy in China and Korea.

Between 1894 and 1898, both Japan and Russia were
endeavoring to dominate Korea,- Russia through diplomacy and
Japan through violence. On October 8, 1895, by the terms of
three treaties between Russia and Japan, namely (1) the
Komura-Waeber memorandum, signed at Seoul on May 4, 1896;
(2) the Yamagata-Lobanov protocol, signed at St. Peters-
burg on June 9, 1896, and (3) the Nishi-Rosen protocol, concluded at Tokyo on April 25, 1898, both countries "recognized
definitely the sovereignty and the entire independence of
Korea, and mutually engaged themselves to abstain from all
interference in the internal affairs of that country." (Collier's History of Nations, Vol. 7, p. 296.

On February 23, 1904, by a Japanese-Korean protocol, Japan agreed, in exchange for the use of Korean territory in its coming conflict with Russia, that,

> "The Imperial Government of Japan shall in
> a spirit of firm friendship ensure the safety
> and repose of the Imperial House of Korea."
> (Art. II).

> "The Imperial Government of Japan definitely
> guarantees the independence and territorial
> integrity of the Korean Empire." (Art. III).

In the early part of 1904, Japan entered into negotiations with Russia concerning Korea. Russia, in order
to preserve peace in the Far East, "declared herself ready
to recognize Japan's privileged commercial and economic
position in the Korean peninsula, with the concession of
the right to protect it by military force in event of disturbances"; but insisted (1) upon the principle of regarding
Korea as a definite sovereignty and with entire independency;
(2) that no part of Korea should be used for strategic purposes, and (3) the preservation of full freedom of navigation of the Straits of Korea.

This did not satisfy Japan and, without even replying to Russia's proposal, she broke off diplomatic relations. Then, without the formality of a declaration of war
and within thirty hours after diplomatic relations were severed,
Admiral Togo led the entire Japanese fleet (6 battleships and
10 armored cruisers) from Sasebo directly to Port Arthur on
February 7, 1904, and in a surprise attack destroyed or dis-
abled practically the entire Russian squadron. The Japanese
then invaded the Korean peninsula and drove the Russian forces
into Manchuria. After the decisive defeat of Russia's main
fleet on May 28, 1905, upon the invitation of President Theodore Roosevelt, negotiations were commenced which ended in the

Treaty of Portsmouth. Korea endeavored to be represented
at Portsmouth but was not permitted by Japan to have a
representative there.

Article II of this treaty provided in substance
that "Japan possesses in Korea paramount political, military
and economic interests" and Russia agreed "neither to ob-
struct nor interfere with measures for guidance, protection,
and control which Japan may find necessary to take in Korea."

(3) Immediately after the signing of the Treaty
of Portsmouth, Baron Ito was sent to Seoul, the Korean capital, where he importuned the Korean Emperor and cabinet ministers to sign a treaty establishing a Protectorate by Japan
over Korea. This was refused even though on various occasions
threats of violence were used by the Japanese having the
Palace surrounded and invaded by armed troops. Through bribery (1,000,000 yen) and the grant of a large estate, Yi Wan-
Yon signed as Minister of Foreign Affairs fraudulently, with
two others, Yi-She-Yong and Yi Kun-Tak, who were Advisory
Ministers.

The Emperor of Korea endeavored to thwart the designs of Japan on Korea by sending an American, Prof. Homer
B. Hulbert, to Washington to inform the United States of
Japan's treachery and to obtain her good offices to deal with
Japan's unjust and oppressive conduct, so as "to bring about
an amicable arrangement" whereby Korea would maintain her
integrity and sovereignty in accordance with the American-
Korean treaty of 1882. In the interim, however, the Korean
acting Charge d'Affaires, who was "Quisling" for Japan, informed Elihu Root, Secretary of State, of the "Declaration
of the Japanese Government" of November 22, 1905: that she

was taking and exercising "a paramount interest in the
political and military affairs of Korea . . . for the general pacification of the extreme East" in order "to safeguard
their own position and to promote the well being of the Government and people of Korea, the Imperial Government (Japan)
has resolved to assume a more direct influence and responsibility than heretofore in the external relations of the
peninsula . . . The Emperor of Korea is in accord with the
. . . necessity of this measure." Japan gave notice to "the
powers having treaties with Korea" that Japan was "assuming
charge of the foreign relations of Korea" and "watching over
the execution of the existing treaties."

Because of the belief in the false claims made by
Japan, the United States did not do anything about the Korean
Emperor's protests. They simply became part of the records
of the State Department.

After the war with Russia, Japan retained the public buildings at Mukden and the Manchurian gold mines, and
took possession of the Manchurian post offices and telegraph
lines, and occupied a portion of the province of Kirin, claiming it as Korean territory, although "it had long been held
as a part of China."

By 1907, Japan, through treachery, violence and
bribery, made "Korea for all practical purposes an integral
part of the Japanese Empire", in contravention of her agreement with Korea soon after the outbreak of the Russo-Japanese War, "to insure the safety of the Imperial (Korean)
household" and to guarantee "the independence and territorial integrity of the Korean Empire."

-7-

In 1907 the Korean Emperor sent a delegation to
The Hague Peace Conference to protest against the signing
under Japanese pressure, by the Korean Minister of Foreign
Affairs, of an agreement giving Japan the control of Korea's
foreign affairs. As a result of this protest, the Emperor
of Korea was forced to abdicate on July 19, 1907, in favor
of his son. This was opposed by the Ministry of Korea.
Thereupon another so-called treaty was forced on Korea on
July 25, 1907, which (1) placed the administration of all
Korean affairs in the Japanese Resident-General; (2) required the approval of Japan to enactment of laws and the
transactions of affairs of state; (3) provided that Japanese subjects recommended by the Resident-General were eligible to Korean government offices, and (4) provided that
foreigners could be employed only with the consent of the
Resident-General. Thereafter the envoys to The Hague were
subjected to cruel punishment; Japanese forces were increased;
the young Emperor was sent to Japan to be educated; and extensive Japanese colonization of Korea ensued and the imperial
assets of Korea were transferred to the national treasury of
Japan. The Koreans in great numbers rebelled against the
cruel treatment inflicted by the Japanese. This was quelled
by Japan by cruel and inhuman punishment. All the Korean
newspapers, which were rightfully virulent in their denunciation of the Japanese government of Korea, were shut down and
the rights of freedom of the press were abolished. All vio-
lators were severely punished.

-8-

On August 29, 1910, Japan, by virtue of a pur-
ported treaty signed by the "Quisling" Yi Wan-Yong, who,
without any right or authority, signed as "Minister President of the State of Korea", annexed Korea as a part of
her empire.

Under the Korean government before annexation,
land was divided into four classes:

1. Private lands, owned by private individuals.

2. Royal lands, belonging to the crown, but
   leased in perpetuity to private persons,
   with the right of sale and privilege of in-
   heritance. The rentals went to the King.

3. Municipal lands, which belonged to towns,
   but the practical ownership of which was in
   private parties or individuals who paid
   fees to the municipalities; and

4. Land belonging to the Buddhist temples, which
   was free from taxation.

On annexation, one of the first of Japan's acts
was to confiscate the royal, municipal and temple lands,
survey the same, dispossess the Koreans and sell or lease
the land to Japanese farmers. All Koreans who protested
"were fastened to wooden crosses and shot." To induce Japanese colonization the Japanese government offered every
Japanese settler free transportation to Korea and provided
him with a home and a piece of land, to be paid for in three
or four years. Koreans were forced to sell fertile lands
at ridiculously low prices and by 1919 one-third of the
best land in Korea was in the hands of the Japanese.

-9-

Then came the World War I period, when Japan took the side of the Allies to grab the German possessions and islands in the Far East, which consisted of Kaiochow on the Shantung peninsula, Marshall Islands, Ladrones Islands and the East and West Caroline archipelagoes. The islands were mandated to her but she took them as her own and has now fortified them. Japan was interested only in what she could grab in the Far East and refused to send any troops to the European battle fronts.

During 1919 the Koreans, chafing under the yoke of Japanese oppression, revolted against Japan. This revolt was suppressed by Japan. "The measures taken by Japan, or at least the way in which they were executed, were so severe that they caused general condemnation throughout the civilized world."

A report of the conduct of Japan toward Korea, given before the United States Senate by Senator Norris of Nebraska (see 1919 Congressional Record, pp. 2735-6; 2844-2956) in a debate, against Japan's claim to take over the German concession on the Shantung peninsula from China, stated the following:

> "One of the most pitiable spectacles in the history of the world is the picture of poor, weak, downtrodden China pleading before the great world tribunal (League of Nations) for justice - yes, for mercy - pleading to be saved the humiliation of turning over 36,000,000 of her people, her industries, her holy land, the sacred dust of her ancestors, to the control and government of the one nation of all the earth she feared the most. China had reason for fear. She had been cruelly punished by Japan before. She had been treated by Japan the same as she had been treated by Germany. She had at her own door an illustration of what could be expected when the Japanese were given power to rule over a foreign people. She had seen Japan cruelly and unmercifully take possession of her

neighbor, Korea. She knew at this very time
Japan was doing everything within her power
to blot out every vestige of Korean literature
and history. She knew the Japanese soldiers
and Japanese officers had cruelly murdered
innocent Koreans who were guilty of ONLY ONE
CRIME - THAT OF LOVING THEIR COUNTRY. She
knew that women and children had been murdered
in cold blood. She knew that every Korean official had been forced out of office, and that
from the bottom to the top, the Korean Government was ruled by the Japanese. She knew that
private residents all over Korea were searched
for books and literature, and whenever such
things were found they were burned, in order
that the rising generation might have no opportunity to learn the history of their own country. She knew the Korean language was being
supplanted by the Japanese language and no
place in all the Empire was a Korean school
permitted to exist. . . . As between the German rule in China and the Japanese rule in
Korea, she knew that even the Kaiser's control,
wrong and unjust though it was, was a bright
and shining light compared with what she
could expect from Japan."

This was followed by innumerable proofs of inci-

dents where Koreans were brutally maimed and murdered for

the slightest display of love of country. Missionaries and

their Christian converts were tortured and the property and

churches burned. A missionary from Korea reported how "in

a village near Seoul the Christian men were all commanded

by the soldiers to go into their own church, and when they

got in, the soldiers commenced to fire upon the church.

Anyone coming out was killed. Then they set fire to the

church and burned it and all the men in it."

Edward W. Thwing, of Boston, Mass., Oriental Sec-

retary of the International Reform Bureau, in a report of

the Japanese atrocities in Korea, stated:

"The following are some of the things that
I have actually seen with my own eyes:

"Small school boys knocked down and cruelly
beaten by Japanese soldiers. This was not
a question of arresting them, but savage,
unjustifiable barbarism.

"Soldiers stop and deliberately fire into a
crowd composed only of girls and women, who
were simply shouting 'Mansai'.

"A small boy of one year shot through the
back.

"An unresisting old man of 65 years pounded,
kicked and beaten by several Japanese soldiers until he could not walk.

"A crowd of about twenty school girls, who
were quietly walking along the public road,
not even shouting, chased by soldiers, beat-
en with guns, knocked down and so shame-
fully treated that it made one's blood boil.

"Japanese firemen chasing boys and girls
with long iron hooks, trying to catch them
with them.

"A Korean in a hospital paralyzed, with his
head crushed in with one of these hooks.

"A man dying, shot through the back.

"One hundred men with torn and bloody clothes,
tied together with ropes, taken to jail.

"An American missionary roughly arrested
while standing in his own yard and looking
on, but doing nothing else.

"Women knocked down with guns and kicked
into the ditch."

The Japanese, in an article in "The Japan Adver-

tiser" of March 9, 1919, quoting Midoru Komatsu, Director

of Foreign Affairs in the Government-General of Korea,

attempted to justify their treatment of Korean mission-

aries. The article is as follows:

"They (the American missionaries) are propa-
gating Christianity in Korea, but pay no
attention to the interests of Japan, the
sovereign of Korea. While engaged in Christian propaganda work, the American Missionaries run schools, and diffuse foreign
political and social ideas among the half-

civilized people. The principle of liberty
is recklessly advocated among them, this
having an evil influence upon their undevel-
oped minds, which are consequently tainted
with excessively radical ideas.

"The American missionaries include in their
number some who have no sound judgment and
discretion. Such people confuse the ideas
of the Koreans, who are in a similar mental
condition as those Japanese students who are
now making an outcry for democracy, without
understanding what this stands for. As a
result, some Korean converts to Christianity
are so senseless as to have recourse to radical action." . . .

"In order to wreak their discontent and bitter feelings, these Koreans, under the mask
of Christianity, I think, have created the
present disturbances. It may safely be declared that missionaries are responsible for
the fact that the advanced ideas of foreign
countries have been diffused without modi-
fication among the Koreans whose state of
civilization is not yet very high, and for
the fact that among those taking part in the
disturbances were girl students."

In May, 1919, after Japanese statesmen, especially

Viscount Kato, urged a more moderate policy and suggested

autonomy or at least civil administration for Korea, the

Japanese Privy Council agreed to grant Korea a certain

amount of self-government and the substitution of civil

for military rule as soon as Koreans gave up their agitation

for complete independence. This the Japanese made pretense

of doing by a statement from the government which "announced

the abolition of military rule in Korea, and the introduc-

tion of civil government and the abolition of all distinc-

tions between Koreans and other Japanese subjects."

The Korean Nationalists were dissatisfied with

this and on August 31, 1919, a proclamation was published in

Washington, D. C., proclaiming to "the people of the world"

the "Republic of Korea".

-13-

<u>OFFICIAL PROCLAMATION</u>

"Korea proclaims to the nations of the world that the people of this land, with a history of 4,000 years, have now, in this age of world progress, asserted the independence and liberty of their nation.

"Although the Japanese troops have overrun our country, as the Germans did Belgium, yet we will not recognize their control, and as a people, in this manner, we repudiate their government and send out these notifications.

"We, the liberty-loving people of Korea, having declared our independence and having chosen our representatives for a Provisional Government, through them make this announcement.

"We extend our most cordial sentiments to the friendly nations that have already had treaty relations with our land and also to the new states which have been recently formed upon principles of humanity and justice.

"PROVISIONAL GOVERNMENT FOR THE
NEW KOREAN REPUBLIC."

<u>PROVISIONAL CONSTITUTION</u>

"By the will of God, the people of Korea, both within and without the country, have united in a peaceful declaration of their independence, and for over one month have carried on their demonstrations in over 300 districts, and because of their faith in the movement they have by their representatives chosen a Provisional Government to carry on to completion this independence and so to preserve blessings for our children and grandchildren.

"The Provisional Government, in its Council of State, has decided on a Provisional Constitution which it now proclaims.

-14-

"2. All powers of State shall rest with the Provisional Council of State of the Provisional Government.

"3. There shall be no class distinction among the citizens of the Korean Republic, but men and women, noble and common, rich and poor, shall have equality.

"4. The citizens of the Korean Republic shall have religious liberty, freedom of speech, freedom of writing and publication, the right to hold public meetings and form social organizations and the full right to choose their dwellings or change their abode.

"5. The citizens of the Korean Republic shall have the right to vote for all public officials or to be elected to public office.

"6. Citizens will be subject to compulsory education and military service and payment of taxes.

"7. Since by the Will of God the Korean Republic has arisen in the world and has come forward as a tribute to the world peace and civilization, for this reason we wish to become a member of the League of Nations.

"8. The Korean Republic will extend benevolent treatment to the former Imperial Family.

"9. The death penalty, corporal punishment and public prostitution will be abolished.

"10. Within one year of the recovery of our land the National Congress will be convened.

"Signed by:

> "THE PROVISIONAL SECRETARY OF STATE,
> AND THE MINISTERS OF FOREIGN AFFAIRS,
> HOME AFFAIRS,
> JUSTICE,
> FINANCE,
> WAR,
> COMMUNICATIONS"

"In the 1st Year of the Korean Republic, 4th Month.
The following are six principles of government:

"1. We proclaim the equality of the people and
the State.

"2. The lives and property of foreigners shall
be respected.

"3. All political offenders shall be specially
pardoned.

"4. We will observe all treaties that shall be
made with foreign powers.

"5. We swear to stand by the independence of Korea.

"6. Those who disregard the orders of the Provisional Government will be regarded as enemies of the State."

The Koreans both in and out of Korea have never submitted to Japanese authority except under duress and compulsion. The Koreans who have openly stated or acted as all Koreans feel, have been promptly executed, tortured, placed in dungeons or jailed, and the jails of Korea are principally populated with political prisoners.

Emigration from Korea has steadily grown since Japanese domination. The migrations, because of economic necessity, have been to areas which are far less physically desirable, to escape this oppression. The principal areas of migration are China, Manchuria and Siberia and those who have settled in Manchuria and Northern China have again, through Japanese piratical aggression, come under this hated yoke. It is estimated that about three and a half millions have left Korea already.

A Korean Provisional Government was established in Shanghai in 1919 and it has been continuously maintained with present headquarters at Chungking, which provisional government has been recognized by China. This Provisional Government declared war on Japan on December 11, 1941.

Because of the alliances of Japan with the United States, Great Britain and France, the Korean Provisional Government received no outside support against Japan to free Korea from Japanese domination and control.

Most of the Koreans throughout North America, including the Hawaiian Islands, are those who have been able, by fleeing their native land, to evade the suppressive and cruel treatment by Japan. They came to America where they could live and work in peace. A check of the immigration records will show that the largest influx of Koreans into the United States was during the period from 1903 to 1905 when Japanese persecution was at its worst. The men, after establishing themselves in the United States, in order to get Korean wives, commenced sending to Korea for picture brides who had to travel under Japanese visas. The greatest influx of Korean women was during the period from 1915 to 1920. The Koreans who have settled in the United States have become a happy, prosperous and law-abiding people. It might be well to note that throughout the United States and its territories no Korean has been picked up or charged with subversive activities in connection with the present American-Japanese war. —

From the foregoing it can be readily seen that Koreans, although unwilling subjects of Japan, are and have been more anti-Japanese than any other nationality on earth, for they have had to bear the cruel yoke of Japanese oppression for more than thirty-six years.

The United States has in a measure recognized this distinction in a number of ways:

1. The Honorable William Jennings Bryan, while
Secretary of State, declared that Koreans in the United
States were not Japanese.

2. During the alien registration in 1940, the
Department of Justice permitted the Koreans to register as
Koreans, and not as Japanese.

3. In the United States census reports, Koreans
are listed separate and apart from Japanese.

4. The State and Labor Departments have granted
Korean refugees and students special entry privileges and
freedom of movement not given to the Japanese.

In the present emergency, Koreans in the United
States have been called upon to obtain licenses as aliens,
from the Foreign Funds Control Board, as they are considered
as Japanese. With the requirement of obtaining licenses
they do not complain in any way; but they do very definitely
object to being classed as Japanese, a race which they in-
tensely and virulently hate.

The Koreans in exile, those settled in other countries, as well as those in Korea proper, are ready and willing
to aid the allied powers in any way that is humanly possible
to subdue and defeat Japan in her viciously illegal and wanton desire for world empire, which history shows to be cruel
and ruthless, without regard for the rights of the persons,
property or countries she has subjugated.

It is the desire of all Koreans that immediate
recognition be given the Provisional Government of the Korean
Republic in exile at Chungking by the Allied powers; that the
United States of America, as the leading democratic nation,

use its good offices to achieve this purpose; that, at the
successful conclusion of the present world conflict Japan be
compelled to renounce its sovereignty over Korea, totally
evacuating its army and government therefrom, and to indemnify
Korea for all property appropriated and rights taken from the
Korean Government and its people.

Overseas Convention And United Korean Committee

Coming as a climax to many months of careful study and concerted effort by responsible leaders of the Korean community here and on the mainland, the first convention of overseas Korean delegates was held in Honolulu April 19-29 this year with 15 representatives from 7 major organizations present.

The convention resulted in a success. All of the important issues bearing on the present and future welfare of the Korean people have been settled and a comprehensive program looking toward materialization of these issues was formulated.

One noteworthy feature of the convention was the birth of the United Korean Committee in America with two co-ordinating headquarters, the first the seat of Directors' committee in Honolulu and the other the seat of administrative committee in Los Angeles.

Mr. Won Soon Lee heads the local committee as general chairman with Mr. Won Kiu Ahn as vice chairman; Mr. Warren Kim, English secretary; Mr. C. H. Tough, Korean secretary; Mr. Henry K. Kim, chairman of the National Defense Aid subcommittee; Messrs .S. W. Sohn and P. Y. Cho co-treasurers: Mr. Shinho Char, auditor. Other members of the Board of Directors include Mr. S. W. Lim, Mrs. Youngsin Shim. Mr. S. H. Kang and Mrs. Yinsik Min.

The staff of the administrative body in Los Angeles include Mr. Ho Kim, chairman: Lee Kyung Sun, secretary; C. I. Song. treasurer and Mr. Sidai Hahn, P. Y. Kim.

The local National Defense Aid Committee. organized soon after the convention with a staff of 9 live-wires, has done and continue to do admirable piece of work in furtherance of the UKC function. This body includes subcommittee on information—David Youth, C. H. Tough. Father Noah K. Cho; subcommittee on training—Walter Jhung. Young Kee Kim, Donald Kang; and subcommittee on relief—Rev. C. H. Min, Thomas Yoon, H. K. Ahn.

FINANCES

To carry on the vast work formulated by the United Korean Committee, a considerable sum of money is needed. The Convention decided to raise at least $20,000 per year—$15,000 from Hawaii and $5,000 from the mainland—to support three institutions dedicated to the independence movement: the Korean Provisional government, the Restoration Army and the Korean Commission at Washington, D. C.

There has been an unexampled manifestation of spontaneous interest and loyalty in responding to the call for Toknipkeum by Hawaii Koreans. To date, over $17,000 has been pledged by local people, an astounding feat! It went over the top by a substantial margin.

CONCLUSION

To the young Koreans of Hawaii, we wish to urge greater loyalty, cooperation and willing service in behalf of America's National Defense program which appears more imperative today in view of rapidly changing world situation. Let the entire Korean community in Hawaii and the mainland put up a united solid front behind the United Korean Committee in America in assisting this important piece of national policy. It is our duty, our privilege as well as our obligation.

With Japan-America relations now strained, to the breaking point, a show-down in Pacific looms almost a certainty. This is the chance we have been praying for since the fateful year of 1910 While the older people are doing their part to support the independence movement, we urge every young Korean in the United States to pitch in and do their share too. This is decidedly a world of youthful activities. Without your active interest and cooperation, our work would fall short of success.

————O————

Resolutions Adopted By The Oversea Convention

I. UNIFICATION OF INDEPENDENCE FRONT

1. Koreans should transcend the "isms" and principles and concentrate all their strength and resources to resist Japan.

(Reason: Regardless of the difference in beliefs among our people, let it be known that Japan is the common enemy of Korean people. Koreans should therefore unite to overthrow her.)

2. All Korean publications should maintain a unified stand on the world situation as it exists today.

(Reason: For cooperative work we need to have the same spirit and plans. Therefore, all publications must agree in spirit, purpose and methods.)

3, Mottos or slogans should be formulated to stimulate team-work.

(Reason: To visualize our program and to accelerate the activity by coining simple suggestive words.)

II. SUPPORTING PROVISIONAL GOVERNMENT

1. All Koreans and their organizations should place absolute trust and faith in the integrity of the Korean Provisional government and support it with spirit and matter.

(Reason: Because of the failure in the past of the people to trust and support the Provisional Government. it had great difficulties. From now on, we should, therefore. trust and support that central organization with all our heart and strength.)

2. Every Korean and every Korean organization should observe the decrees issued by the Provisional Government.

(Reason: By observing the decrees, we may sanctify and strengthen it.)

3. For the sanctity of the government and the discipline of the people we should ask the Provisional Government not to change the form of the present government until the people demand it.

(Reason: We ask this for fear of coup-de-tat and of the diminution of the efficiency of the government.

III. MILITARY ACTION

1. Every Korean political organization abroad should emphasize the idea that every Korean is a unit of the military force and should train himself for it.

(Reason: We know it is our duty to be a soldier for the independence movement. But we need to place strong emphasis on it in this emergency and to train the people to be the vanguards of the movement.)

2. Kwangbokkoon and Euiyondai should come under the control of the Provisional Government without any condition to put up a united front against Japan.

(Reason: We, believing the great significance of unity in our movement, should ask the Government to incorporate these two military units under the control of the Government.)

IV. DIPLOMATIC ACTION

1. We should establish a diplomatic commission in Washington, D. C.

(Reason: Because Washington is the center of word diplomacy, a diplomatic organ at that spot would well serve our purpose.)

2. For the time being we should send one representative to be a full-time worker. According to the development of the work and the situation, the number of officers may be increased.

(Reason: Owing to financial conditions and for simplicity of the procedure, one person takes charge of the work. Later, as conditions warrant, the number of representatives may be augmented.)

3. The diplomatic commission should initiate its action after finishing the legal procedure of the Provisional Government.

(Reason: It is necessary to have the approval of the government for appointment of its staff personnel).

4. The expenses of the diplomatic commission shall be paid by the Koreans abroad.

(Reason: Because the financial power is practically in the hands of the Koreans in America (U.S.A., Hawaii, Cuba, et al), they are to have this responsibility.

5. Dr. Syngman Rhee is elected as the representative of the diplomatic commission

6. The above four items should be presented to the Provisional Government for approval. The commission will start to function when it is approved by the government.

V. AID TO U. S. NATIONAL DEFENSE PROGRAM

1. The United Korean Commission should proclaim to the Koreans to render their services to the United States national defense program, directly or indirectly, both morally and materially.

2. A representative should be elected to be of service to the national defense project. The expense of the representative shall be paid by the Koreans in America.

3. Mr. Kilsoo K. Haan is elected as service man to aid the U. S. National Defense.

VI. FINANCE FOR INDEPENDENCE MOVEMENT

1. All contributions for the Independence movement should be named "Toknipkeum." This should be collected and in a unified method in different organizations of the locality, according to the economical, industrial and labor conditions of the individual. The organization should all cooperate to bring best results in this respect.

2. All other terms used for the contributions in the connection by various organizations should be abolished from now on.

3. The Budget of Toknipkeum: Of the total collection of Topnipkeum two-thirds shall be sent to Provisional Government and the remaining one-third used for the diplomatic and National Defense aid service.

4. The details of the finances will be stated

VII. ESTABLISHMENT OF UNITED COMMITTEE

1. The United Korean Committee in America is hereby established.

2. The committee shall consist of two parts: Directors' Committee and Executive Committee. Directors' Committee is organized by the representatives from Hawaii while the Executive Committee is organized by the representatives from the Mainland.

3. The regulations of the Committee will be stated hereafter.

REGULATIONS GOVERNING THE UNITED KOREAN COMMITTEE

1. This organization shall be called the United Korean Committee in America.

2. The purpose of this committee is to attain the independence of Korea. As the first step toward this goal, the organizaiton will unite the war front to win victory over Japan. Meantime, the organization will do various cooperative work for the betterment of the Korean society abroad.

3. The committee shall cooperate with all Korean political organizations abroad.

4. The committee shall put into practice a representative system. The members of the Committees are all of the delegates to the Convention of Overseas Koreans and the presidents of the Korean National Association of Hawaii, of Dongji Hoi and of the Korean National Ass'n of North America.

5. The Director's Committee shall consist of the representatives in Hawaii. The Executive Committee shall consist of representatives in America. Supplementation is done by the appointment of each particular organization.

6. The unit organization shall make every effort to collect toknipkeum and send same to the United Committee.

7. Every unit-organization shall observe the duty to collect and send toknipkeum cordially.

8. The unit-organizations should be obedient to the regulations and agreements and should not do anything contradictory to the spirit and rules of the Committee.

9. The appointees of the Committee shall follow the supervision of the Committee faithfully.

10. The Committee shall supervise the work of the National Defense Aid service.

11. The financial regulations will be stated hereafter.

12. Details of the expenditures of the Committee shall be paid after the approval of Directors' Committee.

13. The Committee has no regular meeting. Temporary meetings may be held through an agreement made by the Directors' and Executive Committees in time of urgent need.

BY-LAWS OF THE TREASURY

1. The Executive Committee supervises the disposal of Toknipkeum.

2. The Toknipkeum is sent to the Directors' Committee in Hawaii and to the Execuitve Committee in America. Each committee has two treasurers.

3. The minimum amount of Toknipkeum for each individual shall be at least $15 per annum. The method of collection is determined by the respective committee according to local situation.

4. The collection of Toknipkuem shall be operated following the approval of the Committee.

5. The Executive Committee shall report income and expenses of Toknipkeum monthly.

The delegates to the Convention pledge to support all the resolutions of the convention fully and make every effort to fulfill them.

The above 7 resolutions, supplements and by-laws of the treasury shall become operative from May 15, 1941. Donations collected by the unit organizations up to May 14 shall be sent to the treasury of Provisional Government or elsewhere directly by the respective organizations.

———

April 29, the 23rd year of Korean Republic (1941). By the following delegates in attendance at the Convention:

(Sgd) S. D. Hahn, KNA of North America.

   "   Ho Kim, KNA of North America.

   "   C. Y. Song, KNA of North America.

   "   H. K. Ahn, Dongji Hoi.

   "   W. S. Lee, Dongji Hoi.

   "   C. H. Tough, Donji Hoi.

   "   W. K. Ahn, KNA of Hawaii.

   "   H. C. Kim, KNA of Hawaii.

   "   W. Y. Kim, KNA of Hawaii.

   "   S. H. Char, Sino-Korean Peoples' League.

   "   S. H. Kang, Korean National Independence League.

   "   S. W. Lim, Hawaii Chapter, Korean Independence Party.

   "   Doin Kwon, Korean Volunteer League in America.

   "   Y. S. Shim, Korean Women's Relief Society in Hawaii.

   "   Hamna Min, Korean Women's Relief Society in Hawaii.

———O———

In reply refer to
A-B/H 895.01/65

February 4, 1942

My dear Mr. Lee:

By reference from the President your letter of January 23, 1942, and the accompanying "Appeal to the Allied Powers", have been given to me for acknowledgment.

You may be assured that the text of this appeal has been carefully noted and that the views expressed therein will be given due consideration.

Sincerely yours,

Harold B. Hoskins
Executive Assistant

Mr. Won Soon Lee, Chairman,
United Korean Committee in America,
1306 Miller Street,
Honolulu,
Territory of Hawaii.

A-B/H:HBH:RW:JKF   2/4/42

United States Senate

COMMITTEE ON FOREIGN RELATIONS

January 22, 1942

Mr. Maxwell M. Hamilton
Chief, Division of Far Eastern Affairs
Department of State
Washington, D. C.

My dear Mr. Hamilton:

Having in mind your many courtesies to me of the past and also having in mind my own particular interest in the Koreans and their relationship to our interests in the present war situation, I am enclosing herewith a photostatic copy of an excerpt from an article by Geraldine T. Fitch in the publication, "Amerasia".

I recently addressed a letter to Secretary Hull, at the request of one of our Intelligence Units, expressing the fear entertained by them that action such as is contemplated in the enclosed article might seriously jeopardize, if not totally destroy, certain sources of information which are highly valuable to us. I had this in mind in enclosing the excerpt to you, and I also had in mind the statement of this published article that Korean representatives had been assured of help from the United States with "the sky as the limit", if and when we became involved in war with Japan.

Will you kindly return the enclosed for my files after you have read it, and I should welcome any comment or suggestion.

With sincere personal regards, I am

Sincerely,

GUY M. GILLETTE

GMG:HA

Enclosure

KOREA'S HOPE OF FREEDOM

General Lee and granted special permission for the Korean
Army to operate in Chinese territory. The Chinese Government gave some financial assistance for organizational
work, equipment, and training; but reports indicate that
this army still lacks arms and ammunition, and hopes for
some aid under our lend-lease bill.

When the Korean Army was organized in West China to
help the Chinese in their struggle against Japanese domination, the public relations envoy of the Provisional
Government made a trip to Washington to interview officials
regarding the possibility of this lend-lease aid. This
author is reliably informed that State Department
officials informed him that although no lend-lease help
could be proffered at that time, yet if war should eventuate
between Japan and the United States, the "sky would be the
limit." Such help would be justified by Korean aid to the
United States in cooperation, espionage, and information.

Briefly, what aid can Korea today give to the country now at war with her old enemy? The Korean Provisional
Government has issued the following proclamation to its
people at home and abroad:

"The clash between the United States and Japan has
at last come. We Koreans, the first Asiatic victims of
Japanese rapacity, have long tried to warn the American
people of Japan's intentions toward them. . . . And while
the American people did not heed our warnings, they know
now what we have known for nearly half a century; what
the Russians have known since 1904; what the people of
Manchuria have known for ten years and the Chinese for
five, i.e., that no act of treachery, no act of barbarism,
and no act of villainy is beyond the use of the blood-
thirsty savage tribes of Nippon. . . .

Those of you in our homeland, Korea, those of you
in Japan, and those of you in all Japanese-occupied
territories in China, have sacred duties to perform.

You must blow up Japanese ammunition plants.

You must destroy railroads the Japanese use.

You must mine highways over which Japanese troops
pass.

You must shoot and kill every armed Japanese by
day and night.

You

You must commit every act of sabotage and violence
which will hinder, disrupt or destroy any part of the
Japanese war effort.

You must be ready at all times, when the waning
strength of the Japanese permits, to rise up, attack and
to exterminate the enemy."

Coupled with the admonition to Korean-Americans
to serve in the American army, navy, or air corps, the
above outlines what the Government of the Republic of
Korea-in-exile expects of its people. Considering the
fact that many Koreans can pass for Japanese, speak
Japanese perfectly, have had and will have in their
possession information about Japanese plans and movements
helpful to our forces, it may be expected that they will
be useful aides in espionage, in sabotage, and other
subversive activities/wholly compatible with declared
war against their long-standing enemy.

DEPARTMENT OF STATE

DIVISION OF FAR EASTERN AFFAIRS

January 24, 1942

S

Mr. Secretary:

Attached is my letter to Senator Gillette,
acknowledging the receipt of a letter from
him with which was enclosed a photostatic
copy of an excerpt from a recent magazine
article dealing with Korea.

You may care to note the underlying
courteous acknowledgment of Senator Gillette
to your letter of January 19 with regard to
his Resolution offered in the Senate, looking to the investigation of certain pro-
Axis activities, and with regard to the question of Korean independence.

FE:Salisbury:ALM

January 30, 1942

In reply refer to
FE

My dear Senator Gillette:

This will acknowledge the receipt of your letter of January 22 with which you enclosed a photostatic copy of an excerpt from an article entitled "Korea's Hope of Freedom", which was written by Geraldine T. Fitch, and which appeared in the January issue of Amerasia. You state that you would welcome any comment on this.

I appreciate your thoughtfulness in sending us this excerpt. The article had already come to our attention and had been read by various officers of the Department. As you are aware, the military aspects of the Korean situation referred to in the excerpt have no doubt already received the consideration of our military authorities, and there is little which I could say of value in the way of comment.

As

The Honorable
    Guy M. Gillette,
        United States Senate.

As for the statement made by the writer of the article that she had been reliably informed that, in the event that war were to occur between the United States and Japan, assistance under the Lease-Lend Act had been promised to "the public relations envoy of the Provisional Government" by an officer of the Department for use in activities against Japan, it is most unlikely that such assurances have been given by any officer or officers of this Department, and in so far as my own personal knowledge is concerned I am confident that the writer has been misinformed. It is of course obvious that a matter such as this would call for consideration by a number of agencies of the Government.

In accordance with your request I am returning herewith the photostatic copy of the excerpt, a copy having been made for the files of the Department.

With kind regards,

Sincerely yours,

Maxwell M. Hamilton
Chief
Division of Far Eastern Affairs

1942PM

Enclosure:
Photostatic copy of
"Korea's Hope of Freedom".

A true copy of
the signed orig-
inal.

FE:LES:HNS
1/26

FE

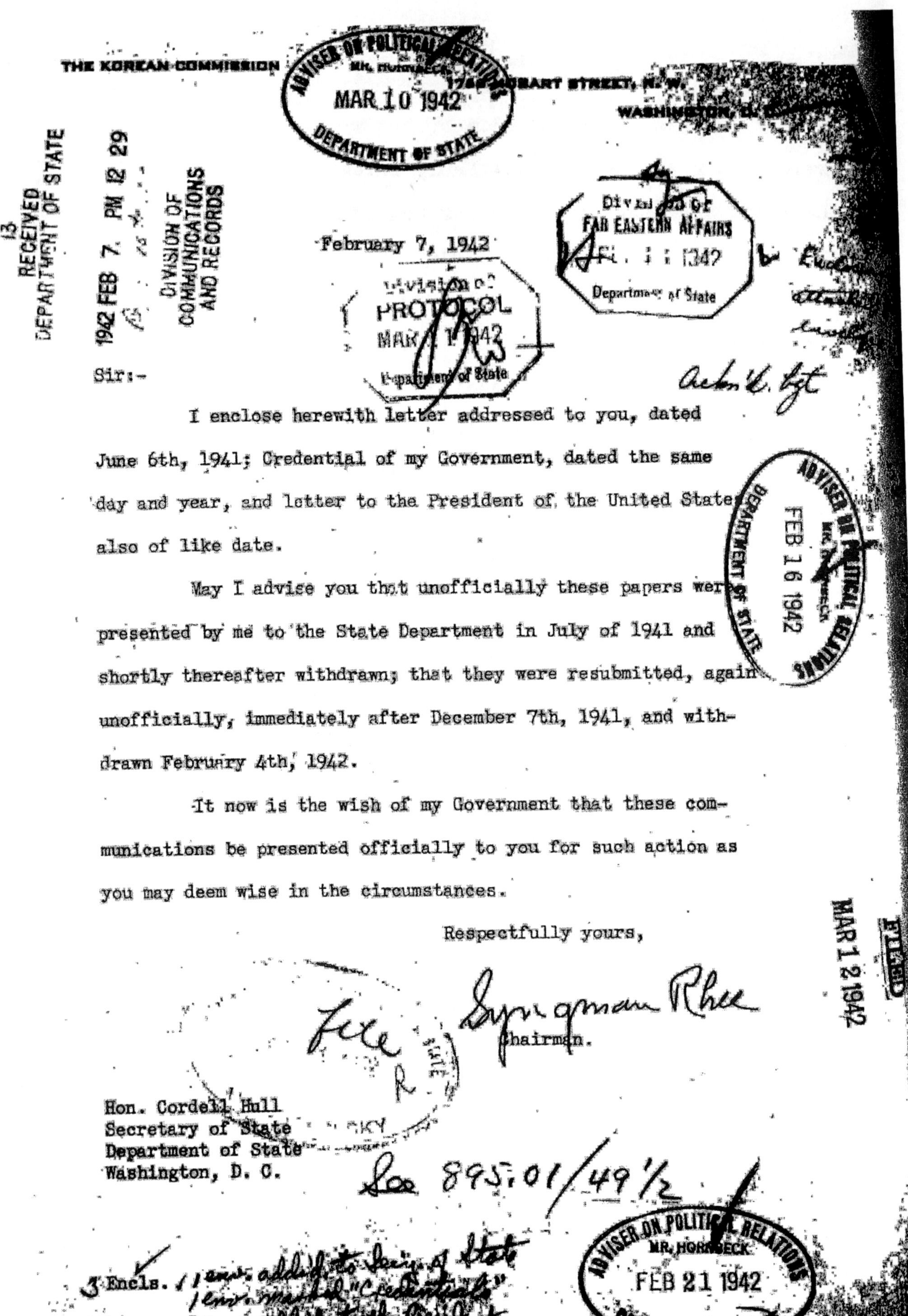

February 7, 1942

Sir:-

I enclose herewith letter addressed to you, dated June 6th, 1941; Credential of my Government, dated the same day and year, and letter to the President of the United States also of like date.

May I advise you that unofficially these papers were presented by me to the State Department in July of 1941 and shortly thereafter withdrawn; that they were resubmitted, again unofficially, immediately after December 7th, 1941, and withdrawn February 4th, 1942.

It now is the wish of my Government that these communications be presented officially to you for such action as you may deem wise in the circumstances.

Respectfully yours,

Syngman Rhee
Chairman.

Hon. Cordell Hull
Secretary of State
Department of State
Washington, D. C.

895.01/49½

3 Encls.

- 323 -

Dear Dr. Rhee:

Reference is made to your letter to the Secretary of State of February 7, 1942 with which there were enclosed a document addressed to the President of the United States dated June 6, 1941, a document addressed to the Secretary of State bearing the same date and a document entitled <u>Credential</u> also dated June 6, 1941.

As you are no doubt aware, the Department has stated in an announcement of its policy toward the activities of foreign political leaders in the United States that it is glad to be informed of the plans and proposed activities of organizations of aliens in this country who wish to assist in the struggle against Axis domination of the world. Accordingly, the Department

is

Dr. Syngman Rhee,
 1766 Hobart Street, N.W.,
  Washington, D.C.

is glad to be informed of the activities of Koreans who are
assisting in the task of defeating Japan and her allies and.
consequently,
is making note of the information conveyed in the
documents under reference regarding the plans and
objectives of the organization to which they relate.

For your convenience there is enclosed herewith
a copy of the Department's press release of December 10,
1941 in which there is set forth a statement of the
Department's policy in matters of this kind.

Sincerely yours,

For the Secretary of State:

ADOLF A. BERLE

Assistant Secretary

Enclosure.

[Dept. of State Press Release No. 600,
dated December 10, 1941]

DCR file no. 895.01/67

FEB 20

PA/H:AHiss:BGT
2-16-42

CROSS-REFERENCE FILE

NOTE

SUBJECT   Tjosowang,Mr.
Application has been made by a German,-,
to visit the U.S. to attend a foreign conference
as the representative of the Provisional Government of Korea at the invitation of Korean
Commission at 1766 Hobart St.Wash.D.C. of which
Dr.Syngman Rhee is understood to be the head.

For the original paper from which reference is taken

See _____ Tel.#80   10am

(Despatch, telegram, instruction, letter, etc.)

Dated January 31,1942   From| Chungking (Gauss)
                          To//|

File No. 811.111 Tjosowang,Mr. Confidential File

TELEGRAM SENT

Department of State

Washington,

February 19, 1942

AMEMBASSY,

LONDON (ENGLAND).

This Government has been approached by various Korean groups in this country which have been and still are working for Korean independence. Some of these people are, moreover, primarily interested in the question of participation by Koreans in the war effort.

The Department is of course desirous of obtaining the active support wherever feasible of opponents of the Axis powers and is naturally sympathetic to the plight of the Korean people under Japanese domination and is anxious to help to strengthen Korean resistance and opposition to Japan. We are not repeat not at this time, however, contemplating a QUOTE recognition UNQUOTE of Korea or the making of any commitment as to future QUOTE recognition UNQUOTE of Korea. Further, we are not repeat not at this moment contemplating recognizing any particular group or organization of Koreans as the dominant or primary movement for Korean opposition to Japanese oppression.

-2-

SETWO --

In connection with the foregoing it would be helpful
to us if you could ascertain whether there is any Korean
organization in England which is pressing the British
Government for some form of QUOTE recognition UNQUOTE of
Korea. We should also like you to ascertain informally
and discreetly the attitude of the British Government
toward the general question of recognition of any QUOTE
Provisional Government UNQUOTE of Korea in exile or of
any QUOTE Free Korean UNQUOTE organization.

Please inform officials of the Foreign Office that
we are at present giving thought to the question of the
advisability of issuing some general statement to the
press expressing the interest of this Government in the
efforts of the Korean people to put an end to Japanese
oppression and to the question whether such a statement
would be likely to be of use in stimulating resistance
by Koreans to the Japanese in Korea, in China (including
Manchuria), and within Japan itself.

We should be glad to be informed of the attitude of
appropriate officials of the Foreign Office on this whole
question. ENMES

Enciphered by _______________________

Sent by operator _______ M., _______ 19 ___

TELEGRAM RECEIVED

HRL
This telegram must be
closely paraphrased be FROM
fore being communicated
to anyone. (MC)

London

Dated February 16, 1942

Rec'd 9:30 p.m.

Secretary of State,

Washington.

Division of
FAR EASTERN AFFAIRS
FEB 17 1942
Department of State

730, February 16, 12 p.m.

SECRET

We have discussed with the Foreign Office the
subject matter of the Department's telegram 552 February
12 midnight and are told by way of preliminary reply
that there are very few Koreans in the United Kingdom
and that there is no active group engaged in advocating
Korean "recognition" or so far as is known even resistance
to the Japanese.

The Foreign Office expresses full agreement of
course with the Department's desire to obtain active
support wherever practicable from opponents to the
Axis powers; it would like however a few days to think
over the questions raised in the Department's telegram
as the problem of "free Koreans" or Korean resistance
has apparently not previously arisen to the British
Government.

WINANT

CSB

P A R A P H R A S E

A telegram (no. 730) dated February 16, 1942, from the American Ambassador at London, reads substantially as follows:

The subject matter of a telegram dated February 12 from the Department has been discussed with the Foreign Office and the Embassy has been informed, in the sense of a preliminary reply, that there is in the United Kingdom no active group which is engaged in the advocation of Korean "recognition", or even resistance, insofar as is known, to the Japanese. It was also stated that the number of Koreans in the United Kingdom is very small.

In as much as the matter of Korean resistance and the question of "Free Koreans" has not previously been considered by the British Government apparently, the Foreign Office stated that it would appreciate a short time, a few days, to consider the various questions mentioned in the Department's telegram under reference; however, the Foreign Office has expressed its complete concurrence in the Department's wish to secure the active support of the opponents of the Axis powers wherever practicable.

FE:EPT:ALM
2-18-42

IMPERIAL MUTUAL LIFE INSURANCE COMPANY
HOME OFFICE -- 700 WEST WASHINGTON BOULEVARD
LOS ANGELES, CALIFORNIA

Dear Mr. Secretary:-

I am heartily in accord with the expression of opinion in favor of your running the State Department - and our foreign relations policy.

The other day I spent several hours with Mr. Seung the head of the National Defence committee of the Koreans in this country.

I was astonished to learn that there are 23,000,000 of their people in Korea, that the Japanese fear them greatly, that all bitterly hate Japan and are ready for a revolution, and that they are situated only 75 miles from Japans backdoor, a dagger pointed at the heart of the Nipponese.

Why can't something

be done toward recognizing the
Provisional Government of Korea,
and utilizing this important
potential source of strength.

Very truly yours,

Frank P. Tibbetts

Frank P. Tibbetts

In reply refer to
A-B/H 895.01/70

My dear Mr. Tibbetts:

The Secretary of State has asked me to acknowledge with thanks your letter to him of February 14, 1942, regarding the potential strength of the Koreans and your suggestion that this Government recognize the Korean Provisional Government.

Your letter has been referred to the responsible officers of this Department, and you may be assured that it will be given due consideration.

Your courtesy in writing and in presenting your suggestions is much appreciated.

Sincerely yours,

Harold B. Hoskins
Executive Assistant

Mr. Frank P. Tibbetts,
Imperial Mutual Life Insurance Company,
700 West Washington Boulevard,
Los Angeles, California.

A-B/H:HBH:MLH:PG:SS

HOUSE OF REPRESENTATIVES U. S.

WASHINGTON, D. C.

February 19, 1942

Respectfully referred to

Hon.Cordell Hull
The Secretary of State
Washington, D.C.

For attention and advice

Very respectfully,

M. C., 5th District.
California

Feb 14

My dear Congressman Welch, — I am in L.A. for a time. I am from your district in S.F.

The other day, I spent several hours with Mr. Sung, head of the Nat'l Defence Committee of the Koreans in this country.

I was astonished to learn that there are 23,000,000 of these people in Korea all bitterly hating Japan and ready for a revolution, and only 95 miles from Japans backdoor, a veritable dagger pointed at the heart of the nipponese.

Why can't some action be taken toward recognizing the Provisional Government of Korea, and thus utilizing this potential source of strength.

Very truly yours,

Frank P. Tibbetts

- 335 -

February 26, 1942

In reply refer to
A-B/H 895.01/71

My dear Mr. Welch:

I have received your note of February 19, 1942 in which you referred to this Department for attention and advice the letter of February 14 from Mr. Frank P. Tibbetts.

As Mr. Tibbetts also wrote to the Secretary of State regarding the question of Korea I am enclosing for your information a copy of the reply sent to him by this Department on February 23, 1942.

Your courtesy in bringing Mr. Tibbett's suggestions to my attention is much appreciated.

Sincerely yours,

Sumner Welles
Acting Secretary

Enclosure:

As stated.

The Honorable

Richard J. Welch,

House of Representatives.

A-B/H:HBH:RW:JKF   2/24/42

DEPARTMENT OF STATE

Memorandum of Conversation

FEB 18 1942
DIVISION OF
COMMUNICATIONS AND RECORDS

SUBJECT: Provisional Korean Government

PARTICIPANTS: Dr. Singman Rhee
                     Mr. Hoskins

COPIES TO: PA/H - Mr. Hornbeck
                          Mr. Hiss

                  FE -

In the course of a telephone conversation with Dr. Rhee
regarding other matters, I had an opportunity to collect from
Dr. Rhee information regarding his reasons for returning to
Dr. Hornbeck various official documents covering a request
for recognition of the provisional Korean Government in Chungking
and of Dr. Rhee's status as the representative of that provisional
government in Washington.

It was clear from his conversation that Dr. Rhee had been
guided in presenting these letters officially to the State
Department by advice of individuals described as "American
friends". He explained that this was a first step in their
program of bringing to the attention of the American people

Korea's claim to independence. The next step aims at getting in touch with friendly Senators and Congressmen on the Hill and he felt they should be in a position at that time to state as a matter of record that they had made an official request for recognition as indicated in these letters to the State Department.

In the course of his conversation Dr. Rhee also mentioned the fact that he had discussed with Dr. Hornbeck the advisability of starting a more aggressive campaign for Korean recognition in the United States and that this had the general approval of Dr. Hornbeck.

Harold B. Hoskins

A-B/H:HBH-gw

February 4, 1942.

Reference, Dr. Syngman Rhee's letter to
me of December 9, my memorandum to FE of
December 16 and FE's memorandum to me of
December 20 regarding papers offered by
Dr. Rhee.

Dr. Rhee called on me at his request
today. Our conversation related to various
matters of concern to Koreans active in the
Korean independence movement which raised
questions of interest and concern to the
American Government.

Having in the interval since December 20
discussed with officers of FE and most recently
with Mr. Hoskins the question of the documents
which Dr. Rhee had offered, I, at an opportune
moment in this conversation, took up with
Dr. Rhee the question of possession of those
documents. I stated that it appeared that the
time had not yet arrived when it would be opportune and would serve a useful purpose for
those documents to be presented to the
President, the Secretary of State and the
Department; and I summarized, in other parts
of the conversation, reasons for that opinion.
Dr. Rhee indicated that he in no way dissented
from that opinion and that he was perfectly
willing to have the documents continue to be
withheld. I then said that it seemed to me
that the documents might either continue to
be held by me or might be given back by me

to

-2-

to Dr. Rhee; that I was willing to follow
either procedure but I thought that it would
be better for Dr. Rhee to take them. I said
that the fact that these documents had been
offered was a matter of record and was known
to Mr. Hamilton, Mr. Hoskins and myself,
and that the matter had been mentioned to the
Secretary of State. Dr. Rhee said that it
would be perfectly agreeable to him for me
to hand the documents back to him. I thanked
Dr. Rhee and gave the documents over to him.

PA/H:SKH:FLB

TELEGRAM RECEIVED

FROM

London

Dated February 28, 1942

Rec'd 12:19 p.m.

WM
This telegram must be
closely paraphrased be-
fore being communicated
to anyone. (MC)

Secretary of State,

Washington.

962, February 28, 3 p.m. (SECTION ONE)

Department's telegram 552, February 12 midnight

and Embassy's 630, February 16 midnight.

I was handed this morning the following

informal memorandum setting forth the views of the

Foreign Office with respect to the Korean question:

MATTHEWS

TELEGRAM RECEIVED

HRL
This telegram must be
closely paraphrased be-
fore being communicated
to anyone. (B)

London
FROM
Dated February 28, 1942

Rec'd 1:15 p.m.

Secretary of State,

    Washington.

    96?, February 28, 3 p.m. (SECTION TWO)

    "In a memorandum dated sixteenth February on
the subject of groups of Koreans in the United
States who are working for Korean independence the
United States Embassy invites an informal and confidential indication of the attitude of the Foreign
Office on the general question of the recognition
of any so called 'provisional government' of Korea
in exile or any organization of 'free Koreans'.

    Two. So far as is known there are no Koreans
in the United Kingdom and certainly not enough to
form any kind of organization.

    Three. The following approaches have been
made to His Majesty's Embassy at Chungking soon after
the outbreak of the war in the Pacific by Mr. Tjoso
Wang purporting to be Minister for Foreign Affairs
in the Provisional Government of the Republic of
Korea who handed in letters addressed to Mr. Churchill
and the Prime Minister of Canada expressing solidarity

        with the

TELEGRAM RECEIVED

TTM
This telegram must be
closely paraphrased be-
fore being communicated
to anyone. (MG)

London

Dated February 28, 1942

Rec'd 12:19 p.m.

Secretary of State,

Washington.

COPIES SENT TO O.N.I. AND
M.I.D. IN CONFIDENCE

962, February 28, 3 p.m. (SECTION ONE)

Department's telegram 552, February 12 midnight

and Embassy's 730, February 16 midnight.

I was handed this morning the following

informal memorandum setting forth the views of the

Foreign Office with respect to the Korean questions

MATTHEWS

TELEGRAM RECEIVED

HRL
This telegram must be
closely paraphrased be-
fore being communicated
to anyone. (B)

London
FROM
Dated February 28, 1942

Rec'd 1:15 p.m.

Secretary of State,

    Washington.

    969, February 28, 3 p.m. (SECTION TWO)

"In a memorandum dated sixteenth February on
the subject of groups of Koreans in the United
States who are working for Korean independence the
United States Embassy invites an informal and confidential indication of the attitude of the Foreign
Office on the general question of the recognition
of any so called 'provisional government' of Korea
in exile or any organization of 'free Koreans'.

    Two. So far as is known there are no Koreans
in the United Kingdom and certainly not enough to
form any kind of organization.

    Three. The following approaches have been
made to His Majesty's Embassy at Chungking soon after
the outbreak of the war in the Pacific by Mr. Tjoso
Wang purporting to be Minister for Foreign Affairs
in the Provisional Government of the Republic of
Korea who handed in letters addressed to Mr. Churchill
and the Prime Minister of Canada expressing solidarity

                  with the

-2- #962, February 28, 3 p.m. (SECTION TWO) from London

with the Allied cause and belief in an Allied victory. Similar messages were received from organizations called the Korean National Revolutionary Party, the Korean National Association for the fight for liberty, the Korean National United Comrades Association and from a Mr. Ching Jo-Shan describing himself as Commander of the Korean Volunteers Corps. His Majesty's Ambassador understood that similar approaches were made to the United States Embassy.

MATTHEWS

CSB

TELEGRAM RECEIVED

AF
This telegram must be
closely paraphrased be-
fore being communicated
to anyone. (B)

FROM

London

Dated February 28, 1942

Rec'd 4:43 p.m.

Secretary of State,

    Washington.

962, February 28, 3 p.m. (SECTION THREE)

Four. His Majesty's Ambassador gained the impression that there was considerable disunity in the
Korean ranks and was informed by the Chinese Ministry of Foreign Affairs that although the Koreans in
Free China were aiming at independence, they differed
widely in their politics from republican radicalism
to reactionary monarchism. The Chinese authorities
found them all useful for anti-Japanese activities
but declared that there could be no question of any
sort of recognition of a free Korean movement until
factional differences were composed to which end they
were lending their good offices.

Five. An approach on the subject of 'recognition'
of the 'Korean Government' at Chungking was also made
by Mr. Yong Jeung Kim of the Korean National Association of North America who wrote to His Majesty's
Embassy at Washington in December, and called there
in January. On the occasion of his call he said that

        the 'Korean

-2- #962, February 28, 3 p.m. (SECTION THREE) from
London.

the 'Korean Government' were anxious to sign the
declaration of the United Nations and to obtain
British recognition. The Embassy gave him no encouragement on these points saying that they were without
instructions. Subsequently, they discussed the
matter with Mr. Haskins of the Department of State.

Six. The Foreign Office note that the Department of State while wishing to stimulate Korean opposition to Japan are not contemplating any 'recognition' of Korea at present or any commitment as to
the future; but that they have been giving thought
to the advisability of some general declaration regarding Korean endeavor to terminate Japanese oppression with the object of stimulating such opposition.

                                    MATTHEWS

NK

TELEGRAM RECEIVED

HRL
This telegram must be
closely paraphrased be-
fore being communicated
to anyone. (B)

FROM London

Dated February 28, 1942

Rec'd 10:05 p.m.

Secretary of State,

Washington.

962, February 28, 3 p.m. (SECTION FOUR)

Seven. The Foreign Office are in general of the
opinion that at present the possibilities of effective
Korean opposition to Japan in Japan itself are very
small indeed and that the possibilities in Korea are
not much greater. The possibilities in Manchuria and
occupied - China are perhaps more considerable, but
it appears to the Foreign Office that so long as the
present successes of Japan continue any formal declaration or act of recognition on the part of the
United States or United Kingdom Government's would be
unlikely to arouse a response on a really effective
scale amongst Koreans generally in the areas where
the Japanese are in control. When the tide turns
against the Japanese, however, a carefully timed
declaration might produce useful results.

Eight. For the time being the Foreign Office
considers that the reply to further approaches from
Koreans outside the Japanese area should be confined

to assurances

48

-2- #962, February 28, 3 p.m. (SECTION FOUR) from London

to assurances of sympathy with the efforts of
Koreans towards the realization of their aspirations
for national freedom and independence. This is
in fact the attitude adopted by the Chinese Minister
of Foreign Affairs in a letter to Mr. Kim dated
25th October 1941 (of which Mr. Kim communicated a
copy to the British Embassy in Washington). The
Foreign Office would suggest also that in view of
the interest of the Chinese Government in Korean
matters it might be well to concert with that
government any action tending towards recognition.

Nine. The Foreign Office would be glad to
have the opportunity of giving their support to any
action which the Department of State may eventually
decide to take and they would accordingly be glad
to learn in due course of any conclusions which the
Department may reach as a result of their review of
this question".

MATTHEWS

NPL

TELEGRAM RECEIVED

TRB
This telegram must be
closely paraphrased be-
fore being communicated
to anyone. ('IC)

FROM
London

Dated February 28, 1942

Rec'd 10:45 p.m.

Secretary of State,

Washington.

262, February 20, 3 p.m., (SECTION FIVE).

In conversation the pertinent official explained
that in indicating a feeling that the issuance of a
"formal declaration" at the present time would be
inopportune there was no intention of implying that
efforts through the radio and the press to stimulate
Korean opposition to Japan should not be engaged in.
In fact it is the Foreign Office feeling that the
history of Korea under Japanese domination and the
long series of violations of Japanese assurances
offer a highly useful field for publicity. They read
me in this connection a quotation from page 214 of
Hornbeck's "Contemporary politics in the Far East"
as cited in "Far Eastern International Relations" by
Morse and McNair. They feel that Korea furnishes
an excellent object lessons of the meaning of Japanese
domination.

(END MESSAGE).

MATTHEWS

KLP

50

P A R A P H R A S E

A telegram of February 28, 1942 from the American
Embassy at London reads substantially as follows:

On the morning of February 28 the Embassy received
from the Foreign Office an informal memorandum setting
forth its opinions concerning the Korean question. The
memorandum is to the following effect:

Reference is made to the American Embassy's memorandum of February 16 concerning the matter of groups of
Koreans in the United States who are working for the
independence of Korea. Reference is made also to the
Embassy's invitation that the Foreign Office indicate
confidentially and informally its attitude in general on
the subject of recognition of any organization of "free
Koreans" or any so-called "Provisional Government" of
Korea in exile.

No Koreans are known to be in the United Kingdom,
and in any case there are not enough of them to organize
in any manner. Soon after the outbreak of war in the
Pacific, Mr. Tjoso Wang, who purports to be Minister of
Foreign Affairs of the Provisional Government of the
Republic of Korea, approached the British Embassy at
Chungking with letters addressed to Prime Minister
Churchill and the Prime Minister of Canada. These letters
expressed belief in the victory of the United Nations and

expressed

expressed solidarity with their cause. Messages of
similar import were received from organizations bearing
the names of the Korean National Association for the
Fight for Liberty, the Korean National Revolutionary
Party, the Korean National United Comrades Association,
and from one Ching Jo Shan, who described himself as
Commander of the Korean Volunteer Corps. The British
Ambassador at Chungking understood that the American
Embassy was similarly approached. It was the impression
of the British Ambassador that a great deal of disunity
existed in the ranks of Koreans, and he learned from the
Chinese Ministry of Foreign Affairs that there was a
wide difference ranging from republican radicalism to
reactionary monarchism in the politics of the Koreans
in free China although their aim was independence. Although the authorities in China found all of the Koreans
useful for activities against the Japanese, they asserted
that, until factional differences were ironed out, which
they were endeavoring to assist in doing, there could be
no question of recognition of any sort of a free Korean
movement.

Mr. Yong Jeung Kim of the Korean National Association of North America approached the British Ambassador
at Washington in December by means of a letter in regard

to

to "recognition" of the "Korean Government" at Chungking.
In January Mr. Yong Jeung Kim called at the Embassy and stated
that the "Korean Government" was desirous of obtaining
recognition from Great Britain and of signing the
Declaration of the United Nations. The Ambassador informed Mr. Kim that it had no instructions in the matter
and gave him no encouragement. Later the Embassy discussed
the matter with Mr. Hoskins (the State Department).

Note has been taken of the fact that, although the
Department does not contemplate "recognition" of Korea
at the present time or any commitment with regard to
the future while desiring to stimulate opposition to
Japan on the part of Koreans, it (the Department) has
been considering the advisability of some general declaration in regard to efforts of Koreans to bring an end
to Japanese oppression in order to stimulate opposition
on the part of Koreans.

In general the Foreign Office believes that there
is very small chance at the present time of Koreans
effectively opposing Japan in Japan itself or that the
chances are much greater of effective opposition in
Korea. Although it is possible that the chances of
effective opposition in occupied China and in Manchuria
are greater, it seems to the Foreign Office that as

long

-4-

long as Japan continues with its present successes
it is improbable that any act of recognition or formal
declaration by the British Government or by the Government
of the United States would call forth any really effective
response from Koreans in general in the regions controlled
by Japanese. However a useful result might be brought
about by a carefully timed declaration when the tide
turns against Japan.

It is the opinion of the Foreign Office that for the
present any further approaches made by Koreans outside the
Japanese area should be confined to assurances of sympathy
with attempts of Koreans to realize their aims for independence and national freedom. As a matter of fact, the
Chinese Minister for Foreign Affairs adopted this attitude in a letter of October 25, 1941, addressed to Mr. Kim,
a copy of which was given the British Embassy in Washington
by Mr. Kim. The Foreign Office suggests that on account
of the Chinese Government's interest in Korean matters,
it might be advisable to act in concert with the Chinese
in any action looking toward the recognition of a Korean
Government. It is the desire of the Foreign Office to
support any action which the State Department may decide
eventually to take, and therefore, the Foreign Office
would be glad to be informed of any decisions which the

State

State Department may arrive at as a result of its review of Korean matters.

The pertinent official of the British Foreign Office during the course of the conversation explained that in expressing the opinion that it would be inopportune at the present time to issue a "formal declaration", it was not the intention of the Foreign Office to imply that attempts by means of the press and the radio to stimulate opposition to Japan on the part of Koreans should not be carried on. The Foreign Office is in fact of the opinion that an extremely useful field for publicity is presented by Korea's history under Japanese control and the long series of violations of Japanese assurances. In this connection a Foreign Office official read to the American Chargé an excerpt from page 214 of <u>Contemporary Politics in the Far East</u> by Mr. Hornbeck as cited in Morse and McNair's <u>Far Eastern International Relations</u>. The Foreign Office is of the opinion that an excellent object lesson of what Japanese domination means is supplied by Korea.

FE:EPC:MJF
3-2 3-3-42

FE

TELEGRAM SENT

Department of State

Washington,

March 18, 1942

AMERICAN EMBASSY,

LONDON.

Your 962, February 28, 3 p.m., Korean question.

Please inform the British Foreign Office that the
Department has found helpful its informal memorandum in
regard to the Korean question and [inform the Foreign
Office] that in general the views of the Department
coincide with those of the Foreign Office. In this
connection it is suggested that the Foreign Office may
be interested in the statement made at my press
conference on March 2 in regard to this question (see
Radio Bulletin of that date).

Acting

CR
MAR 19 1942PM

FE:WRL:MJK/HNS

FE   PA/H   Eu   A—B/H

Enciphered by ___________________

Sent by operator ___________ M.. ___________ 19____

Radio Bulletin No. 51   March 2, 1942

WHITE HOUSE

President today issued Executive Order modifying organization of U.S.
Army in move designed to expedite and better coordinate military action.
Effective March 9 for duration of war and six months thereafter, there will be
established following three basic units under Army Chief of Staff: (1) Army
Ground Force under Army Ground Forces Commanding General; (2) Air Force under
Army Air Forces Commanding General and (3) Service of Supply Command under
Services of Supply Commanding General. In addition there will be such overseas departments, task forces, base commands, defense commands, commands in
theaters of operation and other commands as War Secretary may deem necessary
for national security. All functions, duties and powers of chiefs of infantry,
field artillery, cavalry and coast artillery corps, except those related to
procurement, storage and issue, are transferred to Army Ground Forces. Functions, duties and powers of General Headquarters Air Force including Combat
Command and Chief of Air Corps are transferred to Army Air Forces. Functions,
duties and powers of Chief of Coast Artillery relating to procurement, storage
and issue are transferred to Services of Supply. Officers holding transferred
functions, duties and powers shall be re-assigned to suitable duties. Order
also directed War Secretary to issue from time to time "detailed instructions
regarding personnel, funds, records, property, routing of correspondence and
other matters."

(Later today Secretary Stimson termed reorganization "striking revitali-
zation" to eliminate cumbersome procedure and promote efficient direction of
Army activities, and appointed under over-all command of General Marshall
following commanders of respective basic units indicated above: Lt. Gen.
Henry H. Arnold, Lt. Gen. Lesley J. McNair, Major Gen. Brehon B. Somervell.)

President today issued Executive Order transferring all functions of
Marine Inspection Navigation now in Commerce Department to Coast Guard (now
part of Navy) and Bureau of Customs, and transferring training functions of
Maritime Commission solely to Coast Guard. Order made Coast Guard henceforth
responsible for: (1) safety inspection of every American merchant vessel,
(heretofore responsibility of local inspectors of Bureau of Marine Inspection
and Navigation Service); (2) all marine casualty investigations; (3) signing
on and discharging of merchant crews; and (4) welfare of seamen aboard merchant
vessels (last two of which have heretofore been responsibility of Shipping
Commissioners). Five State nautical schools in California, New York, Massa-
chusetts, Maine and Pennsylvania aided by Federal grants are also transferred
to Coast Guard. White House statement accompanying Order said "move is
designed to facilitate the Government's efforts in the intensive wartime
development of the merchant marine."

CONGRESS

Senate today completed Congressional action on repeal of pensions-for-
Congress legislation including as elective officers, President and Vice President. Bill also provides for allotment of pay for one year to dependents of
members of armed forces captured by enemy, or who are missing and not presumed
dead or deserted; 20 percent and 10 percent pay increase for enlisted men and
officers respectively, serving outside continental U.S., Alaska or on sea duty;
and new set of locks for Sault Ste. Marie Canal to speed ore shipments.

Senate today unanimously passed and returned to House $33,452,000,000 War
Appropriation Bill after accepting amendments therein exempting Filipinos from
provision banning use of funds for payments to non-citizens and increasing
total

total of bill by $690,000,000 above House-approved figure of $32,762,000,000.
(According to press, belief was expressed in many quarters that Senate farm
bloc would attach to mammoth War Appropriation Bill rider forbidding President
to sell surplus farm produce below 110 percent of parity, and that President
would accordingly veto measure regardless of urgency of needed appropriations.
Speaking for farm bloc, Senator Thomas today said issue would not again be
raised until Agriculture Supply Bill reached Senate.)

House today passed and returned to Senate Second War Powers Bill providing
drastic penalties for violation of priority orders and expanding Government's
power to seize private property in furtherance of war effort.

NATIONAL WAR EFFORT

According to press, General Motors' President Wilson stated Saturday
that despite dislocation through conversion, Corporation's payroll of 162,000
factory workers in mid-February was 88 percent of average 1940 figure.

According to press, Korean Liberty Conference, which convened in Washington Saturday, approved resolutions calling on President and Congress to
recognize independence of Korea with 21,000,000 inhabitants, and requesting
State Department to admit petition of Korean Government to subscribe to pact
of 26 United Nations.

OFF Director MacLeish in address yesterday said he believes "tough truth"
can be revealed to nation concerning reports of adverse as well as favorable
nature because strategy of truth is soundest factual basis for formation of
judgments and criticism by public.

According to press, Army and Justice Department representatives in San
Francisco announced Saturday that decision has been made to move all Japanese
citizens as well as aliens out of Pacific Coast combat zones, (designation of
all of which has not yet been announced by Lt. Gen. DeWitt, Western Defense
Commander) despite plea of Governors of six of eight interior States protesting
against "dumping" evacuees therein. DeWitt said military necessity and national
interest outweighed other considerations.

Attorney General Biddle announced that as far as possible contractors,
farmers, lumber operators and other employers of migratory labor will be protected against loss of labor of enemy aliens through measures whereunder, after
obtaining identification certificates, aliens may on good reason, and following
investigation, within discretion of Justice Department be exempted from travel
and other restrictions imposed by Executive Orders.

War Secretary Stimson announced formation of six Negro military police
battalions for service in zone of interior, for guarding factories, warehouses,
bridges, power houses and similar installations.

Assistant War Secretary McCloy in radio address yesterday said Army
needs 75,000 new officers this year who will be selected from 95,000 candidates,
including those of enlisted personnel between ages of 18 and 45 with 4 months'
service and intelligence rating of 110 or better, as well as men from civilian
life with good records, "some education", and "marked qualities of leadership."
Men with dependents may enlist for sole purpose of qualifying as officers and
if they fail to make the grade, be transferred to enlisted reserves and not
called until previous draft classifications come up.

War Department announced that Chief of Ordnance has declined offers of
many U.S. communities to contribute for Army use cannons and other weapons
mounted in public squares, parks, before court houses, etc., salvaged from
Central Powers at conclusion of first World War on grounds of obsolescence,
but suggested such collection be turned over to metal dealers as scrap iron for
use our war effort.

WPB announced it has given can manufacturers permission to deliver until
May 31 can for packing beer, coffee, and hams.

WPB in statement designed to show need for auto rationing, said for every
automobile not made 100 pounds of nickel steel is saved for armor plates,
projectiles, and armor-piercing bullets and enough zinc and copper is saved to
make brass for 2,400 brass cartridge cases; for reducing production by 24
automobiles enough steel and rubber is saved for 27-ton medium tank; and for
reducing production by 700 autos enough aluminum is saved to make one fighter
plane.

Price

Price Administrator Henderson established temporary wholesale price ceilings for 25 varieties of canned fruits and vegetables aimed at stabilizing retail prices. Order, which becomes effective March 2, will be in force 60 days before replacement by permanent maximum price regulations.

According to press, Army Chief of Staff Marshall today said that as "time has now come to carry the war to the enemy" and to discontinue immobilizing troops in continental U.S., nation must expect isolated air raids if for no other purpose than to create public reaction against sound military purpose of defending U.S. by engaging and defeating enemy in distant theatres.

Maritime Labor Board created 1938 and under process of disbanding rendered final report to President and Congress making following three recommendations based on almost four years study of maritime labor conditions: (1) establishment of clear and unequivocal public policy unclouded by "obsolete tradition" to emancipate seamen "from their traditional status of doubtfully competent wards of the state"; (2) improve seagoing morale by insuring seamen against unemployment; (3) completion of development of permanent policy "for the stabilization of maritime labor relations."

ICC today announced it had authorized rail and water carriers to increase freight rates by average of about six percent.

<u>STATE DEPARTMENT</u>

Acting Secretary, questioned in press conference about developments in Vichy situation, said he had nothing on that this morning.

Correspondent said Korean Liberty Conference meeting in Washington had expressed desire to adhere to United Nations pact and he wondered if it would be possible to indicate Department's attitude toward this movement and its adherence to declaration and those of other free movements in country, Mr. Welles replied that in general terms he viewed conference and meetings of other organizations of all other free groups with utmost sympathy but that he knew correspondents would understand there are many problems involved in each particular movement and each particular meeting of that character and for the moment he could only say that whole question including the particular inquiry made is receiving consideration and from time to time we will probably make some announcements.

Questioned about progress of Brazilian negotiations, Acting Secretary said he would have honor of signing agreements reached with Finance Minister during mission here in a meeting tomorrow morning and at that time press release would be given regarding nature of agreements signed. Questioned regarding these agreements, Mr. Welles said he thought he would sign only new lend-lease agreement and one covering a development project and it was his present belief that immediately afterwards there would also be signed with Federal Loan Agency authorities an agreement of different character information regarding which should be obtained from such authorities.

Asked whether authenticity of statement from New Caledonia (see below) could be depended upon, Mr. Welles said he would be glad to make available text of statement issued by New Caledonia High Commissioner. Asked whether it was possible to have doctrine of effective control as manifested by statement applied to all parts of French empire, Mr. Welles said he thought statement as issued was categorical and clear. Questioned regarding its applicability to St. Pierre and Miquelon, he read from last paragraph of statement calling attention to words "in the Pacific." Asked whether negotiations with Vichy are so much less satisfactory as to rock the boat if we called attention to the fact that the announced policy regarding such possessions is limited only to Pacific, Mr. Welles said he had endeavored to best of his ability in last few days to clarify as much as possible our present relationship with French Government at Vichy, and that while he appreciated nature of inquiry, he did not think there was anything to add to his previous statements and would therefore have to leave answer to question to correspondents' judgment.

Asked whether there were any new developments in St. Pierre-Miquelon situation, Acting Secretary said he had nothing on that this morning.

Correspondent inquired whether Soviet Government has recently had occasion to mention Finnish situation to us from diplomatic standpoint and Acting Secretary replied he thought that memorandum of conversations had with Finnish
Minister

Minister last August were given to press at that time and that he had had no
more recent exchanges of views.

Correspondent said considerable publicity has recently been given proposal
to build so-called Burma Road through Canada, Alaska and Siberia to Irkutsk for
delivery of lend-lease supplies to Russia, since Japanese claim that they can
soon cut off Persian Gulf route, and inquired whether Government has been con-
ducting any negotiations or discussing any such proposal with Soviet Union.
Mr. Welles said that since such matters should be discussed by military authorities of United Nations and general staffs of countries concerned, it would be
best to request information from War Department.

Department released text of announcement made public by High Commissioner
of New Caledonia on February 28, reading as follows:

"The policy of the Government of the United States as regards France and
French territory has been based upon the maintenance of the integrity of France
and of the French Empire and of the eventual restoration of the complete independence of all French territories. Mindful of its traditional friendship for
France, this Government deeply sympathizes not only with the desire of the
French people to maintain their territories intact but with the efforts of the
French people to continue to resist the forces of aggression. In its relations
with the local French authorities in French territories the United States has
been and will continue to be governed by the manifest effectiveness with which
those authorities endeavor to protect their territories from domination and
control by the common enemy.

"With the French authorities in effective control of French territories in
the Pacific this Government has treated and will continue to treat on the basis
of their actual administration of the territories involved. This Government
recognizes, in particular, that French island possessions in that area are
under the effective control of the French National Committee established in
London, and the United States authorities are cooperating for the defense of
those islands with the authorities established by the French National Committee
and with no other French authority. This Government appreciates the importance
of New Caledonia in the defense of the Pacific area."

Department acting in conjunction with Treasury and Commerce Secretaries,
Attorney General, BEW and Coordinator Inter-American Affairs issued Supplement
No. 1 to Revision I of Proclaimed List of Certain Blocked Nationals (Radio Bul-
letin No. 33). Part I of Supplement contains 844 additional listings in Amer-
ican Republics and 29 deletions, and Part II contains 81 listings, including
Banco Aleman Antioqueno in Colombia which is being reorganized to eliminate
German influence, and 3 deletions outside Western Hemisphere.

<u>WAR COMMUNIQUES AND REPORTS</u>

War Department reported continuation of lull in Bataan Peninsula, with
General MacArthur's troops holding advance positions gained in recent attack.
Enemy has made no effort to counter-attack, indicating period of positional
warfare may be expected. Among enemy aircraft participating in some bombing
activity behind our lines were three 2-engine planes with white crosses on wings
of black background, believed to have been German-built and held by Japan in
reserve. According to Sunday's communique, small detachment of American and
Filipino guerilla troops operating in mountains has forced enemy to evacuate
Abra valley from Cervantes to Bangued.

Navy Department communique March 1 describes major action occurring
February 27 in which combined Dutch, British, Australian and U.S. naval forces
probably including heavy American cruiser and five American destroyers, engaged
much larger enemy force of combatant vessels covering 40 transports attempting
landing on north coast Java. Japanese heavy cruiser <u>Mogami</u> and 3 enemy destroyers
were put out of action in unsuccessful attempt to land Japanese. Enemy transports
last seen retiring northward. None of our vessels suffered heavy damage in
initial phase of battle for Java.

Reports from U.S. submarines operating in Far East indicate February 23, 2
torpedo hits were effected on 1 large enemy ship and February 24, 2 hits made on
large enemy auxiliary vessel and on February 25, 1 hit on enemy transport and 1
hit on unknown type. One enemy transport was hit on unknown date. All of enemy
ships hit believed sunk.

Navy Department announced that American ore carrier <u>Mararo</u> has been torpedoed
and shelled by three enemy submarines off Atlantic coast without loss of personnel

<u>EDITORIAL COMMENT</u>

Note to Operators: Run usual caption.

<u>New York Times</u> - seven editorials.
1.) Points out Japanese successes in Pacific. Victory depends in large measure on increased production now. We need not exaggerate the seriousness of Japan's successes. Now the critical time has come. It is now time for war industries to work 168 hours a week and each individual -- laborer, farmer and office worker -- to put aside every consideration but the winning of the war. "The time has come for us to work as though our lives depended on it".
2) Declares invasion of Java now in full swing. Japanese fleet of 20 warships convoyed fully 50 transports. At least 27 vessels were hit by allied bombs. Nevertheless, landings have been made. Other drives from new landings may be expected. The defense must depend on accumulated strength, which is considerable, with American and British ground and air forces aiding the Dutch.
3) Concerns congestion in Washington and endorses a redistribution of non-war functions to other cities.
4) Local interest.
5) Welcomes order from War Production Board to make aluminum in New York and other cities where surplus power is obtainable. Production plants should be built where power is available and should not wait upon such long-time undertakings as the St. Lawrence project. Up-State works as far north as Massena should get needed power for production aluminum from Beauharnois, only 50 miles distant. Doubtless Canadian Parliament would grant necessary authority.
6) Discusses reading in England and the objective of the National Book Council of giving English people a little rest and change from the work and worry of war.
7) Local interest.

<u>Baltimore Sun</u> - six editorials.
1) Lauds Byrd committee on non-essential Federal expenditures and declares its scrutiny of OCD ought to result in enabling that agency to get down directly to the tasks for which it was created.
2) Declares "It is easy to believe that, despite their victory in the Senate, the farm bloc leaders are willing now to 'compromise'. For their position is peculiarly vulnerable to mass attack by the consuming public."--Discusses previous advantages already obtained by that bloc and urges that Administration should not compromise with the farm bloc in any way.
3) Concerns announcement of hearings to begin on a new tax bill. British are operating under a budget which calls for defrayment of 42 percent of this year's war costs out of current revenues. There should be no additional taxes without further retrenchment in non-defense expenditure. Urges Congress to grapple decisively and promptly with the problem which the Ways and Means Committee takes up tomorrow, the new tax bill.
4) Local interest.
5) Concerns the battle in Java. "Putting aside the obviously distorted and untruthful Japanese claims, it is plain, however, that both sides have suffered heavy casualties. ... We can be sure that Japanese losses have been much larger, though perhaps not larger relative to the forces which she can immediately bring to bear." By gaining actual lodgments on Java the prospects of defense have darkened considerably but "For the first time the Japanese will be meeting a really large army supported by good roads ... No more than a small down payment on the cost of assaulting the island has yet been made."
6) Discusses as one benefit of war the enormous civilian organization now being formed in Washington and Oregon to fight forest fires. "Professional foresters hereafter will find an intelligent interest taken in their work by many thousands of civilians; and their work will be far more successful on that account."

<u>Washington Post</u> - six editorials.
1) Despite heavy losses Japanese have succeeded in landing at several points on the Javanese coast. The battle for Java has thus begun in earnest. Speculates concerning chances of the Allies of saving Java from the Japanese.
2) Urges

2) Urges a general understanding of what the President aptly calls the "urgency of duty". Stresses importance of public cooperation in the war production effort and endorses program for series of weekly discussions promised by Donald Nelson so that each individual may know how he can help.

3) Announcement from Honolulu that American submarines have sunk at least 44,900 tons Japanese shipping is just a taste of what is in store for Japan when it becomes possible to reinforce American striking power in Pacific. On other hand, we should not overlook the more immediate significant activities of enemy submarines in the Atlantic and Caribbean. We must assure our own routes.

4) Praises radio program of one General Electric short-wave station now broadcasting abroad story of struggle between Nazi regime and Christian churches, Catholic and Protestant. Mentions that one broadcast the other evening informed the world that bold and courageous Bishop von Galen of Muenster in his sermons to his congregation and in letters to high German officials, has revealed both the nature and extent of the Gestapo's campaign for the total extermination of all religion save the religion of Fuehrer worship. Such broadcasts are important not only as a means of counteracting the hypocritical propaganda about the Bolshevist menace manufactured by Dr. Goebbels, but also because they serve to awaken Christians everywhere to the realization that there is a great deal more at stake in this conflict than mere political forms or systems, or even than the survival of particular peoples and nations.

5) Local interest.

6) Declares that decision to try by courts-martial Short and Kimmel was to be expected in view of Roberts Report but recommends a searching inquiry into reported charges. Discusses advantages and disadvantages of the necessity for postponing the trials indefinitely until the conclusion of the war.

61WU G 49 & extra

FROM

WR LosAngeles Calif 345p Feb 28 1942

Hon Cordell Hull

Washn

We Koreans and Americans gathered together at 1368 W. Jefferson Blvd

Los Angeles California in commemoration of 23rd Anniversary of

declaration of independence of Korea and founding of Korean

republic reaffirm our loyalty to America. We are ready to give

our all for America, democracy and freedom.

United Korean Committee in America

P Y Kim, Executor Vice Chairman

911p

TELEGRAM RECEIVED

March 5, 1942

45 wu n 123 Dl 3ex.

WR LosAngeles Cal Mar 2 4

Cordell Hull

Dear Mr Hull:

On March first, 1942, the Koreans of Southern Californi
in a mass meeting, to commemorate the twenty-third anniversary of
the proclamation of the Independence of Korea, have unanimously
adopted a resolution to petition you to formally recognize the
provisional government of Korea, now in exile at Chungking and
whose representative, the Korean Commission, is in Washington DC.

It is our sincere belief that American recognition at this time
will so encourage the Koreans, both at home and abroad that the cau
of the Allied Nation's will be most healthily advanced in East Asi

We beseech your favorable consideration.

All Koreans in America and Hawaii, young and old, are eager to
fight for the UnitedStates and Liberty.

     United Korean Committee in America,

     P Y Kim, Executive Vice Chairman.

1005pm.

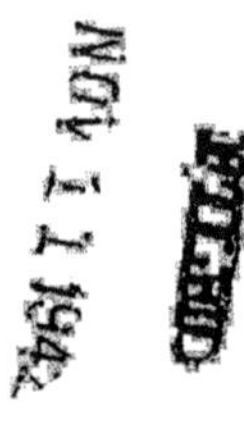

895.01/75

Dear Mr. Kim:

The Secretary has asked me to acknowledge your telegrams of February 28 and March 2, 1942 on behalf of the
United Korean Committee in America. The renewal of your
pledges of loyalty to this Government are much appreciated.
You may be assured that the petition unanimously adopted
by your Committee urging recognition of the Provisional
Government of Korea will be brought to the attention of
the interested officials of this Department and that it will
be given due consideration.

                    Sincerely yours,

                              Harold B. Hoskins
                              Executive Assistant

Mr. P. Y. Kim, Executive Vice Chairman,
    United Korean Committee in America,
        1368 West Jefferson Boulevard,
            Los Angeles, California.

A-B/H:HBH:RW:JKF   3/3/42

PS/BB

CROSS-REFERENCE FILE

NOTE

SUBJECT Government - Korea.
Inquires regarding statement made by the Attorney General
that Koreans who had not owned allegiance to Japan before a
certain date would not be treated as enemies.

For the original paper from which reference is taken

See _________ Telegram #940, 6pm _______________
(Despatch, telegram, instruction, letter, etc.)

Dated __Feb 27,1942______   From⎫ _Great Britain_ (Matthews)
                            To ⎭

File No. __863.01/681 \ ________________________

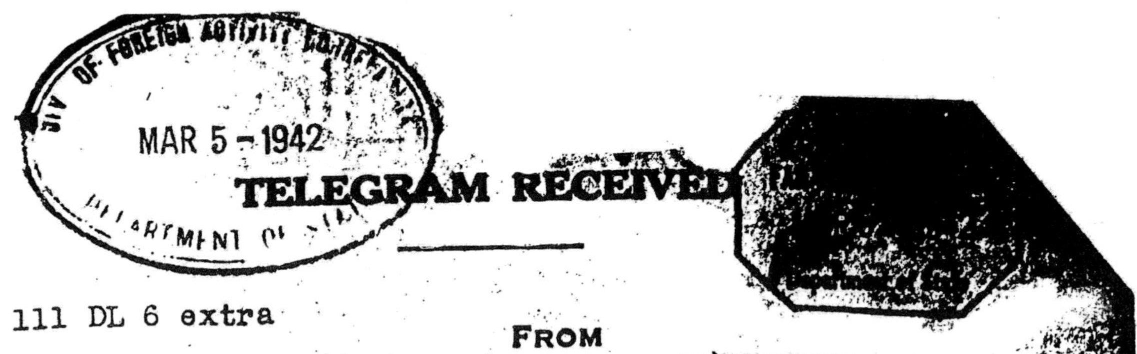

TELEGRAM RECEIVED

63WU G 111 DL 6 extra

FROM

VC LosAngeles Calif 1217p Mar 4 1942

His Excellency Sumner Welles

Acting Secretary of State Washn

All Koreans most deeply grateful for your consideration for recognition of Korea. This is happiest news Korea has had in half a century. God bless you for your righteous stand. Every Korean ready to give his all for United States and her principles. Recognition of their nation will so encourage all Koreans both at home and abroad that it will greatly enhance allied cause on fields of action. We beseech your continued great sympathy and help. Dr. Syngman Rhee, chairman Korean Commission in Washington has support of all Koreans and represents Korean provisional government and will do all to serve freedoms cause of United States and allies.

Officers and Members of Dongjihoi Society,

1119 South SanPedro Street LosAngeles Calif.

615pm

WESTERN UNION

1942 March 5 AM 5:38

8A16 89 NT 6 Extra - Los Angeles, Calif. 4

His Excellency Sumner Welles

Acting Secretary of State, Washington, D. C.

Accept sincere thanks of all officers and men of
the California Korean Reserves. Your Excellency's
statement at the press conference March second that
the State Department is considering recognition of Korea
is most heartening to all Koreans both at home and abroad.
Every son of Korea is a natural born enemy of Japan. This
Korean unit in California is the neucleus of a larger force
eager to see action at the Far Eastern front in service
of America, Korea, and freedom. Command us.

California Korean Reserves   Arthur Kim, Commander

700 Exposition Boulevard

Los Angeles, California.

March 10, 1942.

A/B / H,

Mr. Hoskins: Department of State

You have already seen the original of the telegram, copy of which is attached hereto. It occurs to me that your committee may wish to consider the advisability of obtaining further information about the organization which sent this message.

I have sent a copy of the telegram under reference to Major Moore of MID.

PA/H:A

March 10, 1942.

To: Major Moore

From: Stanley K. Hornbeck

         As of possible interest.

PA/H:SKH:FLB

(Copy of telegram of March 5, 1942 to Acting Secretary Sumner Welles from California Korean Reserves, Arthur Kim, Commander, 700 7Exposition Boulevard, Los Angeles, California.)

在美韓族聯合委員會

United Korean Committee in America

1365 WEST JEFFERSON BOULEVARD
LOS ANGELES, CALIFORNIA

March 2, 1942

His Excellency Cordell Hull,
Secretary of State,
Washington, D. C.,

Your Excellency:

On March 1, 1942, the Koreans of Southern
California, in a mass meeting, to commemorate
the Twenty-third anniversary of the Proclamation
of the Independence of Korea, have unamimously
adopted a Resolution to petition you to formally
recognize the Provisional Government of Korea,
now in exile at Chungking, and whose representative,
the Korean Commission, is in Washington, D. C.

It is our sincere belief that American recognition at this time will so encourage the
Koreans both at home and abroad that the cause
of the Allied Nations will be most healthily
advanced in East Asia. We beseech your favorable
consideration. All Korean in America and Hawaii,
young and old, are eager to fight for the United
States and Liberty.

UNITED KOREAN COMMITTEE IN AMERICA

P. Y. Kim
Executive Vice-Chairman

Encl. 1

RESOLUTION

WHEREAS: On March 1, 1919, the citizens of Korea in every part
of the nation, solemnly and in unison have declared the
indipendence of the Republic of Korea, and have vowed to
drive out the forces of the Imperial Japanese Government
from Korea, and

WHEREAS: The Provisional Government of the Republic of Korea, its
agencies in many parts of the world, and the Korean
people both at home and abroad have been carrying on
the work of liberating their nation from Japanese yoke
with increasing vigor; now

THEREFORE BE IT RESOLVED: That the citizens of Korea and the
American citizens gathered together in the Korean Presbyterian Church of Los Angeles, California, in commemoration of the signing of the Proclamation of the Independence of the Republic of Korea, shall petition the
Government of the United States of America to formally
recognize the Provisional Government of the Republic of
Korea now in exile at Chungking, China, and the independence of the Korean nation; and

BE IT FURTHER RESOLVED: That representations be made by this
gathering to the President of the United States and the
Secretary of State of the United States to use their
good offices to facilitate the formal recognition of
the Provisional Government of the Republic of Korea, by all
the Governments of the United Nations allied against the
Axis countries.

- 370 -

U
Mr. Welles?

A-B
Mr. Hoskins:
Mr. Berle

　　There is attached a memorandum
prepared by Mr. Langdon of FE on the
subject "Some Aspects of the Question of Korean Independence". There
is much of factual information in
the memorandum which it is believed
might profitably be kept in mind by
all officers of the Department
specially concerned with questions
relating to Korea.

FE:MVE:ENS

DEPARTMENT OF STATE

DIVISION OF FAR EASTERN AFFAIRS

February 20, 1942

Social Aspects of the Question of Korean Independence

I.   Social Structure and Intellectual Life
of Korean People

Korean People

The Korean people, a very distinct, homogenous, sturdy race with a language, costume, culture and interesting history of its own, number some 23 million, of which number some 21 million are in Korea, some 1 1/2 million in Manchuria, where they are concentrated in Chientao Province (the population of which is 80% Korean), and about 1/2 million in Japan. There are also unimportant Korean communities in cities of occupied-China. There was a large Korean population in Ussuri and Primorsk Provinces of Siberia, but between 1936 and 1938 this population was resettled in Soviet Central Asia and is no longer a factor in the Korean question—the population of these two Siberian Provinces is now 95% European.

Korean Society

Korea is overwhelmingly rural. There are not more than half a dozen large cities in all Korea and, with the exception of Seoul, these are little more than overgrown market towns. As the Japanese occupy all the administrative and important professional positions and operate all the public services, big industries, banks and big businesses, the occupations

left

left to the Koreans are agriculture, clerical, petty shop-
keeping, fishing, household industries and heavy labor. Thus
Korean society consists of landlords, farmers, tenant farmers,
shopkeepers, artisans, fishermen, mountaineers, laborers,
clerks, and very low-ranking civil functionaries and professional
men. There are three main strata in this society, a thin
upper stratum of landlords and professional men, a middle
slightly thicker stratum of literate classes including the
shopkeepers, artisans, small functionaries and clerks, and a
lower stratum of the great mass of the people. The elements in
the great lower stratum are poor and illiterate, although not
lacking in gentle ways and good manners.

<u>Korean Intellectual Life</u>

There is a fairly active intellectual life in the two
top strata of Korean society. The older people in these strata
have a conventional Chinese classical education, and the younger
people have studied the "national language", as Japanese is
officially designated, either in the Government school system
(Japanese) or in the foreign (mostly American) mission schools.
Both groups, of course, read and write their own language in
addition to Chinese or Japanese as the case may be—young
Koreans must learn Korean in the home as it is officially barred
from the classroom. Government publications and the leading
dailies are in Japanese, and the bookstores and bookstalls are

stocked

stocked with Japanese books and magazines only, but there
are also two or three Korean newspapers. Literate Korean
elements, being largely bilingual, thus have access to the
news of the day and to current Japanese thought, and they
follow such news and thought with lively interest.

Political Thought

It is difficult to know the true feelings of literate
Koreans in political matters as no feelings but those loyal
to Japan are generally expressed. Mere suspicion, let alone
expression, of a treasonable inclination of thought, not
only subjects the Korean to long police inquisitions accompanied frequently by torture, but also ends his prospects
for advancement in his country. Moreover, with so many
detectives and informers in his midst, the Korean cannot
tell friend from foe, so that silence is golden in controversial matters. The Japanese press, of course, represents
the Japanese point of view, while the two or three Korean
papers are closely censored. However, in the latter papers,
as in the advisory councils attached to the central and
local governments, on which there are a few Koreans appointed
by the Governor General, minor grievances of a non-contro-
versial nature are allowed expression. On the other hand,
expression of pro-Japanese sentiment among Koreans is
abundant, as it ensures some freedom from personal molestation

and

and helps one's material standing. However, in confidence
and in moments of despair, Koreans now and then speak their
minds, and from these outbursts it is plain that pro-Japanese
expression is largely false and insincere.

I. Feelings of Koreans toward Japanese

Assuming that intelligent awareness of events begins at
adolescence it is only Koreans over fifty years of age who
remember free Korea. Even the youngest Koreans who remember
the abuses of the Japanese military regime (1905 - 1919) which
ended with the so-called "Mansei" rebellion*/are nearing
                                              (1919)
forty. Persons below thirty remember nothing but Japanese
rule. In addition to these factors militating against Korean
nationalism there is the fundamentally changed position in
international affairs of Japan since 1931.

Before 1931 much of the bitterness of the Koreans came

from

---

*The abuses of the military government led to a well-
organized plan of mass presentation at a given moment at all
administrative offices throughout the country of a petition
for more considerate rule. The plan was concealed from the
police, and at the given moment crowds assembled before the
local office, shouted "Mansei" ("ten thousand generations")
and presented their petition. Subsequently Korean crowds
would gather in public places and yell "Mansei". The Government suppressed the movement by the most ruthless measures,
measures so revolting that the United States Government was
compelled to inform the Japanese Government that reports of
them were having a bad effect on American-Japanese relations.
The Koreans won their point, however, and were given a civil
government when the movement was quelled.

from the feeling that they were subjected/of an inferior ^{to the rule}
race. When the Koreans in 1931-32 saw that Japan was able
not only to wrest Manchuria from China but also to defy the
Western Powers over the seizure, a feeling began to take
root among them that they were a component element of a
great nation. But what was more to the point was that
important material benefits began to accrue to Koreans after
the Manchurian Incident. With the boom in Japanese economic
life that began in 1932, prices of Korean rice (Korea is a
one-crop country) and paddy-land and mined gold (Korea is
the principal auriferous region of the Japanese Empire)
soared and a period of general prosperity set in in Korea.
In addition, the Japanese allowed Koreans to have a good
share in the exploitation of Manchuria, not only aiding them
in settling on new lands, acquiring Chinese-owned rice lands
and advancing them funds for commercial enterprises, but
also appointing them extensively to higher official positions
than they could ever hope to occupy in Korea. Thus broad
fields of opportunity were opened to the literate elements
of Korean society as well as to the masses of tenant farmers,
so that from hated oppressors the Japanese began to be
looked upon by many Koreans as benefactors. In this connection mention also may be made of the opportunities for
profit afforded Koreans by the Japanese in the demilitarized

zone

zone between Peiping-Tientsin and the Great Wall.   In
1934-35 large bodies of Korean smugglers were employed at
good wages by the Japanese Government to move cargo past
the Chinese customs barriers while the Japanese Army disarmed the Chinese customs authorities and prevented them
from functioning.

Then came the China Incident, and after it in 1938 the
Changkufeng and in 1939 the Nomonhan Incidents with the Soviet
Union*, and Koreans looked with increasing amazement and admira-
tion at the military prowess and political daring of their
masters. Conversely, whatever hope of deliverance from Japanese rule may have lurked in the minds of the Korean people
flickered out. Again, with the Japanese occupation of great
Chinese areas and cities, further opportunities for profit
and adventure were opened to Koreans.

For reasons of material interest and because all hope
of deliverance from Japanese bondage seemed dead, the mass
of Koreans have found it to their advantage since 1931 to
join the Japanese parade. Conversely, the wonted aloofness
from the Government's Japanization program of the large
Christian element in Korea, which is perhaps the most
nationalistic, and other irreconcilables became more and
more conspicuous and materially disadvantageous, and in
consequence

---

*Although the fighting at both these battles was inconclusive
at Nomonhan the Japanese actually lost some ground -- it was
reported and generally believed in Japan as favoring Japanese
arms.

consequence decreased progressively. Thus, outwardly at
least, the Korean people in the past decade have become
more and more Japanese in their outlook and sentiment.

An illustration of the apparently increasing rapproche-
ment of Koreans to Japanese in recent years may be found in
the Korean response to the Japanese Government's standing
invitation to Koreens formally to adopt Japanese names. In
Korea the response was considerable; in Manchuria it was
marked. Each daily issue of the "Manchukuo" Official Gazette
since 1939 lists the registration of adopted Japanese names
of dozens of Korean civil servants of "Manchukuo".

The collapse of the great/mission structure in Korea in
the past four years is not altogether due to Japanese pressure.
The native congregations by no means unanimously supported
the stand taken by missionaries in the theological dispute
with the authorities (over the requirement that mission school
students bow at the shrine of the Sun Goddess, foremother of
the Emperor, or assist at Shinto ceremonies), and when this
dispute reached a climax the Korean congregations, for
reasons of self-interest, fear or honest belief, ranged
themselves with the authorities and readily took over the
schools and other institutions involved in the dispute for
operation in conformity with Japanese policy.

A missionary of thirty years experience in Korea in

1940

1940 stated that the prevalent feeling of the Korean
people toward the Japanese had undergone a profound change
in the past three years and had become one of hero worship.
In the young people especially, he said, a growing lack of
sympathy with American missionaries was noticeable. Another
missionary of long experience in Korea asserted that the
Koreans had lost much of the antagonistic spirit they had
at the time of the "Mansei Movement".*

A businessman in Korea whose experience had spanned
both Korean and Japanese regimes stated, as long ago as 1935,
before the "hero worship" set in, that the earlier rancorous
feeling of Koreans toward Japanese had given way to one of
"mild peevishness". He added, however, that Koreans now
had a great deal more pride of race and race solidarity than
they had in the days of the Kingdom.

The outward sympathy and even cooperation with Japan of
most Koreans described in the preceding paragraphs are after
all only natural results of conditions and circumstances, and
Koreans cannot be blamed for them. Koreans want to stay
and make as good a living as possible in the land of their
ancestors, and long experience has taught them that the only
way to do this is to cooperate with the Japanese and act in

pro-Japanese

---

*See footnote page 4.

pro-Japanese ways. It is believed, however, that this
sympathy and this cooperation are only skin deep and that
at bottom there is no love for the Japanese but rather
bitterness and resentment.

The Japanese on their part basically mistrust and
look down upon the Koreans. As illustrations of the abiding
Japanese mistrust of Koreans, even with all their pro-
Japanese posturing, may be cited (1) the consistent failure
to allow Koreans to serve in the Japanese Army except as
volunteers in severely restricted numbers (a few hundred at
most in the whole Japanese Army) distributed individually
in Japanese units, (2) the denial of even sporting firearms
to Koreans except in rare cases, (3) the vast internal
espionage system and police frightfulness used for stamping
out so-called Korean "malcontentism". That Japanese also
have an almost physical abhorrence for Koreans is apparent,
for instance, in the virtual non-existence of any mixed
marriages, in the absence of social intercourse or fellow-
ship with Koreans, and in the designation of other Japanese
as Koreans when it is desired to affront them. "What's the
matter with you? Are you a Korean?" or "Aren't you a Korean
goldfish?" are words used by one Japanese to another when he
wants to pick a fight with him.

Koreans on the other hand reflect their enduring rancor
toward the Japanese by unyielding resistance to assimilation.
A Korean

A Korean will never use the written or spoken Japanese
language if he can avoid it; he resists all Government
campaigns to make him give up his national costume; he
does not seek the company of Japanese; and he lives his
own life in his traditional way as much as the Japanese
will let him. His hurt at his exclusion from any position of consequence in his country--and this is literal,
as the Japanese have not allowed one single Korean to
become eminent or authoritative in their 37 years of rule--
preys on his mind, and medical missionaries have stated
that nervous crises due partly to frustration on this
account are not uncommon among educated Koreans. In a
state of hysteria a Korean frequently will moan that
Koreans are the unhappiest of people and he the unhappiest
of Koreans.

Korean nationalism sometimes expresses itself in
manly ways, as the following instance will show. Koreans
are of good physique and many members of the Japanese team
of the Olympic Games of 1936 were Koreans. Before the
organization of the Japanese team, the Korean athletes
sought to take part in the games as a separate national
unit but the Japanese did not permit this and incorporated
them in the Japanese team. The winner of the Marathon
race was a Korean, and when the news of his feat reached

Korea

Korea, it was an occasion of almost national rejoicing.
The day after the event the editor of the _Dong-A-Ilbo_,
the chief Korean language daily, by trick photography
altered the Rising Sun flag on the chest of the Marathon
winner and substituted the old flag of the Korean kingdom
for it, and printed a whole edition with a full front page
illustration of the athlete with the Korean flag on his
chest. The edition was confiscated after it had found some
circulation, but as the police clamped down on the story,
nothing is known of what the editor or his printers had to
pay for their patriotic outburst.

In the region of Manchuria bordering the upper reaches
of the Yalu River and in the mountain and forest fastnesses
of Chientao Province there are still organized armed bands
of Korean revolutionaries fighting the Japanese and working
for Korean independence. This resistance, which has received
sustenance through the years by recruits among sufferers from
Japanese oppression, nationalistically minded youths, and
outlaws, has survived all Japanese and 'Manchukuoan'
efforts and military expeditions to extirpate. These bands
will be discussed later.

It is believed that if Koreans were given the choice
between being once more independent and remaining subjects
of Japan, even with the full civil rights of Japanese, which
they do not possess at present, they would unanimously

choose

choose independence.

The argument may be put forward that, as in Germany and Russia, Korean youths have been so indoctrinated by Japanese propaganda in schools and colleges and youth organizations that they are in sympathy with Japan and Japanese aims. This argument does not hold good, it is believed, because Korean youths as well as older people think that Korea is their country and not Japan. Another argument is that the Koreans have been faring so well economically of recent years that they might not welcome the confusion of the change to independence. Again it is not believed that this argument holds true because the Koreans do not want relative prosperity but/want full possession of the resources, riches, and opportunities of their country, which are now the property of the Japanese.

III. Question

~~choose independence.~~

III. Question of Korean Independence

Although it is certain that Koreans would unanimously choose independence if it was merely a question of a vote, independence in the case of Korea involves many practical difficulties and considerations. These difficulties and considerations may be classified as political, military and economic.

Political difficulties - It must be borne in mind that in the 37 years of Japanese rule, the Korean people have been emasculated politically. Long excluded from any participation in administration of central and local government, diplomacy, justice, law, police, finance, banking, education, communications and shipping, they would have no experience in managing a state if given their independence.

Military difficulties - The Japanese have never allowed the Koreans to perform military service or to possess arms. Nor have the Japanese taught them or allowed them to teach themselves how to defend themselves. Thus there are not more than a few dozen bird guns among the entire Korean population and it is doubted whether there are more than a few dozen Koreans in Korea who know how to load or aim a rifle or a revolver. Moreover, the Korean people from

decades

decades of being protected have no concept of or deep
will to self-defense.

Economic difficulties - As in the case of administration,
Japanese have excluded Koreans from all banking, big business, mechanical manufacturing, engineering, importing,
exporting, wholesale distribution, and shipping, so that
the Korean population has no training for modern economy.
Furthermore, Korean economy has become thoroughly integrated
with Japanese economy, and Korean production, especially
rice, the great cash crop and mainstay of Korean economy,
has enjoyed a free market in Japan and the high Japanese
prices. Separation of Korean from Japanese economy and
adjustment to competitive status would involve difficult
and painful processes. However, there is an essentially
sound basis for Korean economy. Neighboring countries
cannot subsist without Korean rice and Korean rice would
be ample to pay for imports from those countries. Korean
mined gold, valued at about 50 million dollars annually—
Koreans are unsurpassed gold miners and gold production
would continue almost on the present level without
Japanese assistance— would be adequate to pay for
unbalanced trade with the United States and other countries
not needing Korean products in large quantities.

It is obvious that, because of their political

inexperience

inexperience and defencelessness, the Korean people at
first would neither know how to run their country nor be
able to defend it from reconquest, and that for a generation at least Korea would have to be protected, guided,
and aided to modern statehood by the great powers. It
would seem to be no more than essential justice, however,
that the Korean people should be so protected, guided, and
aided, and given the opportunity they never really had to
be independent and develop along their very distinctive
cultural lines. The Koreans are intelligent, quick and
willing to learn, progressive, and patriotic and it is
believed that, given disinterested protection, guidance,
and aid, they will in a generation be able to stand on
their own feet and contribute to world prosperity and
advancement.

IV. Suggested Procedure to Independence

Anything like a concrete independence movement within
Korea at the present time should not be looked for or
counted upon. As has been stated, police surveillance of
the people is too close to allow any such movement to be
organized or to be effective. Accordingly, preparation
for independence will have to be organized abroad and
liaison with Korean leaders within Korea established.
When organization for independence is satisfactory, that

is

is, when such organization satisfies the sponsoring
government (1) that it is as representstive as can be
under the circumstances, (2) that it has the support of some
reputable leaders within Korea--these leaders are known to
Americans who have lived in Korea--(3) that it has a substantial following and (4) that it is ready and capable of
helping itself and the cause of the United Nations in
positive ways, the sponsoring government might consult with
the American, British, Chinese and Soviet Governments*
about proclaiming the independence of Korea as one of the
war aims of the United Nations and about recognizing the
organization as the Provisional Government of Korea. As
China and the Soviet Union are chiefly concerned in the
practical aspects of Korean independence, the approval at
least by those nations of any plan for independence which
a third government may sponsor is essential. Following
victory of the United Nations, the Provisional Government
could be installed in Korea and could administer the
country with the aid of an international commission pending the adoption of a national constitution and the setting
up of a constitutional government. The sponsoring governments

from

---

*If the Soviet Union should still be at peace with Japan, it
would of course not wish to associate itself with the proclamation, in which case the proclamation would have to lack the
Soviet Union's signature.

from the very beginning should make provision for the functioning of the international commission until such time as they, and not the Koreans, might decide it to be no longer necessary.

By no means should the United States be stampeded into proclaiming the independence of Korea or into recognizing any shadow organization of Koreans as the Provisional Government of Korea prematurely or before consultation with China, Russia and Great Britain and before agreement at least with China and Great Britain. And above all, the United States should avoid promising independence until it scores some substantial victories against the Japanese. It would only do the Korean cause harm, give the Japanese and their allies a good laugh, and irritate our own friends if we promised independence to one Asiatic people as we were being pushed out of our own possessions in Asia by the Japanese.

V. Interim Measures Before Independence

<u>Political</u> — We are being and will continue to be importuned by this Korean group and that claiming to represent Free Korea for a statement of our position with regard to Korean independence and for recognition of some particular group as the Provisional Government of Korea. While we need not dampen hopes of independence, we should avoid

any

any premature commitments in this respect and, until the situation becomes clearer, not go beyond referring these groups to public declarations of national policy having a bearing on the general question of freedom of subjected peoples. In particular, we might invite attention to the third principle for a better world proclaimed in the joint Anglo-American declaration of August 14, 1941, namely, our "respect of the right of all peoples to choose the form of government under which they will live" and our "wish to see sovereign rights and self-government restored to those who have been forcibly deprived of them".

At a later time, when warranted by the progress of the war, we might become more specific with regard to Korean independence and inform Free Korean representatives that, depending on a number of factors, we might positively support the Korean independence movement. These factors might be explained as (1) the capacity of all Korean groups working for independence to unite and organize a committee to speak with full authority for each group and all groups, (2) the capacity of the organization of united Free Koreans to work in positive ways for Korean independence and for the defeat of the enemy and the actual extent of its positive war efforts, and (3) the attitude of the other powers.

<u>Military</u> - The contribution which Free Korean groups

may

may make to the war effort is a matter for our military
authorities to look into. In this connection our military
authorities should avoid attaching importance to Korean so-
called volunteers in China. Numerically these volunteers are
insignificant and, because Koreans in China have been largely
rascals and running dogs of the Japanese Army, they are generally not to be trusted. Rather, these authorities should
endeavor to make contact with and reorganize into distinct
Korean units and equip the Korean revolutionaries, desperados,
and "malcontents" of Chientao and Antung Provinces in Manchuria. These elements run into sizeable numbers and, because
they have been fighting the Japanese and "Manchukuo" forces
for years, sometimes as independent units and at other times
in conjunction with Chinese guerrillas, they are excellent
fighters as well as trustworthy allies. Two "malcontent"
chieftains in the wildernesses of Eastern Manchuria deserve
particular mention. Their names are Kim (given name unknown)
and Tsui Hsien. Their raids on Japanese and "Manchukuo" out-
posts are important enough to be reported in the censored
papers of Manchuria, and the recurrence of such reports indicates that Kim and Tsui are a match for the expeditions sent
against them. Kim's and Tsui's commands are small, three or
four hundred men in each at most, but they form convenient
nuclei for a Korean nationalist army because of the closeness
of their sphere of operations to the Korean border.

FE:Langdon:MJF/ALM

WB41 VIA RCA

F CHUNGKING 33 10 1200

DLT PRESIDENT ROOSEVELT

MAR 10 7 33 AM 1942

GRATEFUL FOR YOUR ASSISTANCE IN KOREAS INDEPENDENCE IN YOUR

FIRESIDE TALK ON WASHINGTONS BIRTHDAY REQUEST YOU RECOGNIZE

KOREAN PROVISIONAL GOVERNMENT IMMEDIATELY

KIM KU CHAIRMAN OF THE KOREAN PROVISIONAL GOVERNMENT.

DEPARTMENT OF STATE

———

DIVISION OF FAR EASTERN AFFAIRS

March 17, 1942

Reference Chungking's confidential air-mail despatch no. 297 of February 12, 1942, entitled "The Provisional Government of the Republic of Korea."

Mr. Gauss reports that Mr. Tjo So-wang, "Minister for Foreign Affairs of the Provisional Government of Korea" requested an interview and was received unofficially by Mr. Gauss. Mr. Gauss states that Mr. Tjo sought American recognition and financial and military aid for the "Provisional Government" but was "most vague and unsatisfactory in his presentation of the case for his 'government'".

Mr. Gauss states that, in response to his inquiry whether the "Provisional Government" had been recognized by the Chinese National Government, Mr. Tjo admitted it had not, "whisperingly" suggesting that this was perhaps due to China's desire to bring Korea eventually under Chinese suzerainty. Mr. Gauss reports that Mr. Tjo, on the other hand, has persistently indicated to others that the "Provisional Government" is "on the point of being recognized" by the Chinese Government. According to Mr. Gauss, there is no confirmation of a report that the "Provisional Government" is being financially supported by Generalissimo Chiang Kai-shek. Mr. Gauss states that officials of the Chinese Foreign Office display no enthusiasm over the "Provisional Government" and do not suggest that it is likely to be accorded recognition by the Chinese National

Government.

Government. Mr. Gauss states that Mr. Tjo
evaded replying to questions as to Korean
independence groups in Manchuria and would give
no definite statement as to the relationship
of the "Provisional Government" and such groups.
Mr. Tjo was also unenlightening on the question
of how the Korean movement is financed and the
question of possible military aid to Korean
independents. Mr. Gauss adds that, as Mr. Tjo
speaks English fairly well, there was no difficulty in having him understand Mr. Gauss'
questions and that Mr. Gauss considered Mr. Tjo
both "evasive and secretive".

Mr. Gauss suggested to Mr. Tjo that he
might care to give Mr. Gauss a written statement of pertinent information regarding the
provisional regime and its affiliations.
Mr. Tjo did this, and a copy thereof is enclosed.

Mr. Tjo's statement gives the impression
to the reader that Mr. Tjo's evasiveness and
vagueness were in part due to the absence of
organization for and correlation of independence
activities on the part of the Korean regime at
Chungking, as well as to a seemingly basic
inchoate condition of the Korean movement.
Mr. Tjo gives an account of the independence
movement, which began with vigor in 1919 but
which weakened during subsequent years and has
seemed to lose sight of that movement's concrete
objectives. The organization of which Mr. Tjo

is a

is a member was, however, behind the best-
known instances of direct action taken by
Koreans against Japanese during the past
several years, including the famous bombing
of the Japanese reviewing stand in Shanghai
in 1932, when Ambassador Shigemitsu lost his
leg and Admiral Nomura lost his eye. Mr. Tjo's
efforts to picture continuity in the independence movement and a relationship between
the various elements of the movement do not
convince the reader that there has been either
cohesion or direction in the movement. When
Mr. Tjo gives figures they are usually man-
ifestly exaggerated. He refers to millions of
Korean Christians, three million Koreans in
Manchuria, two million in China, upwards of
ten thousand Koreans in Hawaii, and seven
hundred thousand Koreans in the maritime
provinces of Siberia. These figures are all
exaggerated. For example, the number of
Korean Christians does not exceed two or
three hundred thousand; the number of Koreans
in Manchuria is in the neighborhood of
1,250,000; there are only a few thousand
Koreans in China and the Koreans in the
maritime provinces of Siberia were re-settled
in central Asia.

The information which Mr. Tjo furnishes
with regard to leading Korean revolutionaries
is of interest. The average age of the nine
men whom he mentions is 62.

The statement

The statement which Mr. Tjo gave to Mr. Gauss gives the reader the feeling that Mr. Tjo is somewhat out of touch with the real situation and with the problems relating to independence and that the movement of which he is a member lacks concrete organization and precision of program.

895.01/81

FE:Salisbury:MHP

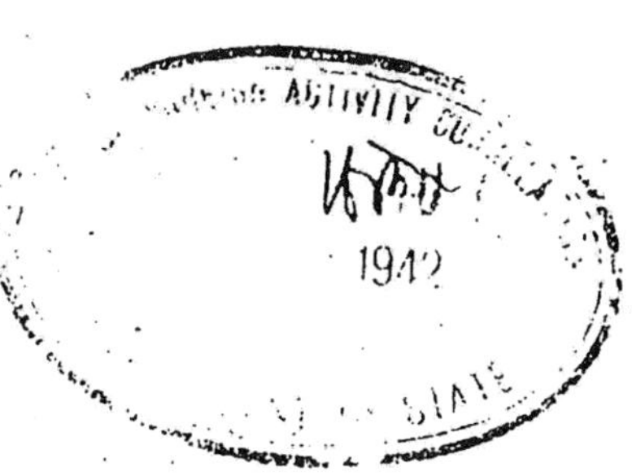

EMBASSY OF THE

UNITED STATES OF AMERICA AIR MAIL

No. 297   Chungking, February 12, 1942

Subject: "The Provisional Government of
          the Republic of Korea."

CONFIDENTIAL

Air Mail

MID

Copy in FE

COPIES SENT TO
O.N.I. AND M.I.D.

895.01/81

The Honorable,
    The Secretary of State,
    Washington, D. C.

Sir:

895.01/62

        With reference to my despatch no. 248 of December
20, 1941, regarding the so-called "Provisional Government of the Republic of Korea", I have the honor to
report that some days ago Mr. Tjosowang, who represents
himself to be the Minister of Foreign Affairs of the
"Provisional Government" requested an interview with
me. I consented to receive him unofficially. He sought
American recognition and financial and military aid for
the "Previsional Government", but was most vague and
unsatisfactory in his presentation of the case for his
"government".

        Asked whether the "provisional government" had been
recognized by the Chinese National Government, he admitted
that it had not, and whisperingly suggested that he felt
that this was perhaps due to the desire of China after
the defeat of Japan to bring Korea under Chinese suzerainty. To others, Mr. Tjosowang has persistently indicated
that the provisional government is on the point of being
recognized

recognized" by the Chinese Government. I have also heard
it credited to Mr. Tjosowang that the provisional government is being financially supported by Generalissimo Chiang
Kai-shek; but there is no confirmation of such report.

Inquiry at the Chinese Foreign Office has produced
nothing of value or interest in reference to the Korean
"Provisional Government". The officials there have indicated that they are "investigating" the Korean set-up, but
they display no enthusiasm regarding it nor do they suggest
that it is likely to be accorded recognition by the National
Government of China.

Questions directed to Mr. Tjosowang regarding the Korean
independence groups in Manchuria - believed to include principally radical, pro-Communist groups - are evaded; and I
was unable to obtain from Mr. Tjo any definite and precise
statement of the relationship between his "provisional government" and such outside groups except his assertion that the
Koreans are now all one in the effort for independence and
that his "provisional government" is the one representative
body of Korean independents.

On the subject of financial aid to the "provisional
government" I avoided any discussion. Mr. Tjo was unable
or unwilling to tell me how the movement is at present
financed.

On the subject of any possible military aid to Korean
independents, Mr. Tjo was likewise unenlightening; he
admitted that it would not be possible for the United
States to supply arms and ammunition to the Korean patriots at this time, but suggested that the situation might
later develop to a point where this could be done.

Mr. Tjo speaks English fairly well, and there was no
difficulty in having him understand my questions. I considered that he was evasive and secretive. I received him
with appropriate cordiality and friendliness and encouraged
him to talk about his provisional government, its organization, the Korean volunteers in China and Manchuria, et
cetera, but the result was unsatisfactory. I then suggested
that perhaps Mr. Tjo would care to give me a written statement of pertinent information regarding the provisional
regime and its affiliations. He undertook to do so, and has
now sent me a letter with enclosures, in English, a copy of
which I enclose for the information of the Department.

Within the past few days Mr. Tjo has approached the
Embassy for a "passport" to permit him to proceed to the
United States. His request has been placed before the
Department by telegraph.

Respectfully yours,

C. E. Gauss

Enclosures:
  copy of letter, with enclosures
Original and two copies to Department by air mail
Three copies to Department by pouch

801 Korea

CEG/gs

<u>C O P Y</u>

THE PROVISIONAL GOVERNMENT OF THE REPUBLIC OF KOREA

Ministry of Foreign Affairs

54 Cable Address:
        KOPOGO

No. 1 Wu Sh Yeh Hsiang,
Hu Ping Road,
Chungking.

February 4th, 1942

Mr. Clarence E. Gauss,

Ambassador to China,

American Embassy,

Chungking.

Dear Sir:

Referring to your request in our interview on
January 7th I am hereby sending you a brief history of our
independent movement, different parties, and the organization
of the Korean Provisional Government. However, they are not
all in detail and adequate description of our cause. But if
your Excellency wishes to know further in regard to our cause
I will be very pleased to have another interview with you
at your earliest convenience. I will take my English secretary this time and I am sure there would not be any incon-
venience in our conversation.

Very truly yours,

(signed) Tjosowang

Minister of Foreign Affairs

Provisional Government of Korea.

THE KOREAN PROVISIONAL GOVERNMENT

I. Introduction

The Korean Provisional Government has been the outcome
of an unprecedented revolution of the masses of the Korean
people. Represented by the leaders of different Korean revolutionary organizations at home and abroad, it receives
support from all sections of the society and the country
as well as from the governments of a number of friendly
nations. For more than twenty years it has been the Korean
patriots' main camp of radical action against Japan!

Thirty-three Korean national leaders were created for
founding the Korean Provisional Government on March 1, 1919.
It was they who first issued the manifesto of the Korean
Independence and who mobilized millions of Korean people in
an anti-Japanese campaign. After several years of struggle
the Korean Provisional Government succeeded in conglomerating
many revolutionaries and it was then found necessary to organize the Supreme Revolutionary Commission. At that time, the
principal personalities of the Provisional Government included
Messrs. Dr. Rhee Syngman, Li Shir-yung, Kim-ku, Cho Sung-
whan, Cho Wan-ku, Tjo Sowang, Liu Tong-viul, Song Biung-
chao, and numbers of others who have either passed away or
still in the Japanese prisons. All of them have most pat-
riotically supported the Provisional Government up to the
present day. They may be regarded as part of the leading
anti-Japanese personalities for racial emancipation in the
Orient.

II. Organization of the Provisional Government

After the declaration of the Korean Independence in
Seoul on March 1, 1919, all those having signed the manifesto were arrested and imprisoned. In order to carry on
their work and activities the Korean revolutionaries secretly
convened the Second National Representatives' Congress to
which the Supreme Revolutionary Council owed its birth.
The Councillors of the S. R. C. were elected from the State
Councillors of the Provisional Government. As a matter of
fact the appellation of the Provisional Government and the
Constitution of the Republic were not decided upon until
April 11, 1919. The delay was caused by the loss in Korea
of freedom which compelled the removal of the Provisional
Government to Shanghai, where efforts were made to effect
close contact with the Koreans living in China and in other
parts of the world for the purpose of intensifying the independence movement.

In accordance with the above-mentioned Constitution of
the Korean Republic over fifty delegates of the people from
the different provinces of the country organized E-Jung-
Wen (Provisional Political Council) which then elected State
Councillors. That process of organization is much similar
to that of the present day democratic nations. The present
Constitution of the Korean Republic is a document of careful revision for five or six times. According to this Constitution, there should be six to ten State Councillors

including

including Ministers of Interior, of Foreign Affairs, of
War, of Law, of Finance, etc. The Ministers are to be
elected from and among the State Councillors whose President is to be elected by the Political Council. The term
of a State Councillor is three years. According to the
Outline of National Reconstruction, the State Council is
the Supreme executive organ in the movement of national
reconstruction.

III. The Government and the Political Council

After March 1, 1919, the Second National Representatives' Congress, because of the enemy's radical action
taken against it, was unable to carry on its work and duty
in Korea. For that reason the Political Council was set
up as a substitute in Shanghai.

Article 1 of the existing Constitution stipulates that
the sovereignty of the Korean Republic is vested in the
people. But during the period of pre-Independence, the
sovereignty rests with the whole body of the Independentists.
According to Article 4, the Provisional Political Council
is to be organized by its Councillors elected directly by
the people of the Korean Republic. But, when election is
impossible in Korea, it may be carried out in the oversea
location of the Provisional Government, provided that there
are Independentists who undertake vote-casting for those
living at home. Article 5 fixes Councillors of fifty-seven
persons who are to be elected from various parts of Korea
and abroad. Article 34 makes the President of the State
Council and the Ministers of the Provisional Government
both responsible to the Political Council in executing
State affairs in accordance with the regulations of the
State Council. Article 14 states that when the Provisional
Political Council finds that the President of the State
Council, or a Councillor of the State Council, or oversea
diplomatic representative has neglected his duty, or acts
in contravention of the Government's orders he shall be,
with the decision of two-thirds of the Councillors of the
Headquarters of the Political Council forming a quorum in
a meeting, sent for impeachment or dismissed from his post.

In brief, it may be surmised that the basic principles
of Korea are to be so carried out and are to so develop
that democratic politics will tend to prevail all over
Korea under the administration of the Government and of
the Political Council.

IV. The Government and Internal Movement

There were three stages of the Korean Government's
internal movement policy which has been pursued for over
twenty years. During the first stage the Government secretly
appointed officers for various political areas of the country
varying from villages to cities as well as appointed ranking
officials in diametrical opposition to those commissioned
by the Japanese Governor-General of Korea. The Korean
people were persuaded to refuse paying taxes and rendering
services to the enemy -- in short, not to observe any law of

the

the enemy. They were, however, advised to perform their
duties and work for the Revolutionary Government. But it
was a regret that, as the campaign was carried out on too
large a scale, it bore no fruitful result, because tens of
thousands of people were thrown into imprisonment.

During the second stage the policy of local destruction
was adopted and practiced. The Government sent radical elements to undertake destruction of the enemy's administration,
buildings, structures of military organizations, iron bridges,
factories manufacturing military supplies, besides carrying
out the assassination of leading personages in the enemy's
military and political circles. It aimed at striking terror
into the enemy, besides creating disorder and confusion. It
also aimed at foiling the policy of emigration and at inciting
the masses of the Korean people to revolutionary feelings and
thought. Some of the outstanding cases of radical destruction are mentioned in the following:

1. Kim Igsang's Bombing of the Japanese Governor-General's
residence in 1926.
2. Kang Ukiew's attempted assassination of the Japanese
Governor-General in 1919.
3. Kim Sangok's bomb throwing into the Japanese military
barracks in Seoul in 1923.
4. Li Suhung, Na Suk-chu, and Pack Kwang-un's surprise
attack on Saito (then Japanese Governor-General in Korea) in
a steam launch in 1925.
5. Li Bongchang's surprise attack on the Japanese
Emperor in Tokyo in 1932.
6. Yun Bong-il's bomb throwing act at the Japanese
military and civil officials in the Hongkew Park in Shanghai
in 1932.

Besides those above-mentioned cases there are hundreds
of different cases which are not recorded here. As can be
seen, mere acts of terrorism have failed and will fail again
to bring success to the movement of independence of Korea
but these heroic acts at least have shown to the world that
the Korean people are not willingly dominated by Japanese.

During the third stage which was begun shortly after the
outbreak of the Sino-Japanese war on July 7, 1937, a comprehensive programme on the preparation of national mobilization
was put into effect and has continued up to the present day.
Action has been taken to secure the support from those having
the abilities of organization as well as from influential
persons of different organizations. For example, the Chun-
Do-Kio religionists, several millions in number, dwelling
in the urban and rural districts, have a sublime history
of revolution behind them and secret organizations of political nature. As to the Christians, both Roman Catholics
and Protestants also several millions in number with their
leaders who are permeated with the ideals of modern democracy had sworn to support our present revolutionary movement. The influence exerted by religious societies to link
up the thought and the action between the dwellers in urban
and rural districts has been both great and far-reaching.
There appears to have no other more effective way of mobil-
izing the masses of the people. Besides the Chun-Do-Kio

religionists

religionists and Christians there are several hundreds of
thousands Buddhism and Dai-Chong-Kio followers who are also
strong anti-Japanese elements.

Before the start of the Great Revolution it is first of
all necessary to train the people in responding to the Provisional Government's call for mobilization. As a matter of
fact, the Provisional Government secretly sent many agents
to help them to set up organizations and to make contacts
with organizations of different shades of nature so that at
an order of the Government those people will readily rise up
against the enemy. Intelligence, espionage, destruction,
assassination, stop of labor, and business are their acts
of violence. Besides, the Government has secretly ordered
that capable men such as military experts, technicians, doctors,
etc., will go abroad so as to enable its gathering of talent
for use. Along with the Pacific War the Provisional Government will be enabled to push its plans abroad in coordination
with those being secretly carried out in Korea.

V. The Provisional Government and the Koreans
in Manchuria

The mass emigration of Koreans to China's Three Northeastern Provinces, otherwise known as Manchuria, began about
a century ago. In those provinces there are over three
million Koreans and under the direction of the Provisional
Government they had, by using their bases in the basins of
the Yalu and the Touman Rivers, waged a battle against three
divisions of Japanese troops. That occurred before the
Mukden Incident of 1931, but following the Incident the link
between the Provisional Government and the Korean fighters
in Manchuria was cut. At this time the Korean combatants
joined the Chinese volunteers and hence arose the name of
the Sino-Korean United Army.

At present, the Provisional Government has at least
twenty thousand troops, but with the aid of equipment and
military expenditure from outside sources the number may
easily swell to one hundred thousand. Geographically
speaking, the Sino-Soviet borderland with its mountains and
forested regions can be advantageously utilized against the
enemy. It is also important to make use of the anti-Japanese
psychology of the Korean and Chinese dwellers there. Secret
contact should be made with the puppet troops of the "Manchukuo" for the purpose of making them "turn over" with their
bayonets pointed against the bogus organization and against
the Japanese invaders.

Most recently, as a result of the direction of the Provisional Government, those taking charge of the secret societies and the peasants' organizations have all the more inten-
sified their activities which, with the aid of military supplies from the Allies, can be pushed on a large scale.

Besides those now living in Manchuria, there are over two
million Koreans scattered in various provinces of China,
notably Kiangsu, Chekiang, Shantung, Hopei, Chahar and Sui-
yuan. Out of this number, two hundred and fifty thousand
Koreans have been forcibly sent to China for war; quite a large
number of them have already come over to the Korean

Restoration

Restoration Army.

At present, the Provisional Government is having three objects in view: first, to make the armed Koreans in the "occupied" areas revolt and "turn over"; second, to make the Korean people in the "occupied" areas psychologically participate in the war of Korean independence; and third, when the above two steps meet with success, action will be taken to "bridge" the work in Manchuria. The execution of all such measures need great moral and material aids from the Allied Government.

VI. The Provisional Government and the Koreans
in America

The Koreans now residing in the Hawaiis number from ten thousand upwards. Those residing in the U. S. A. during the past thirty years have been a vital force in the Korean national movement: for they have rendered a great deal of their spiritual and material support to the government, setting an example which need be followed by overseas Koreans in all other parts of the world. The Oversea Koreans United Commission which forms part of the machinery of the Provisional Government is a central organ for executing and directing all affairs in regard to oversea Koreans. Very recently, the Korean Provisional Government has issued an order calling upon Korean youths to participate in the Pacific war against aggressive Japan, and this is to be believed to be a welcome news to the American military authorities.

The United Korean Peoples Committee in America was formed in Hawaii last April by the representatives of nine organizations from Hawaii and America to strengthen inter-organizational unity in spite of the difference of political and social theory and practice, in order to make united war, united diplomacy, as well as united support of the Korean Provisional Government in China as our main revolutionary organ. During the United Korean Peoples Convention of last May in Honolulu they have passed the following resolutions in regard to supporting the Provisional Government:

(a) All Koreans and the organizations should absolutely trust and support the Provisional Government with spirit and matter.
(b) Every Korean and organization should absolutely observe the decrees issued by the Provisional Government.
(c) For the sanctity of the government and the discipline of the people, we should ask the Provisional Government not to change the cabinet of the present government until the people ask for it.

VII. The Provisional Government and the Koreans
in the U. S. S. R.

The Koreans in the Soviet Union are estimated at a figure of seven hundred thousand, excluding the two divisions of troops under the command of the Soviet military authorities. But under certain circumstances these Korean troops can take orders from the Provisional Government and, after effecting a link with the Korean troops in Manchuria, may

battle

battle under the chief commander of the Korean Restoration
Army against the Japanese forces. It will be recalled that
shortly after the inauguration of the Korean Provisional
Government in 1919 the Koreans living in Soviet territory
gave it their enthusiastic support as was perceived in their
despatch of leading delegates to take part in the new revolutionary organizations.

VIII. The Provisional Government and the Korean
Independence Party

The Korean Independence Party was instituted in 1931 with
the object of pooling together the revolutionary leaders of
the country. Its members have scattered over Korea, "occupied"
China, Free China, the U. S. A. and Mexico, and are commissioned
to engineer the movement of Korean Independence. At present,
the leading personalities of the Provisional Government, the
ranking officers of the Restoration Army and the Councillors
of the Political Council are mostly members of the Korean
Independence Party. The principle and policy of the Korean
Independence Party and of the Korean Provisional Government's
Outline of the National Reconstruction have one common object
in view and receive full support from the people of the whole
country. It may be surmised that the reconstruction plans of
Korea will be carried out on the basis of the three-equality
principles, of politics, economics and education.

IX. The Provisional Government and the Restoration Army

During the early stage of the Provisional Government
there was promulgated a set of rules for the organization of
the Korean Restoration Army, the commanding officers of which
were then active in the Three Northeastern Provinces of China.
In 1940 the Restoration reorganized with General Li Chung-
Chun appointed as its Commander-in-Chief. Towards the end
of 1941, arrangements had been so made with the Chinese military authorities that the Korean Restoration Army was permitted to carry on its activities and work in several provinces of Free China. Before gaining any firm footing in its
own territory, the Korean Restoration Army has to take part
in the Sino-Japanese war and in the Pacific war. In form,
Korea wages a double-fledged war but, substantially, her war
is simply one of independence.

The most important problems at present are measures in
regard to the training up of three divisions or more of Korean
crack troops and the assignment of war areas for their military operations. The solution of these problems relies upon
Allied aids. It can be certain and sure that the success in
this solution will occasion a stirring impulse to the anti-
Japanese feelings of the Korean people in all parts of the
world. It would be a splendid thing if the United States would
by the Land-Lease Bill, help the Korean Provisional Government
to train up three divisions of crack troops in Free China
within a year. With these crack troops the Korean Provisional
Government would easily puff up the latent power of Korea's
revolution. It is significant to note that Korea's revolution
is a fresh force of aid to the democratic bloc in the Pacific
war, but may even go so far as to help deciding the final
outcome of this titanic struggle.

X.

61

X. The Provisional Government and the Allies

During the period of the Korean Independence, the Korean Government concluded a treaty with China in 1882, with the U. S. A. on May 20 of the same year, a treaty with Great Britain in 1883, and a treaty with Russia in 1884.

In 1920 the Soviet Government promised to subsidize the Korean Government with two million Rubles, but only part of the amount was obtained. In 1920 the United States Senate passed the Korean Provisional Government's report and discussed the question of extending recognition to the Korean Provisional Government. In the same year the British House of Commons discussed the independence question of Korea. In 1941 the Chinese Political Council passed the proposition regarding recognition of the Korean Provisional Government. The governments of other countries such as Czechoslovakia, Esthonia and the Netherlands also give support to the Korean Provisional Government.

Some time in the middle of 1941 the Korean Provisional Government issued a manifesto on August 29, in support of the Roosevelt-Churchill Declaration and declared war on the Axis nations. A request was later made to join the 26-Nation Alliance as a member, and action was taken to mobilize armed Koreans to fight shoulder to shoulder with the Allies against the common enemy in the Far East.

Whatever things Korea may do, it will not be without effects on the Allies. At present, what the Korean Provisional Government requests from the Allies is their formal recognition of its existence and their supply of munitions with which the Korean troops and people will be undoubtedly able to deal more telling blows to Japan, thus contributing their part toward the Allies' ultimate triumph.

MANIFESTO OF KOREA'S PROVISIONAL GOVERNMENT

(Issued on August 29, 1941)

"To the governments and peoples of the world's anti-aggressive countries, this Government proposes to declare the determination and hopes of the thirty million Korean people. Since 1919 the Korean people have been single-handedly resisting Japan and despite the loss of several millions of youths, their spirits have remained as high as ever. At the beginning of the struggle it was already firmly believed that aggressors would collapse in the end and that anti-aggressive countries would arise, and might be joined in a common effort.

"With an insatiable desire for territorial conquests the Japanese militarists flared up conflagration of war on the Asiatic mainland on July 7, 1937, when the Luk-ouchiao Incident was precipitated. The people of China all exerted their utmost in resisting the invaders, causing enormous losses to the latter.

"Following

"Following the joint declaration of President Roosevelt
and Premier Churchill on the 14th of August, 1941, many other
countries including the Soviet Union, Australia, Canada and
Holland began to join the U. S. A. and Britain. - As a result,
the front of anti-aggression began to become more consolidated, words being translated into action and national hostilities becoming those of world-wide nature. That the democracies can encircle the Nazis and defeat the Japanese may
certainly materialize as <u>has</u> been desired in the joint
resolution.

"The third and eighth points and the preamble of the
Roosevelt-Churchill Declaration are especially inspiring
to the Korean people. The third point stipulates that
America and Britain respect the rights of all the peoples
to choose the form of government under which they live and
they wish to see sovereign rights and self-government
restored those who have been forcibly deprived of them.
According to the eighth point, all nations of the world,
for realistic as well as spiritual reasons, must come to
abandonment of the use of force. The preamble makes it that
by the Lend-Lease Act munitions of war are to be supplied
to the entire armed forces of Britain and other countries
actively engaged in resisting aggression.

"Not only those principles are necessary to Korea's
struggle for independence and to the defeat of Japan but
they will help to reestablish a desirable order of the world
and to eliminate the prejudicial differences between the
yellow races of the East and the white races of the West.
This Government, in principle, is in whole-hearted support
of the above-said declaration.

"This Government deeply believes in the potential power
and strength of China, the U. S. A., Great Britain and the
Soviet Union as well as takes cognizance that the Korean
nation is occupying an important position in the anti-Japanese campaign. Mutual aid necessitates a crushing defeat of
Japan and her Axis partners as a step towards reconstruction
of the Far East and the world as a whole.'

XI.   Chief Korean Independentists

Mr. Kim Ku, Chairman of the State Council of the Korean
Provisional Government, now 66 years old, is one of the
veteran revolutionary leaders and has devoted more than
thirty years to the cause of Korea's freedom. He is most
respected and widely known leader among the Koreans both
at home and abroad. For his connection with the assassination of Japanese high officials in Korea, he was arrested
and several times received death sentences when the so-called
Protectorial Treaty was forced upon Korea by Japan. But
somehow he safely came to Shanghai and joined the Provisional
Government. Some of the important posts held by him were
Commissioner of Police, Minister of Interior, Minister of
Finance, Director of Special Service of Intelligence, and
President of the Korean Provisional Government. After the
Mukden Incident of 1931, he secretly sent Li Bong-Chang to
Tokyo where he threw a bomb at the Japanese-Emperor while he
was going to inspect the troops. Although the bomb did not

<u>kill</u>

not kill the Emperor, it gave the Japanese people to know
how much we resent their domination over us and we did not
care whether the Emperor is the son of God or not. In 1932,
he again sent Li Bong-Gil, another Korean patriot to Honkew
park in Shanghai where he bombed a number of Japanese army
and navy commanders. He sent many Korean youths to the
Chinese Military Schools and all of them now are in the
Korean Restoration Army.

Mr. Cho Wanku, Minister of Interior, now 62 years old,
was graduated from the College of Law in Seoul. He distinguished himself as a model and wise district magistrate but
after the so-called Protectorial Treaty he organized a political party called Tai Tan Hap.Hui (Great Korea Association)
to fight the Il-chin Hui (Traitor's Group). After the
annexation of Korea by Japan he escaped to Vladivostok
where he became director of the Chungkuo Daily News and
organized Tong Chi Sa, a secret political society to fight
the Japanese. Later he proceeded to Shanghai to join the
Korean Provisional Government and assisted in matters of
organization and movement. Some of the important appoint-
ments held by him were Vice Minister of Interior, Vice Chairman of the Provisional Congress and one of the Executive
Committee of the Korean Independence Party.

Mr. Tjosowang, Minister of Foreign Affairs, graduated
from the Korean National Academy, is now 55 years old. During
the Russo-Japanese war the Korean Government despatched him
to Japan as a Royal Scholarship student. There he organized
the Korean Revolutionary Student's Association and was elected
chairman of it. He was editor of the monthly magazine published by the Korean Revolutionary Student's Association.
Later he was appointed as an instructor in the Law Academy,
but after the Chinese Revolution in 1911 he was compelled
to escape to Shanghai where he organized a secret society
called Tong Chek Sa. There he trained many revolutionary
elements in a special school organized by him during the
First World War. He spared no effort to advocate national
unity of the Korean people, as it could be well seen in the
issue of one of his manifestoes. He was credited with having
made close connection with American and European organizations
and discussed with them on questions of Korea's emancipation.
He organized the Headquarters of the Korean Independence
Volunteer Army, and was appointed vice-president. Then he
was appointed as Secretary-General of the Provisional Government and responsible for the drafting of the Provisional
Constitution which embodied ten articles. He was then again
appointed as President of the Provisional Congress, Minister
of Foreign Affairs (appointed for four times), Minister
of Interior, and one of the founders of the Korean Independence Party. He wrote two famous books entitled "Remains
of Perfume" and "Korean Literature."

General Djo Sung-huan, Minister of War, now 68 years old,
was graduated from the Korean War College. For his opposition to the Korean Imperial Government he was sentenced to
death, but curtailment of his "crime" enabled him to live.
After his release he entered the army, and following the
so-called Protectorial Treaty he organized the Hsin Min Hui
(New People's Society), a secret political organization.

                                                    He

He went to Peking to undertake intelligence service, but
was caught and ordered to return to Korea. He was then
exiled to Siberia. In 1919 he proceeded to Shanghai to
join the Korean Provisional Government. Some of the important posts held by him were Vice Minister of War, Minister
of Education, Director of the Northwest Special Military
Corps and Commander-in-Chief of the Korean Volunteer Corps.
General Dje speaks Chinese fluently.

Mr. Li Shi-yung, Minister of Finance, now 74 years old,
was graduated from Yuk Ying Public Institute. He had held
many important posts in the Imperial Korean Government, but
after the annexation of Korea by Japan he and his family went
to live in Manchuria where he opened schools and trained
Korean youths for the purpose to make them real fighters
for the freedom of Korea. He came to Shanghai in 1919 and was
appointed Minister of Finance by the Provisional Government.
Since then he held this post many times. He sold all his
properties for use in Korea's revolutionary cause.

General Li Chung-Chun, Commander-in-Chief of the Korean
Restoration Army, now 54 years old, was graduated from the
Japanese War College. In response to the Korean Independence of 1919 he took an active part, and distinguished
himself in many battles against the superior Japanese
forces in the Manchurian border. He is one of the ablest
military men Korea has ever had today.

Dr. Syngman Rhee, Korean Republic's plenipotentiary
representative in the United States, now 67 years old,
was graduated from a missionary high school in Seoul. When
the movement of the Korean Independence was afoot, he took
an active part in it, but was caught and sentenced to death.
Curtailment of his "crime" however, saved his life, but
was ordered to do hard labor. During the period of his
imprisonment he wrote a book called "Independent Spirit".
In the early days of the Russo-Japanese War he escaped to
the United States where he furthered his studies and obtained
a Ph.D. degree. In Honolulu he spared no effort in establishing schools, in running press and organizing societies
for the interests of the Koreans. In 1919 he was elected
First President of the Provisional Government in Shanghai.
Now he is Director-General of the Dong Ji-Hui (Comrades'
Society) in Honolulu. His writings in English are "International Public Law", "Drive Away Japan", and "The Problems
of Koreans in Manchuria.".

General Liu Tong-Yiul, Chief of Staff, now 66 years
old, was graduated from the War college in Japan. He was
elected Chairman of the Sin Min Hui (New People's Society)
for several times. He was among the 150 members of the
society who had been arrested by the Japanese police and
was sentenced to hard labor. He too came to Shanghai and
held many important posts in the Provisional Government,
and also directed military activities of the Korean Volunteers in the Manchurian border against the Japanese.

Major-General Lee Bum-Suk, assistant to the Chief of
Staff of the Korean Restoration Army, is 40 years old, and

graduated

graduated from the Central Military Academy in China. In 1921 the Korean Volunteer Corps under his command had a severe engagement with the Japanese forces at Chungsanlee, Manchuria, and won the battle, the details of which were even recorded in the enemy's reports, books and magazines. He has translated a book entitled "History of the Chungsanlee Battle" from Korean into Chinese.

II. The Pacific War and Korea

A review of the Far Eastern situation during the past thirty years, reveal that Japan had six stages of development, in each of which she was able to meet with success owing to the indifference of the democratic powers toward the Far East. For instance, first their indifference to the so-called Protectorial Treaty in 1905; second, their silent allowance of Japan to annex Korea in 1910; third, no substantial aid to Korea during the start of the independence movement in March of 1919; fourth, no sweeping action taken to deal with the Mukden Incident in 1932; fifth, no positive aid given to China following the Lukouchiao Incident in 1937; sixth, the Allies' failure to assume an offensive immediately after the outbreak of the Pacific War towards the end of 1941; and seventh, the Pacific War was being regarded as one of secondary importance.

The lack of vigorous reaction from the democratic Powers must have emboldened militarist Japan to create her so-called "Incidents" one after another, climaxing in the precipitation of the Pacific War. If China, Britain, and the United States had taken concrete action to prevent Japan from dominating Korea, the aggressor would have been unable to so smoothly carry out continental expansion the success in which obviously enabled her to throw the Pacific into turmoil. So how very important is the Korean problem which, as a matter of fact, is only a principal factor in the solution of the Far Eastern War. The only means of solving the Korean problem is to give enormous support and help to Korean Provisional Government, so that it can train up crack troops for the Pacific War against Japan. The independence of Korea is indispensable, because only thus will it cease to be a stepping-stone for any aggressor nation in the East, and moreover it will become a place where all friendly nations can have their equal opportunity of trade. If the Roosevelt-Churchill Declaration applies to Korea, then there will soon rise up a state which will strongly fight for the cause of peace and democracy in Asia and in the Pacific.

The following is the English translation of the first
manifesto issued by the Korean Independence Party upon its
formal inauguration:

"We have by unanimous agreement dissolved the Korean
People's Party, the Korean Revolutionary Party, and the Korean
Independence Party, have established a united body in the
Korean Independence Party, and hereby we announce to the
public the meaning and significance of our joint organiza-
tion.

Comrades and fellow-country men: The main reason for
the amalgamation and unification of our three parties is
fourfold - first, the aims, policy and principles of the
three parties, their endeavors and historical background
have all shown the feasibility and desirability of union.
Second, the time is now mature and opportune for union as
the three parties during recent several decades have made
preparations for such a step. Third, the past several
decades of experience in the independence movement has
enabled us to understand the basic obstacles which have
caused our three parties to be frequently at loggerheads
with one another. We have, therefore, truly realized that
for the exaltation of our common purpose we must unite and
consolidate our efforts. Fourth, the heroic resistance put
up by China against Japanese aggression is entering its
fourth year, and the enemy's foot of clay is sunk deeper
and deeper where they neither could advance nor retreat.
Japan's collapse and China's final triumph are now foregone
conclusions. This is the chance of our life time, as it is
imperative that we must reorganize ourselves and closely
coordinate our activities with China's resistance in order
to hasten the downfall of the Japanese imperialists and the
restoration of our fatherland as a free and independent
nation.

It was our great regret that the three predecessors of
our new party has never until now succeeded in bringing about
the much-desired solidarity. Though several conferences with
that in mind were held, all such endeavors were abortive due
to divergence of opinions. To attain our historic task of
our nationalist movement we have to emphasize the unity and
solidarity of all our revolutionary groups for else, we would
not be able to launch our campaign on a nation wide scale.
With the formation of the united front, therefore, we con-
fidently hope to be able in the very near future to make
greater progress in our revolutionary cause.

Our party welcomes the cooperation of any group that
has as the aim of its struggle the restoration of the freedom and independence of our fatherland and that exerts its
utmost in fighting the enemy for the realization of this
aim. At the same time however, it will be necessary to preserve the dignity and independence of our party. We uphold
all the political principles to which the entire Korean race
attaches its deepest faith and push our movement as far as
the situation allows us. At the merger of three parties, it
is especially important to establish and define our political
beliefs on the basis of the principles, aims and policy which
the three previous parties had in common. With unflinching
and unwavering faith in our party, we shall be able to over-
come all obstacles.

Party

'Party Principles - Korea, our fatherland, was a free
and independent country with a history of 5,000 years. Since
our land was forcibly occupied by Japan who belongs to an
alien race, our people have been suffering from the enemy's
political, economic and cultural oppressions and have become
slaves. There has been for our Koreans no racial self-determination internally and no equality in the family of nations.

Under the circumstances, our party seeks by means of
revolution to overthrow the Japanese regime and to recover
our lost territory and reestablish our country as a new
republic on the basis of equality of opportunity in the
political, economic and educational fields. Within the
country the people's livelihood must be guaranteed and exter-
nally Korea must have an equal footing with other countries
of the world.

Party Aims - 1. Complete restoration of the territorial
sovereignty and the founding of the Great Republic of Korea.
2. The preservation and protection of all the basic
factors that are vital to the life and growth of the nation,
such as territory national sovereignty and privileges and the
propagation of all our good national traits, historical and
cultural.
3. The adoption of popular election so that all citizens
may have an equal chance of participating in government affairs.
In the constitution, all citizens irrespective of sex, religion
and class shall be entitled to equal privileges.
4. The nationalization of land and big productive enterprises so that all the people may have equal rights and privileges in their livelihood.
5. The provision of free education so that all the people
may have an equal chance for education to equip themselves with
the basic knowledge and vocational training.
6. The enforcement of conscription in order to build up
an army for national defense.
7. Enlisting the cooperation of all those countries that
treat our nation with equality and reciprocity in the common
task for world peace and happiness of mankind.

Party Policy - 1. To arouse the national and revolutionary
sentiments for the people by preaching the party's principles
and aims.
2. To concentrate all the revolutionary forces within the
country and abroad with a view to a general mobilization for
the revolutionary campaign.
3. To centralize the training of army officers and men
preparatory to organization of the revolutionary army.
4. To enlarge and strengthen the mass opposition and
armed resistance of the Korean people against Japan and to
organize the international publicity and other means in preparation for the all front war to overthrow Japanese domination.
5. To support and maintain the Korean Provisional Government of the Great Republic of Korea.
6. To enlist the support and cooperation of all those
countries sympathetic and helpful to our independence movement
with a view to enhancing our revolutionary strength.
7. To coordinate our struggle with the heroic resistance
of China against Japan with a view to forming an allied anti-
Japanese force.

Our

Our party shall forge ahead with bravery and unwavering determination for the realization of our historic mission of the revolution in strict adherence to the party principles, aims and policy as outlined above. We shall fight with all might until the alien control of our nation is ousted and the territorial sovereignty of Korea as a free and independent nation restored. Then we shall proceed with the establishment of a new republic in which the citizens shall be entitled to equal rights and privileges in political, economic and educational fields. We take the opportunity to declare to the people of the entire nation that there are responsibilities our party shall seek to discharge.

Comrades and fellow-countrymen: The aggressive designs of Japan spread practically all over Asia during the recent ten years. Driven by her dream of dominating Asia, she has started her most unreasonable aggressive war on China.. The aggressor has trampled over southern and northern provinces of this country and everywhere they went, they lift in the wake of their invasion houses and properties burned and bombed, innocent civilians killed and murdered, women raped and abused. These acts are indeed unforgiveable.

In an attempt to frustrate our independence movement, the Japanese militarists tried every cruel means they could think of throughout the 13 provinces of Korea and among all classes of our people. They seek to kill the national consciousness of our masses by organizing all kinds of "phony" societies.

Comrades and fellow-countrymen: Our enemy Japan has encountered a most stubborn resistance from who during her prolonged war has been able to deal her enemy one blow after another. Now Japan is coming near to the point of exhaustion and her total collapse is close in sight. Her regular troops killed on the China fronts have totalled more than a million men and the number of her wounded is countless.

The total of 20,000,000,000 yen, sinking fund in her national treasury has already been spent for her war in China, and her economic and financial insolvency has reached to its worst stage. Internationally Japan has gone bankrupt.

Within her own country, the livelihood of the Japanese people has become miserable and anti-war feelings are seething among the entire population. Such conditions are reminiscent of those existing in Russia and Germany during the first World War that led revolutionary uprisings in those two countries.

This is an excellent opportunity we must grasp and the time is now opportune for us to launch the general mobilization of our people and to organize on a nationwide scale our revolutionary army. Thus we may be able to hasten the downfall of the Japanese imperialism and to regain the freedom and independence of our country as the first step towards the realization of the happiness of mankind."

Mr. Hornbeck:

The previous correspondence with
Mr. Bird is attached.

F.B.

OCCIDENTAL COLLEGE
LOS ANGELES, CALIFORNIA

OFFICE OF THE PRESIDENT   February 14, 1942

Mr. Stanley Hornbeck
Department of State
Washington, D. C.

My dear Mr. Hornbeck:

     Will you please find en-
closed a copy of a letter which is self-
explanatory.

     Thank you for the courtesy of your
note received some days ago. We need your
wisdom in this matter very decidedly.

     Most cordially,

Dr. Syngman Rhee
The Korean Commission
1766 Hobart Street, N.W.
Washington, D. C.

My dear Dr. Rhee:

Our mutual friend, Mr. S. L. Rhee, is in my office and we are counselling together seeking to be wise and fore-warned in reference to Korean interests and in our hope, Korean freedom.

You will fully comprehend that at a time like this there will arise a multitude of friends and persons pretending to be friends and it will be difficult in the crisis and the emotion of the crisis to know one from the other.

It would seem to me that from some source there should be a careful scrutiny of all persons who may be sponsored by the "Korean for [illegible] Movement" in the United States.

I understand there are about 2000 Koreans in this country, most of them second generation and citizens of the United States.

One would presume that any effort which is made to support [illegible] would need accurate understanding of forces and persons now in Korea. [illegible] urally there can develop suspicion and hostility where there should be [illegible] ity of understanding and full cooperation.

You will recall that the government of [illegible] and [illegible] and fostered in the United States, especially in [illegible] and the [illegible] was to [illegible] degree made possible by the [illegible] and [illegible] country. There [illegible] have been extraordinary [illegible] made so [illegible] for the [illegible] to be so universally and socially adopted.

[illegible]
[illegible]
[illegible]

Dr. Syngman Rhee -2.

          The friends of Korea in this country need to be absolutely sure
that no false move may be made or that anything may be done contrary to
the will of our own State Department.

          I am sending a copy of this letter to Mr. Hornbeck. I would
suggest that you confer with him.

          We have an immediate situation. A man has appeared in this com-
munity who is training Korean volunteers in the Coliseum. He has been
received immediately and quite naturally with great enthusiasm by the local
colony. Let us presume that he is in every respect a desirable person to
render this service. Let us presume that no suspicion whatever should be
entertained concerning him. I rather imagine, however, that there has been
no full investigation and I know that there is no central office which has
sent out word giving complete endorsement to this gentleman. This is an
illustration of what I have in mind.

          I am a personal friend of Mr. Louis Adamic. You may have noticed
that he has recently written a book under the title Two-Way Passage. In
this book he advocates a policy of the building in America of cooperating
groups who can return to their native lands and assist in the recovery of
the blighted areas which have been overwhelmed by enemies and false philosophies. I know that his book has intrigued the interest of President and
Mrs. Roosevelt. He was a guest in the White House a few weeks ago. While
the direction of his own interest would be toward Europe, the need of a
similar development of support for the nations of the Orient is quite as
urgent.

          I would not need to tell you, but you would fully comprehend and
much better than I, that the exile must be exceedingly careful that he does
not assume types of leadership and authority which make him in any way undesirable on the part of these loyal citizens who have endured persecution
within the home land in the period of occupation.

          I am sure there are in Washington in the State Department, in the
Donovan Committee, in the Office of Facts and Figures, and in other cooperating centers, persons who would welcome the opportunity to counsel with you.

          I regret very much that our mutual friend, Dr. McAfee McGume, is
ill and has therefore been unable to leave for Washington to accept the post
to which he has been appointed by the Donovan Committee. I shall try to see
him before he goes. I will give him a copy of this letter and ask him
that I may give whatever wisdom I may possess to our friend, Mr. S. K.
with whom this college enjoys now through many years so happy and helpful
a relationship.

Dr. Syngman Rhee -5.

        May I thank you again for your book which I shall read with
great profit and inspiration.

        I beg to remain

                                Very sincerely yours,

FEB 25 '42

Dear Dr. Bird:

I have received and I thank you for your letter
of February 14 with which you were so good as to
enclose a copy of a letter of the same date which
you had written to Dr. Syngman Rhee.

I have read your letter to Dr. Rhee with much
interest and I shall see that it is brought to the
attention of others in the Department who are
interested in this matter.

Yours sincerely,

STANLEY K. HORNBECK

Stanley K. Hornbeck
Adviser on Political Relations

Dr. Remsen D. Bird,

President, Occidental College,

Los Angeles, California.

[File no. 811.428/27

PA/H:AHiss:BGT
2-27-42

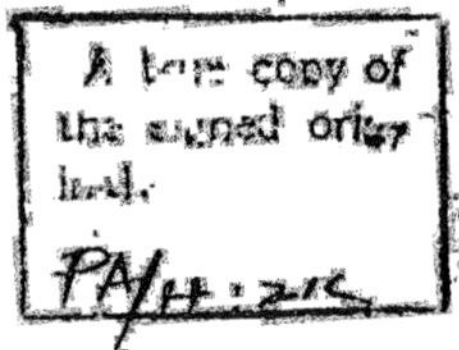

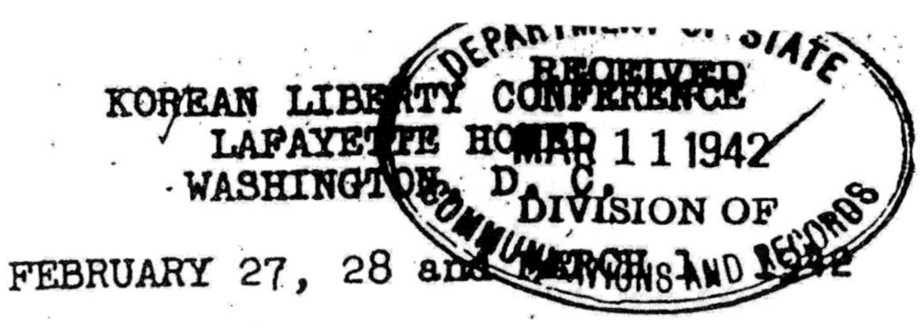

RESOLUTION 1

Mr. Chairman. After hearing the Declaration of
Independence of Korea, adopted March 1, 1919 again read,
I wish to offer the following Resolution:

> BE IT RESOLVED, that we and each of us do this day,
> March 1, 1942 reaffirm the 1919
> Declaration of Independence of the
> People of Korea, and that the Korean
> Commission, the Representatives of
> the United Korean Committee of America,
> Los Angeles, California, and Honolulu,
> T. H.; The Korean-American Council;
> and the patriotic Koreans of Korea,
> China and Manchuria now assembled by
> and through their Representatives and
> Delegates do hereby proclaim that we
> will continue to fight for our free-
> dom and liberty until it has been
> obtained.

KOREAN LIBERTY CONFERENCE
LAFAYETTE HOTEL
WASHINGTON, D. C.

FEBRUARY 27, 28 and MARCH 1, 1942

RESOLUTION 2

Mr. Chairman. The Resolution Committee appointed by
the Chairman wish to submit the following Resolutions.

BE IT RESOLVED, on this 1st day of March, 1942 that we the
Representatives of the United Korean Committee
of America, Los Angeles, California and Honolulu, T. H.; the Korean-American Council and
the patriotic Koreans of Korea, China and Manchuria now assembled by and through their Representatives and Delegates do hereby reaffirm
their wholehearted support and maintenance of
the Provisional Government of The Republic of
Korea, now located in Chungking, China.

KOREAN LIBERTY CONFERENCE
LAFAYETTE HOTEL,
WASHINGTON, D. C.

FEBRUARY 27, 28 and MARCH 1, 1942

RESOLUTION 3

Mr. Chairman. The Resolution Committee appointed by
the Chairman wishes to submit the following Resolution.

BE IT RESOLVED, on this 1st day of March, 1942 that we, The
Korean Commission, Representatives of the
United Korean Committee of America, Los Angeles,
California and Honolulu, T. H.; the Korean-
American Council; and the patriotic Koreans
of Korea, China and Manchuria now assembled
by and through our Representatives and Delegates do hereby reaffirm our adherance to the
Declaration of the United Nations, signed by
twenty-six Nations, January 1, 1942 at
Washington, D. C. and reaffirm and approve
our Provisional Government's formal application submitted to the Department of State
of the United States of America, requesting
that our Government be permitted to become
formally a party to the Declaration of United
Nations.

RESOLUTION 4

Mr. Chairman. The Resolution Committee appointed by

the Chairman wishes to submit the following Resolution.

BE IT RESOLVED, on this 1st day of March, 1942 that we, the
Representatives of the United Korean Committee
of America, Los Angeles, California and Honolulu, T. H.; the Korean-American Council; and
the patriotic Koreans of Korea, China and Manchuri
Manchuria now assembled by and through our Representatives and Delegates do hereby authorize,
direct and propose to memorialize the President
of the United States for the recognition of the
Korean Provisional Government and to give us
the status of an active member in the Declaration of the United Nations.

KOREAN LIBERTY CONFERENCE
LAFAYETTE HOTEL
WASHINGTON, D. C.

FEBRUARY 27, 28 and MARCH 1, 1942

RESOLUTION 5

Mr. Chairman. The Resolution Committee appointed by

the Chairman wishes to submit the following Resolution.

BE IT RESOLVED, on this 1st day of March, 1942 that we, the
Representatives of the United Korean Committee
of America, Los Angeles, California and Honolulu, T. H.; the Korean-American Council; and
the patriotic Koreans in Korea, China and
Manchuria now assembled by and through our
Representatives and Delegates do hereby authorize, direct and propose to petition the
Congress of the United States for the recognition of the Korean Provisional Government.

The Korean Liberty Conference

LAFAYETTE HOTEL, WASHINGTON, D. C.   FEBRUARY 27, 28 AND MARCH 1
Sponsored by the United Korean Committee in America and the Korean-American Council

---

FRIDAY, FEBRUARY 27

AFTERNOON, 2:30 TO 5:30—Registration

EVENING, 7:30

Chairman: C. Ho Kim, Executive Chairman, United Korean Committee in America
Master of Ceremonies: Jay Jerome Williams, Treasurer, Korean-American Council
Star Spangled Banner: Rose Chang
Opening Address: Dr. Syngman Rhee, Chairman, Korean Commission
Speakers: Hon. John M. Coffee, M. C., State of Washington
Miss Inez Kong
RICHARD ~~Bankhead~~ Eaton, Commentator, MBS
Dr. Paul F. Douglas, President of American University
Korean National Anthem—Princess Minn

SATURDAY, FEBRUARY 28

MORNING, 10:00—Korean Session

Chairman: C. Ho Kim
Reading of Declaration of Korean Independence: Sukyoon Chang
Speakers: Kee Young Chang
C. I. Song
C. H. Whang
Resolutions

AFTERNOON, 3:30—Tea at American University

EVENING, 7:00

Chairman: C. I. Song, Executive Member, United Korean Committee in America
Master of Ceremonies: John W. Staggers, Legal Counselor, Korean Commission
Solo: Florence Ahn
Speakers: Yongjeung Kim, Director, Public Relations, United Korean Committee
Mrs. George A. Fitch, writer and lecturer
Violin Solo—Ruth Y. Kim
Sebastian Ugarte, Legal Assistant to the Philippine Resident Commissioner
Dr. Philip Jaisohn, Adviser to former Emperor of Korea

SUNDAY, MARCH 1—Commemoration of Anniversary of Declaration of Korean Independence, 1919

AFTERNOON, 3:00

Chairman: Dr. Syngman Rhee
Invocation: The Rev. Dr. F. B. Harris, Pastor, Foundry Methodist Church
Korean National Anthem—Mrs. Mary Ann Kim
Reading of the Declaration of Korean Independence
Speakers: Dr. Homer B. Hulbert, Personal Adviser and Confidential Envoy of the former Emperor of Korea
Dr. Maurice William, Vice President, American Bureau for Medical Aid to China
His Excellency, Dr. Hu Shih, Ambassador of China
Hon. James Cromwell, Former U. S. Minister to Canada
Star Spangled Banner

EVENING, 8:00—Korean Independence Night at Foundry Methodist Church

---

Through the courtesy of Station WINX the following speakers will be heard over this station: Hon. John M. Coffee, Friday, 8:05 to 8:30 p.m.; Yongjeung Kim, Saturday, 7:30 to 8:00 p.m.; His Excellency, Dr. Hu Shih, Ambassador of China, Sunday, 4:30 to 5:00 p. m.

For Release: Monday, March 2, 1942   March 1, 1942.

        Full text of address by Dr. Homer B. Hulbert, Personal Advi.
and Confidential Envoy of the former Emporer of Korea, before the
Korean Liberty Conference at the Hotel Lafayette, Washington, D. C.,
on the afternoon of March 1, 1942.

K O R E A N   L I B E R T Y

        I deem it a signal honor to be given a few minutes on this
platform, though it ought to be trodden only by Korean feet. It is
a delicate compliment, not especially to me, but to all those of
American birth who in the past have participated in the moral struggle
for Korea's bare existence. It means that you who are bearing the
brunt of this ceaseless and untiring fight believe that we of the
earlier generation who are even now breasting the steeps of the Great
Divide and are looking into a setting sun have abated not one whit of
the interest and solicitude which marked our more active days nor
dimmed by one degree the hope, nay the conviction, of her ultimate
emancipation. In the name of all of these I give you thanks.

        I venture to affirm that if one leaf on one tree in all the
forests of America could defy the law of gravitation and refuse to
fall to earth, the entire universe would presently revert to Chaos
and Old Night. There can be no ordered universe unless there be universal obedience to universal law. If a single bolt in a complicated
machine is flawed it may easily bring the entire structure to ruin.
That is why I say that if at the end of this war Korea be not given
back her God-given right to liberty there will be a festering sore,
a noisome cancer beneath the surface which will sooner or later infect
the whole and bequeath to our childrens' children wars more dreadful
than the one from which humanity now suffers.

        Korea enjoys neither the glamor of Japan's spectacular

revolution of sixty years ago nor the dignity of China's gigantic
imperturbability; but though she lacks these more or less desirable
adjuncts and instruments of advertisement, these so-called "talking points", she has something a thousand times as important - the
right to participate in the solution of the problem of the international status of The Little State.

You may have read what that great speaker, Pere Hyacinthe,
said in Notre Dame, Paris, years ago. "The little states! They are
the radiating centers of the most splendid civilizations, from the days
of ancient Greece which gave us an Aesculus, a Sophocles, a Euripides
and a Plato down to those republics of modern Italy to which we owe
the revival of learning. The little states! They are constituted by
the hand of God and I trust He will not suffer them to be removed.
He has placed them between the great states as a negation of universal
empire, a pacific obstacle to the shocks of their power and the plots
of their ambition". That is where Korea belongs and that is where
some day in the Providence of God she will be found. I and all my
generation will be under the sod ere then, but I assure you, in the
words of one of our minor but yet distinguished poets,

> If Graves may listen then,
> We then shall listening be.

It is true that Korea has to show few of the more startling
and spectacular things which attract the eye of the casual tourist, but
it may be that a careful perusal of her history would disclose
achievements which would demand the consideration of the most cultured
of peoples. Go with me, for instance, to the Congressional Library
here in Washington and I will show you a Korean book in one hundred
and twelve quarto volumes that was published something like five
hundred years ago, when our ancestors were just emerging from the

shadows of the Crusades which cluttered the altars of Europe with
spurious fragments of the Cross of Christ and had hardly recovered
from the horrors of the Black Death; when the dawn of English literature was barely breaking. It is a cyclopaedia which, if put into
English, would hardly be shamed by sharing a shelf with the Cyclopaedia
Brittanica. The very existence of such a book in such an age affords
connotations and implications of a surprising nature as regards the
literary attainments of the Korean people. But we could go back another
five hundred years, almost to the days of Alfred King of Wessex, and
I could introduce you to the great scholar Ch'oe Chiwun who went to
China to complete his education and there made for himself a renounced
name in literature even for China. He came back to Korea and became
the doyen of a coterie of Korean literati. It was over a thousand
years ago that he published his autobiography in thirteen volumes.

I could take you to the Natural History Museum in New York
and show you fifty-three pieces of metal movable printing type which
were invented in Korea in 1406 A.D., fifty years before Guttenberg
invented them in Europe. They were the first of the kind which history
records. But they did a thing far more wonderful. The King of
Korea was dissatisfied that his common people could not learn to read,
for at that time they had only the Chinese characters for their
literary medium, and this was so difficult to learn that only the
wealthy and leisure class had access to it. The King commanded his
scholars to invent a phonetic alphabet. Now, the Chinese characters
appeal almost solely to the eye, while an alphabet appeals only to
the ear. To change from one to the other would be as difficult as it
would be for you to stop reading books and listen to the clicking
off of the book with a telegraph key in the Morse Code. A company of

the best scholars, in one tremendous _tour de force_, evolved an
alphabet of twenty-six letters. They had to go far afield for a model
even to Tibet. But the Tibetan, itself derived from Sanscrit, made
the consonant the basis of the syllable and almost ignored the vowel,
like Hebrew and all the Semitic alphabets. The Koreans, with no
previous knowledge of alphabets declared this to be a error - that
the vowel is the "mother" of the syllable and the consonant is the
"child" for there could be syllables without consonants but none
without vowels, just as you can have women without children but no
children without women. So they made up vowels from the simplest
strokes of Chinese characters. —Every letter had one sound and every
sound one letter and I can give evidence from my personal knowledge
gained by careful experimentation that any Korean of average ability
can take up his alphabet and in two weeks read any book you lay before
him.

Somewhere in the sand on Korea's southern shore lie the
remenants of the first iron-clad war-vessel that was ever made. Under
the lash of Hideyoshis sanguinary invasion the genius of the Korean
people awoke. Admiral Yi Sun-sin invented an iron-backed boat that
the Japanese could neither burn nor board. With a fleet of these he
sailed forth and engaged a fleet of Japanese composed of 60,000
troops and destroyed it in a battle which modern naval experts declare
the equal of Trafalgar. It did for eastern Asia what the battle of
Salamis did for Europe.

There is no time here to dwell at length upon all the forms
of oppression which the Japanese have inflicted upon Korea during
the past fifty years, but there are two or three, of which I was a
personal witness, that must be mentioned if only as a matter of record

and because they are adequately illustrative of the range and scope
of her flagitious encroachments upon Korean rights from the loftiest
to the humblest reaches of society.

When, in 1895, Japan had beaten China to her knees, Korea
was almost within the grasp of her avaricious hands. But, you say,
Korea was poor. There could not have been much to take. You may not
be aware that for the past thousand years the margin of comfort in
Korea had been far higher than in either China or Japan, because the
ratio of arable land to population was twice as high. Korean history
gives numerous instances when countless tons of rice had to be thrown
out to rot in order to make room in the store-houses for the new
crop. It was this teeming wealth that beckoned Japan. There was only
one obstacle to its peaceful acquisition. It was the Queen of Korea
who stubbornly refused to submit to such spoliation. Japan therefore
sent to Korea a Minister by the name of Miura Goto, a protege of the
Military Party in that country, a man whose known proclivities were
those of brutal force. Almost immediately he called in a gang of
the so-called _soshi_, that curious product of Japanese culture whom
even Brinkley, the arch-advocate and apologist of Japan, called a
company of irresponsible ruffians who would take anyone's money to
perpetrate assassination. He told them to enter the palace and kill
the Queen. They broke into the Palace, killed her, wrapped her body
in oil-soaked garments and burned it to ashes within a hundred yards
of the King's apartments. He then forced upon the bewildered King a
cabinet of Korean hirelings and through them caused to be promulgate
an edict, purporting to come from the King's own hand, degrading his
dead Queen to the status of a prostitute.

What should then have happened? You will remember that
when Queen Draga of Servia was assassinated by her own people, not by

aliens, the British Government refused for months to send a Minister to
that country out of horror for that deed. What then shall be said of a
government that will send its representative to a friendly court and
there assassinate its Queen and cause her degradation to the position
of an outcast? Every government in treaty relations with Japan
should have arisen and with one voice said to her "You shall send
your Mikado to Korea where on bended knee he shall beg Korea's pardon.
In earnest of his sincerity he shall pay the Korean Government an
indemnity of one billion yen and swear on his sacred honor never
again to touch Korea with one finger, or else Japan will be isolated
internationally and economically and shall become the pariah among
nations." Am I right? You Koreans do not need to reply. I ask the
People of the United States of America to answer.

Another instance, of less tragic moment but no less illum-
inating. There was a high Japanese official named Tanaka, a gentleman of the most imposing position who might well be supposed to
be instinct with the spirit of that noble concept bushido. He was in
some real sense an avatar of Hideyoshi, for it was he who put in
written words the idental plan of far-reaching conquest which
Hideyoshi had formed and which he followed to complete disaster. This
memorandum of Tanaka's might be called the Mein Kamft of Japan.

Now, this high official, The Minister of the Household to
the Emperor, in 1906 was sent by the imperial court as a representative of the Mikado to the wedding of the Crown Prince in Seoul, Korea.
As such he was, constructively, the very mouth of the Emperor. While
in Korea he contemplated taking back home some little memento of his
imperial visit. What should it be? It must of course be something
rather nice - something befitting the dignity of his mission. In the
center of Seoul there stands a marble pagoda, carved with intricate

Buddhistic designs, admittedly one of the most beautiful monuments
of the past in all the Far East. It was sent by the last Emperor of
the Mongol Dynasty in China as a gift to his daughter, the Queen of
Korea. It was set up in Han-yang, now Seoul, because that city is
near tide-water and the edifice was too ponderous to take overland
to Song-do the Capital. But, lest this should seem a slight to his
queen he caused a replica of the pagoda to be set up in P'ung-dok
near Song-do. It was this replica that Tanaka determined to take to
Japan as a memento of his visit. He would have preferred to take
the original, but this was too much even for his effrontery. In
1592 the Japanese invaders had tried to take the marble pagoda to
Japan and had begun its demolition, but were driven headlong by the
combined Korean and Chinese armies and left the top three stories
of the structure on the ground beside the main shaft. No one knows
why the Korean King did not restore the pagoda to its original shape.
There was something prophetic about it. These fragments were to
remain there on the ground as a mute protest against Japanese vandalism until the Japanese themselves should be compelled to come back
and restore the pagoda to its pristine perfection.

So Tanaka went in and asked the King for the P'ung-dok
pagoda supposing probably that the prestige of his position would
overawe His Majesty and secure assent to the request; but the King
answered mildly that the pagoda was not his to give, that it belonged
to the nation and, specifically, that it antedated his own dynasty
by many decades, and it would hardly do to insult his dynastic pre-
decessor by denuding the land of this monument of his former great-
ness. No, he could not assent. Tanaka left the palace with what
face he could, but he was far from discouraged. There were other ways.
He sent eighty-five armed Japanese who drove the Koreans away, tore

down the pagoda, loaded it on carts, took it to a railway station
and shipped it to Japan where it was finally dumped in Tanaka's back
yard. It was not intended as a monument to Japan's imperial prestige,
like the great mound in Kyoto beneath which lie the ears and noses
of 100,000 Koreans which Hideyishi's generals had sent back three
centuries before to be a fitting symbol of their braggart raid. No,
it was to be for Tanaka's private delectation.

It was a little bit too much for some of us Americans in
Korea mutely to endure. The facts were published in The Korea Review
and they caused something of a flurry in Japanese official circles.
Some of the better people in Japan and a few of the newspapers denounced the act of spoliation and demanded that Tanaka be compelled
to take the pagoda back and reerect it on its proper site, but the
Imperial Government could hardly be expected to give added publicity
to facts which implied its own stultification.

At first, the Japan Mail, the paid advocate of Japan, came
out denouncing the story as fabulous. There could be no truth in
it. It was inconceivable that any formal envoy of Japan could have
perpetrated an act of such damnable vandalism. This, of course,
delivered them into our hands "lock, stock and barrel". I went to
P'ung-dok, interviewed the Korean eye-witnesses, took photographs of
the site still littered with the fragments of stone broken from the
edifice in the frantic haste of its demolition and the cart tracks
which witnesses to its removal. All this was published in the
Japan Chronicle in Kobe, and it proved to the hilt the truth of the
indictment. The Japan Mail thereupon changed its mood. It said
"After all, it amounted to nothing. A pagoda! A mere pin-prick!"
It certainly added to "The gaiety of nations". The Japanese Government had been protesting that the unrest in Korea was caused by a few

irresponsible rough-necks who had crossed to Korea and were taking
advantage of her weakness to perform certain petty acts of oppression,
much to the annoyance of the authorities in Japan, and it feared that
these ruffians could be held in check only by policing the whole
country with Japanese! Nothing was said about sweeping all this
riff-raff out of Korea. After Tanaka had identified himself with
them as a super-roughneck the Japanese government stopped making ex-
cuses.

Hundreds of Koreans brought me the deeds of their farms and
sold them to me for one cent a farm that I might put my name on
the boundary-marks to save them from seizure by Japanese for little
if any pay. I gave each man a written promise to sell the farm back
to him at cost price and meanwhile he should be tenant without rent
in perpetuity. I had a bushel-basket full of deeds. When I left
Korea I put them in the hands of an American agent to give back to
the owners when things should quiet down. The last I heard from him,
many years ago, was that they were almost gone, that he had only a
scant half-peck left.

A distinguished professor of one of our prominent universities, a personal friend of Marquis Ito, the Governor-general, came
to Seoul. I went to him and begged him to use his influence with
the Marquis to secure just the most elementary justice for the common
people of Korea, but there was no response, in fact, he denounced
me as a charlatan. In Part I of his book he said that the history
of Korea had never been written and in Park II he quoted a dozen
times from my History of Korea, acknowledging his source in foot-notes.
Pardon the touch of humor. I plead with other distinguished Americans
who were persona grata with the Japanese but not one of them would

raise a finger. The American residents in Korea, the permanent ~~one~~
were not expected, nor were they asked, to jeopardize their business
connections or their professional commitments by openly opposing
Japan, but numbers of them sent to me privately cases of gross injustice some of which I was able to bring to a successful issue,
but not many.

There is one matter of prime importance which must be
inscribed on the pages of history. It is this. The King of Korea
never surrendered to the Japanese. Never did the soil the sanctity
of his regal office by voluntary consent. He bent but he never
broke. At the risk of his life he appealed to us for aid - without
effect. At the risk of his life he approached the Peace Conference
at The Hague - without effect. At the risk of his life he sent
appeals to every chancellery in Europe but his enforced abdication
prevented their delivery. He was marooned upon a throne. I say to
the Korean People everywhere that they can cherish through all the
ages to come the undying loyalty of their last King.

But I must hasten to close. One final picture. At a late
hour on a Summer night down at my summer-house beside the river I
was awakened by a plaintive cry. I went out and found a Korean baby
some three months old lying on the grass beside my house. I called
one of my servants and said "What does this mean?" He said "Look".
I looked and saw a Korean woman hurrying away through the trees.
"Well, what's the answer?" I demanded. "She is a widow" he said.
"She has four or five small children. Tomorrow morning the Japanese
are tearing down her hut without payment or a place to go. She is
desperate. So she has brought the baby here and left it and has
gone back to bring the rest". But why here?" I asked. "Because she

knows that you are a friend of Koreans"? "Yes, buy why on the grass? Why did she not bring it in and ask for shelter". "Oh" he said, "Oh Master, she wouldn't dare do that. She's too timid". Ah God! Too timid! And the tears started from my eyes to think that in our day, in this twentieth century, there could be tyranny like that.

Sometimes in the long night watches I wake and think about that land. I see before me Hagar. Driven out of the tents of Abraham, she took her little boy by the hand and led him out into the desert and laid him down to die. But an angel came and gave them water. Even so this modern Hagar; driven out of the family of nations that some great plan of god may not miscarry, she took her little children by the hand and led them out into a cruel, blinding desert. But when wrong and calumny and shame had done their worst and she laid her little ones upon the ground to die I knew that some archangel, looking in the face of God and seeing there the shadow of this mother's agony, with an insubordination unrebuked would leap from his place to bring her help. Aye, he has already leaped. God needs no winged angels to work his will on earth. He uses men. This messenger, charged with the duty of leading Korea out of the desert back into the family of free nations is

The United States of America.

FOR RELEASE MONDAY, March 2, 1942.

FULL TEXT OF ADDRESS DELIVERED to Korean Liberty Conference
March 1, 1942., BY Mrs. George A. Fitch, Past President of American
Association of University Women, Shanghai, now of United China Relief,
New York City.

-ooOOoo-

KOREA, "PATTERN" OF JAPANESE AGGRESSION.

by

Mrs. George A. Fitch of China.

Most Americans date the beginning of totalitarian aggression,
as they date the collapse of collective security, with the invasion of
Manchuria by Japan in 1931. They forget Korea. The Hermit Kingdom,
which had enjoyed over 4000 years of remarkably democratic culture, fell
victim to Japan in 1905, became her practise ground for world conquest,
the pattern for Japanese aggression, forerunner of Hitlerism. So completely did Korea become a "black-out" in the international firmament
that the Japanese Navy could practise the Pearl Harbor "surprise attack'
in Korea's Chemulpo Bay unsuspected by the rest of the world.

It is nearly four decades since Japan invaded, conquered and
then annexed Korea. This means that a generation that knew not Korea
has grown up in America. Young people read "Korea for Victory with
U. S." on the coat-lapel button of Dr. Syngman Rhee in Washington, or
Mr. Yongjeung Kim in Los Angeles, and ask:

"Where is Korea?"

Imagine! A nation of 23 million liberty-loving people in
almost total eclipse, almost without mention in the teaching of history,
geography and international affairs, sinned against and forgotten. God
forgive us.

So we must ever so briefly review history. The small country
of Korea held a people who were industrious and peace-loving, largely
agricultural, but also adept at arts and crafts, including sericulture,
silk-weaving and embroidery. So highly civilized were the Koreans that
in 285 A.D. they sent a cultural mission to Japan in order to civilize
the wild tribes of that country. Mostly, however, they remained detache
from other nations and, like China, desired only to be left alone - in
dignified isolation.

In 1592 under Emperor Hideyoshi, Japan invaded Korea, but
Admiral Yi Soon-sin built iron-clad warships which annihilated the entir

- 433 -

Japanese fleet and saved Korea from Japanese domination. But the country never fully recovered. Three million men, women, children - 90% of whom were noncombatants - had been massacred. [illegible] had been plundered, books had been burned, cities had been sacked, [illegible] culture was almost obliterated. From that day to this the Koreans have looked upon the "dwarfs from the East" as their implacable foes.

In 1876 Japan paid lip-service to Korea's sovereignty, promising then and repeating later her hollow intent to respect it. But in 1882 we concluded a Treaty of Amity and Commerce with Korea under President Chester A. Arthur. I think it very significant that when our Admiral Shufelt knocked at the door of the Hermit Kingdom - as Commodore Perry had done 30 years earlier at the portals of Japan - the Korean Government declined the offer of trade and friendly intercourse on the ground that they "had too much trouble with their neighbors, especially Japan, and chose to remain detached." Korea did not seek our trade. We sought hers. On the promise of assistance in case of trouble, Korea signed the treaty of 1882 with us. The record needs to be kept clear on this point, because of what happened later. Remember that Korea put her trust first in isolation, and then in the sanctity of her treaties!

Korea's cultural ties with China were strong. In fact, historically, geographically, politically, their interests have been almost identical. During the Ming Dynasty, China referred to Korea as the "brother state", the Oriental counterpart of our expression: "sister nation". When Korea was conquered by Japan in 1905, deep gloom settled over the Chinese people. When the Korean patriot, Ahn Chung-ken, shot Prince Ito at the Harbin railroad station as he was en route to Russia to negotiate a secret treaty vis-a-vis China in 1908, all China was stirred and deeply gratified. Similarly, the Koreans rejoiced when China threw off the Manchu yoke and established her republic in 1911. Having by this time been annexed by Japan, they looked upon Manchuria as their base for future operations in a war of independence. When Japan moved into Manchuria in 1931 the Koreans were almost more disheartened than the Chinese themselves.

There is still a close bond between the Koreans and the Chinese. Since 1919 China has received political refugees from that oppressed country. It is in "Free China" that the first Korean Independence Army was open organized under the famous patriot, Kim Koo, and commanded by General Lee Tseng-chen. General Lee is a former colleague of General-issimo Chiang Kai-shek in the military academy of Japan. Because of this long acquaintance General Chiang had confidence in General Lee and granted special permission for the Korean Army to operate in Chinese territory. News dispatches this week have related some of their suc-cessful operations. The Chinese Government has given some financial assistance for equipment and training, but reports indicate that this army still lacks arms and ammunition and needs help under our lend-lease bill, as does every army resisting aggression, East or West.

Much has been said of our commercial and cultural relations with Korea. After the Treaty of 1882, Americans went to Korea, built the first railroad there, electric tramways, electric lighting-plants, waterworks, steamboats, operated mines and furnished machinery and other equipment. American missionaries were welcomed. Modern schools, churches and hospitals were established. In fact, Korea became more nearly a Christian nation than any other in the Orient.

At the turn of the century - when Hitler was still a babe-in-arms - Japan began to covet the resources: the iron and coal, the copper and silver, even more the gold - and the rich rice-lands of Korea. Japan invaded Korea, having coerced Korea into being the passage-way for her military campaign against Russia, conquered Korea in 1905 and annexed that country in 1910.

Now what I am going to say may hurt. But it must be said. We were Korea's "sister nation", we had insisted that she desert her isolation and detachment, we had opened the door, we had promised "in case of trouble" we would protect her. What did we do to fulfill our promises? We acquiesced in Japan's crime. I say it must be said, be-cause this was the beginning of totalitarianism which today darkens the whole world. This was the beginning of disregard of international treaties. The United States of America helped usher in the era where treaties are no longer binding, wars no longer declared, and human life no longer sacred. He who runs may read. Scan the pages of modern his-tory and you may see at a glance the progressive disregard for inter-national promises, until in 1940, the First Lady of China, Madame Chiang Kai-shek, could write - scathing, but well-deserved rebuke to the

"What has happened - and more important what has not
happened - is another bitter lesson for the Chinese people,
a painful lesson which will be taken to heart by every child
of school-age: never again to believe in international promises and professions, no matter how many imposing-looking
seals may adorn the documents."

When this World War II is over, and we again build our structure of
world peace, let us remember that this is something that must be changed,
a wrong that must be righted, the keystone to the arch of international
peace which must be replaced. And facing up to our guilt in the Treaty
of Portsmouth, which President Theodore Roosevelt later acknowledged to
have been a mistake because it violated the promises of the treaty of
Amity and Commerce, the sooner we make restitution to the Korean people
by recognizing the Provisional Government of the Republic of Korea with
its headquarters in Chungking, China, the better! And if we mean the
"four freedoms", and if the Atlantic is to have its counterpart in the
Pacific, and if we hope to have the cooperation of all peoples of the
world who love freedom in the overthrow of totalitarian aggression any-
where on the globe, the time to give that recognition is NOW!

Do you realize the secret - the keynote at least, for it
should be no secret - to the success of the Chinese who have beaten
the Japanese to a standstill, of the Russians who are breaking the
backbone of the German army, and of MacArthur in a stand that will make
glorious the pages of history as long as time shall last? Is it that
they "fight to the last ditch"? Not that. The brave British are doing
that, and yet retreating: from Hongkong, from Singapore, in Burma. No,
it is something else, and I don't think the British have quite learned
it yet. It is "fighting to the last villager". It is enlisting the
cooperation of the people, indoctrinating the people, so that every man,
woman and child knows what he is to do as war approaches. We call it
the "scorched earth" policy. It is that, and more. It is no longer
leaving the fighting of the war to armies, anymore than aggressors today make war on armies only. In China when the Japanese entered a
village every bit of food was gone, even the pots and pans to cook food
they carried had disappeared, there was no scrap of fuel. The water of

the wells was polluted. The Japanese can carry food [illegible]
This means they can never advance more than 80 miles [illegible]
without being in danger of being without food and water. [illegible]
have cut their way down the Malay peninsula as rapidly as they did [illegible]
they had not been able to live off the country?

Unless the United Nations utilize the experience of the
Chinese in successfully resisting the Japanese, utilize their manpower
to the full, regard them as "comrades-in-arms" and trust them, I doubt
we can win the war in the Far Eastern theater. Today the Chinese
troops go over the border into Burma by permit only. If the British
estimate that it will take 5,000 Chinese troops to hold a sector of
the road or railroad assigned to them, and the Chinese say it will take
40,000 - only 5,000 get into Burma. And it is in northern Burma only
that the Chinese are being used, while the British continue to retreat
in southern Burma. Tens of thousands of seasoned troops, well-equipped,
are still in Yunnan province awaiting the word of permission.

I devoutly hope, and pray, that the United States may not be
so slow to see the aid that Korean patriots can give us in this common
cause. I am not thinking so much of the 23 millions of people in
Korea. Though I know they are no more subjugated than the enslaved
Danes, Norwegians, Belgians, Dutch or Poles, I would not have the heart
to ask them to rise again unarmed to be slaughtered by the Japanese as
they were 22 years ago this day. A peaceful demonstration of kindly
people who having heard of President Wilson's "self-determination of
nations" carried banners saying "We would like our country returned to
us!" I do not want 23 million people, hearing of President Roosevelt's
"four freedoms" to rise in peaceful demonstration. This time let them
bide their time until we can get arms and ammunition to them.

I am thinking rather of the Koreans in exile. Those patriots
who have kept Freedom's candle of hope, a flickering flame at times but
never extinguished, burning in the hearts of their compatriots at the
price of imprisonment, torture and martyrdom! Black-listed by the
Japanese, they have lived in exile in every friendly country, working
quietly, persistently, in China, in France (before this war), in Cuba,
Mexico, Hawaii and the United States. Some of these brave spirits I
have known personally.

There was W. H. Liu, surrounded at a ball-game, bundled into a waiting car, kept in solitary confinement in a jail for three and a half years. Released for "good conduct", more truly because he was ill and unable to speak, he was refused permission by the Japanese authorities (though supposedly a free man) to visit his son, dying of tuberculosis in Shanghai. Ahn Chang-ho, arrested on a faked warrant in the French Concession of Shanghai, was sent to Korea on a trumped-up charge, put into solitary confinement. His health also broke from the treatment, and he was released lest he die on their hands. On March 11, 1938 this telegram came to me from his actor son in Los Angeles: "Cable received from Korea: Ahn Chang-ho passed away in Seoul University hospital". An unnamed patriot came to my husband's office in Shanghai with his face covered by a mask. The lower half of face and jaw were gone from phosphorous poisoning. He was the only survivor of twelve who had been caught in revolutionary activities, imprisoned, and fed phosphorous with their food.

Dr. Syngman Rhee, head of the Korean Commission in Washington, D. C. spent seven years in a Korean prison, and was being hunted down again when he escaped to the United States. Here and in Honolulu he has continued to work for Korean independence. His well-documented book "Japan Inside Out" has recently been published.

Perhaps the highest price on the head of any living Korean patriot rests on the head of Kim Koo, the quiet, kindly, courteous gentleman, who was one of four in our home in Shanghai in 1932 when the Japanese military police began raiding Korean homes. He is the man who at the age of 19 with his own hands killed Captain Tsuchida, who had assassinated the Korean Empress. When he had done so, he wrote his reasons for this patriotic act on a near-by wall with his name and address, and continued on his way until arrested. Under Japanese pressure a Korean court sentenced Kim to death, but news of the sentence rocked the country like an earthquake. His patriotic and daring act had so fired a smouldering nation that the sentence had to be commuted to imprisonment. He has been in and out of prison several times. He was freed by a general amnesty accompanying the coronation of a new Emperor in Japan. Now at 64, he carries a bullet in his lung from an attempted assassination only three years ago, but organized the Independence Army

and established the Provisional Republic of Korea at its ▐▐▐▐▐▐▐
in Chungking, China.

The greatest hope of freedom in this generation came to us
Koreans with the outbreak of war between Japan and the United States.
On December 11, four days after Japan's treacherous attack on Pearl
Harbor, previously rehearsed in a harbor of Korea, the Provisional
Government of the Republic of Korea formally voted a declaration of
war upon Japan. This pronouncement may not materially affect the out-
come of the war for the United States, any more than the token army of
35,000 Koreans in China may determine the fate of China's millions, but
the fact that Japan's aggression, begun nearly forty years ago in
Korea, had at last encompassed the United States brought to shackled
Korea the hope of emancipation in this generation.

When in 1592 Japan tried to invade Korea under Emperor
Hideyoshi Admiral Yi Soon-sin of Korea built iron-clad warships which
annihilated the entire Japanese fleet. The Koreans today cry, "Give us
arms and we can do it again!" A glance at the map will show Korea's
strategic importance as the Gibraltar of Asia, the military highway to
Manchuria and Siberia, or in reverse a "dagger pointed at the heart of
Japan". It is to be noted that the 23 million people of that peninsula
are no more subjugated today than the enslaved Danes, Norwegians, Dutch,
or Belgians in Europe. There is still burning in their breasts that
fierce love of liberty which once-free people never lose. They are the
original haters of Japanese military oppression, the under-cover
enemies of Japanese officialdom throughout the years, the potential
allies of the United States today. If the United Nations secure a foot-
hold in Korea, with the cooperation of her people the destruction of
Japan would be a foregone conclusion.

Whatever we do for the Koreans, as for the Chinese, we are
doing for ourselves. So many of them speak Japanese fluently, look
like Japanese, know the psychology of the Japanese, that their value to
us in counter-espionage and sabotage is in calcucable. Moreover, what
nationals of Korea, China and the Philippines could do to counteract
over short-wave radio Japan's present propaganda to alienate Oriental
peoples from the Occidental should not be overlooked.

The first of March, 1919 was Korea's day of crucifixion. Let
the first of March, 1942 become Korea's day of recognition!

DEPARTMENT OF STATE 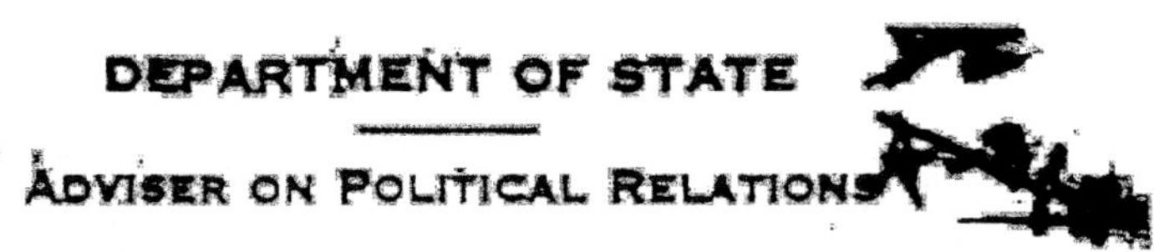

ADVISER ON POLITICAL RELATIONS

February 28, 1942.

I wonder whether someone in
the Department might not to
advantage find time to look in
at the Conference of the Koreans
(to which the public is invited)
at the Lafayette Hotel today or
tomorrow.

PA/H: SKR: FLB

You are respectfully invited to attend

THE KOREAN LIBERTY CONFERENCE

February 27, 28 and March 1, 1942, at the Hotel Lafayette, Washington, D. C.

The purpose of this conference is to (A) Solemnly commemorate the 1919 Revolution, reaffirm the 1919 Declaration of Independence, and plan for the Revolution of 1942 against the Japanese; (B) Request the Government of the United States to recognize the Provisional Government of the Republic of Korea; (C) Declare adherence of the Korean people and their Government to the Declaration of the United Nations; (D) Examine and report on Japan's terrorism in Korea.

United Korean Committee in America   Korean-American Council
Los Angeles, California and Honolulu, T. H.   Washington, D. C.

RSVP: 327 Colorado Building   Republic 6119
WASHINGTON. D C

DEPARTMENT OF STATE
DIVISION OF FAR EASTERN AFFAIRS
March 3, 1942

KOREAN LIBERTY CONFERENCE
(Held on February 27-28, March 1 at Lafayette Hotel,
Washington, D. C. under sponsorship of United Korean
Committee in America and the Korean-American Council,
see program attached.)

Reference PA/H's memorandum of February 28, suggesting that someone in the Department look into the above-captioned conference.

In accordance with the suggestion contained in Mr. Hornbeck's memorandum, Mr. Langdon of FE proceeded on the afternoon of February 28 to the Lafayette Hotel to attend whatever meeting might be in session at that time. There was no session that afternoon, but a Korean gentleman in the Hotel gave Mr. Langdon a program which indicated that a meeting would be held at 7 o'clock of the same evening. As this meeting appeared to be unimportant, both because of the little-known personalities addressing the meeting and because so much of it was devoted to music, Mr. Langdon did not attend. He obtained, however, a copy of the main address of this meeting, given by Mrs. George A. Fitch of China. A copy of this speech attached hereto.

Mr. Langdon attended the final session of the conference

on the afternoon of March 1. This was probably the most important meeting on account of the eminence of some of the speakers. Mr. Langdon arrived shortly before 3 o'clock and found about 30 Koreans awaiting their American speakers and guests. He observed that Mr. Staggers, legal counselor of the Korean Commission, was speaking somewhat sternly to Dr. Syngman Rhee, and overheard him telling Dr. Rhee that there is a lot of criticism in this country about the lack of unity among Koreans and that Koreans today would have to show a united front. Mr. Langdon asked a Korean gentleman sitting beside him whether the Koreans present came from Hawaii or from the Pacific Coast or from different parts of the world. This Korean replied that the Koreans present were all from Atlantic Coast cities, chiefly businessmen from New York.*

The meeting opened by a reading by Dr. Rhee of a sheaf of telegrams of congratulation and good wishes, including one from Admiral Yarnell, and followed the order shown in the program, except for an unscheduled address of congratulation and best wishes for Korean freedom by Delegate King (in Congress) of the Territory of Hawaii. In Dr. Hu Shih's absence, Counselor Liu of the Chinese Embassy read the Ambassador's message. In this message Ambassador Hu

said

said that the message represented "the considered view
not only of himself but of the National Government of China",
and that the message had the approval of the National
Government of China. The message, however, while expressing
hope for Korean freedom, sympathy for the Korean cause and
appreciation of the current Korean contribution to China's
fight against Japan, made no mention of the recognition of
Korean independence or of the so-called Provisional Government of the Republic of Korea.

The address of Mr. Cromwell, former U.S. Minister to
Canada, was broadcast over station WINX. There was nothing
unusual in Mr. Cromwell's speech (outside of an indication
of little study or knowledge of the problems of the Korean
question), but it ended with words to the following effect:
"We Americans demand to know what is keeping our Government
from recognizing Korea. We want recognition of Korea NOW.
What are we waiting for?"

Dr. Rhee then took the floor and made an impromptu
passionate plea to the Americans present to press their
representatives in Congress for recognition of Korea NOW.
The "now" was shouted by both Mr. Cromwell and Dr. Rhee
and got much applause from Americans as well as Koreans.

The speech of Dr. Hulbert, the noted historian of Korea,
was highly interesting and was well delivered, although of historical value only. Dr. Hulbert three times broke down

from

from the emotional strain of reciting the tragedy of
Korea's last days as a nation. Of particular interest was
his final conclusion that the United States is God's messenger
charged with "the duty of Leading Korea out of the desert
back into the family of free nations" (see speech attached).
Dr. Hulbert told off the record of the secret message the
Korean King gave him in the last days of the Kingdom to
deliver to the United States Government calling upon the
United States to save Korea from the Japanese; of how the
then American Minister, E. V. Morgan, acted suspiciously
indifferent to this message, and how upon arrival in
Washington the message was said not to have been received
by the State Department, and that when it was received it
was too late, the King already having ceded his sovereignty
to Japan.

In closing the conference Dr. Rhee invited Americans
to observe for themselves, by looking around the room, how
united Korea was. He said that he had heard charges of
lack of unity among Koreans, and refuted these charges by
pointing to the Koreans present and saying that they represented all elements working for independence.

Attached to this memorandum are the following items of
literature prepared for the conference and distributed to

American

American persons attending it:

(1) Declaration of Korean Independence, March 1, 1919.

(2) The Korean Liberty Conference, February 27, 28 and March 1.

√(3) The Proclamation of Korean Independence.

.(4) Korea Must Be Free.

.(5) Korea, "Pattern" of Japanese Aggression, by Mrs. George A. Fitch of China.

(6) Korean Liberty, by Dr. Homer B. Hulbert.

- -

Impressions of Meeting

Dr. Hornbeck was among the American guests. He and Mr. Langdon seemed to be the only persons from the State Department in the audience. Two or three members of the Chinese Embassy and their wives were also observed.

The Koreans in the audience gave a favorable impression from the point of view of physique, alertness and bearing. Outside of this feature, however, there was little about the meeting to encourage hope of Korean independence. In the meeting under discussion not a word was said of plans or organization for resistance to Japan or for independence.

The

The meeting was well attended by professional publicists
and by press representatives, and impressed one as a
publicity stunt. As for the addresses, they dealt with
the past and showed no knowledge of the problems of the
present and were totally lacking in constructiveness.
Moreover, not a note of self-help was sounded. In fact,
there were many allusions to the opportunity which was
now presented to the United States for "atoning" for its
failure in 1905 to defend and save Korean independence.
An objective stranger would have gathered the impression
from the meeting that the independence of Korea is entirely
an American problem and not one with regard to which Koreans
need put forth concrete efforts to assist in winning the
war and thereby gain independence for themselves.

FE:Langdon:MBW

The Korean Liberty Conference

LAFAYETTE HOTEL, WASHINGTON, D. C.   FEBRUARY 27, 28 AND MARCH 1
Sponsored by the United Korean Committee in America and the Korean-American Council

FRIDAY, FEBRUARY 27

AFTERNOON, 2:30 TO 5:30—Registration

EVENING, 7:30

Chairman: C. Ho Kim, Executive Chairman, United Korean Committee in America
Master of Ceremonies: Jay Jerome Williams, Treasurer, Korean-American Council
Star Spangled Banner: Rose Chang
Opening Address: Dr. Syngman Rhee, Chairman, Korean Commission
Speakers: Hon. John M. Coffee, M. C., State of Washington
Miss Inez Kong
Eaton, Commentator, MBS
Dr. Paul F. Douglas, President of American University
Korean National Anthem—Princess Minn

SATURDAY, FEBRUARY 28

MORNING, 10:00—Korean Session

Chairman: C. Ho Kim
Reading of Declaration of Korean Independence: Sukyoon Chang
Speakers: Kee Young Chang
C. I. Song
C. H. Whang
Resolutions

AFTERNOON, 3:30—Tea at American University

EVENING, 7:00

Chairman: C. I. Song, Executive Member, United Korean Committee in America
Master of Ceremonies: John W. Staggers, Legal Counselor, Korean Commission
Solo: Florence Ahn
Speakers: Yongjeung Kim, Director, Public Relations, United Korean Committee
Mrs. George A. Fitch, writer and lecturer
Violin Solo—Ruth Y. Kim
Sebastian Ugarte, Legal Assistant to the Philippine Resident Commissioner
Dr. Philip Jaisohn, Adviser to former Emperor of Korea

SUNDAY, MARCH 1—Commemoration of Anniversary of Declaration of Korean Independence, 1919

AFTERNOON, 3:00

Chairman: Dr. Syngman Rhee
Invocation: The Rev. Dr. F. B. Harris, Pastor, Foundry Methodist Church
Korean National Anthem—Mrs. Mary Ann Kim
Reading of the Declaration of Korean Independence
Speakers: Dr. Homer B. Hulbert, Personal Adviser and Confidential Envoy of the former Emperor of Korea
Dr. Maurice William, Vice President, American Bureau for Medical Aid to China
His Excellency, Dr. Hu Shih, Ambassador of China
Hon. James Cromwell, Former U. S. Minister to Canada
Star Spangled Banner

EVENING, 8:00—Korean Independence Night at Foundry Methodist Church

Through the courtesy of Station WINX the following speakers will be heard over this station: Hon. John M. Coffee, Friday, 8:05 to 8:30 p.m.; Yongjeung Kim, Saturday, 7:30 to 8:00 p.m.; His Excellency, Dr. Hu Shih, Ambassador of China, Sunday, 4:30 to 5:00 p. m.

The Proclamation of Korean Independence.

"We herewith proclaim the independence of Korea and the liberty of the Korean people. We tell it to the world in witness of the equality of all nations and we pass it on to our posterity as their inherent right.

"We make this proclamation, having back of us 5,000 years of history, and 20,000,000 of a united loyal people. We take this step to insure to our children for all time to come, personal liberty in accord with the awakening consciousness of this new era. This is the clear leading of God, the moving principle of the present age, the whole human race's just claim. It is something that cannot be stamped out, or stifled, or gagged, or suppressed by any means.

"Victims of an older age, when brute force and the spirit of plunder ruled, we have come after these long thousands of years to experience the agony of ten years of foreign oppression, with every loss to the right to live, every restriction of the freedom of thought, every damage done to the dignity of life, every opportunity lost for a share in the intelligent advance of the age in which we live.

"Assuredly, if the defects of the past are to be rectified, if the agony of the present is to be unloosed, if the future oppression is to be avoided, if thought is to be set free, if right of action is to be given a place, if we are to attain to any way of progress, if we are to deliver our children from the painful, shameful heritage, if we are to leave blessing and happiness intact for those who succeed us, the first of all necessary things is the clear-cut independence of our people. What cannot our twenty millions do, every man with sword in heart, in this day when human nature and conscience are making a stand for truth and right? What barrier can we not break, what purpose can we not accomplish?

"We have no desire to accuse Japan of breaking many solemn treaties since 1636, nor to single out specially the teachers in the schools or government officials who treat the heritage of our ancestors as a colony of their own, and our people and their civilization as a nation of savages, finding delight only in beating us down and bringing us under their heel.

"We have no wish to find special fault with Japan's lack of fairness or her contempt of our civilization and the principles on which her state rests; we, who have greater cause to reprimand ourselves, need not spend precious time in finding fault with others; neither need we, who require so urgently to build for the future, spend useless hours over what is past and gone. Our urgent need today is the setting up of this house of ours and not a discussion of who has broken it down, or what has caused its ruin. Our work is to clear the future of defects in accord with the earnest dictates of conscience. Let us not be filled with bitterness or resentment over past agonies or past occasions for anger.

"Our part is to influence the Japanese government, dominated as it is by the old idea of brute force which thinks to run counter to reason and universal law, so that it will change, act honestly and in accord with the principles of right and truth.

"The result of annexation, brought about without any conference with the Korean people, is that the Japanese, indifferent to us, use every kind of partiality for their own, and by a false set of figures show a profit and loss account between us two peoples most untrue, digging a trench of everlasting resentment deeper and deeper the farther they go.

"Ought not the way of enlightened courage to be to correct the evils of the past by ways that are sincere, and by true sympathy and friendly feeling make a new world in which the two peoples will be equally blessed?

"To bind by force twenty millions of resentful Koreans will mean not only loss of peace forever for this part of the Far East, but also will increase the ever-growing suspicion of four hundred millions of Chinese—upon whom depends the danger or safety of the Far East—besides strengthening the hatred of Japan. From this all the rest of the East will suffer. Today Korean independence will mean not only daily life and happiness for us, but also it would mean Japan's departure from an evil way and exaltation to the place of true protector of the East, so that China, too, even in her dreams, would put all fear of Japan aside. This thought comes from no minor resentment, but from a large hope for the future welfare and blessing of mankind.

"A new era wakes before our eyes, the old world of force is gone, and the new world of righteousness and truth is here. Out of the experience and travail of the old world arises this light on life's affairs. The insects stifled by the foe and snow of winter awake at this same time with the breezes of spring and the soft light of the sun upon them.

"It is the day of the restoration of all things on the full tide of which we set forth, without delay or fear. We desire a full measure of satisfaction in the way of liberty and the pursuit of happiness, and an opportunity to develop what is in us for the glory of our people.

"We awake now from the old world with its darkened conditions in full determination and one heart and one mind, with right on our side, along with the forces of nature, to a new life. May all the ancestors to the thousands and ten thousand generations aid us from within and all the force of the world aid us from without, and let the day we take hold be the day of our attainment. In this hope we go forward.

THREE ITEMS OF AGREEMENT

"1. This work of ours is in behalf of truth, religion and life, undertaken at the request of our people, in order to make known their desire for liberty. Let no violence be done to anyone.

"2. Let those who follow us, every man, all the time, every hour, show forth with gladness this same mind.

"3. Let all things be done decently and in order, so that our behaviour to the very end may be honorable and upright."

The 4252nd year of the Kingdom of Korea 3d Month

Representatives of the people

The signatures attached to the document are:
Son Byung Hi, Kil Sun Chu, Yi Pil Chu, Paik Long Sung, Kim Won Kyu, Kim Pyung Cho, Kim Chang Choon, Kwon Dong Chin, Kwon Byung Duk, Na Long Whan, Na In Hup, Yang Chun Paik, Yang Han Mook, Lew Yer Dai, Yi Kop Sung, Yi Mung Yong, Yi Seung Hoon, Yi Chong Hoon, Yi Chong Il, Lim Yei Whan, Pak Choon Seung, Pak Hi Do, Pak Tong Wan, Sin Hong Sik, Sin Suk Ku, Oh Sei Chang, Oh Wha Young, Chung Choon Su, Choi Sung Mo, Choi In, Han Yong Woon, Hong Byung Ki, Hong Ki Cho.

KOREA MUST BE FREE

Historical Sketch of Korean Independence Movement from March 1, 1919 to March 1, 1942

By Kei Won Chung

PART I

Before March 1, 1919

Korea is an old and civilized country with a background of four thousand years in which the Korean people enjoyed peace, freedom and prosperous living in absolute independence. The complete sovereignty of Korea was recognized by all nations of the world. Korea is also noted for a very distinguished language, its literature and culture, and ts morality. These things have long set the standard of civilization.

The Korean government concluded treaties with foreign countries as long as sixty years ago. Korea was recognized as an independent nation, and countries showed much friendship toward her. On May 22, 1882, a Treaty of Amity and Commerce was signed between the United States and Korea. Article 1 states: "If other powers deal unjustly or oppressively with either Government, the other will exert their good offices on being informed of the case, to bring about an amicable arrangement, thus showing their friendly feelings."

Since then, American missionaries have come over to Korea and have preached the Gospel to the Korean people and the principles of Christianity which were well received. There are over 400,000 Christians in Korea, and Korea has become the center of Christian civilization and the center of the foreign mission field in the continent of Asia.

Korea made a treaty of "lip and tooth" with China, and these two nations have long worked together in all problems. In 1894, Japanese Ambassador, Ino-ue Kaoru, came to Korea with the policy of strengthening the independence and protecting the territory of Korea. He proposed to the Korean ministers that they should sever the intimate relations with China, stating that China's actions were detrimental to the welfare of Korea. He further added that Japan will fight against China for the benefit of Korea.

After the Shino-Japanese War, Japan concluded the Treaty of Shimonoseki with China, on April 17, 1895. The first clause of this treaty states: "The two High contracting Parties hereby recognize and confirm the complete independence of Korea." However, on August 8, 1895, Japanese Mi-ura and Okamoto attacked the palace with an army and killed the Queen, Myung-sung, of Korea.

On January 30, 1902, the Treaty of Anglo-Japanese Alliance was concluded. This reads: "The High Contracting Parties, having mutually recognized the independence of Korea, declare themselves to be entirely uninfluenced by an aggressive tendency in the country." Japan further declared that she would recognize the Independence of Korea.

In 1904, when the Japanese declared war on Russia, the Emperor of Japan stated in the Imperial Edict: "The independence of Korea is our Empire's real and unfaltering aim and successity." With this declaration, the Korean government, opened her country for the Japanese soldiers and helped them in every way. The Russo-Japanese Agreement of 1898 states in the first clause: "Russia and Japan hereby confirm the recognition of Korea's sovereign rights and her complete independence." But after the

See Page Four

Russo-Japanese War, Japan broke and discarded those treaties as one would throw away waste paper. Prince Ito came to Korea and assumed control of the gold mines, silver mines, copper mines, and the coal mines. He ruled communications, was the police authority, director of finance, assumed control of the military administration, ruled the board of justice, the educational department and ran the postal system.

In 1905, Ito exercised the use of a trick and concluded the Treaty of Protectorate, against the wishes of the Korean government, by force of military power. The Emperor of Korea and all the ministers, refused to the point of death, to sign the treaty. All the Korean leaders backed the government and protested against the unjust treaty concluded by the Japanese.

In 1907, three envoys were sent to a peace conference held in Holland. The Korean emperor sent the representatives to join in a peace conference at which all countries of the world participated. Unfortunately, the Japanese envoy at the conference asked the other delegates to forbid the Koreans from speaking. Mr. Lee Choon, one of the three Korean envoys, was so disheartened that he committed suicide by slashing his stomach in front of all the delegates. This did not deter the Japanese delegates from having their own way. The Japanese Prime Minister, Ito, had discovered that the Korean emperor had sent three envoys to this peace conference, in an attempt to explain the wickedness of the Japanese, so the Japanese authority forced the Korean Emperor to resign his throne. The Korean Emperor continued to rule Korea until 1919. Also in 1907, the Japanese once again vent their hatred on the Koreans by attacking it and urged the emperor, Kwang-moo, to abdicate his throne. Kwang-moo's young son was set on the throne of Korea.

On August 29, 1910, the Japanese forced seven traitors to make the Treaty of Annexation by the means of deception and by force. The whole powers of sovereignty of Korea were then transferred to the Japanese emperor for all time. Twenty-three million Korean people were placed directly under Japanese control. Japan severed all diplomatic relations between Korea and all outside nations, and assumed control of the courts of justice and exercised police authority. The Korean army was scattered and all the weapons were gathered from the Korean people. This subjugation of a whole nation of people against their wishes is certainly the greatest treachery known to the civilized world. The entire country of Korea became angry, and the people were most furious. The match burst into flame, when Chaimyung Lee attacked the head of the seven traitors, Wan-yong Lee, on the streets of Seoul. Choong-keun Ahn shot the Japanese Prince, Ito, at Harbin and killed him. Ito had formulated the imperialistic policy of Japan and had led the troops during their vicious assaults.

The Korean patriots attempted to break the Japanese vise-like grip, but the patriots were eventually driven out of their own country of Korea, and wandered all over the world, where they served as soldiers in a desperate struggle against the invaders of their native lands. The Japanese army could not be beaten in this way, because these irregulars could not muster sufficient arms and ammunition. Then all Korean people rose up and protested against the Japanese rule, with no success, and were accorded brutal punishment for their efforts. Since it annexed Korea, Japan's policy has been increasingly atrocious. The policy should be termed a barbaric one, for that is exactly what it is.

The education in Korea was now the routine of learning the Japanese language only, and the teaching of Korean history and geography were absolutely prohibited. Freedom of speech was forbidden, even in the class room. Korean young people were not permitted to travel to foreign countries for study. In fact, Korean people had no freedom of the press, no freedom of gathering, for the Japanese officials watched all intelligent Koreans and restricted them in thought and work. Even though Koreans did not rob, they received the maximum penalties for those things, and it did not matter particularly to the Japanese whether or not the guilty one was caught as long as some one was convicted. Attempted assassinations were blamed on innocent people to set an example. Many prostitutes and opium were imported. The young people were forced to associate with these things. In such an atmosphere, the moral and physical condition of the people deteriorated at a fast rate.

Then the Japanese established an organization for the development of Western farms, and money was loaned to the people. When the money could not be returned, the Japanese assumed control of the farms. Finally, all the Korean people became poor. Most of the Koreans went to either China or Manchuria and wandered around in foreign countries. The Japanese had a fine time destroying private houses and farms or turned them into barracks for Japanese troops.

On January 20, 1919, the Japanese poisoned the Korean Emperor, Kwangmoo, because he was brave enough to try and avenge the Japanese brutalities. It was during this time that all remaining rights of Korean sovereignty were taken over by the Japanese and oppression of the Koreans went on unabated. Influential or rich Koreans were forced to be governed by a Japanese superintendent. The superintendent governed the properties, exercised control over the spending of money, and nothing of importance could be done by the Korean without the consent of the superintendent. Thus the Korean people struggled to cancel the treaty of annexation and to escape from the heavy Japanese yoke so as to reestablish the independence of Korea.

PART II

The terrible days of March, 1919

On March 1, 1919, all the Korean people rebelled and declared their independence by parades and speeches throughout Korea. In Tap-dong Park in Seoul, Korea, over one thousand men and women students gathered and read the proclamation of Korean independence which was signed by thirty-three representatives of the Korean nation. They declared that Korea was an independent nation. The unreasonable annexation of Korea by Japan was refused. They shouted "Long live Korea—independent Korea" beneath the flying flags. This is known as the beginning of the independent movement. Later on, Korean leaders and all people gathered in their towns and cities and followed the same action.

In reprisal, the Japanese soldiers resorted to treatment the likes of which cannot be comprehended by those who have not experienced such suffering. The soldiers burned church buildings, private houses, and schools. In Tai-ku, four thousand Korean people were lined up five abreast in a march throughout the city, and the soldiers overtook them and killed them. The soldiers continued with their destruction by razing all the churches that remained.

In another city, Chung-choo, two thousand people gathered and shouted "Long live Korea—Independent Korea,"

while parading through the city. Likewise, the Japanese soldiers killed them. Since most of these Koreans were Christians, the soldiers burned their churches to the ground. Three hundred churches were destroyed in this fashion in one hundred different cities and towns. In Soo-won Japanese soldiers called all Christians to gather in churches and burned the churches to the ground. When the Koreans attempted to leave the burning buildings, the soldiers shot them and bayonetted them. In addition to that, the Japanese soldiers burned the other fifteen towns near Soo-Won and killed over a thousand Koreans on one day. In Chung-choo, there was a beautiful high school, called O-san High School. Japanese soldiers entered that school and destroyed the laboratories, the piano, and later on burned the entire school to the ground.

There were thirty-one girls from schools and colleges who were thrown into jail by the Japanese soldiers. The girls were attacked, beaten and mistreated in every way. Then the policemen tore off the girls' clothes. Their legs and hands were tied together like pigs for the slaughter. The girls were placed in a trough and kept there overnight without clothes or covering. It was an extremely cold night. At midnight, Japanese policemen took several beautiful girls of this group and committed the act of rape on them. Later on, the girls were returned with their companions. After the policemen asked them why they had shouted for such a patriotic movement, the girls were set up on wooden crosses. Then the policemen said, "You girls are Christians, so you may be punished on the cross." The cross was placed on the ground, and the policemen made the young ladies lie down on the cross. Pieces of wire were heated on charcoal flames until red hot, then were branded on the breasts several times on each girl. Then the policemen untied the girls, who were next subjected to a beating with an iron bar until bloody. After the wooden cross was moved, the clearer girls were tied by their long hair with their hands tied behind their backs. Plaster was made and poured on the head of the girls. The plaster hardened, and the hair was yanked off with the plaster. The policemen again asked, "Are you still going to have that sort of movement?" The girls again answered "if we do not have independence, we will continue our movement until we are dead." The policemen on each side of each girl grasped the girls arms and another policeman took a bamboo sliver and thrust it through each girl's head until they were unconscious. Just before this treatment was accorded the girls, they had been starved for two days to make them even weaker. Until the end, the girls persisted in their patriotism. Even while under such brutal hardship, one of the girls said, "don't ask such foolish questions anymore, we will keep our movement going." After this, the Japanese policemen knew that nothing more could be done to these girls to convert them to the Japanese way of thinking, so the girls were released.

There was another big jail in Seoul, and the Japanese policemen threw thousands and thousands of Korean men and women into that jail. At least fifty persons were confined in nine by twelve foot rooms. When the Japanese policemen interrogated the Koreans, one by one, about their movement, the policemen removed the clothes from the prisoners.

One arm was tied behind the neck, the other one was tied behind the back. The two thumbs were tied together, and the prisoners' hands were tied on a cord to the ceiling for several hours. This method forced the blood to the head, and the captives became near dead. A box was made, about four feet in height, and three feet in width, with nails projecting through on the three sides. The Japanese policemen put one man in a bending position in the box for four hours. Later on, the policemen brought those Koreans who had undergone punishment in the box, and these were hanged from the ceiling before the eyes of the Chief of Police. Triangular shaped sticks, used as whips, were slashed against the prisoners from head to toe, until all were unconscious. When unconscious, the policemen poured cold water on them, so that they began to revive. This was the punishment for the men. In the case of the women, the policemen tied the ladies' hair with strong rope, and the rope was affixed to the ceiling. Often the hands were put together behind the back and tied from the ceiling. The heads were twisted around and tied in a reverse and uncomfortable position. Then hot water was poured on each person's nose. Then the women were made to lie down without clothes and a strong stick made of bamboo was used to beat them. Water was kept from them, and neither food or water was allowed them for two days, and the dying captives were so thirsty that urination was used as drinking water. Some of them could not stand such brutal punishment and collapsed. Next the policemen took big sticks and beat the captives again. Further cruelty was inflicted on the men when an oily paper was placed on the most sensitive portions of the body and lighted and burned. In the case of women, heated wires were jabbed into organs of the body and breasts. Sharp bamboo needles were shoved deep into the fingers to the joints, into the legs and the arms. The policemen made the naked ladies stand before a mirror and teased them and beat them. After that the ladies were forced to crawl before the mirror, where they could view themselves. The captors teased them by comparing them with dogs. The captives were made to lie down without clothes and hair was pulled from their body. With such barbaric treatment, the Japanese mistreated thousands and thousands of Korean men and women.

When the Japanese policemen entered private houses, especially rich men's homes, they broke all furniture, utensils, beat the families and looted the money boxes. The families were forced to surrender the key to the policemen and the soldiers who took twenty thousand dollars from one home. The Roman Catholic priest deposited money, in the amount of two hundred thousand dollars at the First National Bank of Seoul, which was taken by the Japanese. The priest was a rich man and the Japanese took seven hundred thousand dollars from him. At another place, one hundred thousand dollars was taken from Koreans. In this manner, thousands and thousands of dollars were taken all over Korea from homes, churches and banks.

The Japanese soldiers scattered throughout Korea, where they met patriotic Korean people who were parading and shouting "Long live Korea—an Independent Korea." The soldiers would not tolerate this and shot these Koreans, although they possessed no weapons. In Mang-san, which was a town, there was a Roman Catholic Church. Fifty-three Roman Catholic worshippers were taken to the police station where they were lined up against the wall of the station. These people were shot, one by one, and killed. In various towns and cities, sometimes a thousand people were ruthlessly killed, sometimes a hundred in some places.

Japanese soldiers met one young man on the highway and killed him. His wife saw the shooting and ran to her husband's side. She fell on him and cried. She had a baby on her back, but the soldiers jabbed their swords through the baby and on through the wife and man, several times.

One of the great leaders in the Korean movement conducted a parade which passed through the city. Japanese soldiers punished him by cutting his right arm off at the elbow, and the flag dropped to the ground with his arm. Then the leader boldly picked up the flag in his left hand and shouted "Long live Korea." The enemy then cut off his left hand, but he continued to shout "Long live Korea." The soldiers stabbed him in the chest and killed him. As he was dying, he said, "I am helping our government by my death."

In Seoul, there was a small girl who followed the men in the parade. She held the Korean flag in her right hand and shouted "Long live Korea." A Japanese soldier drew out his sword and severed her right arm from her body. In spite of her condition, she took the flag in her left hand, and the soldiers cut off her left arm. She continued to shout "Long live Korea." Then the soldier stabbed her and killed her. One American newsman tried to photograph these incidents, but the soldiers took away his camera and put him in jail. He was later released.

Five different methods were used by the Japanese soldiers in their brutal killings, and these were: (1) the spear, (2) slitting the mouth and the gums, (3) the sword, (4) firemen's implements, (5) and the gun. Iron sticks were also used to kill Koreans. Wooden sticks were often resorted to in the killing of Koreans, and with these sticks, the soldiers beat each Korean person ninety times. Miss Kim, representative of I-wha Girls College of Seoul, Korea, came to Pyeng-yang Police Headquarters and made an impressive speech about the Korean independence before an audience of several thousand. It was so impressive that the audience cried and began a patriotic movement. She went to the police station and called the chief and asked him: "I had two husbands, one is my husband and one is my sweetheart, whom shall I serve and tell me what should I do." The Chief said, "You may better serve your own husband, but don't serve the other one." Therefore Miss Kim explained to the Chief, "From now on, I will not serve Japan as my husband, but I will serve Korea as my own sweetheart." Therefore, the Chief was mad and took off her clothes, and he poured ice water on her. Then the Chief used the hot iron on her body. The chief again poured ice water on her body, but she did not obey his words. The she

was cast into jail and was subjected to cruel punishment for one month. After that she came from the jail and was extremely sick in a hospital. Later on she recovered her strength, and her mother tried to persuade her to return home, but Miss Kim went instead to the Korean people and planned to continue her patriotic movement. Her mother told her that if she continued with her patriotic movement, you will be dead, so I won't see you anymore." Miss Kim told her mother that she would not complain if she died for Korea. "If I died for our country that would be glory to my mother and father, and it wouldn't be disgraceful to my mother and father."

The Japanese soldiers took many Koreans to the Japanese church in Seoul and gave them drastic punishment on the wooden cross. The people were tied to the crosses and left there for three and four hours at a time.

Japanese soldiers and regular merchants scattered to all cities in Korea and placed poison medicines in all the drinking water, in fishing waters, and in salt and sugar. In this cruel way, they attempted to kill all Koreans. Fifty thousand Koreans were killed in the above way. Another ten thousand Korean leaders were jailed for a half year or a year in the bloody purge in 1919. When these captives were turned loose from their brutal captors, dozens of them died or became insane as a result of their treatment while in prisons. In my home town, when I was still a young boy, I saw at first hand the results of th treatment accorded the prisoners, for the released prisoners soon died of their wounds.

Our patriotic movement could not be successful within one morning or one evening, so to succeed, many Korean patriots made Shanghai the headquarters for their patriotic movement. The provincial government was organized with new officers who totalled seven in number. For the past twenty-three years since the provincial government has been established, military schools have been instituted in China and these schools have produced many soldiers who have fought against the Japanese on the borders of Manchuria.

PART III.

The years following March 1919.

In 1923, many Korean peoples lived in Japan, and between five and nine thousand of these people were killed. The Koreans were blamed for fires resulting from the terrible earthquake at that time. The bodies of the slain Koreans were piled up in the streets of Tokyo and made a river of blood that flowed through the streets of that City in a stream.

The enemy went on with their cruel and wicked treatment and even gave Korean people Japanese names. Now all Korean people have Japanese names, instead of Korean names. Now the Koreans do not know themselves, for they are confused by their new names and those of their friends. The Koreans resent these things.

There is a Japanese law which runs like this: "Religion is free. If anyone wants to believe Buddhism, he could become a Buddhist; if anyone wants to believe he could become a Christian." In spite of such a law, the Japanese persecute the Korean Christians. They force all Korean Christians to worship the Japanese Shinto Shrine. All Christians refused to worship idols, so many of them were cast into jail. They are not

now permitted a free worship service. Church service for the Christian is permitted only following the ceremony of the Japanese Shintoism.

In 1932, on January the 8th, the Provincial Government of Korea in Shanghai planned to avenge the Japanese slaughter. They sent one of their members, Bong Chang Lee, to Tokyo, Japan, in an attempt to kill the Japanese emperor. Lee acquainted himself with the lay of the land and found that the Emperor made an annual trip through Tokyo. Lee placed bombs in a water jar so that no one would become suspicious. He thought it better to wait for the Emperor on the return trip before using his bomb. However, Lee was of the opinion that the Emperor was in the third car when he was in the fourth car. The bomb was so weak that it slightly damaged the third car and did not affect the fourth car, so the Japanese Emperor was saved. Lee expected to be caught so he thought it was wise to wave the Korean flag before he died and shout out the independence of Korea. The Japanese soldiers seized him and eventually killed Lee for his daring escapade. The Korean leaders reasoned that since the Japanese people looked on their Emperor as one from heaven, it might be a good idea to exterminate the Emperor and prove him to be a mortal. In that way, the divine Empire of Japan could be eliminated.

In 1929, Japan was dissatisfied with Korea only under its control, so Japan tried to conquer Manchuria. In three years of fighting, Manchuria was finally conquered. Many Korean soldiers fought against the Japanese at that time. At the end of this war, the Japanese soldiers were happy and reveled in their victory. Before returning home to Japan, the soldiers had a large celebration at Hang-kou Park in Shanghai. The soldiers drank and sang and celebrated their victory. Speeches were mainly on the topic of future invasions in Asia. The chairman of the Provincial Government in Shanghai, Kim Koo, planned to kill all the Japanese Generals at that gathering. Kim sent a brave young man, Yun Bong Kil, to this gathering, with intentions of killing all the generals. This time, to be on the safe side, the Provincial government supplied Yun with two powerful bombs, but the soldiers guarded the entertainment so carefully that Yun could not get in to do his work. He purchased a Japanese water bag and placed a bomb inside. On the one side, he carried a lunch box, which held a bomb, and on the other side of him he carried his water bag, and he gained admittance. He covered himself with Japanese flags to further impress the Japanese. When he was close enough to the platform, on which the generals were speaking, he threw one of the bombs on the platform. That bomb snuffed out the life of General Kawa-hata, who underwent the rather unpleasant sensation of having his stomach blown from his body. Hundreds of pieces of iron were absorbed by Shirakawa, the Commander-in-Chief, who died in a short time. General Nomura, whose name today spells treachery, lost one eye and the sight of his other eye. He regained the sight in the one eye after some time. General Ueda had both legs fractured. General Shige-mitsu had both feet broken as a result of the bomb. The last three mentioned generals did not die from the explosion, but Japanese Consul-general, Mura-i and Secretary, Tomo-no, and five Japanese ladies were wounded severely. This bombing incident occurred in April 29th, 1933 at 11:40 A.M.

What had appeared to be a remarkable Japanese victory now became a defeat, since the Generals were vital to the future successes of the Japanese. This bombing was a major success to the Koreans who had waited thirty years for such a thing to happen.

In 1937, Japan tried to conquer China in what they called an incident. Hundreds and thousands of Korean soldiers joined the Chinese armies in the field and fought against Japan and continue to fight to this day. A recent radiogram received from Kim Koo, shows that ten thousand Korean soldiers are actually fighting against the Japanese on all fronts. The New Korea recently reported that thirty thousand Korean soldiers are fighting against the Japanese, which is far in excess of the ten thousand hitherto reported. At this very time, thousands of Koreans are gathered in Chungking from Siberia and Manchuria where they are training for the express purpose of exterminating the Japanese.

A recent article in the February 18th New York Times reads as follows:

"The Chungking radio declared today that, by guerilla tactics and behind-the-lines propaganda work, Korean rebels are waging an active campaign in North China against their Japanese rulers. The broadcast was recorded by the Columbia Broadcasting System. 'Scores of the Koreans have had clashes with the Japanese, of which one of the most recent took place in Hopeh Province', the broadcast said. In this battle heavy casualties were inflicted on the enemy and a considerable quantity of equipment was captured. It is expected the victory will afford fresh stimulus to the work of Korean volunteers in North China."

For the past twenty years, the Korean people in Hawaii and in North America have supported the Provincial Government and the Korean army in China. General and Madame Chiang Kai-shek have helped the Korean army with great contributions of money, amounting to over a million dollars.

Several years ago, the Provincial Government of Korea moved to Chungking in spite of repeated bombings of that city by the Japanese planes. They continue to formulate war plans with the aim of destroying the Japanese Empire. These things have all been done for the past thirty years in an attempt to defeat Japan. Now the Provincial Government of Korea has sent one representative to Washington, D. C. He is Dr. Syngman Rhee, who is helping the Provincial Government in diplomatic procedures.

Koreans in the United States are buying Defense Bonds and Stamps, helping with Red Cross work, raising money for the Korean Army in China, adding in specialized translating work for the Federal Bureau of Investigation, drilling for future duties in actual combat, and can be found at many crucial posts in this War. They are helping the United States Government to make this a world where peace and freedom reign supreme.

The twenty-six allies have been fighting against the Japanese for but a short time, but the Koreans have been fighting for over thirty-two years against them and are still in the fight. We Korean people pray that the Korean people will be formally acknowledged as one of the allies, when or before this war is finally won by all of us.

The Provincial Government is extremely active at this time in printing and distributing propaganda leaflets by aeroplane and dropping them on Korea, for the Koreans inside Korea have no clear or accurate picture of what is happening, for everything is so closely censored by the Japanese machine in Korea.

Lee Soon Shin and His Tortoise Boat
By Kei Won Chung

In Korea there lived a very famous and able naval commander by the name of Lee Soon Shin. On March 8, 1545, A. D. he was born at Keun-chun-dong, Han-yang (Seoul), Korea. As a boy he studied hard at school and was especially fond of naval and military science. He enjoyed playing out of doors and also liked to ride horses. With other boys, he would play that a military camp was being put up. Calling himself a captain, he ordered his playmates to fight against each other. He would often make wooden bows and arrows which he let his playmates use in military tactic plays.

He attended school until he was twenty-one years of age. When he had learned a good education in literature, he entered a military school and began to learn a military science. He always practised how to use weapons and how to ride horse back. Although he lived in a busy market street, he never went out to close the door and went on busily studying his military books. At the age of twenty-eight he went to the barracks to take his examinations. As a part of the examination he galloped his horse about but fell from the horse and broke a bone in his left leg and became unconcious. The onlookers believed that Lee Soon Shin had died. Lee Soon Shin listened to their shouting and suddenly got up and walked out on one leg and broke one branch of a willow tree. He stripped the bark from the branch and tied up his wounded leg with the bark of the willow branch and jumped upon the horse's back and once more galloped the horse. This the many people saw and cheered Leen Soon Shin and clapped their hands. When he was thirty-two years of age, he took the government examination in a military course and passed the difficult examination and became captain in the army.

His book, Tong-sa Chei-kang (V.3. pp. 46) tells us that, when his school days were over, he planned to build a very unusual boat. In 1591 he finally succeeded in building the boat which he called the "Tortoise-boat" because of its tortoise-like shape. Inside of this boat there were twelve rooms and two store houses for metal objects, three store houses for weapons, and nineteen rooms for the resting place of the Army. On both sides of the top deck there were two rooms for the captain and the commissioned officers. Above the boat there were two narrow cross-ways, and men could go through the cross-roads. On the back side of the boat awls and knives were placed so that they would impede the enemy should they attempt to board ship. On the front of the boat was a dragon head with tortoise body and tail. There were twelve holes from which guns were used in battle with doors of great importance. Its length from stem to stern was one hundred and thirteen feet. Its width was fourteen and a half feet. The boat could go backwards or forwards, and crosswise very adeptly. This boat could also submerge much like our present day submarines. The History of the British Navy says that the battleship of Korea was wrapped with metal plates as the tortoise shell, and that it could defeat Japanese wooden battleships, and the first iron clad battleship of the world was in reality invented by the Koreans. The year that this History of the British Navy gives us this information was in 1883.

During Lee's time the enemies of Korea were planning to conquer all of Korea. The enemies were planning to cross the South Sea of Korea with 300,000 soldiers and his navy of many thousands of wooden ships. The news reached Korea and the people were very worried over the defense of their country. Lee Soon Shin was made Commander in Chief of the army and navy. He organized the navy and army and ordered them to guard all fortifications and harbors. When the many thousands of enemy ships were close to the Korean coast, Lee Soon Shin bravely sailed in his tortoise boat toward the enemy warships. The enemies saw the tortoise boat coming and tried to destroy it. Suddenly the tortoise boat sunk into the water and began to upset the enemy ships from under the water causing great losses for the enemy invaders. Lee Soon Shin continued his upsetting of enemy ships for several days and this resulted in the sinking of a large number of enemy ships. Then the tortoise boat suddenly appeared on the surface of the sea and sailed back to its harbor. The harbor was on a river. The remaining enemy ships followed him to the harbor and anchored downstream.

Lee Soon Shin then planned many surprises on the enemy. The result was disaster for them. He collected many hundred of bee hives each containing many thousands of furry honey bees. He set the hives afloat down the river pass the enemy ships. When the enemies saw the hives floating down to them, they were curious to see what they were. They took out all the bee hives into their ships and opened them up. The enraged bees then flew out and began to sting everybody on the ships. As a result everybody had sores and were swollen all over their bodies.

Lee's men then prepared a large number of containers shaped similar to bees nests and filled them with gun powder. These he also floated down the river to the enemy. They saw what appeared to be bee's nests floating down to them and were sure the Koreans meant to fool them with bees again. They said to themselves, "O Poor Lee, you could cheat us yesterday, but not today. We will not open them up and we shall burn the bees." They brought the nests into the ships and threw them into big fires on the ships to destroy the bees. But suddenly the gunpowder exploded and the casualties were disastrous. Many lives were lost and many were wounded.

Lee Soon Shin then moved upstream to the narrow river channel and anchored there. The enemy followed and anchored there. While some of his men were cutting trees on the bank of the river, he sent his divers to cut holes with hatchets on the bottom of the enemy boats. The enemy could not distinguish the noise of the tree cutters from that made by the divers cutting holes in the bottom of their boats. Water sprung through holes and many more ships were sunk.

Farther upstream Lee's men tied many wires across the narrow river channel. That part was very narrow and the water was very swift and rough, making it almost impossible to anchor boats there. Lee Soon Shin then moved up to this part of the river and cast wooden anchors into the water. The enemies followed and cast their iron anchors. The anchors entangled themselves on the wires under the water. The enemy could not loosen their anchors and as a result the boats were being upset in swift running water. A handful of the majestic enemy fleet returned to their homeland.

TELEGRAM RECEIVED

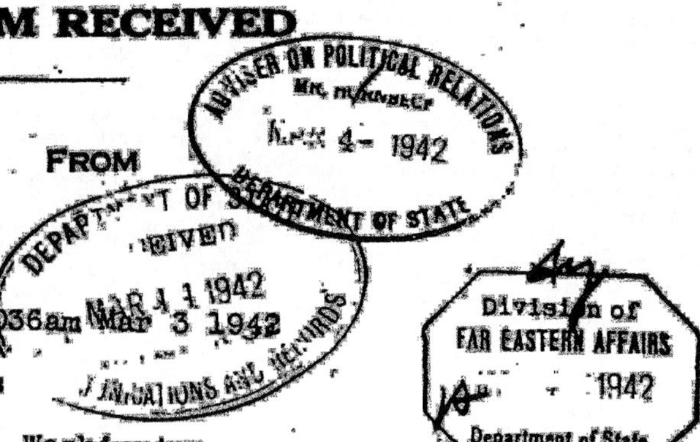

FROM

98wu p 18 VIA RCA

HONOLULU 1036am Mar 3 1942

Under Secretary Summer Welles

Washington

We express our hearty appreciation for your sympathy towards
Korean independence.

SINOKOREAN PEOPLES LEAGUE.

1010pm Mar 3

DEPARTMENT OF STATE

Memorandum of Conversation

DEPARTMENT OF STATE RECEIVED MAR 2 5 1942 DIVISION OF COMMUNICATIONS AND RECORDS

DATE: March 6, 1942

SUBJECT:

PARTICIPANTS: Mr. Soon K. Hahn

Mr. Hamilton

Mr. Salisbury

Division of FAR EASTERN AFFAIRS 1942 Department of State

ADVISER ON POLITICAL RELATIONS DEPARTMENT OF STATE

COPIES TO:

895.01/86

PS/ET

Mr. Soon K. Hahn, a Korean, called today at FE, having been referred to Mr. Hamilton by the Acting Secretary.

895.01

Mr. Hahn was received by Mr. Salisbury and during their conversation Mr. Hahn explained that he had resided in the United States since 1925, having studied at Northwestern University, having then become a peddler, and having finally become an importer and manufacturer. Mr. Hahn stated that he was given the visa status of international trader in 1933, that he now employs 20 Americans in his factory in Chicago, where he makes oriental perfumes and slippers and that he maintains a substantial summer hotel at Lake Geneva, Wisconsin,

named

FILED MAR 14 1942

named "Korean Village". Mr. Hahn's wife is at present in
Pyengyang, Korea, where she is head of a girls' school.
Mr. Hahn stated that he had done a little work for the
Office of the Coordinator of Information and had submitted
a war plan to President Roosevelt, in response to which
he had received an acknowledgement indicating that genuine
interest had been displayed in the plan. Referring to his
work for the Office of the Coordinator of Information, he
referred to a draft broadcast which had been written for
Dr. Rhee to give over short-wave radio. Presumably this
is a draft of the same proposed broadcast which was
recently seen by PA/H and FE. Mr. Hahn, in commenting
on the broadcast, said that he could not see its value
as no Korean in Korea had access to short-wave radio.

Subsequently Mr. Hamilton joined the conversation.
Mr. Hahn stated that the purpose of his call was to obtain Mr. Hamilton's "advice" as to how Koreans in the United
States might best achieve unity among themselves and how
best they could serve the United States and Korea. Mr. Hahn
said that he regretted that the Koreans active in the United
States were not unified and that one of his purposes in
coming to Washington was to affect a reconciliation between
Dr. Syngman Rhee and Mr. Kilsoo Haan. He said that he did
not believe that the Koreans should ask something

("recognition")

("recognition") of the United States until the Koreans had done something to deserve being helped. In response to Mr. Hahn's request for "advice", Mr. Hamilton pointed out that the composing of differences existing among Koreans in the United States was not a matter on which he was in a position to give "advice" although it was, of course, obvious that the achieving of unity would enhance the effectiveness of Korean efforts in the prosecution of the war.

After some general conversation, Mr. Hamilton suggested that Mr. Hahn might like to tell his views to Mr. Hoskins and subsequently come again to FE for further conversation. Mr. Salisbury then made an appointment with Mr. Hoskins to receive Mr. Hahn at 10:15 on March 7.

FE:S/Salisbury:MJF/NHS

CONFIDENTIAL   DATE: March 7, 1942

SUBJECT:

PARTICIPANTS: Mr. Soon K. Hahn

                Mr. Salisbury

COPIES TO:

Reference memorandum of conversation of March 6, 1942
between Mr. Soon K. Hahn and Mr. Hamilton and Mr. Salisbury
with regard to the objectives of Koreans in the United
States.

Mr. Hahn called on Mr. Salisbury this morning, saying
that he had just had a conversation with Mr. Hoskins.

During his conversation with Mr. Salisbury, Mr. Hahn
made a number of interesting statements about Koreans and
Korean activities in the United States. Mr. Hahn stated
that he is the chief financial supporter of Mr. Kilsoo Haan,
supplying him with probably eighty per cent of his funds.
Mr. Hahn showed Mr. Salisbury the original of a letter
received by Mr. Hahn from Kilsoo Haan in March 1939 in

which

which Mr. Haan asked for Mr. Hahn's financial support
in order to enable him to work on behalf of Koreans.
Mr. Hahn showed Mr. Salisbury a copy of his telegraphic
reply, sending Mr. Haan $400. (Later Mr. Hahn showed
Mr. Salisbury a copy of a telegram which he sent to
Mr. Haan in December 1941 sending the latter $500.)
Mr. Hahn stated that he had supplied funds to Mr. Haan
because he felt that Mr. Haan was energetic, well-inten-
tioned, and, on the whole, honest. Mr. Hahn said that one
of the reasons why he had come to Washington was because
he had become dissatisfied with the way in which Mr. Haan
was trying to build up his own reputation rather than
devoting himself entirely to the Korean situation. He
said that Mr. Haan had tried to persuade him not to come
to Washington. With regard to Mr. Haan's honesty, Mr. Hahn
said that, although he believed Mr. Haan to be honest, he
could not be entirely sure of the honesty of anyone who had,
as Mr. Haan had, worked for Japanese and that he was also
afraid he had once found Mr. Haan telling him an untruth.

With regard to Dr. Syngman Rhee, Mr. Hahn said that he
regarded Dr. Rhee as sincere but ineffective, lacking breadth
of view and energy. He said that the Koreans around Dr. Rhee
are not the best type of Korean in the United States but
are largely Koreans who attempt to use Dr. Rhee's prestige
for

for their own purposes. When asked whether Mr. Staggers
had ever received any money from Dr. Rhee, Mr. Hahn
laughed, evidently expressing disbelief in Mr. Staggers'
claim. Mr. Hahn asked: "What American lawyer ever
worked like that?"

Mr. Hahn said that he himself had never contributed
any money to Dr. Rhee except ten or twenty dollars each
Christmas time. These contributions he made because he
believed in Dr. Rhee's sincerity, but he made no other
contribution because he felt that Dr. Rhee was doing
nothing worthwhile to help Koreans. Mr. Hahn said that
he had asked Dr. Rhee why, in all these years, he had
never built up any economic establishment which would be
helpful to the Koreans and that he had further asked
Dr. Rhee what assistance he had been to Koreans during
all these years. Mr. Hahn said that Dr. Rhee had had
no reply other than to say that he was an old man and
that young men would have to do such things. Mr. Hahn
expressed the view that Dr. Rhee and Mr. Haan had injured
themselves by making untrue or exaggerated statements.
Mr. Hahn said that, for example, when they make claims to
the effect that there are large numbers of Koreans fighting
under Chiang Kai-shek, Dr. Rhee and Mr. Haan ought to
remember that the United States has consular officers

abroad

abroad who report the facts on such matters.

Mr. Hahn said that he had come to Washington because he felt that not only was the disunity existing among Koreans in the United States harmful to the Korean cause but because the best Koreans in the United States are not associated with any of the existing Korean organizations. Mr. Hahn said that Mr. Haan had not one follower and that Dr. Rhee's followers were unimportant and lacked the brains which some Koreans in the United States possess. Mr. Hahn said that it should be remembered that the best Koreans have never come to the United States as many of the Koreans now in this country were selected in Korea by American missionaries from among bright boys but that these same boys did not really represent the best in Korea. Mr. Hahn expressed the hope that he would be able to form a strong unified group which would include Dr. Rhee and Mr. Haan and also a number of intelligent Koreans. He said that such a group would resemble a political party and might achieve something concrete.

Mr. Hahn evidently anticipates association between such group and Koreans in Asia, especially those along the Siberian border of Manchuria and Korea. Mr. Hahn referred to the war plan which he had submitted to Mr. Roosevelt and said that he expected to see the War Department in

connection

connection therewith.   Evidently this plan envisages
association between the Korean group which he would form
and the groups mentioned above.

FE:Salisbury:MJF

DEPARTMENT OF STATE

Memorandum of Conversation

DATE: March 14, 1942

SUBJECT:

PARTICIPANTS: Mr. Soon K. Hahn
Mr. Salisbury

COPIES TO:

During a conversation with Mr. Hahn on March 14,
Mr. Hahn referred to the possibility of the American
Government recognizing the "Korean Provisional Government
at Chungking", of which Dr. Syngman Rhee is the Washington representative. Mr. Hahn said that, if recognition
were granted to that regime prior to unification of the
various Korean groups in the war effort, including those
groups along the Siberian-"Manchukuo" border, the possibility existed that the Korean bands along that border
would not join with the Provisional Government at Chungking but would be oriented toward the Soviet Union and
thus there might be set up a rival of the Korean

Provisional

Provisional Government. Mr. Hahn added that one factor
in the situation was that the bands of Koreans along the
Siberian-"Manchukuo" border regard the Korean regime at
Chungking as too much under Chinese domination.

M.M.H.

FE:Salisbury:HNS

Mar. 6

Soon K. Haan, a Korean, called on the telephone. He was told by Mr. Welles to see
you. He is staying at the Plaza Hotel,
Room 219, TRinidad 6500. I told him that
we would call him when you came in. He
would like to see you this afternoon.

M.J.K.

3:45 p.m.

March 24, 1942

My dear sir:-

Further in regard to my communication to you of February 7th:

There accompanied that letter a request of the Provisional Government of the Republic of Korea for recognition by the Government of the United States of America; a request addressed to the President of the United States of America, seeking his good offices regarding the aforementioned plea for recognition, and my credential as the accredited representative of the Provisional Government of the Republic of Korea.

I am in receipt of a letter, dated February 19th, 1942, signed by the Hon. A. A. Berle, Assistant Secretary, wherein he refers to the declared policy of the Department of State toward the "activities of foreign political leaders in the United States" and adding that the Department "is glad to be informed of the plans and proposed activities of organizations of aliens in this country who wish to assist in the struggle against Axis domination of the world", etc., etc.

There was further enclosed with this letter a release by the Department of State, dated December 10th, 1941, entitled "Policy Regarding 'Free Movements' in the United States."

May I respectfully suggest that the matters accompanying my communication of February 7th do not seem to fall within the purview either of the reply of Mr. Berle or the press release referred to.

The Provisional Government of the Republic of Korea is the sole representative of the Korean people, whether they are resident in Korea proper, Manchuria, Siberia, China or elsewhere, and regards itself, on the basis of the treaty of 1883 negotiated between the Government of Korea and the Government of the United States, not as a free movement in any sense whatever of that phrase, but as the only governmental agency of Korea that is in existence.

It is the desire of my Government to be advised how the Government of the United States regards the aforementioned treaty between our two countries. It is the plea of my Government that the existence of this treaty be noted by the Government of the United States for anything to the contrary would seem to further countenance the act of wanton aggression perpetrated by the Japanese Government upon the people of Korea.

Respectfully yours,

The Secretary of State,
Washington, D. C.

Syngman Rhee

DEPARTMENT OF STATE

DIVISION OF FAR EASTERN AFFAIRS
April 1, 1942

Reference: Chungking's strictly
confidential telegram no. 285, March 28,
9 a.m. in which Ambassador Gauss states
that he does not believe that a general
statement of the American attitude toward
Korea would serve any useful purpose at
present either in China or in Korea and
suggests that, if any general statement is
determined on, it would be advisable to
consult with the Chinese Government prior
thereto. Reference also: Chungking's
strictly confidential telegram no. 287,
March 28, 11 a.m. in which Mr. Gauss
comments on Dr. Sun Fo's views with regard
to independence of Asiatic colonial peoples
and states that the Chinese Foreign Office
has made it clear to the Embassy that it
is not yet prepared to accord recognition
to the Korean Provisional Government.

FE is of the opinion that the Department should not make any further statement
with regard to the ultimate independence
of Korea until such time as a statement
regarding Korea could be made either (1)
as a part of a statement referring to
certain other dependent Asiatic peoples
or (2) as a result of significant concrete
developments in the Korean independence
movement. FE also feels that the Department should take no action for the time

being

being with regard to recognition of any
Korean group as the "government" of Korea
in view of (1) the present reluctance of
the National Government of China to recognize the "Provisional Government of Korea";
(2) the fact that information available
to the Department indicates that the recognition of one group by this Government might
result in the establishment of a rival "government" of Korea (see attached memorandum
of conversation); and (3) the existing possibility that current efforts of certain
Koreans might achieve unification of the
various disunified Korean groups in the not
distant future.

FE suggests that no instruction be
sent to Mr. Gauss for the present to discuss the question of a statement concerning
Korea or to discuss Korean independence
in view of Mr. Gauss' statements made in
the two telegrams under reference and in
view of the fact that Mr. Gauss was authorized in the Department's telegram of
March 20, outlining this Government's views
and the views of the British Government
with regard to the Korean question, to use
such portions of the information contained
in that telegram as he might consider advisable in any conversations which he might
have on the subject with the Chinese Government. FE suggests that a telegram be
sent to Mr. Gauss informing him that his

views

views as expressed in the two telegrams
under reference have been helpful and suggesting that he continue, without making
any commitment, to obtain from the Chinese
Government such information or views of
interest as they may have with regard to the
Korean question, letting the Chinese authorities know that we shall bear in mind the
desirability of keeping them informed in
regard to any significant developments here.
A draft telegram along these lines is attached for consideration.

FE:Salisbury:MS/MJK

TELEGRAM RECEIVED

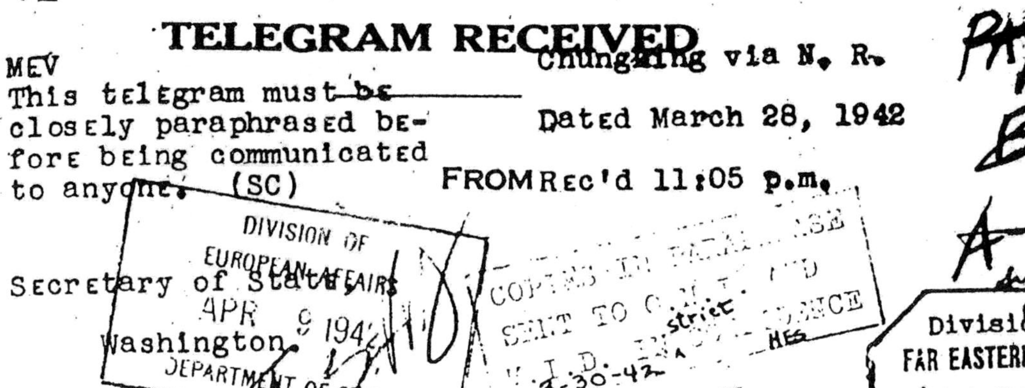

Chungking via N. R.

Dated March 28, 1942

FROM Rec'd 11:05 p.m.

Secretary of State

Washington.

285, March 28, 9 a.m.

Reference Department's 199, March 20, 9 p.m.
regarding Korea.

'The Embassy has continued to follow this subject
and finds no substantial change in the situation
as understood by the Department.

I do not believe that the proposed general statement of American attitude would serve any useful
purpose here at the moment; nor in Korea,' until we
take the offensive and the tide of military fortune
begins to turn against Japan.'

I make the suggestion that if any general statement of American attitude is determined upon, the
Department might make the gesture of consultation,
which China craves as one of the United Nations, by
advising with the Chinese Government in advance in
regard thereto.

It seems to me here, however, that the subject
of Korea is not entirely unrelated to the problem of
the independence aspirations of other Asiatic colonial
peoples

72.

-2- #285, March 28, 9 a.m., from Chungking via N. R.

peoples including the Indians. The Chinese seem to
be sympathetic toward outright independence for India.
In view of this situation an American statement on
Korea with no indication of the American attitude
regarding other Asiatic colonial peoples might
be inopportune.

                                        GAUSS

WWC

73

<u>**P A R A P H R A S E**</u> M.I.D. IN CONFIDENCE
3-30-42 H.S.

A telegram of March 28, 1942 from the ~~American~~ Ambassador at Chungking reads substantially as follows:

No substantial change in the Korean situation as the Department understands it has been found by the Embassy, which has continued to follow the subject in Chungking. The Ambassador is of the opinion that until we take the offensive and the tide of war begins to turn against the Japanese no useful purpose would be served in Chungking at the present time nor in Korea by the proposed general statement of the attitude of the United States. The Ambassador suggests that in case it should be decided to make a general statement of our attitude, we might, by discussing the matter in advance with the Chinese Government, make the gesture of consultation which the Chinese Government so greatly desires as a member of the United Nations. Viewing the matter from his post in China the Ambassador is of the opinion, however, that the Korean question is not altogether without relation to the question of the independent aspirations of the Indians and other Asiatic colonial peoples. It appears that outright independence for India is regarded sympathetically by the Chinese. In the light of this situation it might be inopportune for our Government to make a statement concerning Korea without indicating our attitude concerning other Asiatic colonial peoples.

FE:EMC:MHP   FE
3/30/42

TELEGRAM SENT

Department of State

74

Washington,

April 1, 1942.

AMERICAN EMBASSY,

CHUNGKING (CHINA).

263

Reference your telegrams 285, March 28, 9 a.m., and
287, March 28, 11 a.m.

These expressions of your views have been helpful to
the Department and the Department would appreciate your
continuing, without of course making any commitment,
to obtain from the Chinese Government such information or
views of interest as they may have with regard to the
Korean question. You may in this connection let the
Chinese authorities know that we shall bear in mind the
desirability of keeping them informed in regard to any
significant developments here.

Acting

FE:MJK   FE   PA/H   A-B/H

CR
APR 6 1942

March 9, 1942

Reference attached five telegrams from Korean organizations congratulating the Acting Secretary on the stand he has taken with regard to the Korean question.

Mr. Hoskins' office states that these have not been acknowledged, as a considerable number of similar telegrams have already been acknowledged, originating from the same addresses, and as on a telegram similar to the attached telegrams Mr. Welles had made a notation that it seemed unnecessary to make an acknowledgement.

FE:Salisbury:MJF

March 17, 1942.

Mr. Owen Lattimore makes an interesting suggestion, worth considering, regarding possible handling of pressure put upon us for "recognition" of Korea. He states that the Chinese Government is, of necessity and wisely, being very cautious in regard to the Koreans. There are, he says, at Chungking, as in this country, different and competing groups of Korean patriots. Owing to the fact that Koreans have been for more than thirty years under Japanese domination, it is very difficult to know which Koreans can be relied upon for complete sincerity in connection with their representations regarding themselves, and which of them may be grinding some special ax--even a Japanese ax; also, to know whether and to what extent each group is representative of any group, especially any substantial element, in Korea. The Chinese Government, therefore, is pursuing a "watch and see" policy. Dr. Lattimore's suggestion is that we might say that, being sympathetically disposed toward the movement for a free Korea, we intend to consult and confer with the Chinese Government* in view of the close relationship which long existed between China and Korea and of the fact that China is Korea's nearest neighbor, regarding this subject.

---

*I would phrase it "the Chinese and other Governments".

PA/H:MKH:DGT

March 18, 1942

PA/H - Dr. Hornbeck:

Please answer this for
me. I see no reason for me
at this stage to see this
gentleman. Please say that
the pressure of official
business is such as to make
it necessary for me to ask
that another official of
the Department receive him
in my stead.

U:SW:GES

KOREAN VILLAGE

LAKE SHORE DRIVE, SOUTH

LAKE GENEVA, WIS.

Suite 210 - 245 Fifth Ave.,
New York City, N. Y.,
March 17th, 1942

Hon. Sumner E. Welles,
Acting Secretary of State,
Department of State,
Washington, D. C.

My dear Sir:

I am glad to take this opportunity to thank you for your sympathy with the Korean cause. We Koreans sincerely appreciate your kind consideration in granting Korea the privilege of being one of your allies in the near future.

I was also very much pleased to read your magnificent statement denouncing Hitler's deceitful speech.

I have absolute confidence in the American Democratic principles, which are the true political philosophies for international peace and decency.

In compliance with your suggestion I have had very interesting interviews with Messrs. Hamilton and Hornback of your Department.

I am returning to Washington the latter part of the week and would appreciate very much if you would grant me a personal interview as I have some important matters to discuss with you.

With my kindest regards, I am,

Respectfully yours,

SOON K. HAHN.

SKH/MH

My dear Mr. Hahn:

The Acting Secretary, Mr. Welles, has asked me to acknowledge the receipt of your letter of March 17, 1942, in which you request a personal interview with him, and to express his regret that pressure of official business makes it necessary for him to ask that you see some other official of the Department in his stead.

I take this opportunity to acknowledge the receipt of your letter addressed to me under date March 17, 1942 and to say that I shall look forward to seeing you.

Yours sincerely,

Stanley K. Hornbeck
Adviser on Political Relations

Mr. Soon K. Hahn,
Suite 210,
245 Fifth Avenue,
New York, New York.

FE (LEB:MJK/MJF   FE   PA/H
3-20 3-23-42

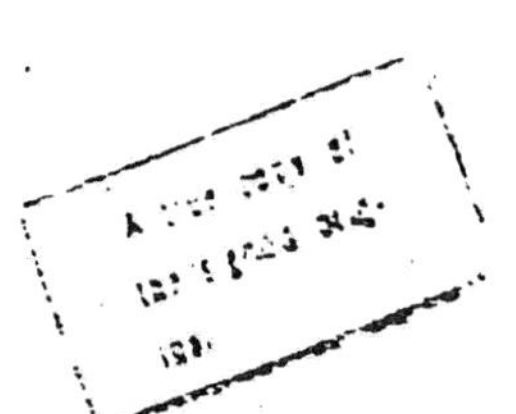

February 18, 1942.

Dear Mr. Haan:

I acknowledge receipt of your letter of February 12 in which you offer comments and suggestions regarding activities of various persons.

I have noted your comments and I shall see that your letter is brought to the attention of those officers of this Department who are especially concerned with matters to which the comments relate.

Yours sincerely,

Stanley K. Hornbeck
Adviser on Political Relations

Mr. Kilsoo K. Haan,

    Washington Representative,

        Sino-Korean Peoples' League,

           101 D Street, Northeast,

             Washington, D. C.

PA/H:AHiss:FLB:ZMK

<u>Personal</u>

"To Help China, Let's Help Korea Too!"

SINO - KOREAN PEOPLES' LEAGUE

101 D Street, N. E.   WASHINGTON, D. C.   Lincoln 5187

Feb. 12, 1942

Honorable Stanley Hornbeck
Advisor - Far Eastern Division
Department of State
Washington D.C.

My dear Hon. Hornbeck :

I note the Chairman of the Korean United Committee, Mr. N. S. Lee - the right hand man of Dr. Syngman Rhee has once more published in his report Jan. 21, 1942 - that

Congressman Charles I. Faddis has introduced a House Resolution in the Congress to recognize the Korean Provisional Government in Chungking, China

Yesterday, Congressman Faddis - denied this - he said he never have introduced any resolution as alledged by Dr. Rhee's friend.

Dr. Rhee tells all the Koreans that you are his best friend and he seem to convey the idea to the Koreans that he has your full consent and backing in all of his activities here in Washington.

Request.

Would you - if you are his close friend as he claims you are - please tell him not to

2

misrepresent U. S. Congress — U. S. Courts and other Department — particularly the State Department — and use this type of lie to collect large sums of money and to force Koreans to pay him or his organizations — certain sums of money.

If this is continued I will be forced to take legal action in the U. S. Courts to protect the freedom and rights of my fellow Koreans.

On Jan. 1, 1942 — the New Korea published that a certain Senator Bgeuse introduced a Senate Resolution to Recognize the Korean Provisional Gov. — Jan. 30, 194_ his Legal Counsel John C. Staggers — wrote me, that the State Dept. has recognize the Korean Commission as official ~~recognition~~ representation of the Korean Provisional Government.

Dr. Rhee's controlled United Korean Committee recently published that Koreans who are financially able to refuses to pay 5 to 20 to their organizations will be branded as "Enemy of Korea". He also sent out official statement saying that when any Koreans are found in taying with Japanese or deal with them will be brought before the U. S. Court and be punished. I am opposing his effort to advise Koreans to keep away from the

SINO-KOREAN PEOPLES' LEAGUE

3.

Japs — but to misrepresent the U.S.
Court — giving the Korean public the idea
that he has such authority to bring Koreans before
the U.S. Courts and meet out punishment.
Ten of thousands of dollars are being subscribed
by the Korean public — believing that the so leader
have all these power and the backing of the State
Department. He official publications continue to
publish such — news items as — Congressman — etc. and
the — Senator so and so — have introduced in the
houses to recognize the Korean Provisional Gov.

Only last January 18, 1942 his own Pacific Week
editorialized advising the Koreans — cautioning them
not to report anti-American Japanese activities in
Hawaii to U.S. officials, because Koreans will
receive the same alien status as Japanese aliens, if
emergency comes to Hawaii.

Dr. Rhees sudden handshaking with the pro-Jap
delegate Samuel W. King of Hawaii and trying to cl
such power, seem that the State Department should
warn and advise the Korean Commission that they
should stop — deliberate misrepresenting the State
Department and the U.S. Congress — Very truly You
in the interest of National Defense
Kilsoo K. Haan

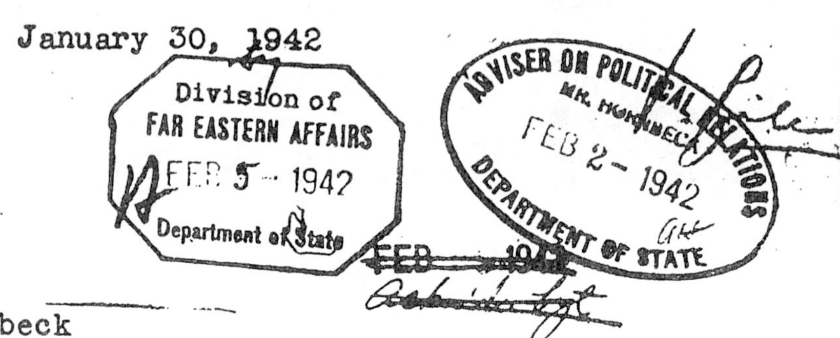

JOHN W. STAGGERS
ATTORNEY AND COUNSELLOR AT LAW
201-204 COLUMBIAN BUILDING
WASHINGTON, D.C.

January 30, 1942

Dr. Stanley K. Hornbeck
State Department
Washington, D. C.

Dear Doctor Hornbeck:

I have been instructed by Dr. Syngman Rhee, Chairman of the Korean Commission to mail you, for your information, a copy of the enclosed letter. This letter was addressed by me to Mr. Kilsoo K. Haan and is self-explanatory.

Sincerely yours,

J. W. STAGGERS

JWS:e
Encl.

                      January 30, 1942

Mr. Kilsoo K. Haan
101 D Street, N. E.
Washington, D. C.

Dear Mr. Haan:

       As Counsel for the Korean Commission, I have been
asked to write you in reference to your activities in
behalf of the Korean cause.

       In your earnest and enthusiastic efforts to help
you have in some instances caused confusion and misunder-
standing.

       One recent incident is the publication by you of
information on the registration of Koreans. This was
made public by you without consulting with the Korean
Commission which had an understanding with the officials
in the Department of Justice that it would not be released until the Department saw fit to do so.

       The Korean Commission is recognized by the State
Department as the official representative of the Provisional Government of Korea. It, therefore, follows
that the proper procedure would be for you to submit to
the Korean Commission, to be forwarded through official
channels, any communication which you wish to address to
any of the Departments in Washington.

       This letter is to further advise you unless you
are willing to conform to the Commission's wishes in
this matter you will be requested by it and the Provisional Government of Korea to cease all activities in connection with the Korean cause.

       I am sure you recognize the necessity for a con-
certed and harmonized effort on the part of the Koreans
at this time and that you would not knowingly do anything
which would cause or bring about confusion.

       A copy of this letter will be filed with the State
Department, War Department, Navy Department and Department
of Justice.

                         Very truly yours,

                         J. W. STAGGERS

JWS:e

February 4, 1942

TO: PA/H - Mr. Hornbeck

On re-reading your letter to Mr. Staggers in
the light of our conversation, I think so as to
keep the record clear that it should be sent as
written.

As to Mr. Kilsoo K. Haan's letter to Mr. Hamilton,
I am enclosing a suggested answer which consists of
a brief covering note together with a copy of your
letter to Mr. Staggers.

Harold B. Hoskins

Enclosure:

Letter as stated above.

A-B/H:HBH-gw

DEPARTMENT OF STATE
WASHINGTON

February 3, 1942.

Dear Mr. Staggers:

I acknowledge receipt of your letter of January 30 in which you state that you have been instructed by the Chairman of the Korean Commission to mail to me for my information a copy of a letter addressed by you to Mr. Kilsoo K. Haan, and of the enclosure, a copy of your letter to Mr. Haan of January 30.

Your courtesy and that of Dr. Rhee in imparting to the Department the information thus conveyed is appreciated.

It is noted that in your letter of January 30 to Mr. Haan, you make the statement that "the Korean Commission is recognized by the State Department as the official representative of the Provisional Government of Korea", and you continue, "It, therefore, follows that the proper procedure would be for you [Mr. Haan] to submit to the Korean Commission, to be forwarded through

official

Mr. John W. Staggers,
    201-204 Columbian Building,
    Washington D.C.

official channels, any communication which you wish to
address to any of the Departments in Washington.' You
also state that "A copy of this letter will be filed
with the State Department, War Department, Navy Department
and Department of Justice.' In the light of the above, it
becomes necessary for me to call your attention to the fact
that no agency of the American Government has at any time
recognized any commission or agency or person as the official representative of a provisional government of Korea.
Officers of this Department and, it is understood, of
other agencies of the Government have over a period of
many years received and talked with persons understood to
represent or to speak for Korean organizations in exile.
Officers of this Department and of other agencies of this
Government have also received and talked with American
nationals associated with or employed by Korean groups.
This, however, has not constituted recognition or an
attribution of an official status or a selective discrimination as among such persons or groups. Further, the Department of State has not taken any action from which it could
with warrant be said, so far as this Government is concerned, that communications which persons of Korean race
might wish to address to "any of the Departments in Washington" must be submitted to the Korean Commission and come
forward only through that channel.

In

In calling attention to these points, I am not undertaking to pass upon either the purpose or the substance of your letter to Mr. Haan under reference in its further particulars.

Copies of this letter are being sent to the War Department, the Navy Department, the Department of Justice, the Coordinator of Information, and Dr. Syngman Rhee.

Yours sincerely,

Stanley K. Hornbeck
Adviser on Political Relations

My dear Mr. Attorney General:

In view of the fact that there apparently was sent
to the Department of Justice recently a copy of a
letter addressed by Mr. John A. Staggers under date
January 30 to Mr. Kilsoo K. Haan, there is sent herewith, for your information and other officers of the
Department of Justice who may be concerned with the
question to which it relates, a copy of a memorandum
commenting upon certain statements made in that letter.

Sincerely yours,

Under Secretary

Enclosure.

The Honorable

Francis Biddle,

Attorney General.

CR
14 1942

PA/H:SKH:ZMK   FE   A-B/H
2-11-42

Memorandum

1. Reference is made to a letter addressed to
Kilsoo K. Haan by John W. Staggers under date January 30,
1942, in which it is stated that copies were to be filed
with the Department of State, the War Department, the Navy
Department and the Department of Justice.

In that letter it is stated, _inter alia_, that "The
Korean Commission is recognized by the State Department
as the official representative of the Provisional Government of Korea. It, therefore, follows that the proper
procedure would be for you to submit to the Korean Commission, to be forwarded through official channels, any
communication which you wish to address to any of the
Departments in Washington".

2. For purposes of record and to obviate confusion,
statement is made of pertinent facts as follows: Officers
of the Department of State and, it is understood, of other
agencies of the Government have over a period of many
years received and talked with various persons understood
to represent or to speak for various Korean organizations
in exile. Such officers have also received and talked
with various American nationals associated with or employed
by such organizations. This, however, does not constitute
recognition of an official status nor should it be construed

as implying a selective discrimination as among such organizations or persons. Officers of the Department of State are not aware of any action taken by the American Government from which it could with warrant be said, so far as this Government is concerned, that communications which persons of Korean race may wish to address to officers or agencies of the American Government must first be submitted to any specified organization and come forward only through that channel.

Copies of this memorandum are being sent to Mr. Staggers, the War Department, the Navy Department, and the Department of Justice.

February 11, 1942.

Dear Mr. Bundy:

In view of the fact that there apparently was sent
to the War Department recently a copy of a letter addressed
by Mr. John W. Staggers under date January 30 to
Mr. Kilsoo K. Haan, there is sent herewith, for the information of the Secretary of War and other officers of
the War Department who may be concerned with the question
to which it relates, a copy of a memorandum commenting
upon certain statements made in that letter.

May I ask that you please be so good as to see that
this communication reaches the appropriate office.

Yours sincerely,

Stanley K. Hornbeck
Adviser on Political Relations

Enclosure.

The Honorable
    Harvey H. Bundy,
        Special Assistant to the
        Secretary of War,
            Room 2035, Munitions Building,
            Washington, D. C.

PA/H:SKH:FLB

Reg. U. S. Pat. Off.
"All the News That's Fit to Print."
ADOLPH S. OCHS, Publisher 1896-1935.

Published Every Day in the Year by
THE NEW YORK TIMES COMPANY.

ARTHUR HAYS SULZBERGER,
President and Publisher.
JULIUS OCHS ADLER,
Vice President and General Manager.
GODFREY N. NELSON, Secretary.

SUNDAY, JANUARY 18, 1942.

ORIENTAL FANTASY

The curtain rises with Japan, played by a man wearing two masks—one representing peace and the other depicting war—contemplating his destiny. The central character, with his mask of peace still turned to the audience, decides in a long soliloquy that before this destiny, calling for hegemony over all of East Asia and the seas which wash its shores, can be fulfilled, the last vestige of American influence in the Pacific must be eliminated. His mask of war still concealed, suddenly he orders his admirals and generals to attack the American stronghold at Pearl Harbor.

Thus opens the first act of the drama of the Pacific as it was conceived by Japanese warlords and placed between the covers of a book filched from a member of the Black Dragon Society in Los Angeles a year ago by a Korean patriot who had dedicated his life to destroying the conquerors of his own country. The whole thing—the Japanese war plan as carefully formulated as a play in three acts, and the manner of its discovery and disclosure—sounds like a rather feverish Oriental melodrama. The first phase of the program of conquest, or the first act, with its stab in the back and the effort to wrest the Philippines, Guam, and Wake, and Hong Kong from Western control, has gone pretty much according to schedule. But Midway is still ours and Borneo and Malaya, whose surrender was to mark the falling of the first curtain, are still fighting.

The second act was to depict the capture of the Netherlands Indies, Australia and New Zealand, the fall of India and Burma and the seizure of Kamchatka from Russia. For the third-act curtain, Japan's militarists had prepared a scene with the banner of the Rising Sun flying over the Panama Canal Zone, Alaska and the three Pacific States of Oregon, Washington and California, and the United States suing for peace on Japan's terms.

A year ago, when presumably the plan first came to the attention of the State Department, it conceivably seemed too fantastic and implausible for consideration. But the play has already gone into production. It is badly in need of rewriting, and the rewriting must be done by Americans.

> Kilsoo Haan, the man behind the spy story in the adjoining column, is "front man" for the Sino-Korean People's League, described as an underground espionage organization which long has attempted to warn the United States of Japanese war aims. Made up of thousands of Korean patriots, fired by hatred of Japan, the organization bases its aims on the belief that only American domination of the Pacific will give Korea its freedom.

for Korean Aliens

"Happy Am I" sings Kilsoo K. Haan today on receiving news from the Justice Department that Koreans do not have to register as enemy aliens, provided they have never voluntarily become German, Italian or Japanese citizens or subjects.

Mr. Haan heads a Korean organization which has furnished information on Japanese war plans. When war struck, however, the State Department ruled that Koreans—natives of a Japanese possession—must register as Japs and suffer the restrictions of enemy aliens. Mr. Haan went to bat for his people, who he says are passionately opposed to Japanese domination in the Far East, and for the life of his information-gathering organization.

Biddle's Alien Orders Exempt Three Groups

Austrians, Austrian-Hungarians and Koreans—if officially registered as such—are exempt from the order requiring German, Italian and Japanese nationals to apply for certificates of identification.

Announcing this yesterday, Attorney General Biddle said:

"Austrians, Austrian-Hungarians and Koreans who involuntarily or mistakenly registered (under the 1940 Alien Registration Act) as Germans, Italians or Japanese are required to apply for certificates of identification, but they may state in their applications that they are Austrians, Austrian-Hungarians or Koreans. After they obtain their certificates of identification, they will be given an opportunity to correct their alien registrations following suitable investigation."

A recent order directed that all German, Italian and Japanese nationals 14 years of age or older must apply at post offices for certificates of identification.

U. S. Exempts Coreans From Enemy-Alien Rolls

10,000 Need Not Register; Leader Pledges Aid in War

From the Herald Tribune Bureau

WASHINGTON, Jan. 20.—Coreans in the United States and Hawaii, numbering 10,000, including 300 in New York, will not be required to register as enemy aliens, according to a ruling given today by Earl G. Harrison, chief of the alien registration bureau of the Department of Justice.

This assurance was given to Kilsoo K. Haan, Washington representative of the Sino-Corean Peoples League, when he sought to clarify the status of his people in this country. Mr. Haan, who said his nation's sympathies lie with the United States, said: "I am sure every Corean alien in the United States and Hawaii will be very grateful and will endeavor to do more to help United States national defense."

Corea is a peninsula jutting out from Manchukuo (formerly Manchuria) with Siberia to the northeast and China to the northwest, and has a population of 23,000,000. Although subjugated by Japan in 1910, all efforts to impress Coreans into the Japanese Army have failed and only a small part of the population is engaged in Japanese labor. Coreans are descendants of the Mongolians and are closely related to the Chinese.

from Japan. Mr. Haan lived from childhood in Hawaii, working in sugar cane fields and going to Salvation Army school.

In a 5000-word impassioned plea to President Roosevelt, Mr. Haan wrote: "If I have erred in writing you please punish me and send me to hell for I would be happier in hell than be forced to be officially classified as a Jap."

EARL G. HARRISON.

YASUTARO SOGA   President and Editor

Sam King Challenges Haan

Under the headline, "Haan's Right to Speak for Hawaii Challenged," the Honolulu Star Bulletin in a dispatch from its Washington bureau yesterday carried a story saying, in part:

"Delegate Sam King's private irritation against the efforts of Kilsoo Haan, agent of the Sino-Korean Peoples' League, to speak authoritatively on Hawaii, often making backhanded slaps of the entire territory, flared into the open today at a hearing before the house immigration committee

The Korean

Jan. 27-1942 Wash. Daily

Neck...

showing...
hito ha...
with th...
the wa...
poster,...
Korean...
the Pr...
now on...

DEPARTMENT OF JUSTICE
Washington, D.C.

January 23, 1942

Mr. Kilsoo K. Haan
Sino-Korean Peoples League
101 D Street, N. E.
Washington, D. C.

Dear Mr. Haan:

I am now in position to answer your letter of January 14.

The regulations, just adopted, governing Certificates of Identification for aliens of enemy nationalities provide that Koreans who, under the Alien Registration Act of 1940 registered as Koreans, are not required to apply for Certificates of Identification, providing that such persons have not at any time voluntarily become German, Italian or Japanese citizens or subjects.

I am sure you will be glad to learn of this official action..............

With best regards, I am

EARL G. HARRISON
Special Assistant to the
Attorney General

○ 한인을 일으며 뿔간 [표십칠일]
하와이 대표 킹씨의 주장

[十七일 와싱톤] 하와이 선출 국회 대표 킹씨는 대일 말록기를 자기가 일족이 정부 중오 인곡을 대하야 적의하기를 허나 미국 경너에 잇난 한국 거류민을 일본 거류민과 반간하야 한국 거류민을 동맹국 거류민으로 인정하고 전국 거류민으로 보지 말며 아욱너 한국을 독맹국으로 승이하전고 하야달을 리승 만씨 와 함갓 지요?

Slant

Neckie Party—Staff Photo.—A poster showing Hitler, Mussolini and Hirohito hanging from a "V" scaffold with the "V" symbols at the base is the way Koreans view the war. The poster, painted by Ilyup Chooh (left), Korean artist, is for presentation to the President on his birthday. It's on exhibit at The Hecht Co.

Merry-Go-Round

(Trade Mark Registered)

By DREW PEARSON and ROBE[RT]

The numerous charges of fifth column activity in Hawaii do not impress one man in Congress.

He is short, gray-haired Samuel W. King, Republican delegate from Hawaii. Ordinarily, King has little to say, but he waxes very voluble when the "loyalty" of his Jap-American constituents is questioned.

King has been telling House colleagues that "all this commotion" about a fifth column in Hawaii is the bunk. However, his most interesting statement was made the other day behind closed doors to the House Military Committee, of which he is a nonvoting member.

King admitted that there had been a "very extensive and active" axis espionage system in Hawaii, but as for a fifth column—"No, no, gentlemen, there is none."

"American citizens of Japanese ancestry in Hawaii are patriotic," King insisted. "Even the older, retired Japanese aliens are all right. Why, they think it's a real compliment for their citizen-children to be drafted in United States armed forces. They usually throw a big party the night before a boy is inducted into the service."

King revealed that after the Pearl Harbor attack the FBI and Military Intelligence rounded up 400 spies and subversive agents and put them in concentration camps. Three hundred were Jap aliens and Jap-American citizens, and the rest Germans and Italians. A number of the Japs were priests of the Shinto (nationalist) cult and wealthy aliens close to the Jap consulate.

Asked if the Army and Navy were accepting voluntary enlistments of young Jap-American citizens, King said no, but that many of the youths had been drafted.

"They make excellent soldiers," he declared. "In fact all people of Jap blood born in Hawaii, and therefore citizens, are patriotic. The suspicion that they are real, or potential, fifth columnists is absurd."

Committee members listened to King in polite silence. Afterwards, some of them privately indicated they considered his views "too optimistic." Several jokingly intimated that they thought King's views might be influenced by the fact that he had a large number of Japanese-American constituents, a dig that King haughtily ignored.

NOTE: One thing King did not tell the committee was that the Hawaiian Territorial (Home) Guard of 3,900 men included a large number of American-born Japs under draft age who are armed, while the white civilian population has been disarmed by the establishment of martial law.

Japanese Obsession

The Department of Justice ruled last week that Koreans need not register as enemy aliens. Austro-Hungarians and Hungarians are also exempt, but Koreans are a special case. About the only people who know Koreans in the U.S. are other Koreans. The U.S. knows little about them; it does not know, for example, that Koreans have the unique distinction of getting on Japanese nerves.

The Korean peninsula, thrusting down into the Yellow Sea to within 100 miles of Japan, is more than a Japanese problem. It is a Japanese obsession. With an older culture than the Japanese (whom they helped civilize), Koreans are traditionally pastoral, home-loving. Since 1910 Japan's policy has been a queer combination of savage repression and grotesque attempts to mollify the people.

Japanese crushed "uprisings" when observers could see none. Soon—in 1919, 1923, 1931—they had to deal with the real thing. The Society of Heroes worked for independence by violence, especially assassination, if possible by the knife; the Exploding Party, also working for independence, chose the bomb. Most shocking revelation of Japan's fear of Koreans came in the Tokyo earthquake. Then, because the rumor grew that Koreans were taking advantage of the disaster to blow up bridges, cut wires, Japanese went into a wave of hysteria that made the Orson Welles broadcast scare look like a session of the Supreme Court. When it was over, at least 500 (perhaps as many as 5,000) Koreans living in Tokyo had been slaughtered.

Since there are only 9,000 Koreans in the U.S. and Hawaii, last week's ruling did not directly affect many people. But it told the world—and especially the Far East—that anybody who so unnerved the Japanese could not be counted an enemy alien.

KOREAN BUDDHIST
He makes some people...

- 492 -

February 6, 1942.

    Mr. Williams, who came to
me with Messrs. Rhee and Staggers
this afternoon, gave me the
paper here attached, and, upon
my inquiring whether the original
had already been sent to the
Secretary of the Navy stated that
it had been sent.

PA/H:SKH:FLB

1700 Eye Street, N. W.
February 4, 1942

Dear Mr. Secretary:-

Our country will lose a great opportunity unless a decision --
and it is a _military_ decision -- is made at once.

We beg of you, in our role first of all as American citizens,
to give this communication and its accompanying data, the most careful
consideration and to bring it, should you agree with us, to the immediate
attention of our commander-in-chief, the President.

General MacArthur and his men constitute our flaming outpost in
the Far East, an outpost glorious in courage, but desperate in its need of
help. At the moment we lack the ability to supply adequate assistance, yet
help lies close at hand and is ours even without the asking.

Help may be had from the 23 million people of Korea in the form
of a revolution against the Japanese.

Their leader, Dr. Syngman Rhee, is in Washington. He is ready to
act on the slightest encouragement from the United States. His character,
his integrity, his devotion to the cause of Democracy, are known to us. His
ability and his service to his homeland are known and feared by the enemy who,
for four decades, has had a price of $100,000 posted for his head.

Believe us, our dear Mr. Secretary, when we tell you the Korean
situation is not a development of the moment. These people have risen once
before to Dr. Rhee's call to revolt. They will do it again and in so doing
will provide a blazing backfire to the Japanese in the Orient. We reiterate
our supplication that this opportunity not be lost or a decision on our part
be further delayed.

We submit copy of our letter of January 10, 1942 to Secretary of
State Hull (Exhibit A) and copy of the State Department acknowledgment
(Exhibit B); copy of radio broadcast by Dr. Rhee to the Korean people requested by the office of the Coordinator of Information (Exhibit C) and
copy of memorandum by the Korean-American Council (Exhibit D).

We have been in person to the State Department several times since
December 7th but never have received word of a definite nature save that the
Korean matter is under consideration. We have been advised, however, that
the Department is unwilling to act now because of the view (a Departmental
view) that to act now might be offensive to the Japanese.

This communication is not meant to be critical of the State Department for we realise the processes of diplomacy are necessarily deliberate. But diplomacy ceases when war begins and may God grant our army and navy the power to visit offense overwhelmingly upon the Japanese.

And it is because diplomacy has ceased and war is on that we appeal to you.

Do we want the weapon the Koreans offer us? Do we want the physical and moral force, supplied by an inspired leader, of a people and a nation which would rank eighth in order of population in the signataries to the Declaration of United Nations?

Mr. Secretary, our interest in the cause of Korean independence covers a span of more than a quarter of a century. In that period none of us has received a penny of compensation, nor would we have accepted one. And there is no hope nor promise of pecuniary reward now. We, therefore, beseech you with all the sincerity we possess not to disregard this plea or delay action on it. Every hour, every minute, every second counts.

Let Dr. Rhee's voice ring out to the Korean people. Our national policy has ever been to help the oppressed. As a nation, we have never recognised the Japanese annexation of Korea. In fact, the treaty we originally made with Korea never has been abrogated.

But most of all, every Japanese concerned with a Korea aflame with revolution is one less Japanese to attack the embattled forces of the United States and the United Nations in the Pacific area. That's why the decision to act must be a military one.

Awaiting your advice, we are,

Respectfully yours,

____
Frederick Brown Harris

____
John W. Staggers

____
Jay Jerome Williams

Hon. Frank Knox
Secretary of the Navy
Washington, D. C.

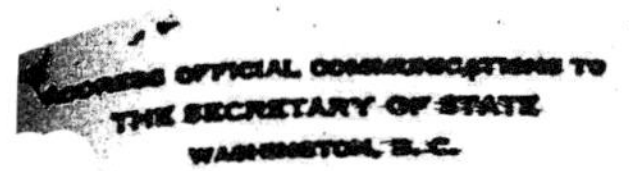

DEPARTMENT OF STATE
WASHINGTON

n reply refer to

My dear Mr. Secretary:

I refer to a letter addressed to you under date of February 4, 1942 by Dr. Frederick Brown Harris, Mr. John W. Staggers and Mr. Jay Jerome Williams in regard to the question of a Korean revolution against the Japanese and the question of Korean independence. A copy of this letter was left with an officer of the Department by Messrs. Staggers and Williams during a call made by them on February 6.

The eighth paragraph of the letter under reference reads as follows:

"We have been in person to the State Department several times since December 7th but never have received word of a definite nature save that the Korean matter is under consideration. We have been advised, however, that the Department is unwilling to act now because of the view (a Departmental view) that to act now might be offensive to the Japanese."

The statement that "the Department is unwilling to act now

because

The Honorable

Frank Knox,

Secretary of the Navy.

because of the view (a Departmental view) that to act
now might be offensive to the Japanese" is not accurate.
In conversations with persons who have called on officers of the Department and expressed an interest in the
question of Korean independence, officers of the Department have mentioned that there were of course a number
of factors to be considered in connection with that
question and that one of those/factors was our interest
in the welfare of American citizens now in Korea and
other parts of the Japanese Empire and the efforts which
this Government is making to/ effect arrangements covering the repatriation from Japan of American officials
and other American nationals now there.

The officer of the Department upon whom Messrs.
Staggers and Williams called on February 6 explained
to them the error in their letter to which reference
is made above.

Sincerely yours,

ESA

IN REPLY
REFER TO AG 095 Haan, Kilsoo K.
(2-11-42)MB

February 22, 1942.

Mr. Stanley K. Hornbeck,
Adviser on Political Relations,
State Department,
Washington, D. C.

Dear Sir:

I am directed by the Secretary of War to acknowledge
your letter of February 11, 1942, inclosing a memorandum relative to "The Korean Commission".

The War Department appreciates the information furnished
and it has been noted in the interested agencies.

Very truly yours,

E S Adams

Major General,
The Adjutant General.

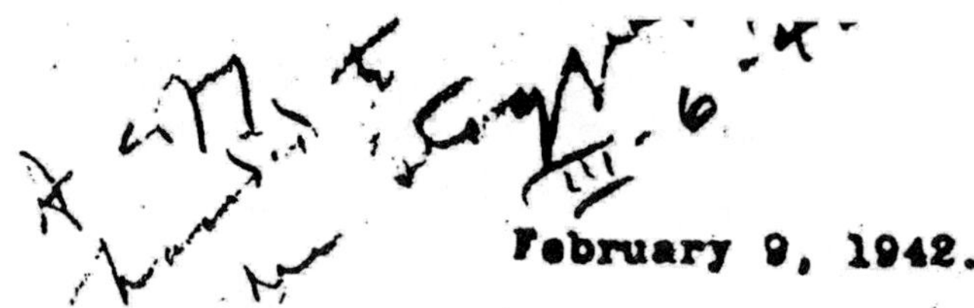

February 9, 1942.

<u>Memorandum</u>

1. Reference is made to a letter addressed to Kilsoo K. Haan by John W. Staggers under date January 30, 1942, in which it is stated that copies were to be filed with the Department of State, the War Department, the Navy Department and the Department of Justice.

In that letter it is stated, <u>inter alia</u>, that "The Korean Commission is recognized by the State Department as the official representative of the Provisional Government of Korea. It, therefore, follows that the proper procedure would be for you to submit to the Korean Commission, to be forwarded through official channels, any communication which you wish to address to any of the Departments in Washington".

2. For purposes of record and to obviate confusion, statement is made of pertinent facts as follows: Officers of the Department of State and, it is understood, of other agencies of the Government have over a period of many years received and talked with various persons understood to represent or to speak for various Korean organizations in exile. Such officers have also received and talked with various American nationals associated with or employed by such organizations. This, however, does not constitute recognition of an official status nor should it be construed

as

as implying a selective discrimination as among such
organizations or persons. Officers of the Department of
State are not aware of any action taken by the American
Government from which it could with warrant be said, so
far as this Government is concerned, that communications
which persons of Korean race may wish to address to officers or agencies of the American Government must first
be submitted to any specified organization and come
forward only through that channel.

Copies of this memorandum are being sent to Mr. Staggers,
the War Department, the Navy Department, and the Department
of Justice.

TELEGRAM RECEIVED

EJ
This telegram must be
closely paraphrased be-
fore being communicated
to anyone. (SC)

Chungking via N. R.

FROM Dated April 10, 1942

Rec'd 7:14 p.m.

Secretary of State,
Washington.

381, April 10, 10 a.m.

The Political Vice Minister of Foreign Affairs
told me yesterday in strict confidence that at a
meeting of the Supreme National Defense Council on
April 6 a proposal for immediate recognition of the
Korean Provisional Government was submitted by Sun Fo
and supported by some other party members. After a
three hour discussion it was decided to refer the
matter to General Chiang for decision.

While the attitude of the Chinese Government toward
the Koreans here has been sympathetic and they have been
urged to compose their factional differences, the major
considerations in this matter are: (one) concern as to
possible Soviet reaction to recognition of the provisional
government. This is described as a matter of great delicacy. It was pointed out that there are two divisions
of Koreans in the Soviet forces in Siberia and that in
event of a Soviet-Japanese war these divisions would
probably be used in any drive into Korea and might be

used

-2-#381, April 10, 10 a.m., from Chungking via N. R.

used by the Soviet to set up some sort of Government
in the country. If meanwhile the provisional government at Chungking had been recognized, a difficult
situation would arise. While the Koreans in the Soviet
armies are said to have been naturalized as Soviet
citizens it is pointed out that they nevertheless remain Koreans. (Two) Concern as to possible British
and other reaction at this time to proposals for independence for colonial peoples, having in mind Malaya,
the Netherlands East Indies and other areas.

I will inform the Department of any further developments.

GAUSS

EMB

P A R A P H R A S E

381

A telegram of April 10 from the American Ambassador at Chungking reads substantially as follows:

On April 8 the Ambassador was informed strictly confidentially by the Political Vice Minister for Foreign Affairs that a proposal for recognizing the Korean Provisional Government immediately was submitted by Sun Fo at a meeting on April 6 of the Supreme National Defense Council and that some other party members supported the proposal. It was decided, after the subject was discussed for three hours, to refer the matter for decision to the Generalissimo.

Although the Chinese Government has been sympathetic in its attitude toward Koreans in Chungking and has urged the Koreans to settle their factional differences, the principal considerations in this matter are (a) concern in regard to reaction, especially British, at this time to proposals for independence for colonial peoples, having in mind among other areas Malaya and the Netherlands East Indies; (b) concern with regard to possible reaction of the Soviet Government to recognition of the Korean Provisional Government. This is looked upon as a very delicate matter. The point was made that in the Soviet forces in Siberia there are two divisions of Koreans and that in case of war between Japan and the Soviet Union it was likely that these divisions would be used in any drive into Korea and might be used by the Soviet Government to set up in Korea some sort of government. A difficult situation would arise, if in the meantime the Korean Provisional Government at Chungking had been recognized. It is pointed out that the Koreans in the Soviet Armies remain Koreans although they are said to have been naturalized as citizens of the Soviet Union.

The Ambassador will report any further developments to the Department.

FE:ECC:MJF
4-13-42

PARAPHRASE

A strictly confidential telegram of April 11, 1942 (283) to the American Ambassador at Chungking reads substantially as follows:

The Ambassador is instructed, as an indication of the spirit of cooperation which underlies the desire of this Government to exchange with the Chinese Government information concerning the Korean situation, to inform the Vice Minister for Foreign Affairs urgently that it is the hope of the American Government that the Chinese Government will be so good as to let us have its views and conclusions in regard to the question of recognition of a provisional government of Korea, before it (the Chinese Government) takes any definitive action in the matter. The Ambassador is instructed, in his discretion, to mention that of course any matter which bears upon free movements against Axis powers is a matter in which other Governments among the United Nations are interested and with regard to which it would be desirable for the interested Governments, so far as practicable, to take cooperative and parallel action.

A short time ago Dr. T. V. Soong handed a memorandum concerning the Korean situation to the President. It is expected that at some time during the week of April 12 the President will discuss the Korean situation with Dr. Soong.

FE:EC:MJF
4-13-42

TELEGRAM SENT

Department of State

"SC"

TO BE TRANSMITTED
X CONFIDENTIAL CODE
NONCONFIDENTIAL CODE
PARTAIR
PLAIN

Washington,
April 11, 1942

AMEMBASSY,

CHUNGKING (CHINA).

283

STRICTLY CONFIDENTIAL.

Reference Department's telegrams no. 199, March 20, 9 p.m.
263, April 7, and your 381, April 10, 10 a.m.

As a manifestation of the cooperative spirit underlying
this Government's desire to exchange information with the
Chinese Government in reference to the Korean situation,
please inform the Chinese Vice Foreign Minister urgently that
we hope that, before the Chinese Government takes any
definitive action with regard to the question of recognition
of a Provisional Government of Korea, it will be so good as to
make available to us its views and conclusions in this matter.
You may, in your discretion, mention that any question which
has bearing upon free movements against the Axis powers is,
of course, one in which other governments among the United
Nations have interest and in regard to which parallel and
cooperative action by the interested governments would be
desirable so far as practical.

Dr. T. V. Soong recently handed to the President a
memorandum on the Korean situation and it is expected that
the President will discuss that situation with Dr. Soong
at some time during the coming week.

Confidential File

such as the reaching of an accord between the British

Government and the leaders of India in regard to the

independence of India, thus achieving greater substance

and scope than would be the case in an isolated reference

to Korea.

Six. . In making the foregoing comments to the

Chinese Government, please emphasize that we are aware of

the fact that geographical and racial factors render the

question under reference of more immediate concern to China

than to the United States; that in presenting our views to

the Chinese Government we are motivated solely by a desire

to give a responsive and frank reply to the question which

the Chinese Government has been so good as to take up with

this Government; and that we do not repeat not desire to

stand in the way of the Chinese Government's taking any

step which, after careful and full consideration of all the

factors, seems to that Government the wisest step to take.

Please mention to the Chinese Government also that there are

certain special factors in the Korean situation to which

this Government must give particular attention because of

their possible effect on a number of other free movements in

this country which also desire formal recognition as governments

by the United States. You may also recall to the Chinese
Government that the President in his radio address of
February 23 referred to the people of Korea and said that they
QUOTE know in their flesh the harsh despotism of Japan UNQUOTE
and that the President also stated later in that address that
QUOTE We of the United Nations are agreed on certain broad
principles in the kind of peace we seek. The Atlantic Charter
applies not only to the parts of the world that border the
Atlantic but to the whole world; disarmament of aggressors,
self-determination of nations and peoples, and the four
freedoms — freedom of speech, freedom of religion, freedom
from want, and freedom from fear UNQUOTE.

FE:LES:RLS
A-B/H:HRH
PA/H:AH:FLB   FE   PA/H   A-B   U   S

Enciphered by _______________________________

Send by operator _____________ M., _____________ 19_____

1—1442   U. S. GOVERNMENT PRINTING OFFICE

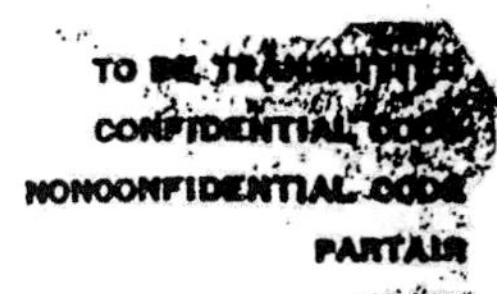

TELEGRAM SENT

Department of State

Washington,

PREPARING OFFICE
WILL INDICATE WHETHER

Collect
- Full rate
- Day letter
- Night letter

Charge Department:
- Full rate
- Day letter
- Night letter

Charge to
$

—4—

such as the reaching of an accord between the British
Government and the leaders of India in regard to the
independence of India, thus achieving greater substance
and scope than would be the case in an isolated reference
to Korea. However, in view of the Generalissimo's views,
this Government is prepared to join at once with China
and others of the United Nations who are immediately
concerned with Korean matters, in announcing support for
Korea's aspirations to ~~independence~~ freedom.

Six. In making the foregoing comments to the
Chinese Government, please emphasize that we are aware of
the fact that geographical and racial factors render the
question under reference of more immediate concern to
China than to the United States; that in
presenting our views to the Chinese Government we are
motivated solely by a desire to give a responsive and frank
reply to the question which the Chinese Government has been
so good as to take up with this Government; and that we do not
repeat not desire to stand in the way of the Chinese
Government's taking any step which, after careful and full
consideration of all the factors, seems to that Government

the

Enciphered by _______________________

Sent by operator _______________ M., _________, 19_____, _______________

1—1462   U. S. GOVERNMENT PRINTING OFFICE

TELEGRAM SENT

Department of State

Washington,

-5-

the wisest step to take; and that, if the Chinese Government, in addition to announcing its support for Korean efforts to achieve ~~independence~~, should accord recognition to a Provisional Government of Korea, this Government would of course expect to re-examine its position in the light of that new step. Please mention to the Chinese Government also that there are certain special factors in the Korean situation to which this Government must give particular attention because of their possible effect on a number of other free movements in this country which also desire formal recognition as governments by the United States.

Seven. Especially important: In as much as Foreign Minister Soong, as mentioned in the Department's telegram no. 283 of April 11, 6 p.m., brought up the question of Korea with the President, would the Chinese Government have objection to the President's taking up the matter at the next meeting of the Pacific War Council which, in view of its composition, would be a convenient forum for consideration of such a question?

FE:LES:RLS   FE PA/H A-B U S
A-B/H:HRH
PA/H:AH:FLB

Enciphered by ___________________

Sent by operator ___________ *M.,* ___________ *19____,* ___________

April 23, 1942

<u>STRICTLY CONFIDENTIAL</u>

<u>MEMORANDUM FOR THE PRESIDENT</u>

As reported in Ambassador Gauss' telegram of
April 18, General Chiang Kai-shek feels that it is desirable to recognize without delay the "Korean Provisional Government" now at Chungking.

The Chinese Government has requested an expression
of our views. There is attached for your consideration
the draft of our proposed reply.

We feel that this whole matter is one which might
to the advantage of all governments concerned be discussed at a meeting of the Pacific War Council, provided of course that the Chinese Government has no
objection to such procedure. We propose raising this
question with the Chinese Government.

The Soviet Union is also specially interested in
the question of Korea. An approach to the Soviet Government in the matter might, however, be embarrassing

to

to that Government in view of the fact that the Soviet
Union is not at war with Japan. There remains the
possibility, in case the "Korean Provisional Government"
at Chungking is recognized by the Chinese Government,
that the Soviet Union may support some other Korean
group associated ideologically with the Soviet Union.
The Chinese Government may be motivated in its desire
to accord recognition to the "Korean Provisional Government" by a wish to nip in the bud the development of any
Soviet-supported Korean group.

This whole question of Korean independence and the
recognition of a Korean government has many complicated
and delicate aspects. In view of China's geographical
position and historic association with its neighbors,
it is doubted whether this Government should interpose
strong objection to any course which the Chinese Government may decide upon. It would seem appropriate,
however, for this Government to lay before the Chinese
Government a complete exposition of its views.

You will note that we have, for reasons explained
in the proposed reply, preferred not to respond at this
time in the affirmative to the Chinese suggestion that
the "Korean Provisional Government", now at Chungking,
be recognized and have, instead, included in the proposed

reply

reply a statement that this Government is prepared to
join at once with China and others of the United Nations
which are immediately concerned with Korean matters in
announcing support for Korea's aspirations to independence.

A decision to favor Korean independence is, of course,
a significant step and involves important considerations
of foreign policy, especially in relation to the post war
settlement.

Enclosure:
  Draft telegram.

FE:MMH:HNS

DEPARTMENT OF STATE

PARAPHRASE

CONFIDENTIAL

Telegram no. 381

Dated: April 10, 10 a.m.

From: Chungking

Rec'd: April 10, 7:15 p.m.

In confidence I was told yesterday by the Political Vice Minister of Foreign Affairs that Sun Fo submitted on April 6 at the meeting of the Supreme National Defense Council a proposal for the immediate recognition of the Provisional Government of Korea, and that other party members supported this proposal. The matter was discussed for three hours, after which it was decided that the subject would be referred to the Generalissimo for decision by him.

Although the Government of China looks upon the Koreans here with sympathy and has urged them to reach an agreement regarding their sectional differences, the principle considerations with regard to this subject are as follows: (a) Concern as to how the U.S.S.R. might react were the Provisional Government recognized (this is considered to be a subject of extreme delicacy.) It was drawn to their attention that in the Russian forces in Siberia there are two divisions of Koreans. It was pointed out that should war develop between Japan and the U.S.S.R., in all events these divisions would be employed in any drive into Korea and furthermore might be employed by the Russians to establish a government of some kind in the country. A difficult situation would result, if in the meantime recognition had been given to the Provisional Government in Chungking. It is pointed out that the Koreans who serve in the Russian armies remain Koreans even though they have been naturalized as citizens of the U.S.S.R. (b) Bearing in mind the Dutch East Indies, Malaya, et cetera, concern as to how Great Britain and other nations might react at this moment to any proposal for the independence of colonies. I will keep the Department of State informed regarding any subsequent developments.

GAUSS

U-L:SM:AB 4-14-42

Copy to Navy - Ensign Macauley Copy to War - Major Sands

THE WHITE HOUSE
WASHINGTON

12

April 8, 1942.

MEMORANDUM FOR THE

ACTING SECRETARY OF STATE:

I enclose a memorandum
handed me by Dr. Soong. Please speak
to me about it before Tuesday the 14th.

F.D.R.

MEMORANDUM

Held down by a large Japanese army of occupation,
the mood of the Korean people is that of sullen sub-
mission, with memories of historic injustice rankling,
and having been dispossessed of the rich South Korean
rice-growing areas by Japanese landlords and oppressed
by the present civil and economic disabilities.

Except for sporadic assassinations in Korea itself,
Korean discontent is manifest only among their nationals
living in China and Russia, while ideologically existent
among Koreans in the United States.

The principal leaders of the Korean revolutionaries
are living in Chungking, on the one hand the members of
the Korean Provisional Government Party, which is the
historic party of Korean disaffection, and on the other
the Korean Revolutionary Party which is made up of
younger and supposedly left-wing elements. Korean revolutionaries in the United States are adherents of one
of these two parties. With the limited aid of the
Chinese Government, there is in existence a small Korean
Peoples Army, which is operating with Chinese guerrillas
in North China and numbers a few thousand.

In Siberia the Russians have incorporated for many
years two or three regiments of Koreans in the Russian
Far East army, but until hostilities commence between
Russia and Japan, no step-up in this activity can be

expected.

If the United Nations, particularly the members of the Pacific Council, desire to foster Korean independence, two measures are indicated:

1. After promoting a fusion of the two rival revolutionary parties by promising help to a united Korean revolutionary organization, which appears easily feasible, undertake to raise, arm and support a Korean irregular army of, say, 50,000 men, which will be located in the guerrilla areas of North China, and which will be the rallying center for all Korean revolutionary activities both within and outside Korea. The purpose of such an army would be:

    (a) to operate in Korea at some opportune moment to be selected by the United Nations;

    (b) to be headquarters for sabotage activities by Korean workers in munition works and vital communications centers in Korea and Japan;

    (c) to constitute an intelligence service through Koreans working in the lower ranks of civil servants and police in Korea, North China and Japan.

The prospect for irregular activities will be particularly promising because, owing to the shortage of labor in Japan similar to that in Germany, large numbers of Koreans have been recruited for munition works in Korea, Manchuria and Japan. In addition, large numbers of

Koreans are working as agents in North China in such
instruments of Japanese policy as monopolies in opium,
morphine and heroin, prostitution and gambling, to
demoralize the Chinese population. With a well-
organized system, these Japanese activities could
prove a boomerang.

2. As a political measure, in order to encourage
Korean aspirations at some opportune moment the Pacific
Council could announce its determination to effect the
independence of Korea after the war. Recognition of a
Korean Provisional Government might be effected either
simultaneously or at some time later.

April 13, 1942

My dear Mr. President:

In your memorandum to me of April 8, enclosing a
memorandum handed to you by Dr. Soong, you asked me to
speak with you about Dr. Soong's memorandum before
Tuesday the 14th.

I am returning herewith the original of Dr.
Soong's memorandum regarding which I should like to
offer the following comment.

I fully concur in the suggestion that the United
Nations, particularly the members of the Pacific War
Council, should assist in organizing and equipping a
Korean irregular army. Geographical factors would
seem to make China the logical place from which such
activity could best be carried on, with the suggestions and assistance of the United States and other
military missions at Chungking. Should you wish me
to do so, after the Pacific War Council has approved
this suggestion, I shall be glad to take the matter
up with my Liaison Committee in order that recommendations may be formulated by the General Staff and by

The President,

    The White House.

Naval Operations for your consideration covering the practical steps involved.

With regard to the suggestion that a fusion of rival Korean revolutionary parties be promoted and that recognition of a Korean Provisional Government be granted at an appropriate time, I am informed that the principal Korean revolutionary organizations are the one existing in Chungking (apparently supported by most of the Koreans in the United States) and the Korean bands in Manchuria and other parts of China. The latter have apparently no close connection with the organization at Chungking.

I have sent a telegram to our Embassy in Chungking asking for further information on this point and also asking for information from the Government of China with regard to its views concerning the possibility of a fusion of these groups.

With regard to an announcement by the Pacific War Council of its determination to effect the independence of Korea, in principle I am heartily in accord with such a step, but I question the wisdom of making an announcement of that character at this moment. If such an announcement were made today, it seems to me that the announcement would lack reality.

Temporarily the tide of war continues to be in Japan's favor. No armed revolt in Korea against Japan can be expected at this time. Furthermore, the question of the independence of India has recently held and still holds the center of attention among the peoples of the Pacific area and the failure of the Cripps negotiations makes it unfortunately impossible for us to utilize the announcement of an agreement between the British Government and the peoples of India, providing for the freedom of India, as a platform upon which to base an announcement of broader policy.

If the Cripps negotiations had been successful, I would have recommended to you an announcement by the Pacific War Council affirming the determination of the countries represented to recognize the independence of the Philippine Islands and to bring about the independence of Korea and the expulsion of the Japanese invaders from all territories which they had temporarily overrun in order that the liberty of the peoples of those regions might be reestablished. In brief what I had in mind was to recommend the announcement of a broad policy of general liberation, insofar as the peculiar circumstances covering the Netherlands East Indies and Burma might make such an announcement possible, but, unfortunately, the breakdown of the Indian negotiations eliminates, at least temporarily, that possibility.

My suggestions for the moment with regard to
Dr. Soong's memorandum would consequently be to do
everything possible to further the organization and
equipment of a Korean army and to further in every
way possible, in consultation with the Chinese and
the British, the fusion of the Korean revolutionary
parties and to postpone until a more propitious time
any recognition of a Korean provisional government
and any announcement with regard to the future independence of Korea.

    Believe me

        Faithfully yours,

        Sumner Welles

Enc.

U:SW:DMK

DEPARTMENT OF STATE

ADVISER ON POLITICAL RELATIONS

April 11, 1942

U - Mr. Welles:

My misgivings, with which you are aware, regarding the matter of this Government's making a commitment at this time that Korea shall be made independent persist. I feel it my duty to inform you of that fact.

By coincidence, it happens that in my reading of last evening I came across a record, in a confidential report of one of the meetings (at which I was not present) held on March 17 of the study group of the Council on Foreign Relations which is interesting itself in the question of bases for the peace settlement to come between the United States and Japan, of a brief discussion of the problem of Korea. That record, which is in the nature of a digest, reads (with omission of names) as follows:

"<u>Korea</u>. The question of the disposition of Korea after the war baffled the group even more than the disposition of Manchuria. The chairman presented five possibilities: (1) it might continue as part of the Japanese Empire, (2) be controlled by China, (3) be controlled by the U.S.S.R., (4) be controlled by an international organization, or (5) be independent. He noted that there were two types of Japanese officials in Korea: the typical bureaucrats and those trained abroad with fairly liberal ideas. If Korea was governed by the latter group, good government might be the result. However, if the United Nations are completely victorious, Korea would probably revolt and an unstable situation would ensue. A similar state of flux would exist under an international mandate and if it was independent, it would be subject to easy conquest.

"Mr.   emphasized the complexity of the Korean problem with its present struggles among the various Korean groups. These groups are centered in Hawaii, Chungking, and the Maritime Provinces; and it is impossible to tell which has the closest connection with the independence movement at home. Though he did not discount the possibility of effectively using the Koreans to strike at Japan, thus giving them a legitimate claim for a different form of government, he felt Korea incapable of self-government. Mr.   said that since Korea geographically was an appendix of Manchuria, the solution of the Manchurian problem would bring

about-

about the solution of Korea's future status. He
agreed that Korea was not ready for self-government
politically or economically. Mr.   suggested it
be placed under a system of international control but
Mr.   said such a contingency would only result in
economic warfare in that area with Japan eventually
winning control. Mr.   wondered about the possibility of some sort of dominion status with the
ultimate aim of independence for Korea.

"In general, the group was perplexed over the
solution of the Korean problem but agreed that Korea
was not capable of self-government at the present
time."

The expressions of opinion thus indicated are those
of six persons each of whom has special knowledge of the
subject and two of whom are at present in service (temporary)
of the Government.

The question what to do for and with and about Korea
will be, when the peace settlement is made, a perplexing
question; and it will be a question which should be
decided in the light of conditions which then exist and
of disposals which are being made of far larger questions.
I assume that all thoughtful persons who are reasoning
objectively on the subject of the peace settlement to come
will agree that it is desirable that the work of the peace-
makers be not impeded by hampering antecedent commitments
to a greater extent than is necessary. A commitment now
that the Korean people shall be made free would be one
thing, but a pledge that Korea shall be made an independent
state might become a source of most embarrassing involve-
ment.

PA/H:SKH:FLB

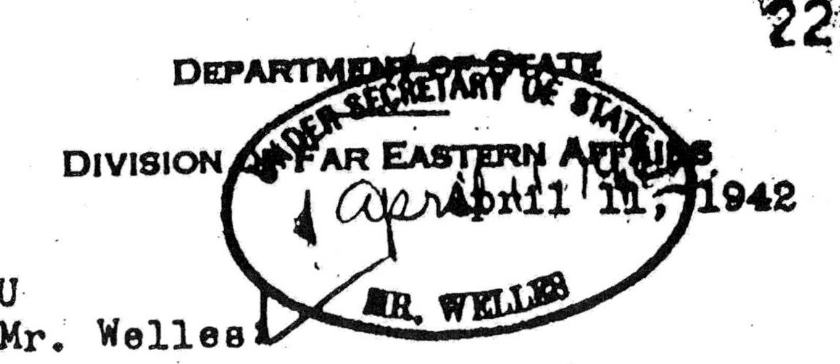

DEPARTMENT OF STATE

DIVISION OF FAR EASTERN AFFAIRS

April 11, 1942

U
Mr. Welles:

Herewith a memorandum, as requested by you on April 9, in regard
to the question of Korea as raised
in the memorandum handed to the
President by Dr. Soong.

We have tried to see
Mr. Berle on this but
have not been able
to do so.

FE:MMH:HNS

April 11, 1942

Reference the memorandum handed to the President by Dr. T. V. Soong in regard to the question of Korea.

With regard to the suggestion that the United Nations, particularly the members of the Pacific War Council, assist in organizing and equipping a Korean irregular army, it is believed that every feasible effort toward this end should be made. Geographical factors would seem to make China the logical place from which such activity could best be carried on, with the suggestions and assistance of the United States and other military missions at Chungking. The plan and method of operations would revolve about military considerations, and it would seem that such operations would require very careful planning by the military authorities with all possible secrecy.

With regard to the suggestion that a fusion of rival Korean revolutionary parties be promoted and that recognition of a Korean Provisional Government be effected at an appropriate time, this Government's information has been that the principal Korean revolutionary organizations are the one existing at Chungking (which most of the politically active Koreans in American territory are understood to support and the Korean

bands

bands in Manchuria and other occupied parts of China.
Both of them are very limited in membership as compared
with the population of Korea, and it is doubtful whether
the organization at Chungking has definite or close connections with the people in Korea or has the support of
the Korean bands in occupied China. As Dr. Soong indicates,
Korean discontent does not manifest itself actively in
Korea. It is of course desirable that fusion of the major
Korean revolutionary elements take place before recognition is accorded to a Korean Provisional Government.
In the absence of an effective fusion, the recognition of
one group might cause another group to set itself up as a
self-styled Korean government. This is an important point
for consideration, because one of the leading groups is
located at Chungking and has some support from the conservative elements of the Chinese Government while the
other, which is reportedly radical in character, is stated
to have association with the Soviet Union. Accordingly, it
seems advisable to leave in abeyance the question of
recognition and to leave the question of fusion of the
Korean organizations largely to the Koreans themselves, with
full interchange of views among the principally interested Governments and with the giving by each such Government of friendly counsel to those Korean organizations
with which it is in contact.

With

With regard to an announcement by the Pacific War Council of its determination to effect the independence of Korea,
under the present situation an announcement with regard to
Korea alone would be lacking in reality. The tide of war
continues to be in Japan's favor. Korea is in the center of
areas controlled by Japan. No armed revolt in Korea against
Japan can be expected at this time. The informal discussions
which this Government has had with the British Government at
London and with the Chinese Government at Chungking indicate
that those Governments have held similar views that the
present is not an opportune time for such a declaration.*
The question of the independence of India now holds the
center of attention among the peoples of the Pacific area.
If the status of India is not satisfactorily adjusted, a
declaration at this time in regard to the independence of
Korea alone would emphasize the failure to reach a satisfactory agreement in regard to India.

The President has already made clear that the Atlantic Charter and the four freedoms apply not only to
the Atlantic but to the whole world. In his address of
February 23 the President stated:

> "We of the United Nations are agreed on cer-
> tain broad principles in the kind of peace we seek.
> The Atlantic Charter applies not only to the parts
> of the world that border the Atlantic but to the
> whole

---

*Note: A telegram which has just been received from our
Embassy at Chungking reports that a proposal for immediate
recognition of the Korean group at Chungking has been
referred to Chiang Kai-shek for decision.

whole world; disarmament of aggressors, self-
determination of nations and peoples, and the four
freedoms -- freedom of speech, freedom of religion,
freedom from want, and freedom from fear."

Although a declaration relating to Korea alone would
not seem to be opportune, the Governments represented on
the Pacific War Council might, should the status of India
be satisfactorily adjusted, use that fact as an occasion
for expressing their deep gratification at the adjustment
of the India question and at the same time affirm their
determination to bring about the independence of the
Philippine Islands and the independence of Korea and to
expel the Japanese invaders from all territories which
they have temporarily overrun.

A draft of a possible joint declaration by the Governments members of the Pacific War Council is attached.

In case any such declaration is to be made, it would
probably be desirable, because of the proximity of Soviet
territory to Korea and because of the Soviet interest in
Korean bands in occupied areas of China, to inform the
Soviet Government of the proposed action with a view to
ascertaining whether that Government perceives objection
thereto.

Enclosure:
 Draft of possible
 joint declaration.

The Governments represented on the Pacific War Council express profound gratification over the conclusion of the agreement between British and Indian leaders in regard to the status of India. Thus again do the peoples of the world have fresh evidence of the peaceful evolution of democratic processes. Not by resort to arms, not by dictation and oppression, but by the give and take of friendly conference and by sincere mutual effort to understand each other's problems and difficulties, has an agreement been arrived at which is of the deepest significance not only for the millions of India and of the British Empire but for those many other millions of freedom-loving people everywhere.

Concomitantly with this history-making solution by peaceful means of an extremely complicated and difficult question and with this concrete manifestation of the application of the principles and purposes of the Atlantic Charter and of the Declaration by United Nations, the Governments represented on the Pacific War Council pledge themselves to secure the final freedom and independence of the Philippine Islands and of Korea and to expel the Japanese invaders from all areas which they have temporarily overrun.

The fruits of the final victory over the savage and brutal forces which are seeking to subjugate the world shall accrue to all peoples of Asia as well as to all peoples throughout the world.

TELEGRAM RECEIVED

NWN
This telegram must be
closely paraphrased be-
fore being communicated
to anyone. (SC)

Chungking via N. R.

FROMted April 15, 1942

Rec'd. 8:36 a.m.

Secretary of State,

Washington.

411, April 15, 10 a.m.

Department's 283, April 11, 6 p.m.

Action taken as directed.

Vice Minister has given assurances that Embassy
will be kept currently informed of developments and
of Chinese Government's views in regard to Korean
question, and that it will be notified in advance of
any contemplated action.

G.USS

RR

AF
This telegram must be
closely paraphrased be-
fore being communicated
to anyone. (B)

Chungking via N. R.

FROM Dated March 28, 1942

Rec'd 7:42 a.m.

Secretary of State,

Washington.

287, March 28, 11 a.m.

Department's/218, March 2ß, midnight.

The United Press report is based upon an address
made by Sun Fo before a local cultural association
which subsequently appeared in the Chinese language
press in abbreviated form. The extracts reported by
the United Press correspondent are substantially correct although Dr. Fo rather than announce the adoption
of a Pacific Charter stated that the Atlantic Charter
should, and expressed confidence that it did apply to
all parts of the world.

The Embassy believes that Dr. Sun (one) in bespeaking independence for Indians, Indochinese,
Koreans and other peoples and (two) in asking recognition of the Korean Provisional Government was not
acting under the instructions of his Government or
with its foreknowledge. With respect to (one) there
is little reason to doubt however that the Chinese

favor

- 531 -

-2- #287, March 28, 11 a.m., from Chungking via N. R.

favor independence for India and other eastern
countries, but with respect to (two) the Chinese
Foreign Office has made it clear to the Embassy
that it is not yet prepared to accord recognition
to the Korean Provisional Government.

Dr. Sun Fo by virtue of his family position
assumes and apparently is to procure greater freedom
of expression on political matters than is the case
with other party and Government officials. It is not
believed, however, that his influence in party councils is commensurate with his position or that declarations by him are necessarily recognized by the
Chinese Government responsible officials.

GAUSS

WWC

TELEGRAM RECEIVED

DM
This telegram must be
closely paraphrased be-
fore being communicated
to anyone. (B)

FROM

Chungking via N.R.

Dated March 28, 1942

Rec'd 7:42 p.m.

Secretary of State,

Washington.

287, March 28, 11 a.m.

Department's 218, March 23, midnight.

The United Press report is based upon an address

made by Sun Fo before a Vocal cultural association

which subsequently appeared in the Chinese language

press in abbreviated form. The extracts reported by

the United Press correspondent are substantially

correct although Dr. Fo rather than announce the

adoption of a Pacific Charter stated that the

Atlantic Charter should, and expressed confidence

that it did apply to all parts of the world.

The Embassy believes that Dr. Sun (one)

in bespeaking independence for Indians, Indo-

Chinese, Koreans and other peoples and (two) in

asking recognition of the Korean Provisional

Government was not acting under the instructions

of his Government or with its foreknowledge with respect

to one there is little reason to doubt however that

the Chinese favor independence for India and other

eastern

- 533 -

-2- #287, March 28, 11 a.m. from Chungking via N.R.

Eastern countries but with respect to two the
Chinese Foreign Office has made it clear to the
Embassy that it is not yet prepared to accord
recognition to the Korean Provisional Government.

Doctor Sun Fo by virtue of his family position
assumes and apparently is to procure greater freedom
of expression on political matters than is the case
with other party and Government officials. It is
not believed, however, that his influence in party
councils is commensurate with his position or that
declarations by him are necessarily recognized by
the Chinese Government responsible officials.

GAUSS

WWC

A telegram of March 28, 1942 from the American
Ambassador at Chungking reads substantially as follows:

An address which Mr. Sun Fo made before a cultural
association at Chungking was the basis for the United
Press report mentioned in the Department's telegram of
March 23. Later the address in an abbreviated form
appeared in the Chinese vernacular press. The extracts
from the address as reported by a correspondent of the
United Press are in the main correct. However, rather than
suggesting that the adoption of a Pacific Charter be
announced, Mr. Sun stated that the Atlantic Charter should
apply to all sections of the world and he expressed confidence
that it did so apply. It is the opinion of the Embassy
that in asking that the Korean Provisional Government be recognized and in bespeaking independence for various peoples,
including Indians, Indo-Chinese and Koreans, Dr. Sun was
not acting with the foreknowledge of the Chinese Government
or under its instructions. With regard to the question of
recognition of the Korean Provisional Government, the
Chinese Foreign Office has given the Embassy to understand
that as yet it is not ready to accord such recognition.

However

However, with regard to independence for India and other Eastern countries there is little reason to doubt that the Chinese Government favors such independence. On account of his family connections Dr. Sun Fo assumes and seemingly is able to act with greater freedom of expression in regard to political matters than other Government officials and party officials are able to do. However, Sun Fo's influence in party councils is not believed to be commensurate with his position nor are declarations which he makes believed to be of necessity recognized by responsible officials of the Chinese Government.

FE:E?C:MS
3/30/42

FE

ADVISER ON POLITICAL RELATIONS

August 17, 1942.

Mr. Secretary:

Herewith the paper on Korea.

You would not need to

bother with the first two and

one-half pages.

PA/H: SKH: FLB